尾田栄一郎

It is said that prior to the Meiji Era, the Japanese walked left foot, left arm forward and right foot, right arm forward. This is called "nanba aruki."

If that is so, I think the Japanese of old were always very nervous.

The reason for being nervous is, of course, that at the piano recital to be held tomorrow, Mariko, whom Takashi secretly admires, will be coming to watch.

Takashi has short fingers that don't reach the black keys on the piano, so in order to overcome this weakness, he will venture into the mountain once again to battle a bear!! And now let's start volume 35!!!

—Eiichiro Oda, 2004

Eiichiro Oda began his manga career at the age of 17, when his one-shot cowboy manga **Wanted!** won second place in the coveted Tezuka manga awards. Oda went on to work as an assistant to some of the biggest manga artists in the industry, including Nobuhiro Watsuki, before winning the Hop Step Award for new artists. His pirate adventure **One Piece**, which debuted in **Weekly Shonen Jump** in 1997, quickly became one of the most popular manga in Japan.

**ONE PIECE VOL. 35
WATER SEVEN PART 4**

SHONEN JUMP Manga Edition

STORY AND ART BY EIICHIRO ODA

English Adaptation/Megan Bates
Translation/JN Productions
Touch-up Art & Lettering/Elena Diaz
Design/Fawn Lau
Supervising Editor/Yuki Murashige
Editor/Alexis Kirsch

ONE PIECE © 1997 by Eiichiro Oda. All rights reserved.
First published in Japan in 1997 by SHUEISHA Inc., Tokyo.
English translation rights arranged by SHUEISHA Inc.

The rights of the author(s) of the work(s) in this publication to be
so identified have been asserted in accordance with the Copyright,
Designs and Patents Act 1988. A CIP catalogue record for this book is
available from the British Library.

Printed in the U.S.A.

Published by VIZ Media, LLC
P.O. Box 77010
San Francisco, CA 94107

10 9 8 7 6 5 4 3 2
First printing, March 2010
Second printing, June 2010

www.viz.com

THE WORLD'S
MOST POPULAR MANGA
www.shonenjump.com

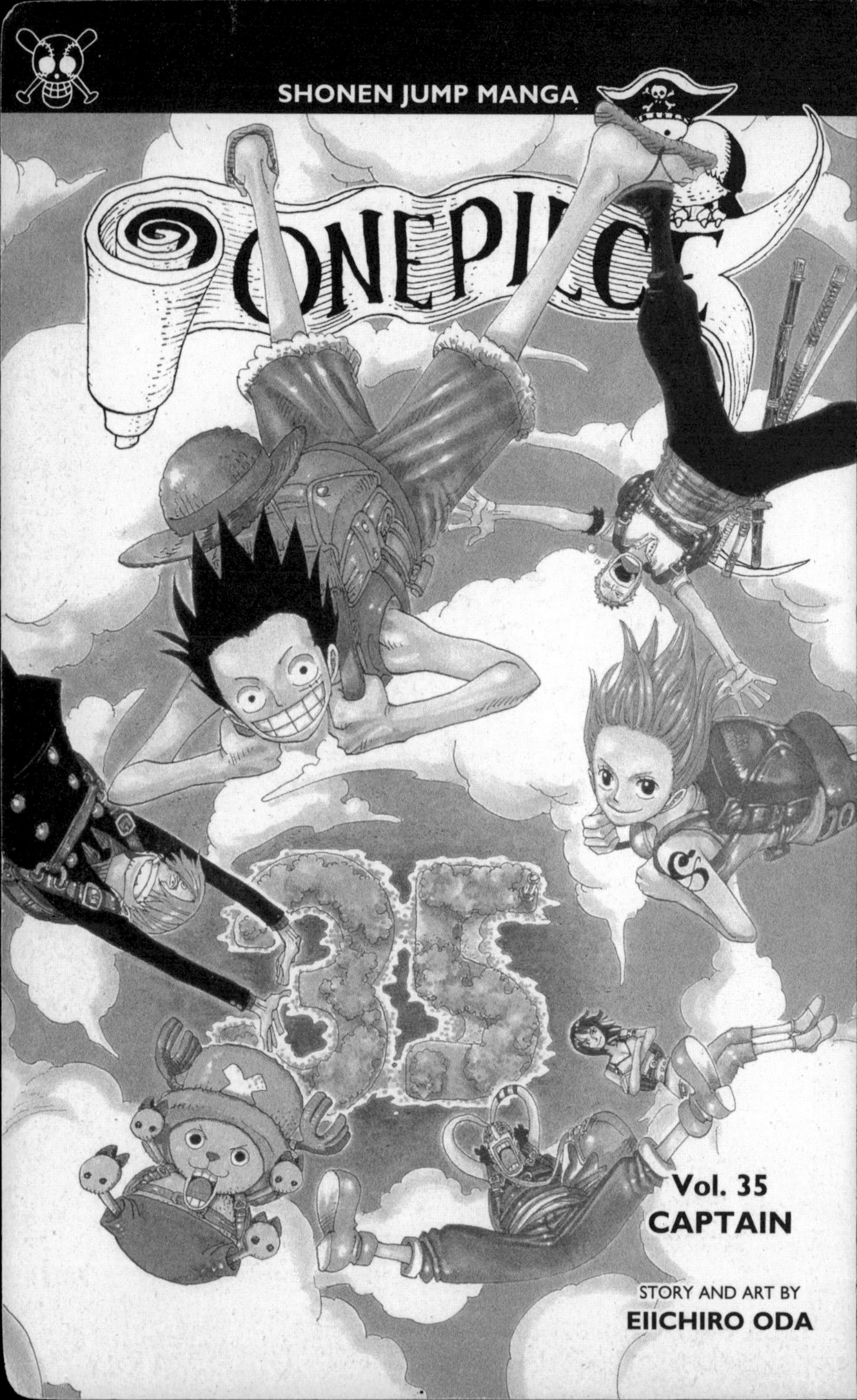
SHONEN JUMP MANGA
ONE PIECE
35
Vol. 35
CAPTAIN
STORY AND ART BY
EIICHIRO ODA

The Straw Hats

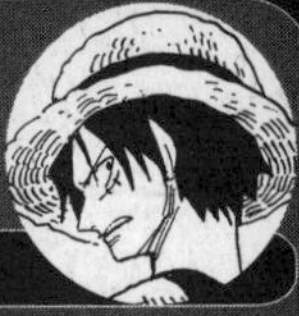

Boundlessly optimistic and able to stretch like rubber, he is determined to become King of the Pirates.

Monkey D. Luffy

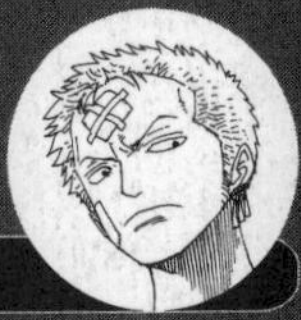

A former bounty hunter and master of the "three-sword" style. He aspires to be the world's greatest swordsman.

Roronoa Zolo

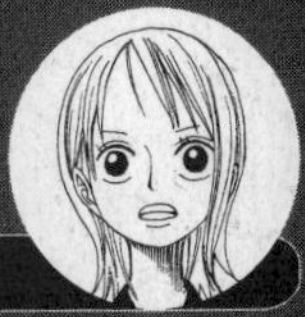

A thief who specializes in robbing pirates. Nami hates pirates, but Luffy convinced her to be his navigator.

Nami

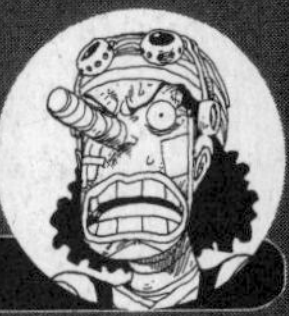

A village boy with a talent for telling tall tales. His father, Yasopp, is a member of Shanks's crew.

Usopp

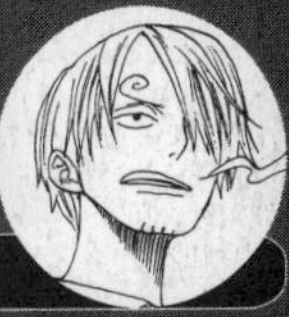

The bighearted cook (and ladies' man) whose dream is to find the legendary sea, the "All Blue."

Sanji

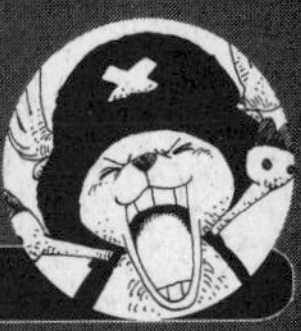

A blue-nosed man-reindeer and the ship's doctor.

Tony Tony Chopper

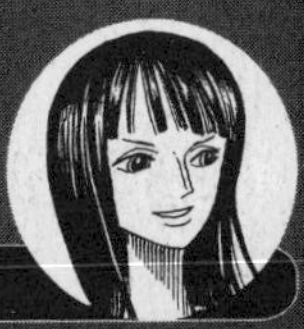

A mysterious woman in search of the Ponegliff on which true history is recorded.

Nico Robin

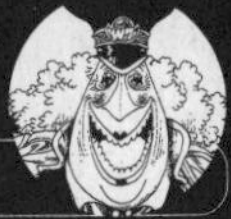

Stationmaster of Sea Train's Shift Station

Kokoro

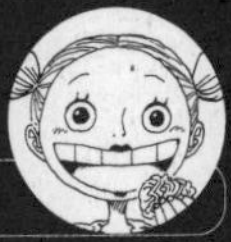

Kokoro's granddaughter

Chimney

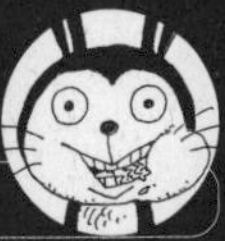

Cat (but actually a rabbit)

Gonbe

The Franky Family

Professional ship dismantlers, they moonlight as bounty hunters.

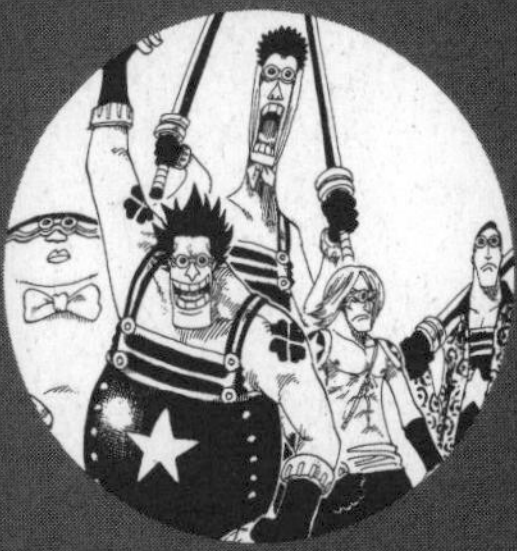

THE STORY OF ONE PIECE

Volume 35

Monkey D. Luffy started out as just a kid with a dream—to become the greatest pirate in history! Stirred by the tales of pirate "Red-Haired" Shanks, Luffy vowed to become a pirate himself. That was before the enchanted Devil Fruit gave Luffy the power to stretch like rubber, at the cost of being unable to swim—a serious handicap for an aspiring sea dog. Undeterred, Luffy set out to sea and recruited some crewmates—master swordsman Zolo; treasure-hunting thief Nami; lying sharpshooter Usopp; the high-kicking chef Sanji; Chopper, the walkin' talkin' reindeer doctor; and the mysterious archaeologist Robin.

After Luffy and his crew enter the Grand Line and have an adventure in El Dorado in Skypiea, they begin looking for a ship's carpenter for the *Merry Go*, which is badly in need of repairs. On an island, they encounter the Foxy Pirates and are challenged to a frightening game called the Davy Back Fight. The three-game contest is tied, and the final match begins. Although he is pushed to the limit by his opponent's enormous strength, Luffy emerges victorious with his Afro power. Then a man who knows of Robin's past appears—Aokiji, an Admiral of the Navy—and a battle ensues! What will this encounter bode for the future?! Robin seems to be disturbed about something...

Luffy and the crew make landfall on the island known as Water Seven. With the gold they managed to find in Skypiea, they go straight to the company that employs the island's best shipwrights to make repairs on the *Merry Go*. Around that time, Zolo, who remained on board, is attacked by the bounty-hunting "Franky Family." Meanwhile, Robin, who has gone her own way, hears a mysterious word, "CP9," and disappears...

After undergoing a thorough check, it is discovered that the *Merry Go* has sustained irreparable damage on her keel. "*Merry*, aren't you able to sail anymore...?"

Galley-La Company

Shipbuilding company that is a purveyor to the World Government

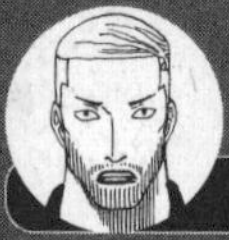

Mayor of Water Seven and president of Galley-La Company

Iceberg

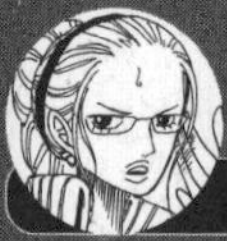

Beautiful secretary

Kalifa

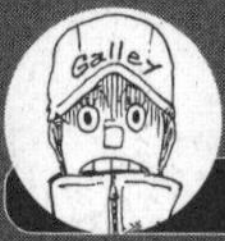
Galley

Carpentry Foreman

Kaku

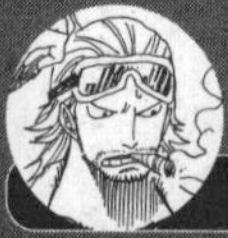

Rigging and Mast Foreman

Paulie

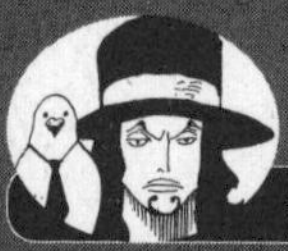

Sawyer and Treenail Foreman, with his pet pigeon

Rob Lucci & Hattori

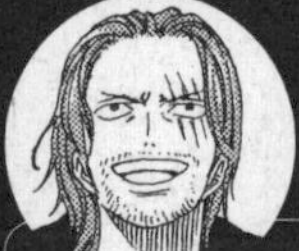

A pirate that Luffy idolizes. Shanks gave Luffy his trade-mark straw hat.

"Red-Haired" Shanks

Vol. 35
Captain

CONTENTS

Chapter 328:
THE PIRATE ABDUCTION INCIDENT

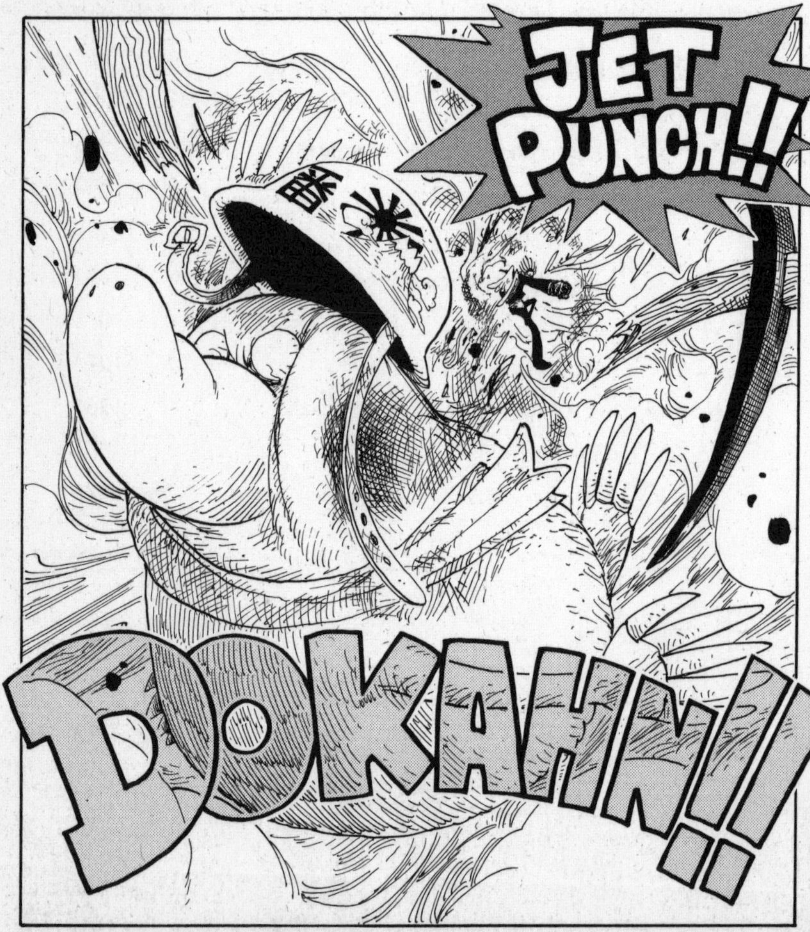
JET PUNCH!!
DOKAHN!!

GEDATSU'S UNEXPECTED LIFE ON THE BLUE SEA, VOL. 13:
"THE SKY BOSS VS. THE EARTH BOSS"

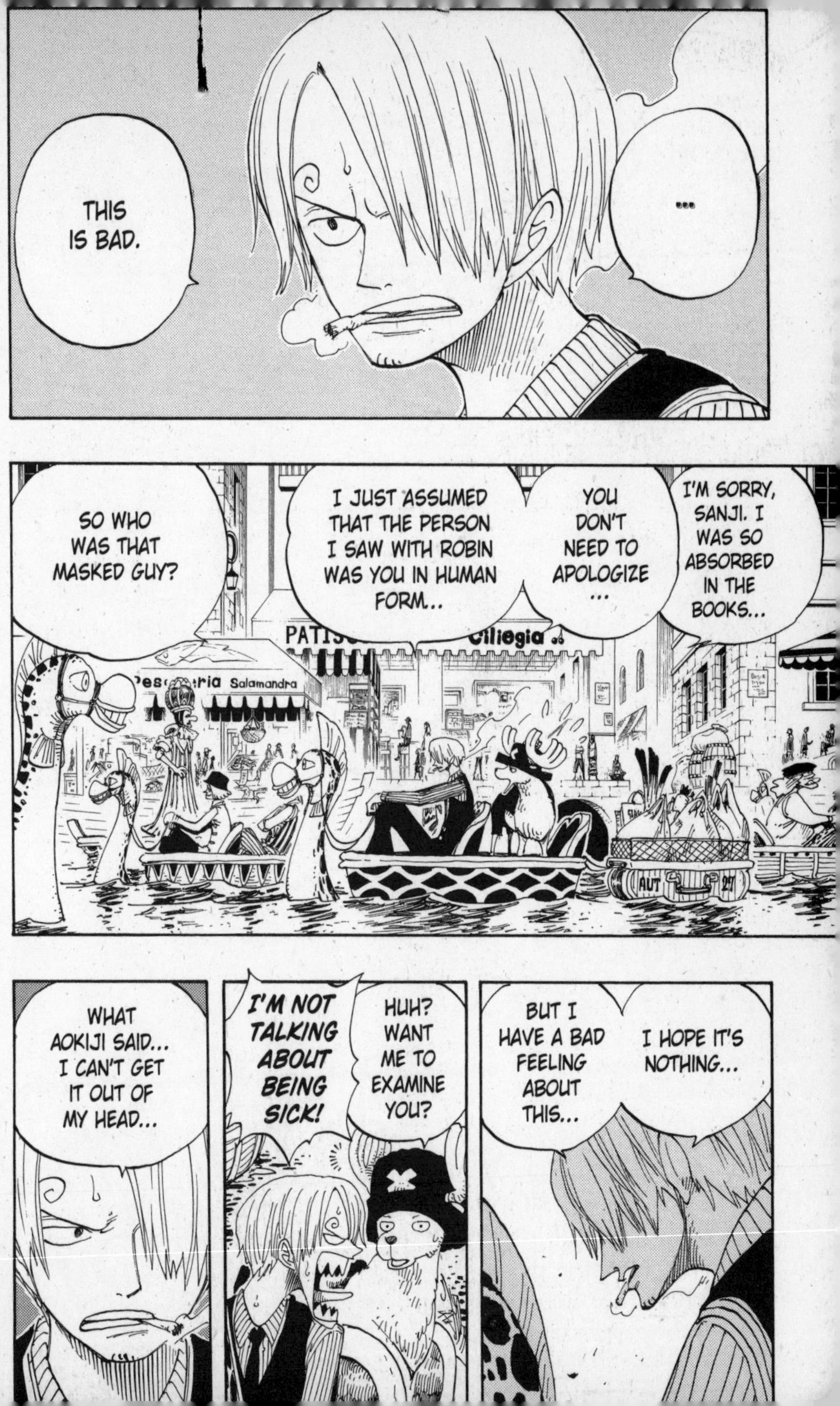
...
THIS IS BAD.
I'M SORRY, SANJI. I WAS SO ABSORBED IN THE BOOKS...
YOU DON'T NEED TO APOLOGIZE...
I JUST ASSUMED THAT THE PERSON I SAW WITH ROBIN WAS YOU IN HUMAN FORM...
SO WHO WAS THAT MASKED GUY?
Ciliegia
Salamandra
I HOPE IT'S NOTHING...
BUT I HAVE A BAD FEELING ABOUT THIS...
HUH? WANT ME TO EXAMINE YOU?
I'M NOT TALKING ABOUT BEING SICK!
WHAT AOKIJI SAID... I CAN'T GET IT OUT OF MY HEAD...

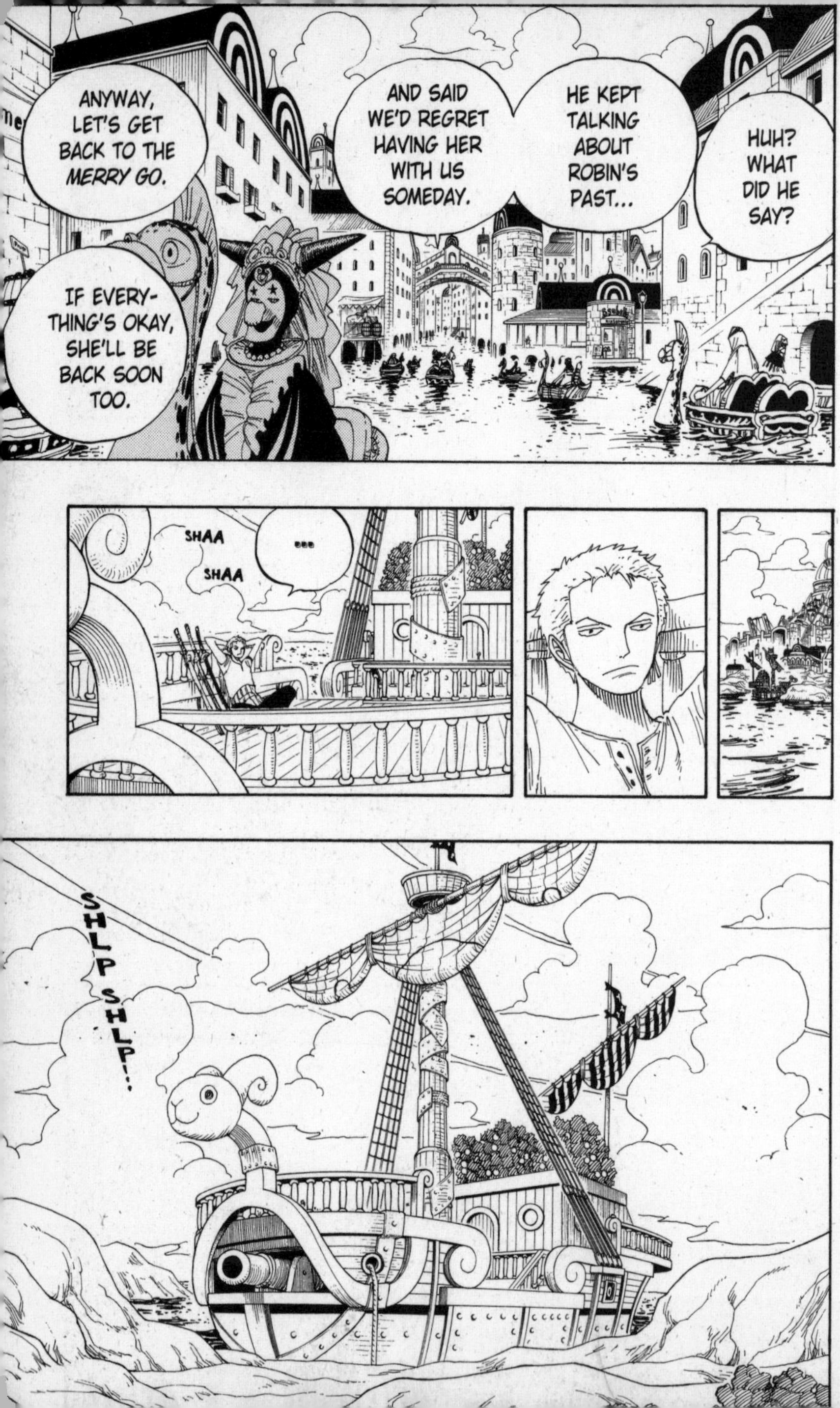
HUH? WHAT DID HE SAY?
HE KEPT TALKING ABOUT ROBIN'S PAST...
AND SAID WE'D REGRET HAVING HER WITH US SOMEDAY.
ANYWAY, LET'S GET BACK TO THE MERRY GO.
IF EVERY-THING'S OKAY, SHE'LL BE BACK SOON TOO.
...
SHAA
SHAA
SHLP SHLP!!

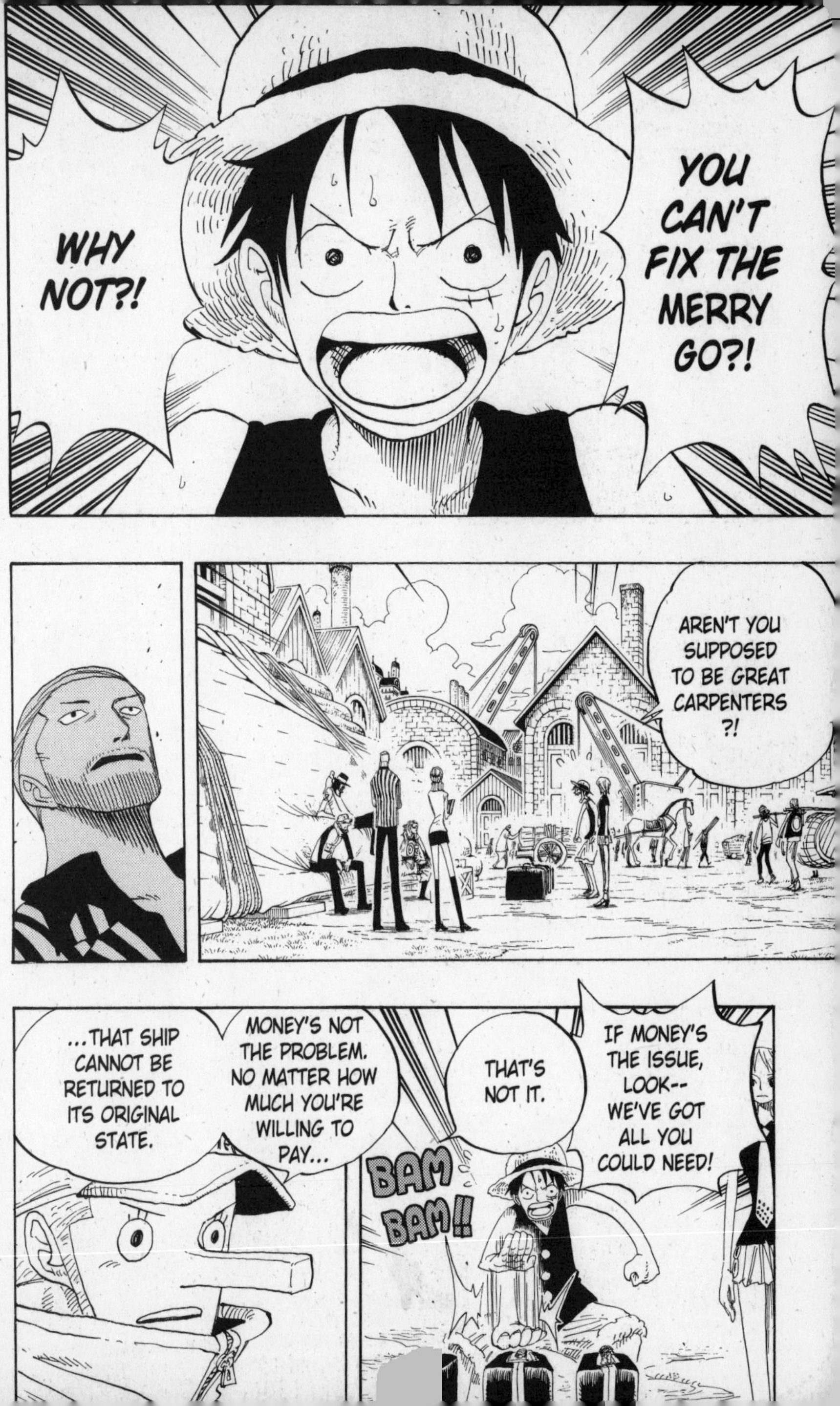
YOU CAN'T FIX THE MERRY GO?!
WHY NOT?!
AREN'T YOU SUPPOSED TO BE GREAT CARPENTERS ?!
IF MONEY'S THE ISSUE, LOOK-- WE'VE GOT ALL YOU COULD NEED!
THAT'S NOT IT.
BAM BAM!!
MONEY'S NOT THE PROBLEM. NO MATTER HOW MUCH YOU'RE WILLING TO PAY...
...THAT SHIP CANNOT BE RETURNED TO ITS ORIGINAL STATE.

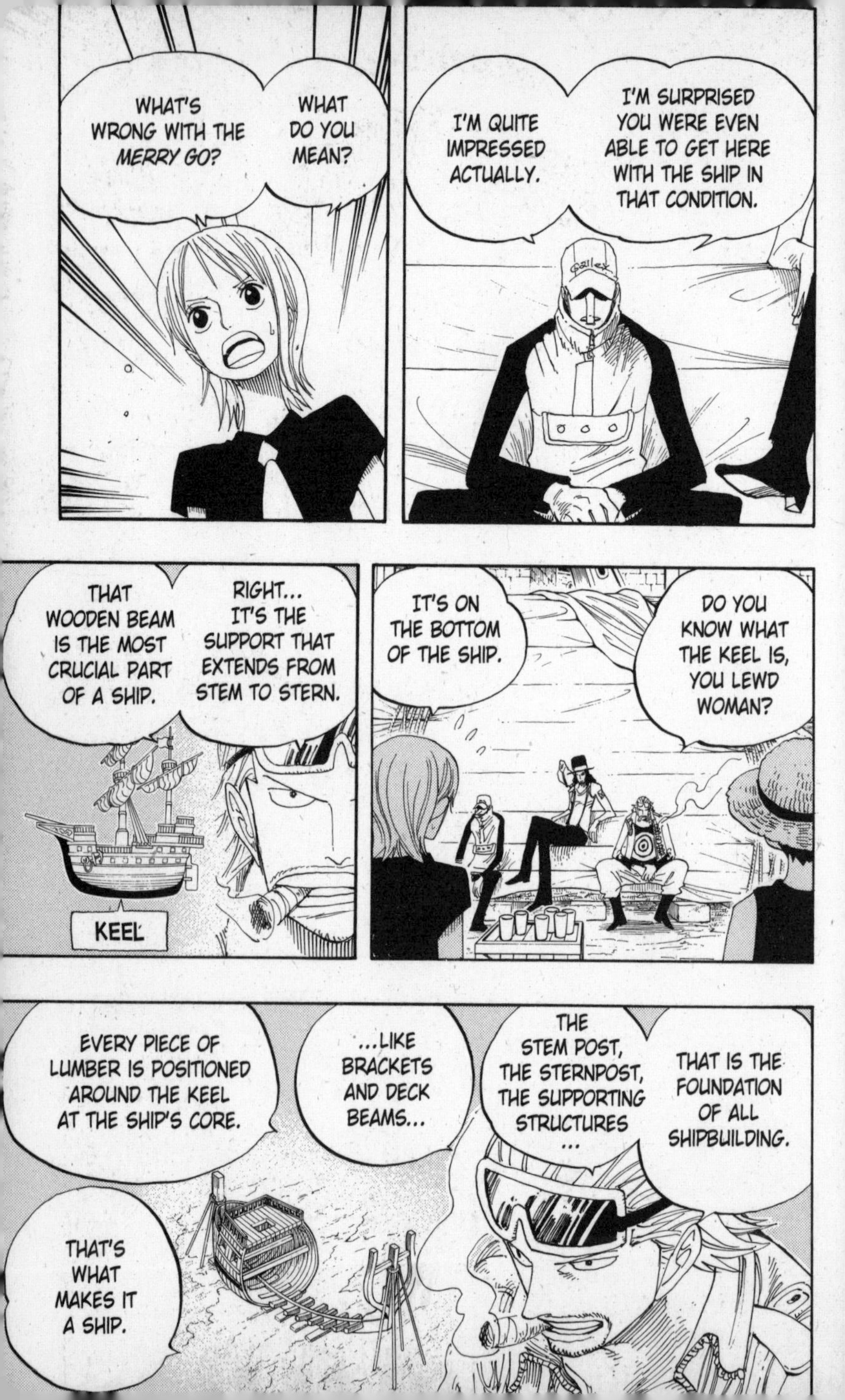
I'M SURPRISED YOU WERE EVEN ABLE TO GET HERE WITH THE SHIP IN THAT CONDITION.
I'M QUITE IMPRESSED ACTUALLY.
WHAT DO YOU MEAN?
WHAT'S WRONG WITH THE *MERRY GO?*
DO YOU KNOW WHAT THE KEEL IS, YOU LEWD WOMAN?
IT'S ON THE BOTTOM OF THE SHIP.
RIGHT... IT'S THE SUPPORT THAT EXTENDS FROM STEM TO STERN.
THAT WOODEN BEAM IS THE MOST CRUCIAL PART OF A SHIP.
KEEL
THAT IS THE FOUNDATION OF ALL SHIPBUILDING.
THE STEM POST, THE STERNPOST, THE SUPPORTING STRUCTURES ...
...LIKE BRACKETS AND DECK BEAMS...
EVERY PIECE OF LUMBER IS POSITIONED AROUND THE KEEL AT THE SHIP'S CORE.
THAT'S WHAT MAKES IT A SHIP.

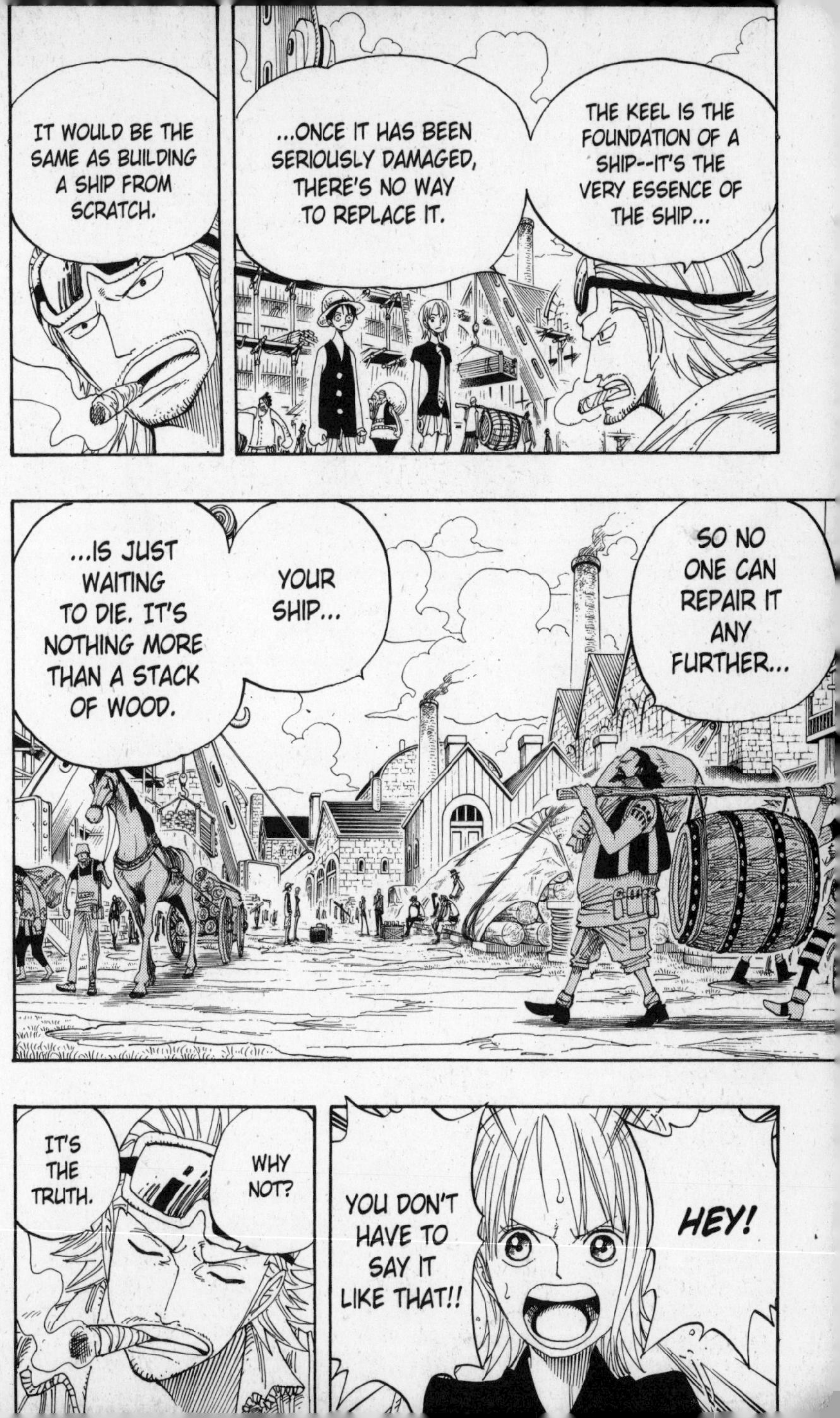
THE KEEL IS THE FOUNDATION OF A SHIP--IT'S THE VERY ESSENCE OF THE SHIP...
...ONCE IT HAS BEEN SERIOUSLY DAMAGED, THERE'S NO WAY TO REPLACE IT.
IT WOULD BE THE SAME AS BUILDING A SHIP FROM SCRATCH.
SO NO ONE CAN REPAIR IT ANY FURTHER...
YOUR SHIP...
...IS JUST WAITING TO DIE. IT'S NOTHING MORE THAN A STACK OF WOOD.
HEY!
YOU DON'T HAVE TO SAY IT LIKE THAT!!
WHY NOT?
IT'S THE TRUTH.

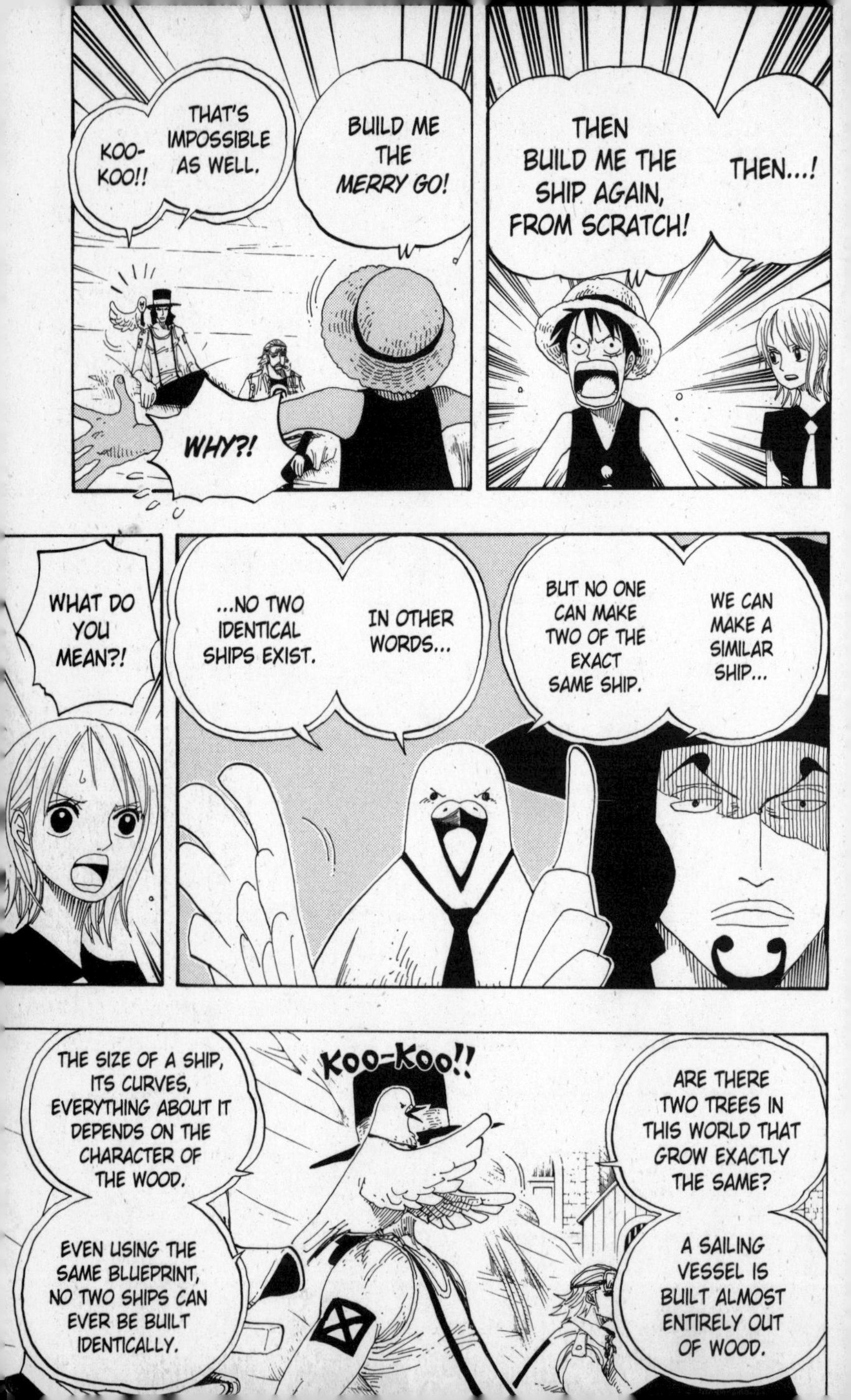
THEN...!
THEN BUILD ME THE SHIP AGAIN, FROM SCRATCH!
BUILD ME THE MERRY GO!
THAT'S IMPOSSIBLE AS WELL.
KOO-KOO!!
WHY?!
WE CAN MAKE A SIMILAR SHIP...
BUT NO ONE CAN MAKE TWO OF THE EXACT SAME SHIP.
IN OTHER WORDS...
...NO TWO IDENTICAL SHIPS EXIST.
WHAT DO YOU MEAN?!
ARE THERE TWO TREES IN THIS WORLD THAT GROW EXACTLY THE SAME?
A SAILING VESSEL IS BUILT ALMOST ENTIRELY OUT OF WOOD.
KOO-KOO!!
THE SIZE OF A SHIP, ITS CURVES, EVERYTHING ABOUT IT DEPENDS ON THE CHARACTER OF THE WOOD.
EVEN USING THE SAME BLUEPRINT, NO TWO SHIPS CAN EVER BE BUILT IDENTICALLY.

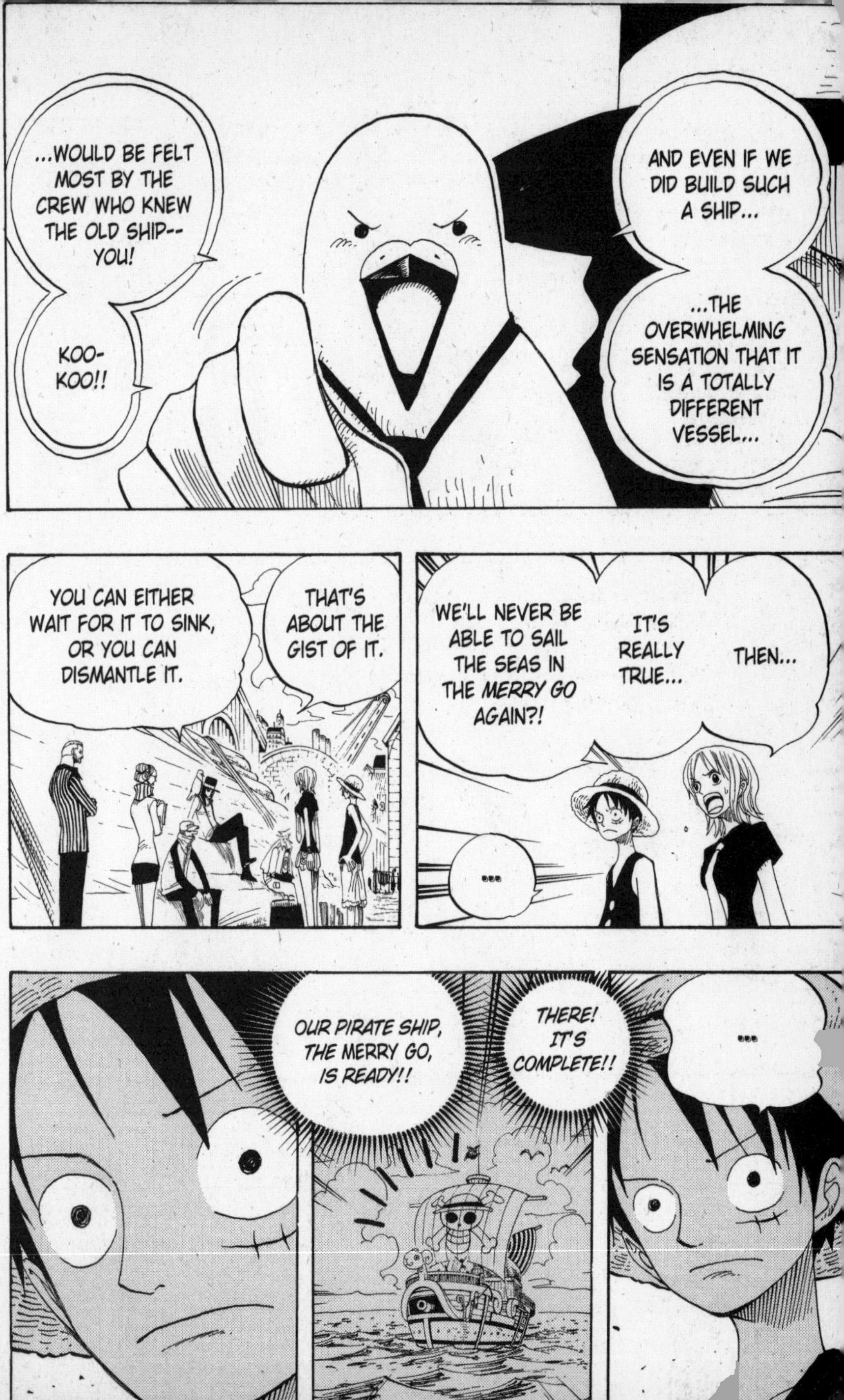
AND EVEN IF WE DID BUILD SUCH A SHIP...
...THE OVERWHELMING SENSATION THAT IT IS A TOTALLY DIFFERENT VESSEL...
...WOULD BE FELT MOST BY THE CREW WHO KNEW THE OLD SHIP-- YOU!
KOO-KOO!!
THEN...
IT'S REALLY TRUE...
WE'LL NEVER BE ABLE TO SAIL THE SEAS IN THE *MERRY GO* AGAIN?!
...
THAT'S ABOUT THE GIST OF IT.
YOU CAN EITHER WAIT FOR IT TO SINK, OR YOU CAN DISMANTLE IT.
...
THERE! IT'S COMPLETE!!
OUR PIRATE SHIP, THE MERRY GO, IS READY!!

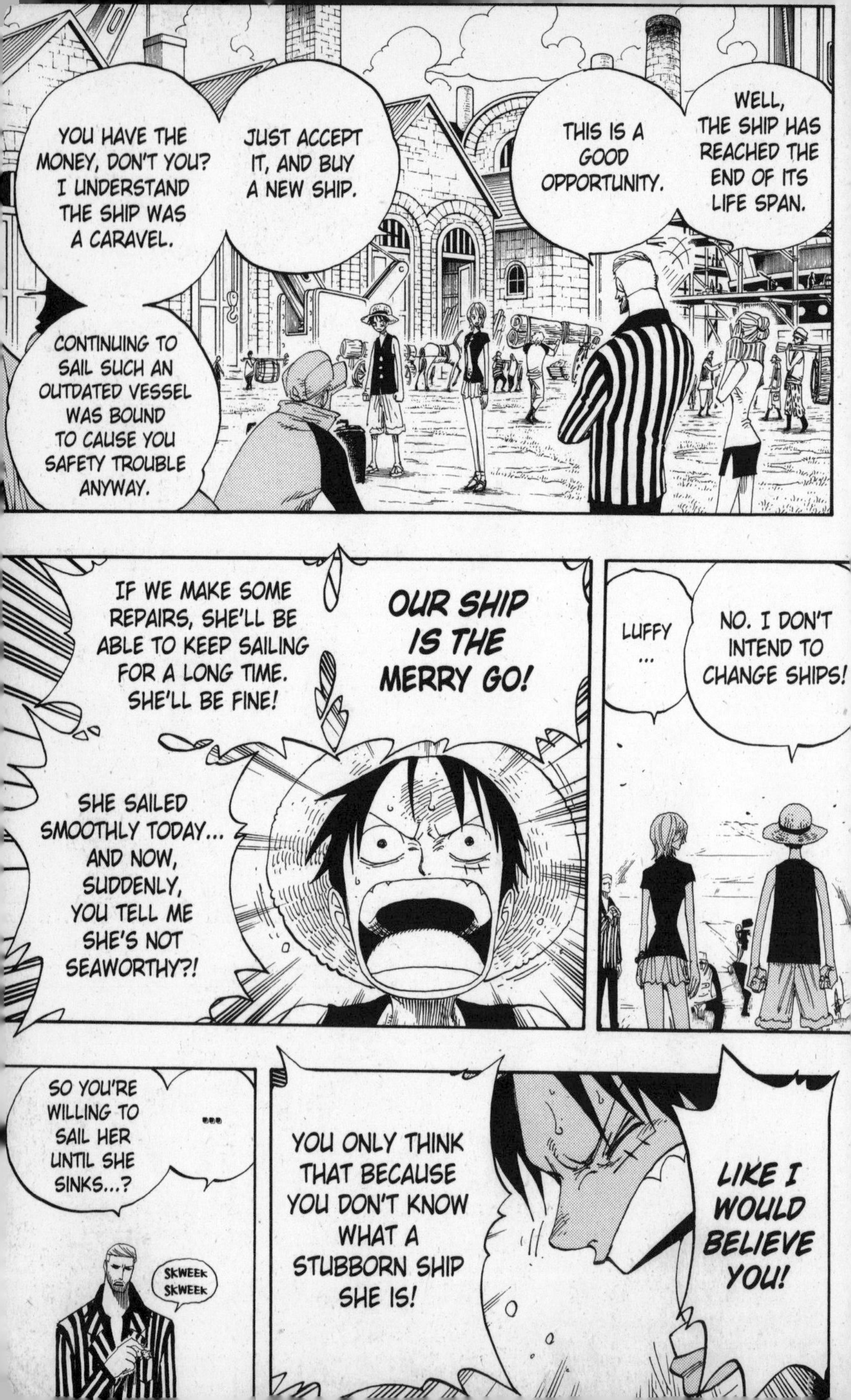
WELL, THE SHIP HAS REACHED THE END OF ITS LIFE SPAN.
THIS IS A GOOD OPPORTUNITY.
JUST ACCEPT IT, AND BUY A NEW SHIP.
YOU HAVE THE MONEY, DON'T YOU? I UNDERSTAND THE SHIP WAS A CARAVEL.
CONTINUING TO SAIL SUCH AN OUTDATED VESSEL WAS BOUND TO CAUSE YOU SAFETY TROUBLE ANYWAY.
NO. I DON'T INTEND TO CHANGE SHIPS!
LUFFY ...
OUR SHIP IS THE MERRY GO!
IF WE MAKE SOME REPAIRS, SHE'LL BE ABLE TO KEEP SAILING FOR A LONG TIME. SHE'LL BE FINE!
SHE SAILED SMOOTHLY TODAY... AND NOW, SUDDENLY, YOU TELL ME SHE'S NOT SEAWORTHY?!
LIKE I WOULD BELIEVE YOU!
YOU ONLY THINK THAT BECAUSE YOU DON'T KNOW WHAT A STUBBORN SHIP SHE IS!
SO YOU'RE WILLING TO SAIL HER UNTIL SHE SINKS...?
...
SKWEEK SKWEEK

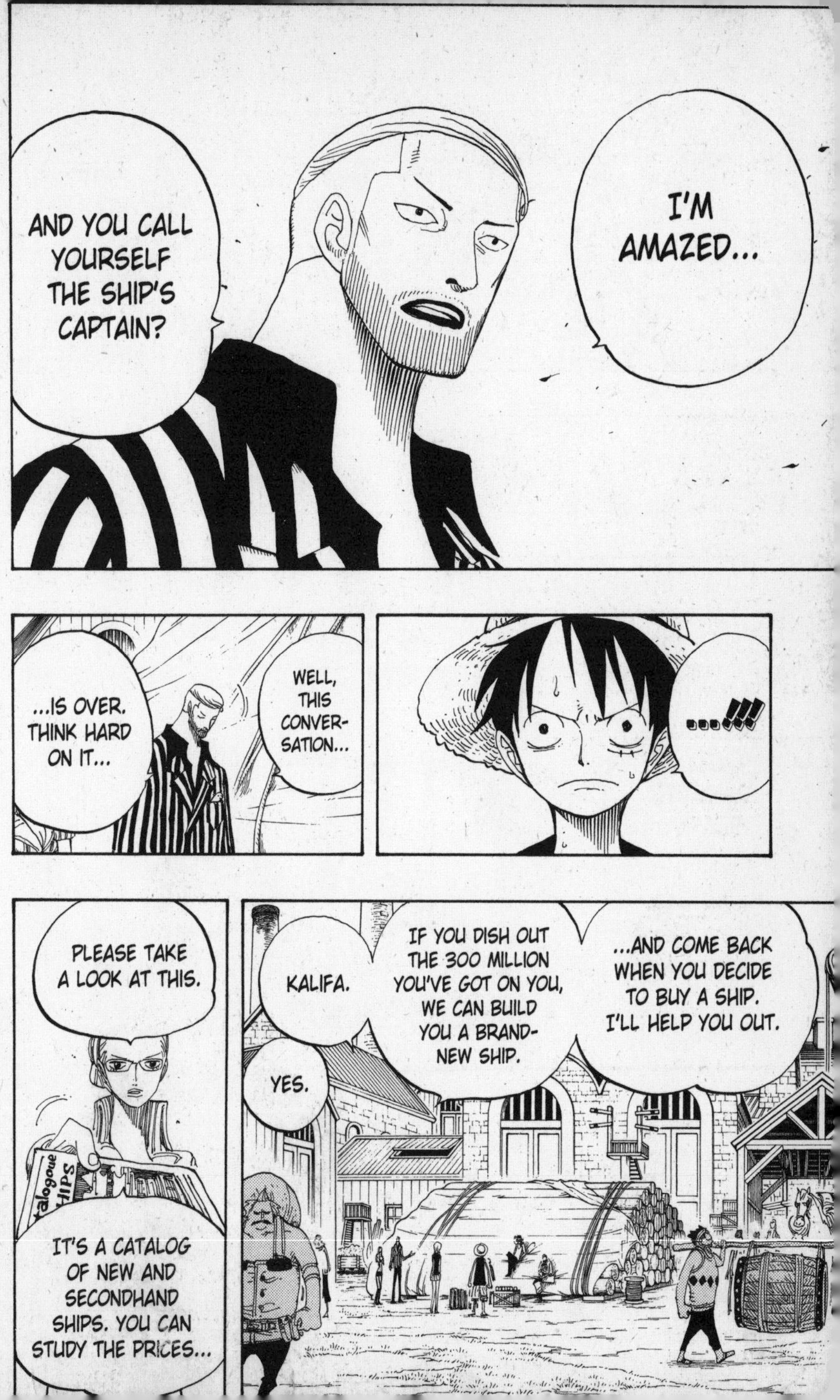
I'M AMAZED...
AND YOU CALL YOURSELF THE SHIP'S CAPTAIN?
...!!!
WELL, THIS CONVER-SATION...
...IS OVER. THINK HARD ON IT...
...AND COME BACK WHEN YOU DECIDE TO BUY A SHIP. I'LL HELP YOU OUT.
IF YOU DISH OUT THE 300 MILLION YOU'VE GOT ON YOU, WE CAN BUILD YOU A BRAND-NEW SHIP.
KALIFA.
YES.
PLEASE TAKE A LOOK AT THIS.
IT'S A CATALOG OF NEW AND SECONDHAND SHIPS. YOU CAN STUDY THE PRICES...

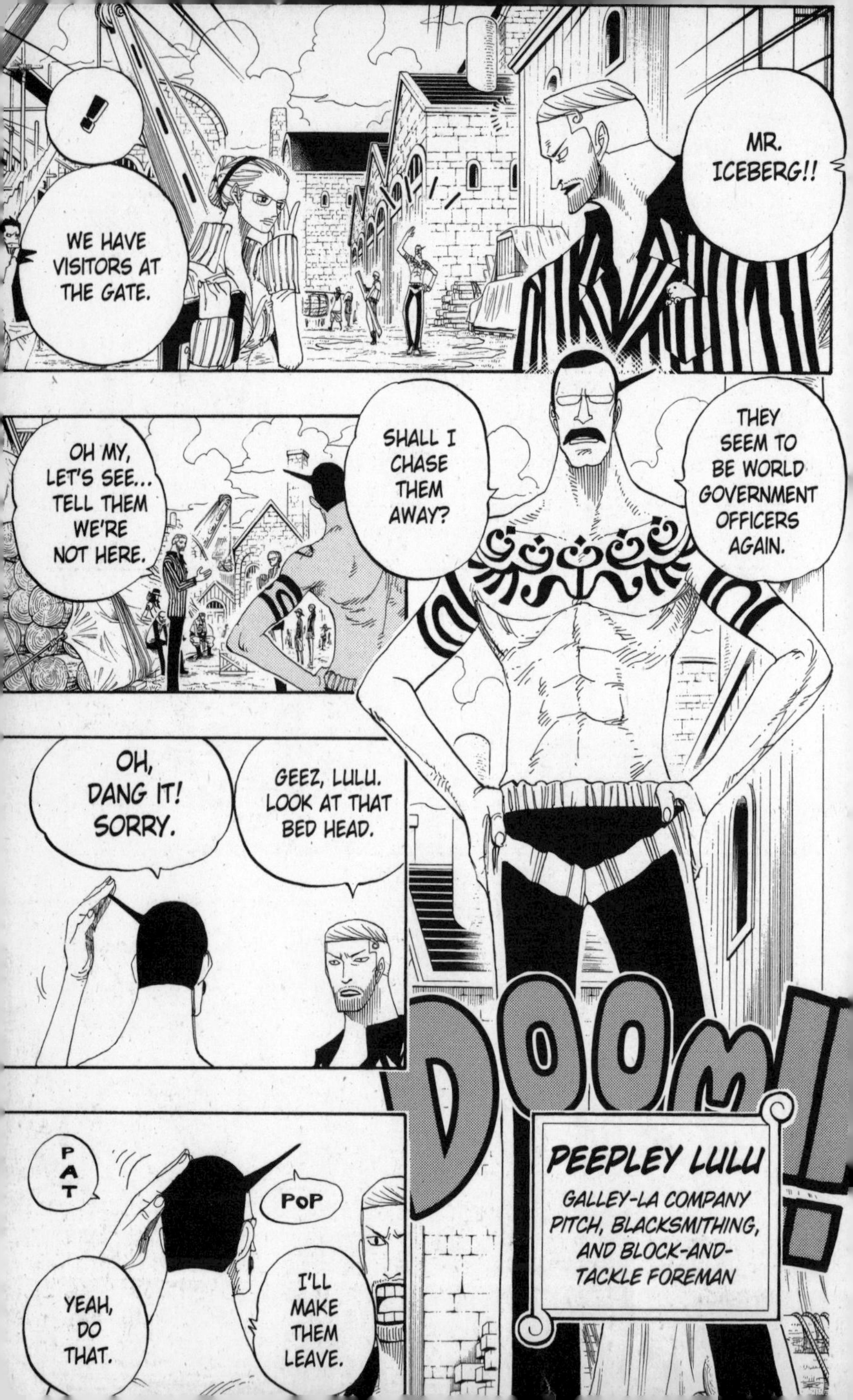
MR. ICEBERG!!
!
WE HAVE VISITORS AT THE GATE.
THEY SEEM TO BE WORLD GOVERNMENT OFFICERS AGAIN.
DOOM!
PEEPLEY LULU
GALLEY-LA COMPANY PITCH, BLACKSMITHING, AND BLOCK-AND-TACKLE FOREMAN
SHALL I CHASE THEM AWAY?
OH MY, LET'S SEE... TELL THEM WE'RE NOT HERE.
GEEZ, LULU. LOOK AT THAT BED HEAD.
OH, DANG IT! SORRY.
POP
PAT
I'LL MAKE THEM LEAVE.
YEAH, DO THAT.

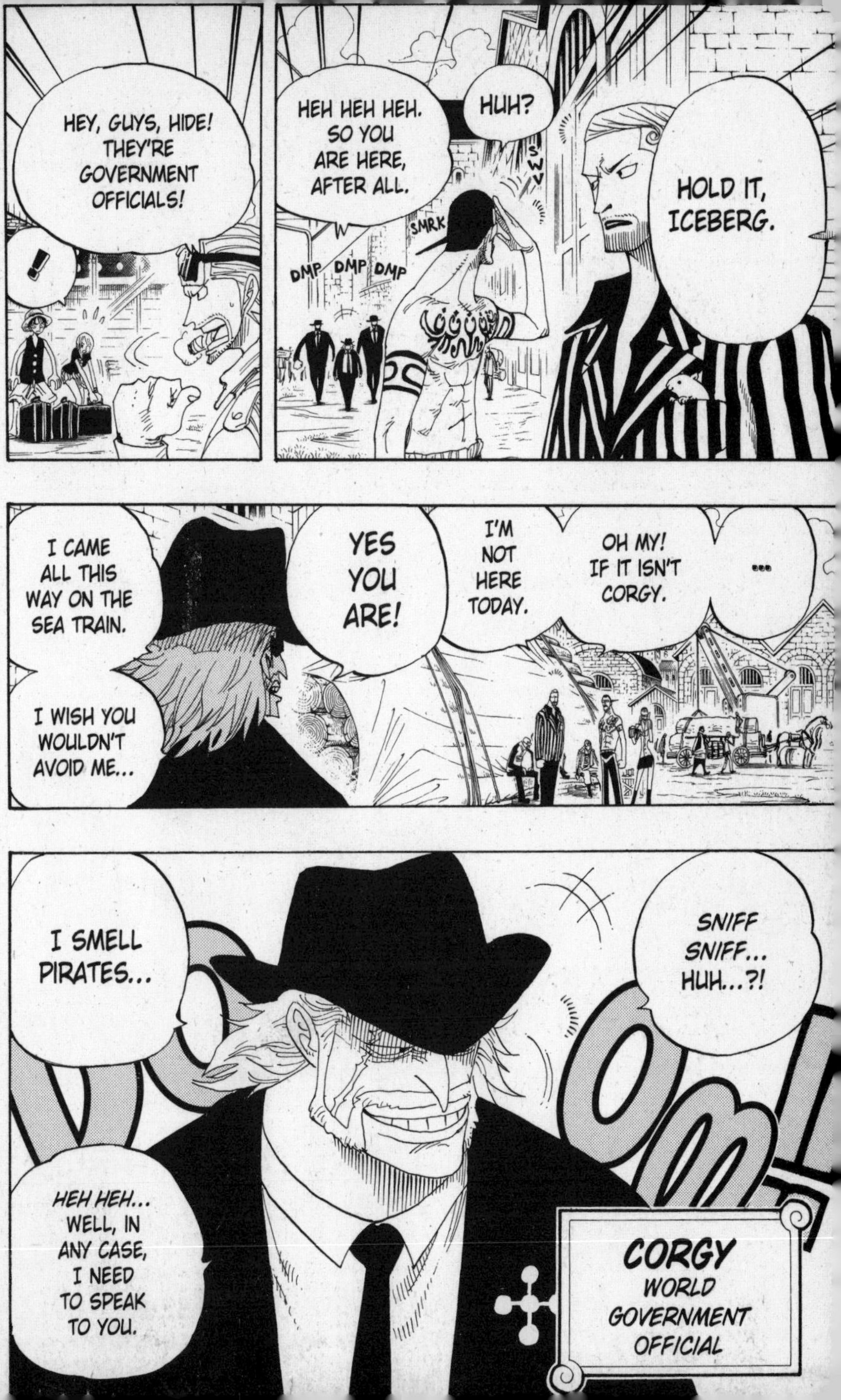
HOLD IT, ICEBERG.
HUH?
SWV
HEH HEH HEH. SO YOU ARE HERE, AFTER ALL.
SMRK
DMP DMP DMP
HEY, GUYS, HIDE! THEY'RE GOVERNMENT OFFICIALS!
!
...
OH MY! IF IT ISN'T CORGY.
I'M NOT HERE TODAY.
YES YOU ARE!
I CAME ALL THIS WAY ON THE SEA TRAIN.
I WISH YOU WOULDN'T AVOID ME...
SNIFF SNIFF... HUH...?!
I SMELL PIRATES...
CORGY
WORLD GOVERNMENT OFFICIAL
HEH HEH... WELL, IN ANY CASE, I NEED TO SPEAK TO YOU.

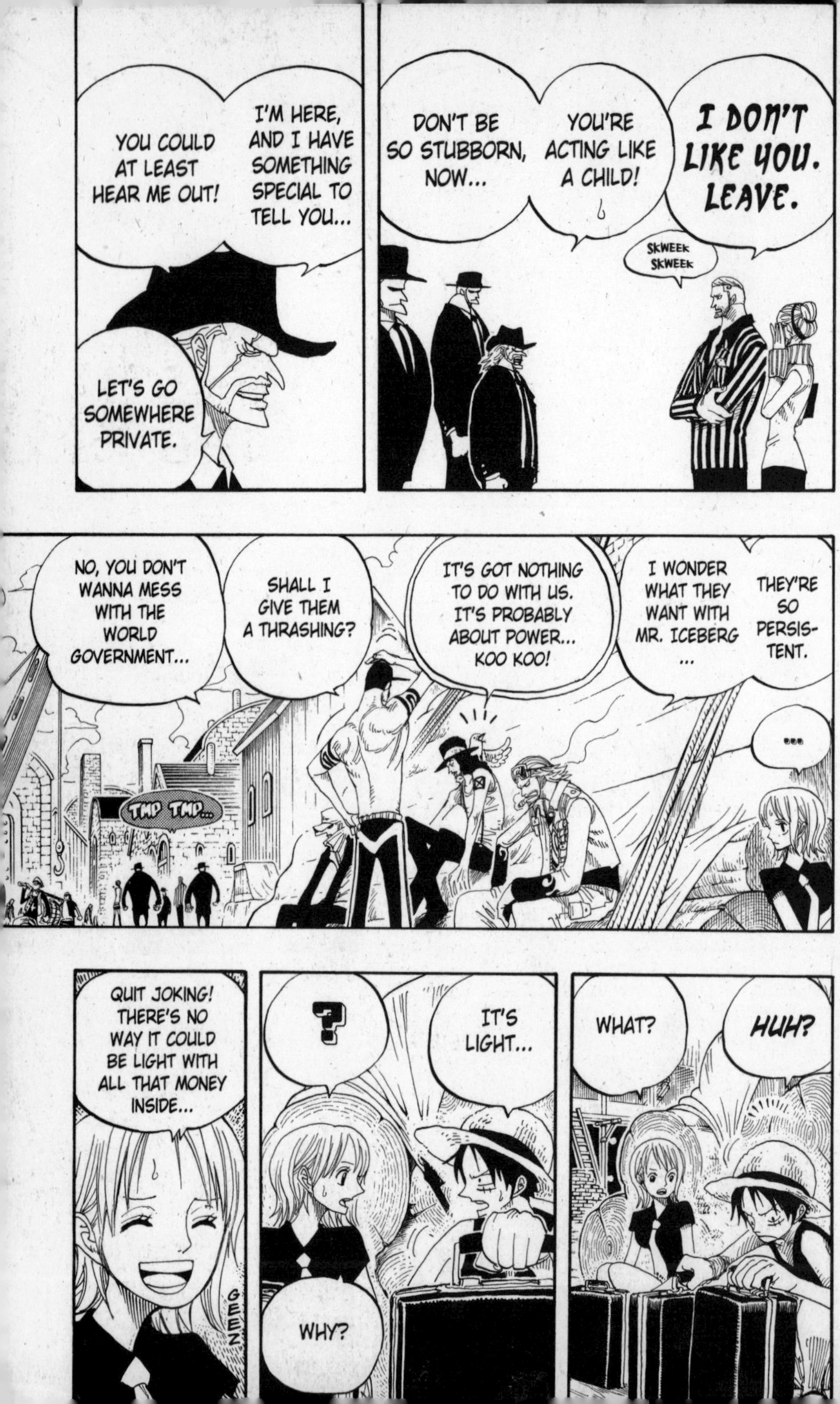

I DON'T LIKE YOU. LEAVE.
SKWEEK SKWEEK
YOU'RE ACTING LIKE A CHILD!
DON'T BE SO STUBBORN, NOW...
I'M HERE, AND I HAVE SOMETHING SPECIAL TO TELL YOU...
YOU COULD AT LEAST HEAR ME OUT!
LET'S GO SOMEWHERE PRIVATE.
THEY'RE SO PERSIS-TENT.
I WONDER WHAT THEY WANT WITH MR. ICEBERG ...
IT'S GOT NOTHING TO DO WITH US. IT'S PROBABLY ABOUT POWER... KOO KOO!
...
SHALL I GIVE THEM A THRASHING?
NO, YOU DON'T WANNA MESS WITH THE WORLD GOVERNMENT...
TMP TMP...
HUH?
WHAT?
IT'S LIGHT...
?
WHY?
QUIT JOKING! THERE'S NO WAY IT COULD BE LIGHT WITH ALL THAT MONEY INSIDE...
GEEZ

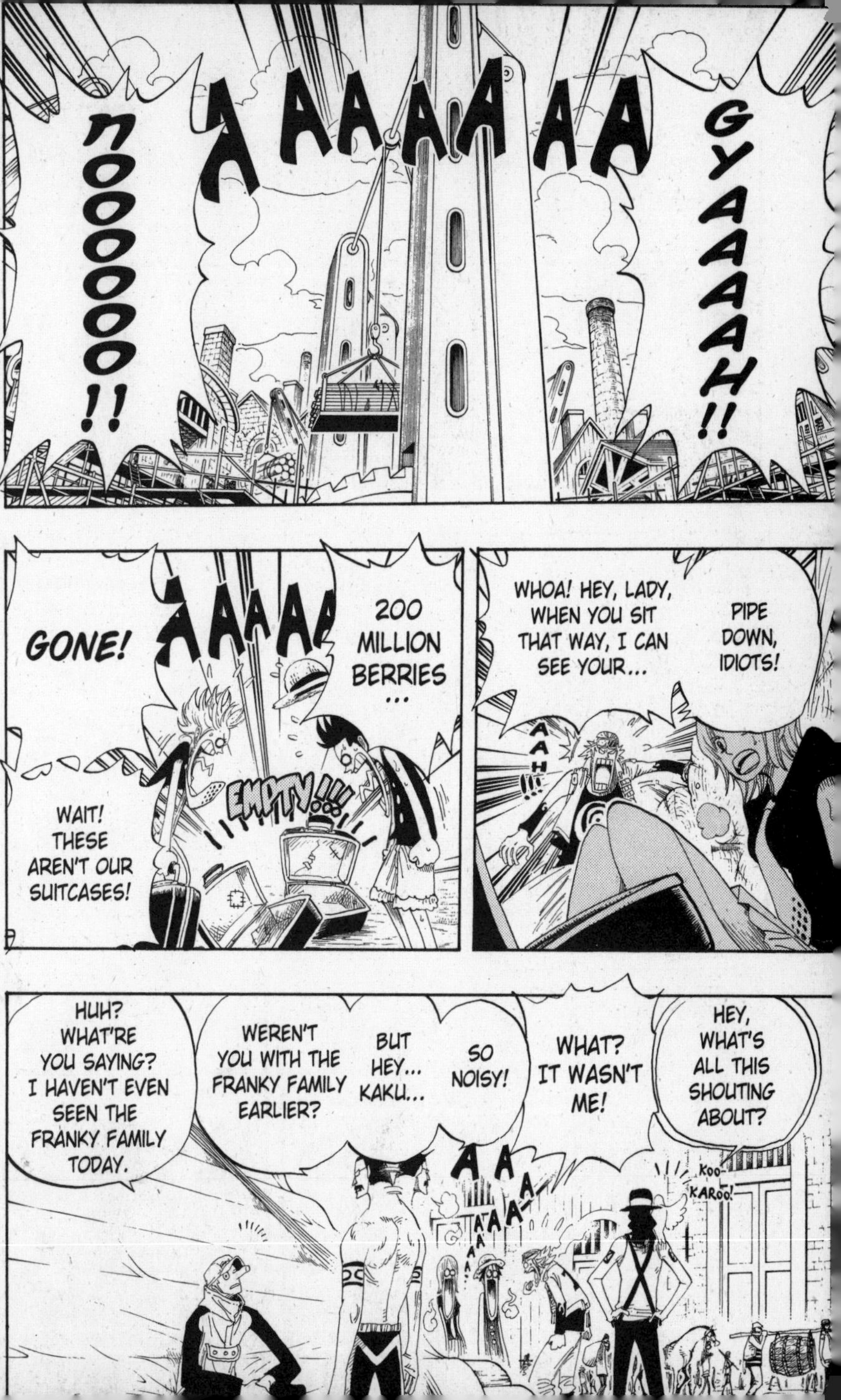
GYAAAAAH!!
AAAAAAA
NOOOOOOO!!
PIPE DOWN, IDIOTS!
WHOA! HEY, LADY, WHEN YOU SIT THAT WAY, I CAN SEE YOUR...
AAH!!
200 MILLION BERRIES...
AAAA
GONE!
EMPTY!!!!
WAIT! THESE AREN'T OUR SUITCASES!
HEY, WHAT'S ALL THIS SHOUTING ABOUT?
KOO-KAROO!
WHAT? IT WASN'T ME!
SO NOISY!
BUT HEY... KAKU...
WEREN'T YOU WITH THE FRANKY FAMILY EARLIER?
HUH? WHAT'RE YOU SAYING? I HAVEN'T EVEN SEEN THE FRANKY FAMILY TODAY.

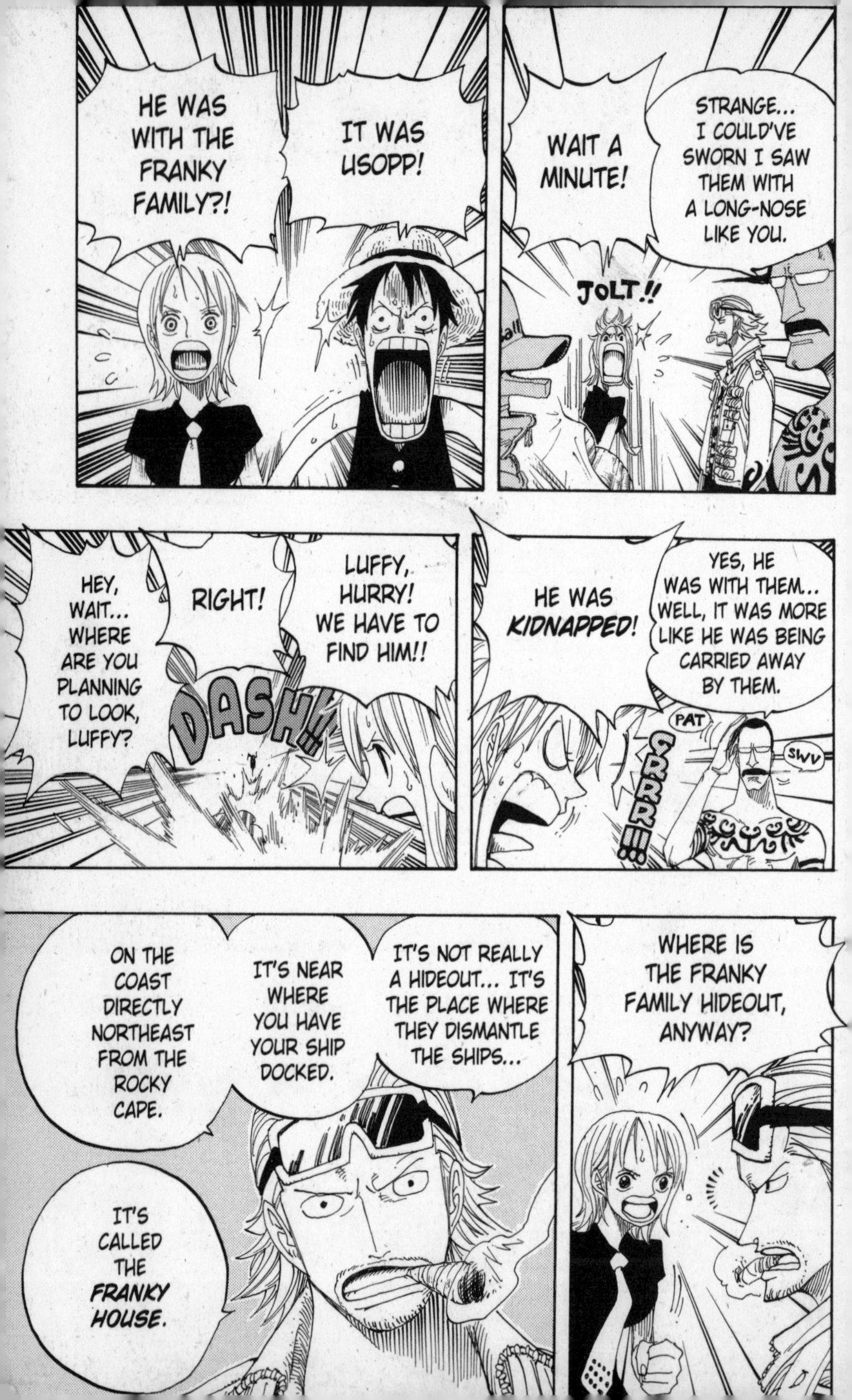
STRANGE... I COULD'VE SWORN I SAW THEM WITH A LONG-NOSE LIKE YOU.
WAIT A MINUTE!
JOLT!!
IT WAS USOPP!
HE WAS WITH THE FRANKY FAMILY?!
YES, HE WAS WITH THEM... WELL, IT WAS MORE LIKE HE WAS BEING CARRIED AWAY BY THEM.
HE WAS KIDNAPPED!
PAT
SWV
GRRR!!!
LUFFY, HURRY! WE HAVE TO FIND HIM!!
RIGHT!
DASH!!
HEY, WAIT... WHERE ARE YOU PLANNING TO LOOK, LUFFY?
WHERE IS THE FRANKY FAMILY HIDEOUT, ANYWAY?
IT'S NOT REALLY A HIDEOUT... IT'S THE PLACE WHERE THEY DISMANTLE THE SHIPS...
IT'S NEAR WHERE YOU HAVE YOUR SHIP DOCKED.
ON THE COAST DIRECTLY NORTHEAST FROM THE ROCKY CAPE.
IT'S CALLED THE FRANKY HOUSE.

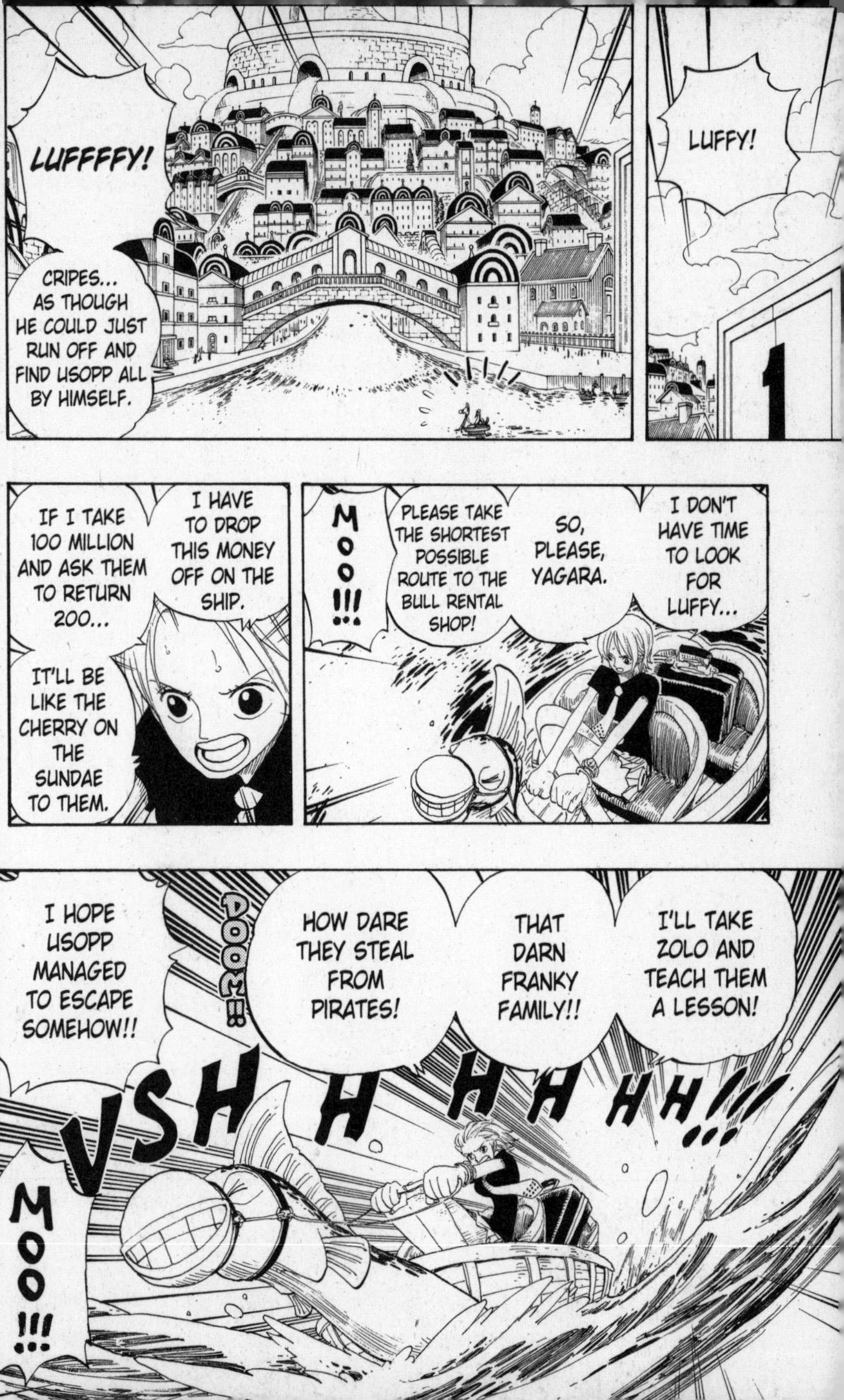
LUFFY!
LUFFFFY!
CRIPES... AS THOUGH HE COULD JUST RUN OFF AND FIND USOPP ALL BY HIMSELF.
I DON'T HAVE TIME TO LOOK FOR LUFFY...
SO, PLEASE, YAGARA.
PLEASE TAKE THE SHORTEST POSSIBLE ROUTE TO THE BULL RENTAL SHOP!
MOO!!!
I HAVE TO DROP THIS MONEY OFF ON THE SHIP.
IF I TAKE 100 MILLION AND ASK THEM TO RETURN 200...
IT'LL BE LIKE THE CHERRY ON THE SUNDAE TO THEM.
I'LL TAKE ZOLO AND TEACH THEM A LESSON!
THAT DARN FRANKY FAMILY!!
HOW DARE THEY STEAL FROM PIRATES!
DOOM!!
I HOPE USOPP MANAGED TO ESCAPE SOMEHOW!!
VSH H H H H!!!
MOO!!!

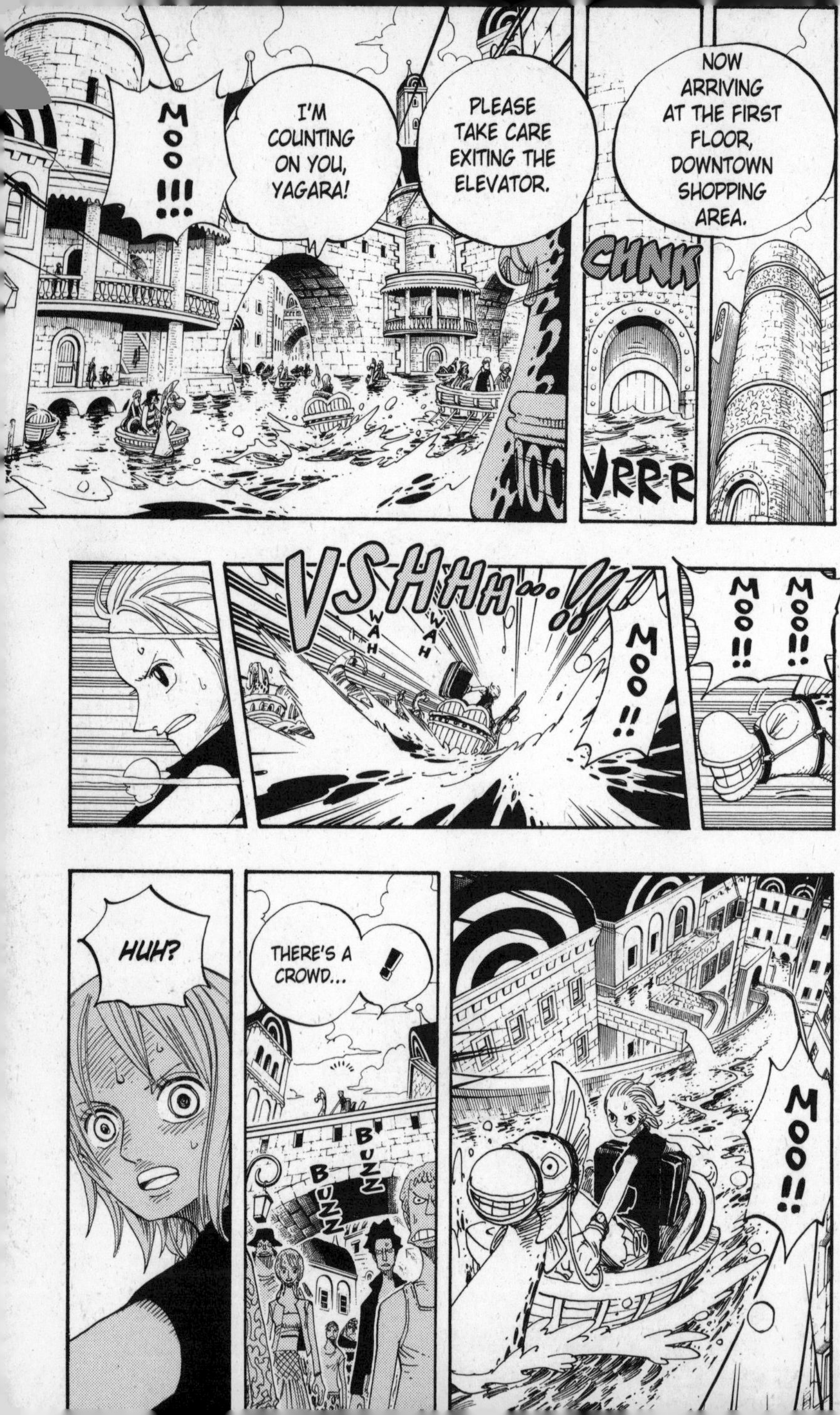
NOW ARRIVING AT THE FIRST FLOOR, DOWNTOWN SHOPPING AREA.
CHNK
VRRR
PLEASE TAKE CARE EXITING THE ELEVATOR.
I'M COUNTING ON YOU, YAGARA!
MOO!!!
MOO!!
MOO!!
VSHHH...!!
WAH
WAH
MOO!!
MOO!!
THERE'S A CROWD...
!
BUZZ
BUZZ
HUH?

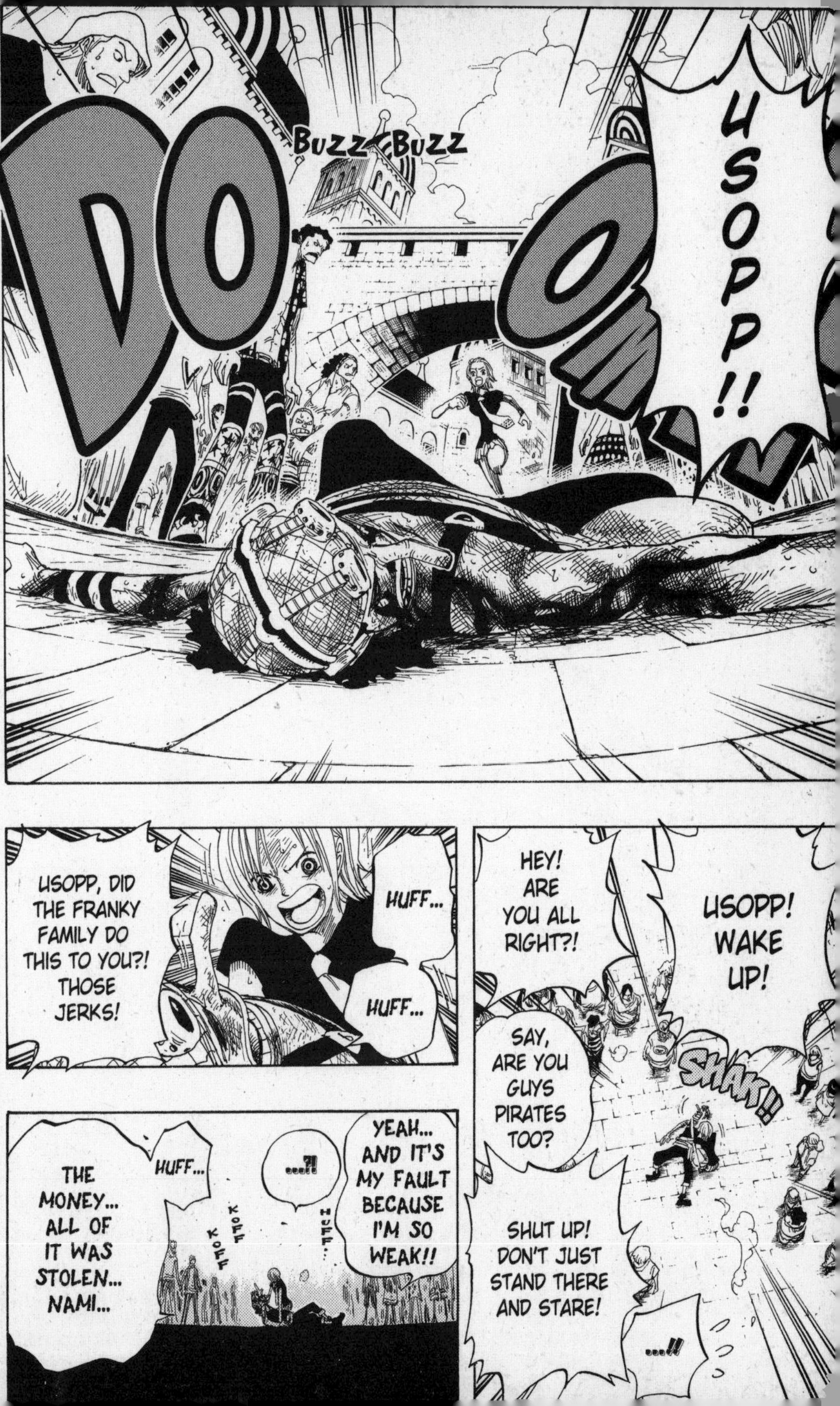
USOPP!!
DO
BUZZ BUZZ
USOPP! WAKE UP!
HEY! ARE YOU ALL RIGHT?!
SAY, ARE YOU GUYS PIRATES TOO?
SHAK!!
SHUT UP! DON'T JUST STAND THERE AND STARE!
...!!
HUFF...
HUFF...
USOPP, DID THE FRANKY FAMILY DO THIS TO YOU?! THOSE JERKS!
YEAH... AND IT'S MY FAULT BECAUSE I'M SO WEAK!!
HUFF...
...?!
KOFF KOFF
HUFF...
THE MONEY... ALL OF IT WAS STOLEN... NAMI...

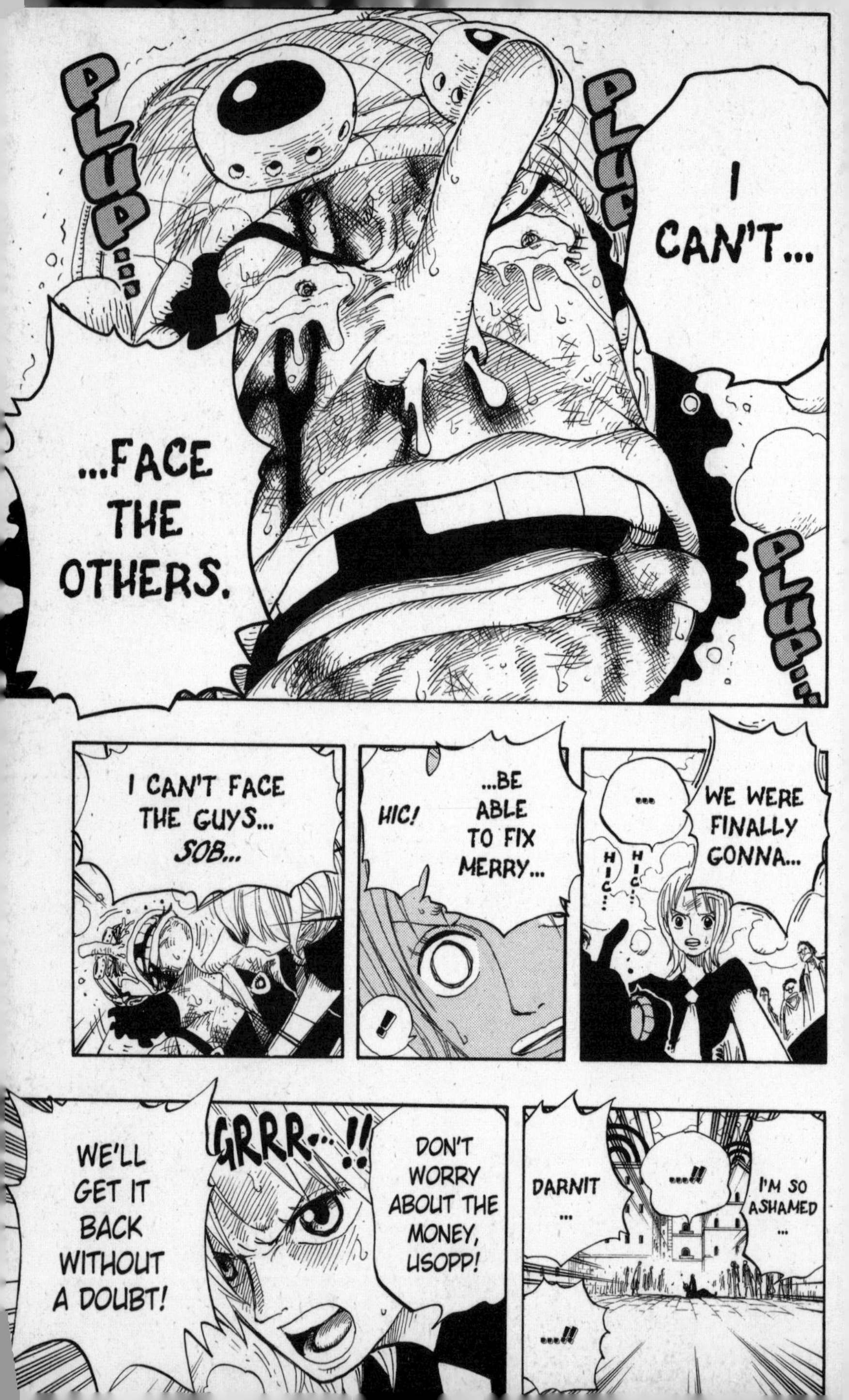
PLUP...
I CAN'T...
PLUP...
...FACE THE OTHERS.
PLUP...
WE WERE FINALLY GONNA...
HIC...
HIC...
...
...BE ABLE TO FIX MERRY...
HIC!
!
I CAN'T FACE THE GUYS... *SOB...*
I'M SO ASHAMED ...
...!!
DARNIT ...
...!!
DON'T WORRY ABOUT THE MONEY, USOPP!
GRRR...!!
WE'LL GET IT BACK WITHOUT A DOUBT!

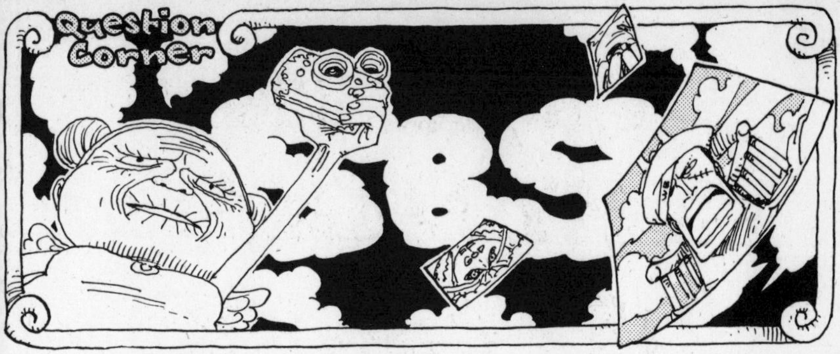
Question Corner

Q: Ding Dong ♪

Oda-san, I have a delivery. It's a beautiful flower bouquet.

Oh! There's a card. Hmm, let's see.

It says, "The Question Corner will now begin,"

Well, please do your best. KACHAK --Nananko Miimi

A: Oda: Thank you very much. Oh my, I received flowers. Yup. Hey now...

The Question Corner has already Begun! (Doom!!)

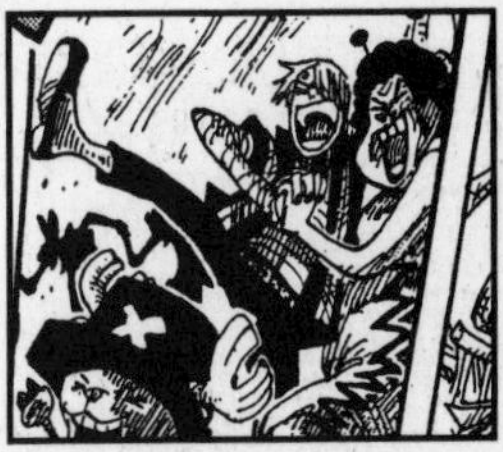

Q: I know this is sudden, Oda Sensei, but in vol. 32, on page 104, panel 6, Chopper and Sanji are dancing. And Sanji is dancing with some strange middle-aged woman!! Just who is she?! Did she just show up out of the blue? --Amirin

A: Oh... You mean Marilyn? Forty years ago, she was Miss Skypiea...the beauty of Skypiea. (past tense) Kami Eneru is scary, but the passage of time is also scary. (Wise words.)

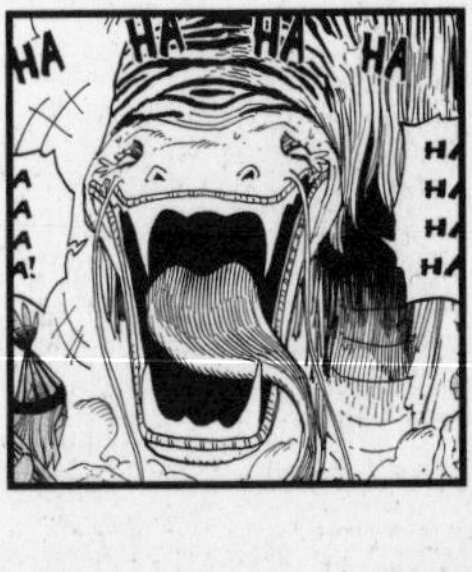
HA HA HA HA

Q: About Nola, who lives in Skypiea: Is the origin of its name from *nora* as in "*norainu*" (stray dog)? Or is it *nola* from "Noland Mont Blanc"? And did Kalgara, who longed to see Noland, give it that name? Please tell me!

--Norashufu (stray housewife)

A: Nola is derived from Noland. Seto chose the name.

Chapter 329:

MY NAME IS FRANKY

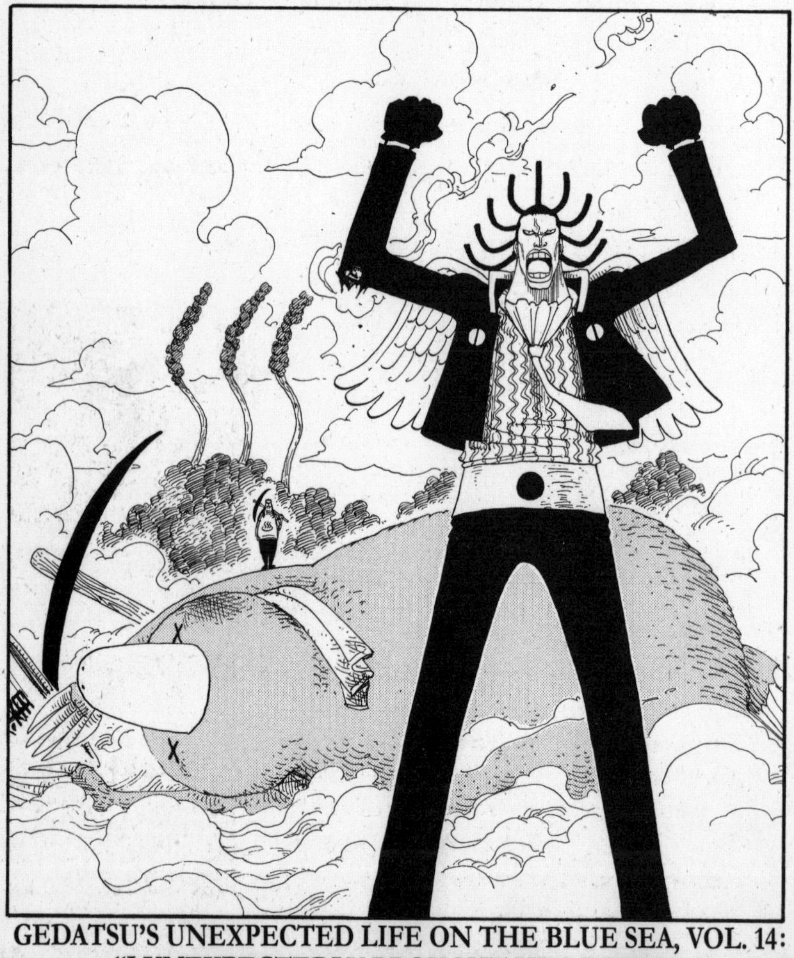

GEDATSU'S UNEXPECTED LIFE ON THE BLUE SEA, VOL. 14:
"I UNEXPECTEDLY BROUGHT HIM DOWN"

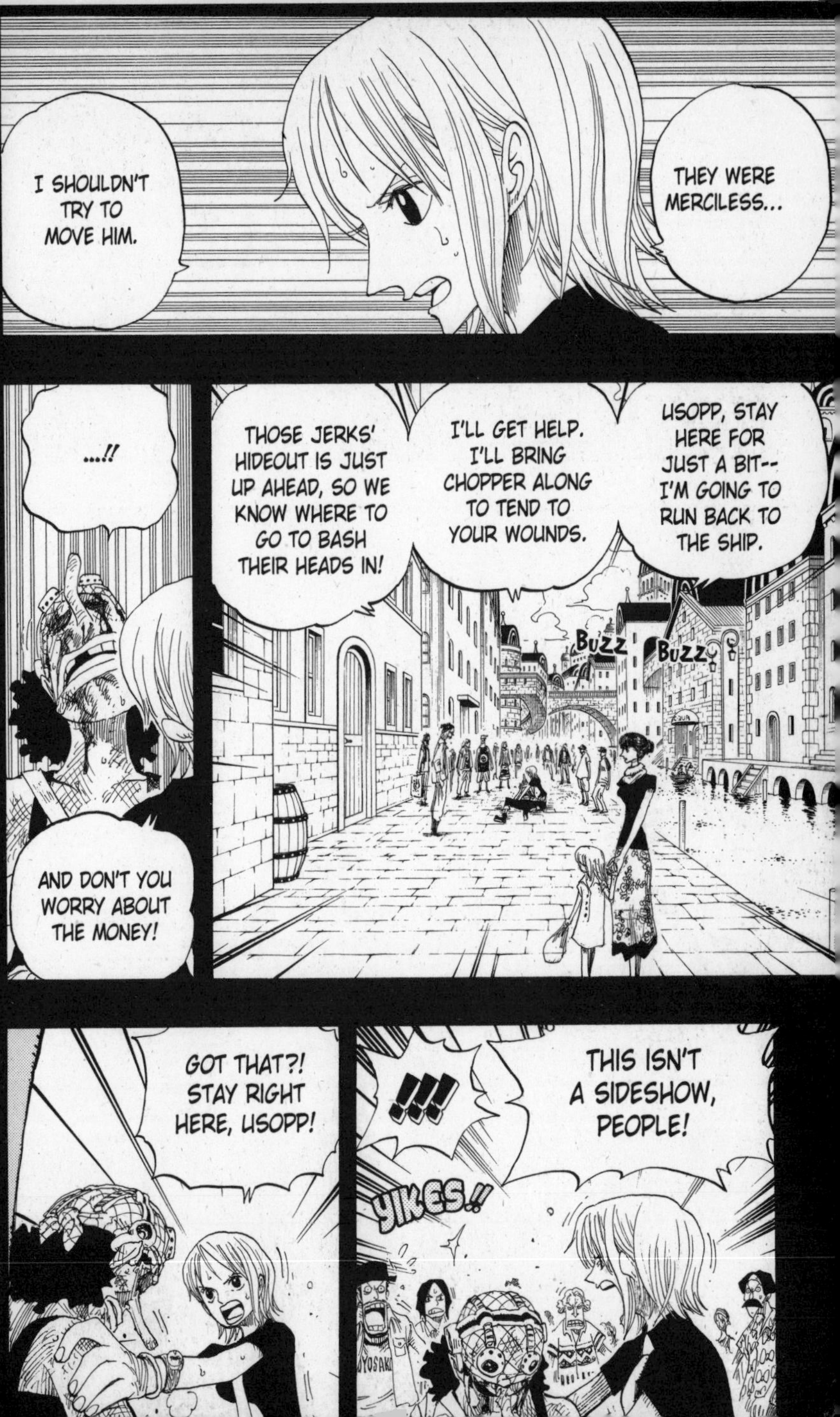
THEY WERE MERCILESS...
I SHOULDN'T TRY TO MOVE HIM.
USOPP, STAY HERE FOR JUST A BIT-- I'M GOING TO RUN BACK TO THE SHIP.
I'LL GET HELP. I'LL BRING CHOPPER ALONG TO TEND TO YOUR WOUNDS.
THOSE JERKS' HIDEOUT IS JUST UP AHEAD, SO WE KNOW WHERE TO GO TO BASH THEIR HEADS IN!
BUZZ
BUZZ
...!!
AND DON'T YOU WORRY ABOUT THE MONEY!
THIS ISN'T A SIDESHOW, PEOPLE!
!!!
YIKES!!
GOT THAT?! STAY RIGHT HERE, USOPP!

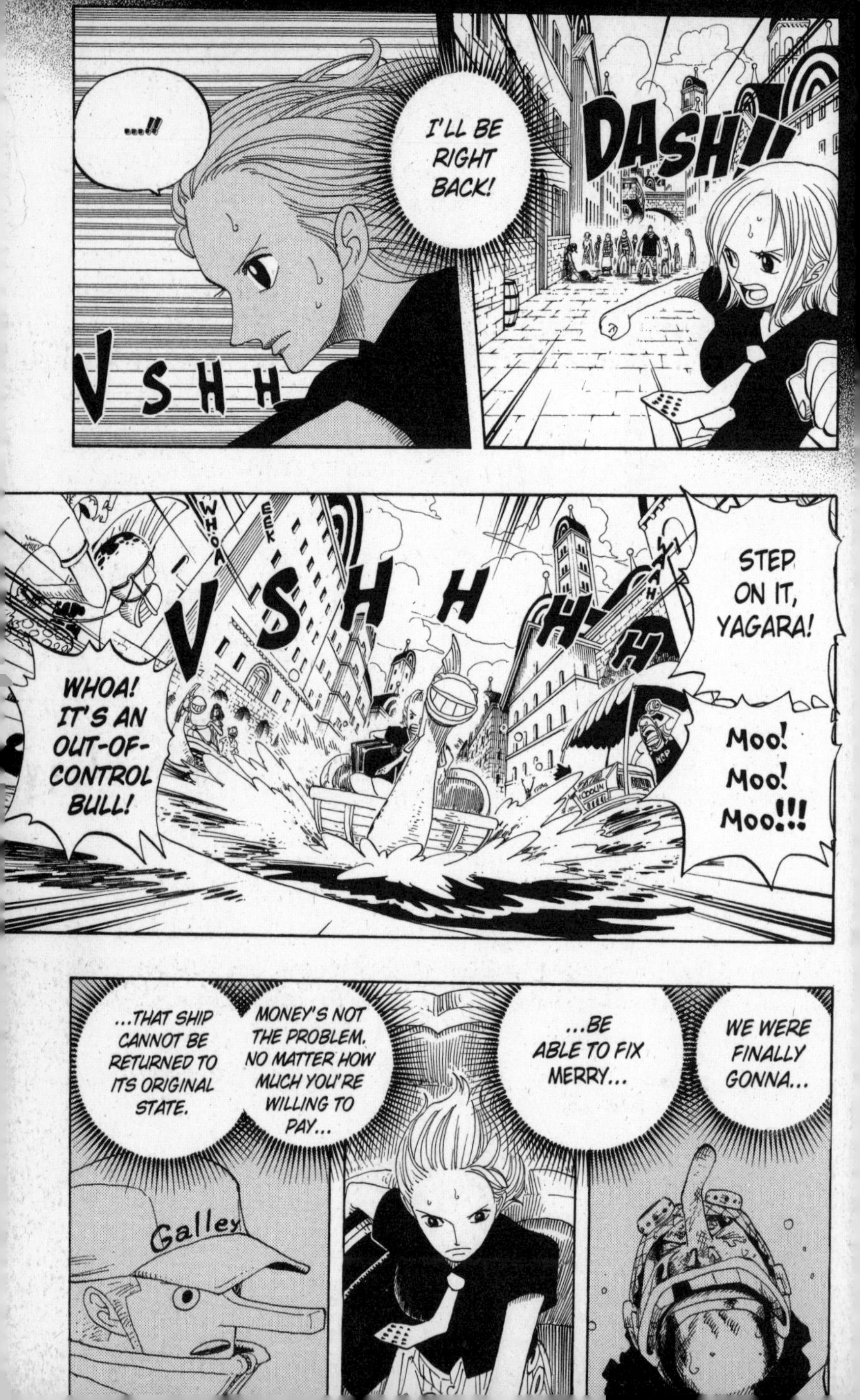
DASH!!
I'LL BE RIGHT BACK!
...!!
VSHH
STEP ON IT, YAGARA!
Moo! Moo! Moo!!!
WAAH
VSHHHH
EEK
WHOA
WHOA! IT'S AN OUT-OF-CONTROL BULL!
WE WERE FINALLY GONNA...
...BE ABLE TO FIX MERRY...
MONEY'S NOT THE PROBLEM. NO MATTER HOW MUCH YOU'RE WILLING TO PAY...
...THAT SHIP CANNOT BE RETURNED TO ITS ORIGINAL STATE.
Galley

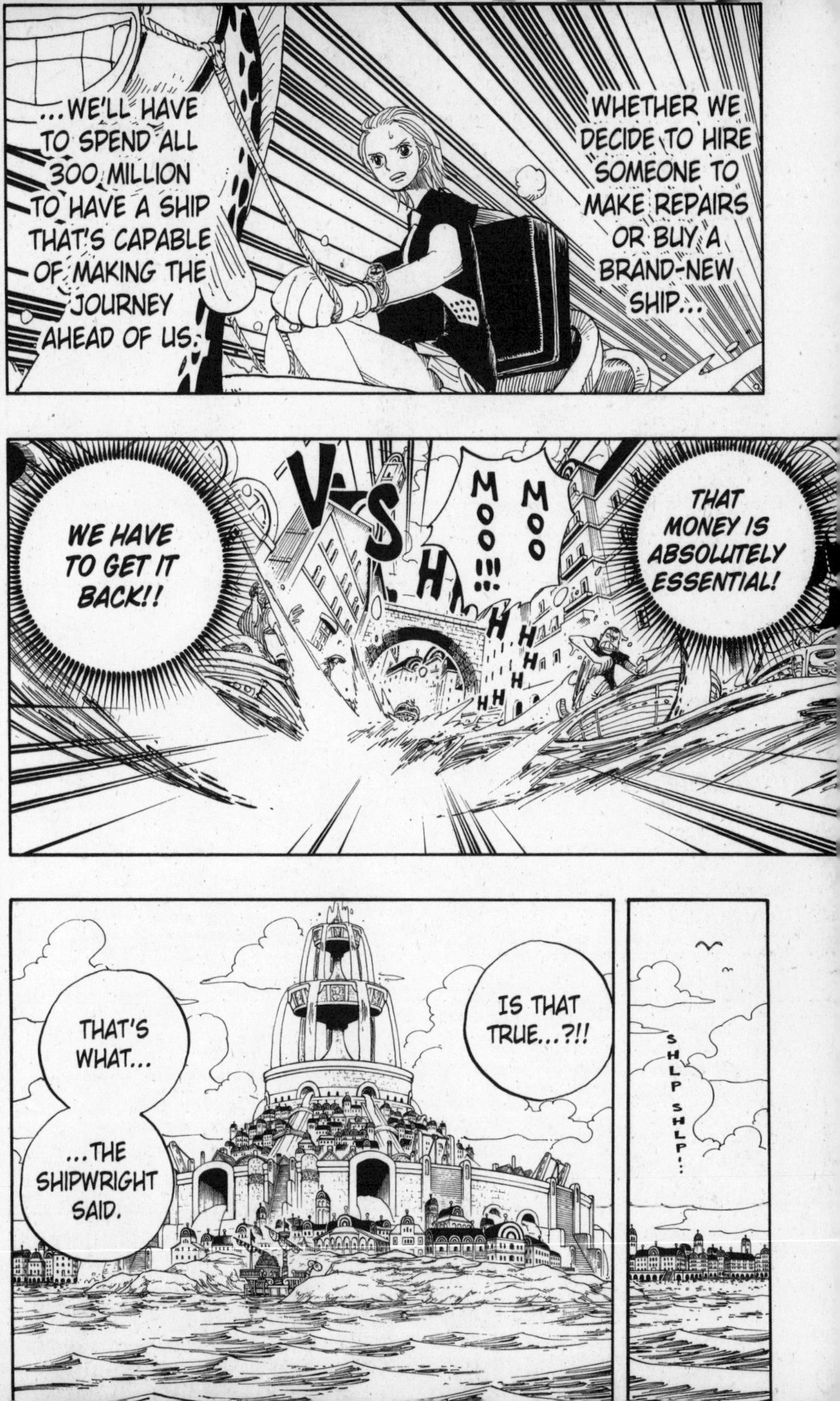
WHETHER WE DECIDE TO HIRE SOMEONE TO MAKE REPAIRS OR BUY A BRAND-NEW SHIP...
...WE'LL HAVE TO SPEND ALL 300 MILLION TO HAVE A SHIP THAT'S CAPABLE OF MAKING THE JOURNEY AHEAD OF US.
THAT MONEY IS ABSOLUTELY ESSENTIAL!
MOO
MOO!!!
WE HAVE TO GET IT BACK!!
SHLP SHLP!..
IS THAT TRUE...?!!
THAT'S WHAT...
...THE SHIPWRIGHT SAID.

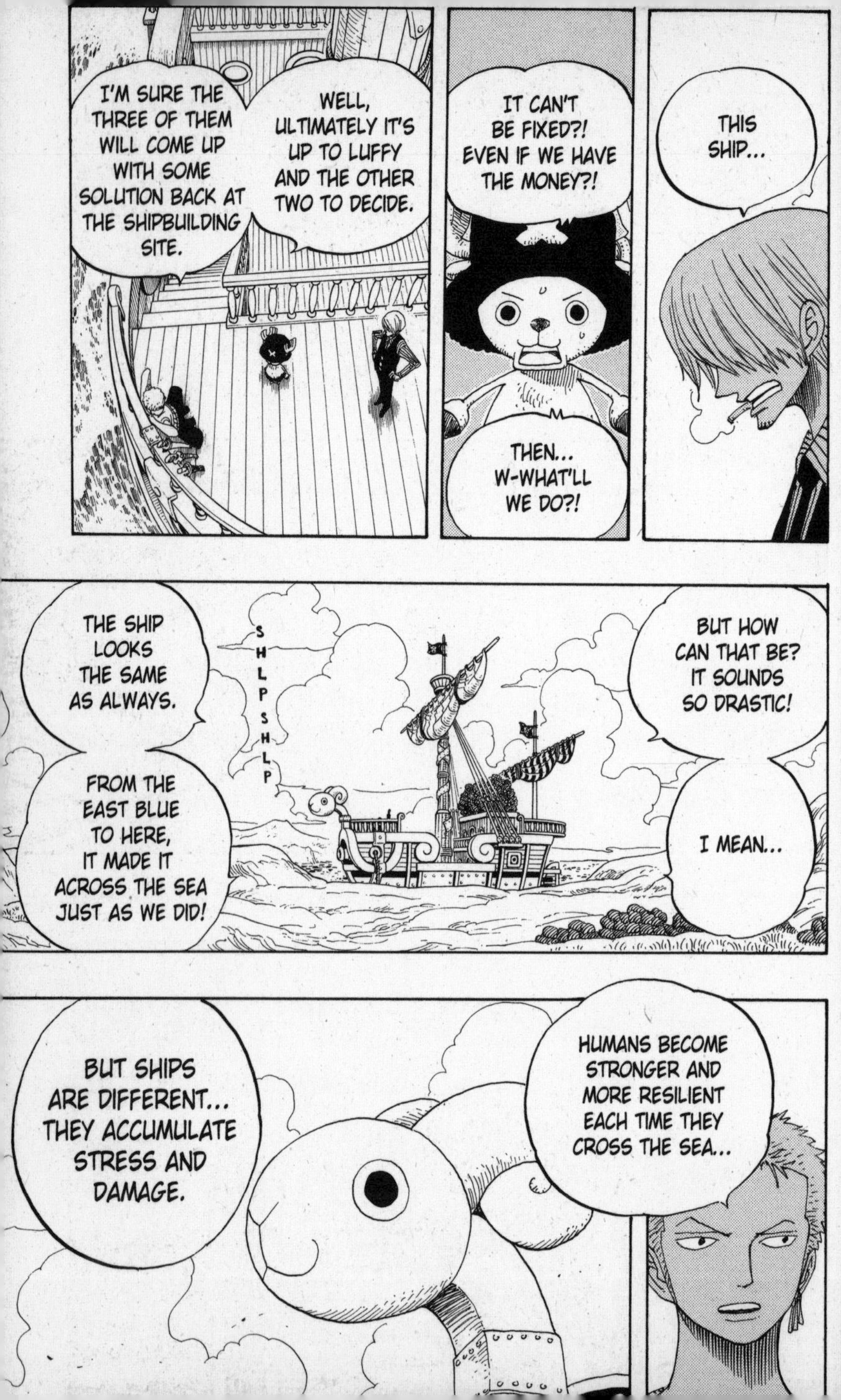
THIS SHIP...
IT CAN'T BE FIXED?! EVEN IF WE HAVE THE MONEY?!
THEN... W-WHAT'LL WE DO?!
WELL, ULTIMATELY IT'S UP TO LUFFY AND THE OTHER TWO TO DECIDE.
I'M SURE THE THREE OF THEM WILL COME UP WITH SOME SOLUTION BACK AT THE SHIPBUILDING SITE.
BUT HOW CAN THAT BE? IT SOUNDS SO DRASTIC!
I MEAN...
SHLP SHLP
THE SHIP LOOKS THE SAME AS ALWAYS.
FROM THE EAST BLUE TO HERE, IT MADE IT ACROSS THE SEA JUST AS WE DID!
HUMANS BECOME STRONGER AND MORE RESILIENT EACH TIME THEY CROSS THE SEA...
BUT SHIPS ARE DIFFERENT... THEY ACCUMULATE STRESS AND DAMAGE.

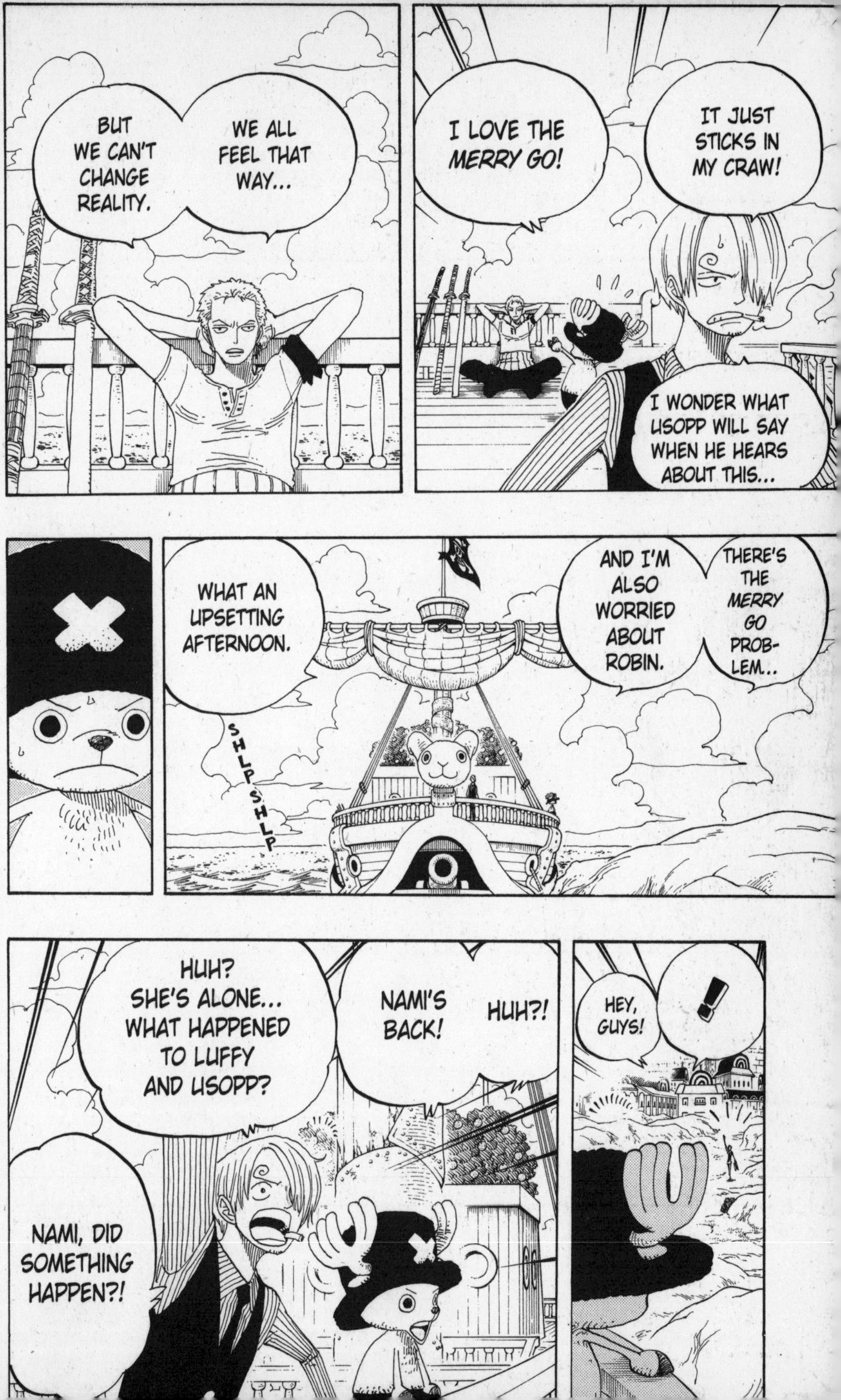
IT JUST STICKS IN MY CRAW!
I LOVE THE MERRY GO!
I WONDER WHAT USOPP WILL SAY WHEN HE HEARS ABOUT THIS...
WE ALL FEEL THAT WAY...
BUT WE CAN'T CHANGE REALITY.
THERE'S THE MERRY GO PROB-LEM..
AND I'M ALSO WORRIED ABOUT ROBIN.
WHAT AN UPSETTING AFTERNOON.
SHLP SHLP
!
HEY, GUYS!
HUH?!
NAMI'S BACK!
HUH? SHE'S ALONE... WHAT HAPPENED TO LUFFY AND USOPP?
NAMI, DID SOMETHING HAPPEN?!

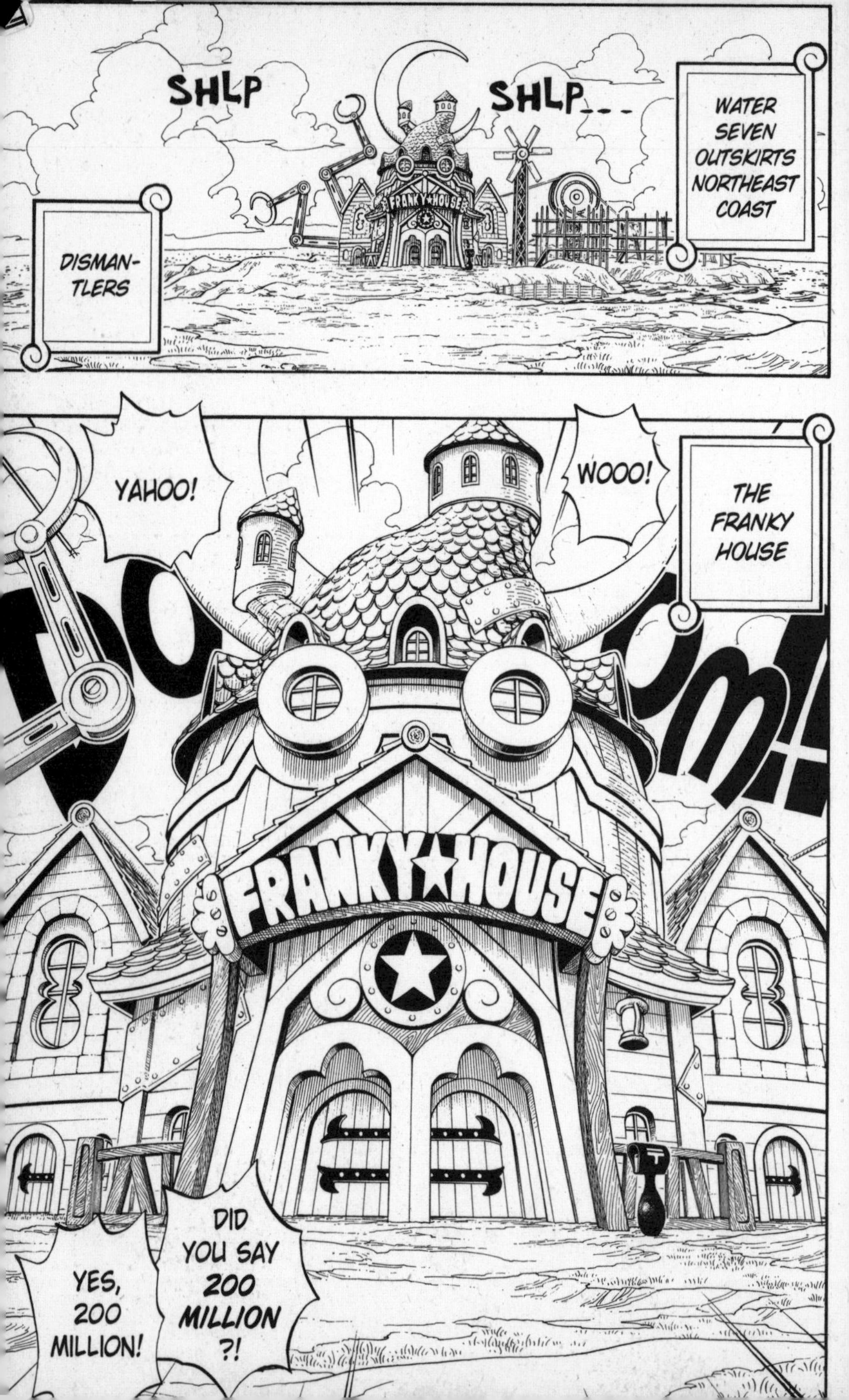
WATER SEVEN OUTSKIRTS NORTHEAST COAST
SHLP SHLP...
DISMANTLERS
FRANKY HOUSE
THE FRANKY HOUSE
WOOO!
YAHOO!
FRANKY★HOUSE
DID YOU SAY 200 MILLION ?!
YES, 200 MILLION!

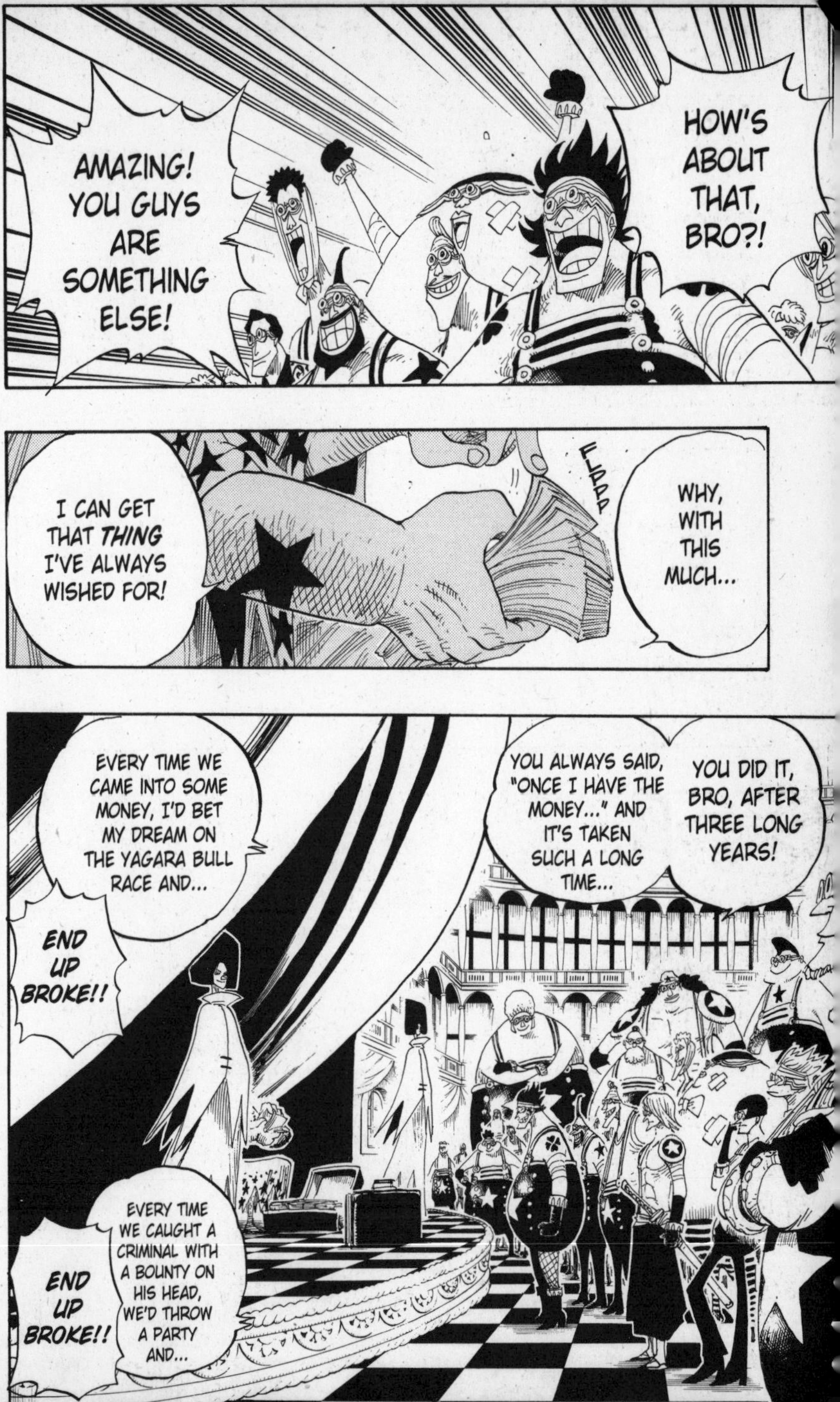
HOW'S ABOUT THAT, BRO?!
AMAZING! YOU GUYS ARE SOMETHING ELSE!
FLPPP
WHY, WITH THIS MUCH...
I CAN GET THAT *THING* I'VE ALWAYS WISHED FOR!
YOU DID IT, BRO, AFTER THREE LONG YEARS!
YOU ALWAYS SAID, "ONCE I HAVE THE MONEY..." AND IT'S TAKEN SUCH A LONG TIME...
EVERY TIME WE CAME INTO SOME MONEY, I'D BET MY DREAM ON THE YAGARA BULL RACE AND...
END UP BROKE!!
EVERY TIME WE CAUGHT A CRIMINAL WITH A BOUNTY ON HIS HEAD, WE'D THROW A PARTY AND...
END UP BROKE!!

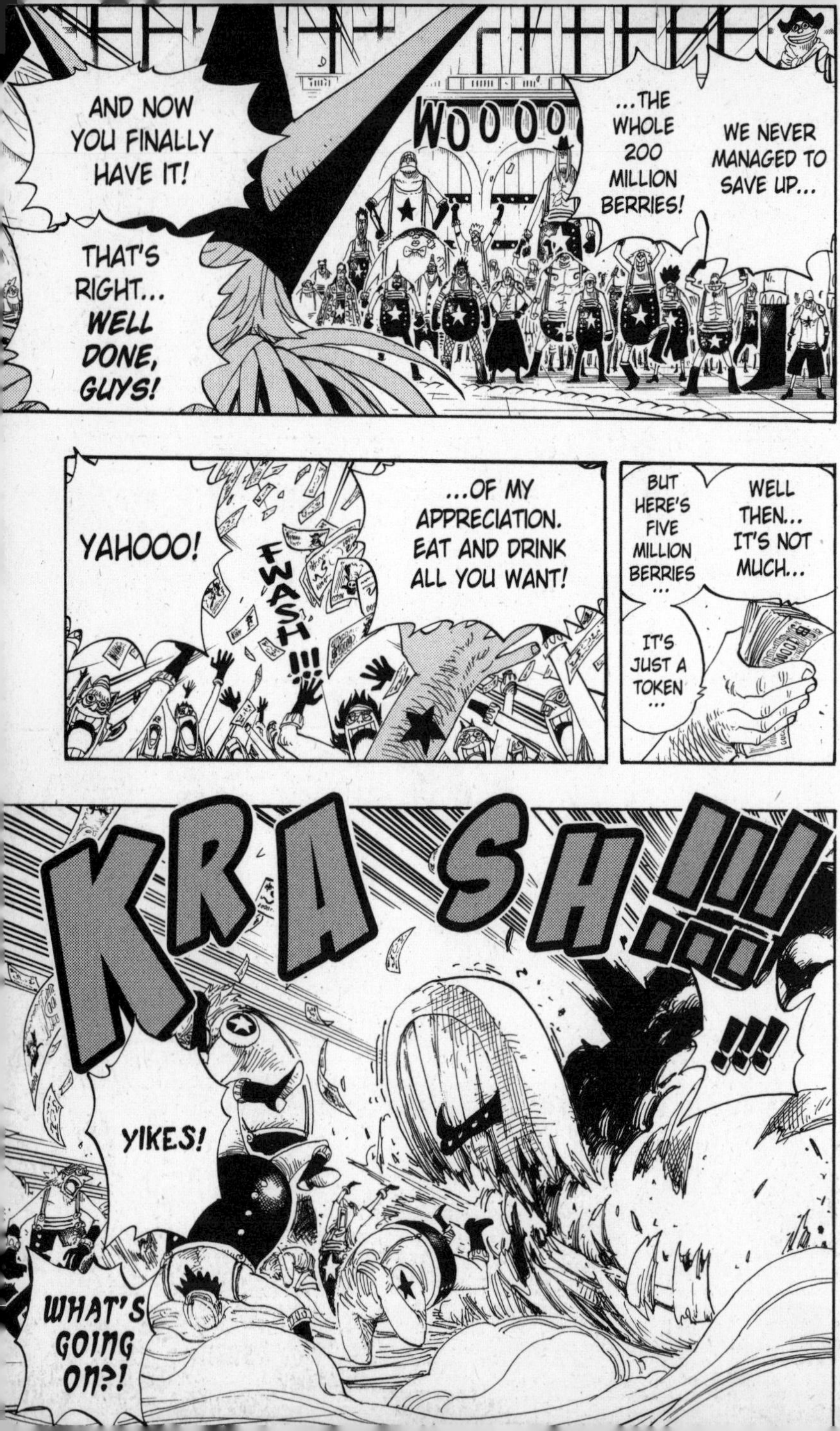
WE NEVER MANAGED TO SAVE UP...
...THE WHOLE 200 MILLION BERRIES!
WOOOO
AND NOW YOU FINALLY HAVE IT!
THAT'S RIGHT... WELL DONE, GUYS!
WELL THEN... IT'S NOT MUCH...
BUT HERE'S FIVE MILLION BERRIES...
IT'S JUST A TOKEN...
...OF MY APPRECIATION. EAT AND DRINK ALL YOU WANT!
FWASH!!!
YAHOOO!
KRASH!!!
!!!
YIKES!
WHAT'S GOING ON?!

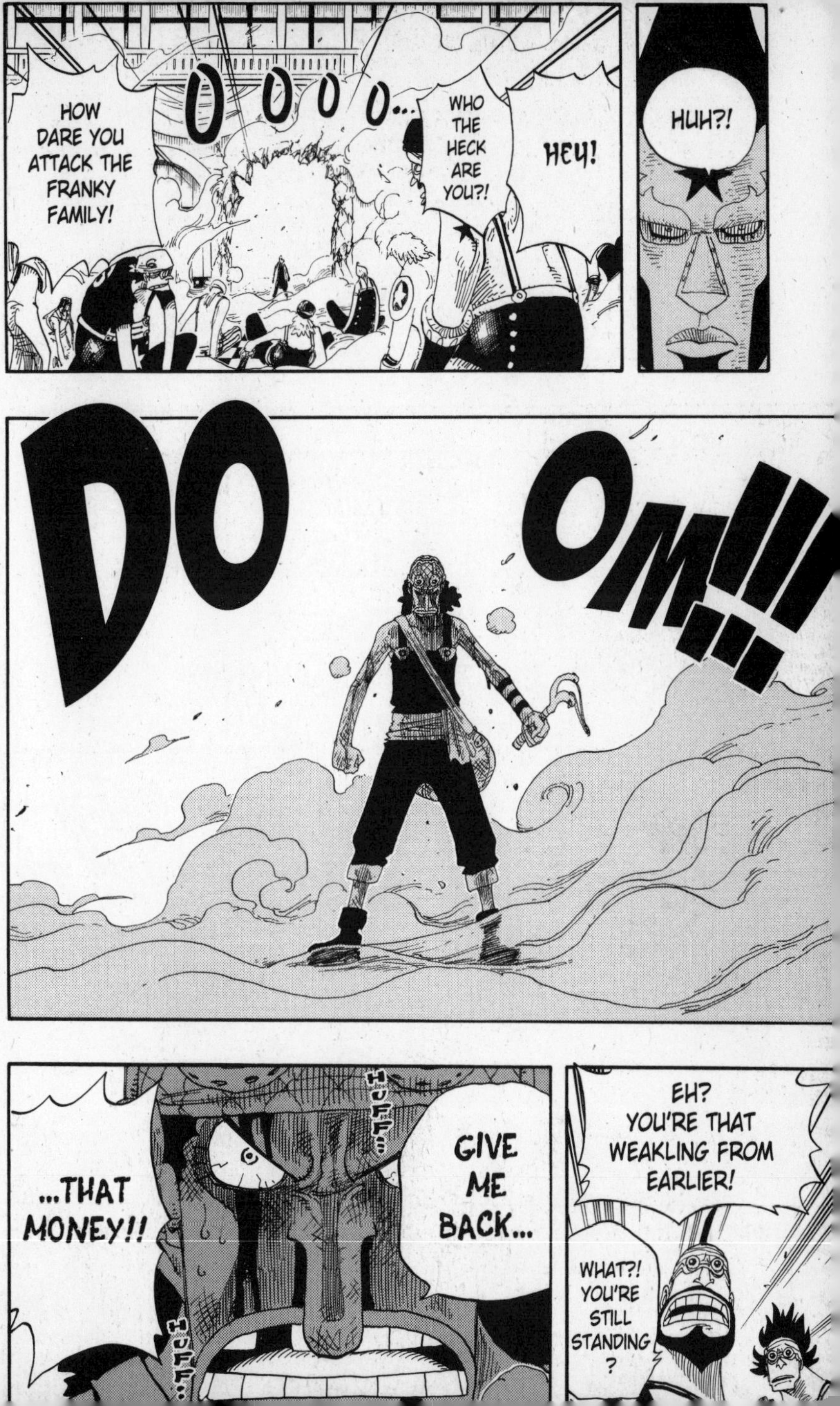
HUH?!
HEY!
WHO THE HECK ARE YOU?!
OOOO...
HOW DARE YOU ATTACK THE FRANKY FAMILY!
DOOM!!!
EH? YOU'RE THAT WEAKLING FROM EARLIER!
WHAT?! YOU'RE STILL STANDING?
HUFF
GIVE ME BACK...
...THAT MONEY!!
HUFF

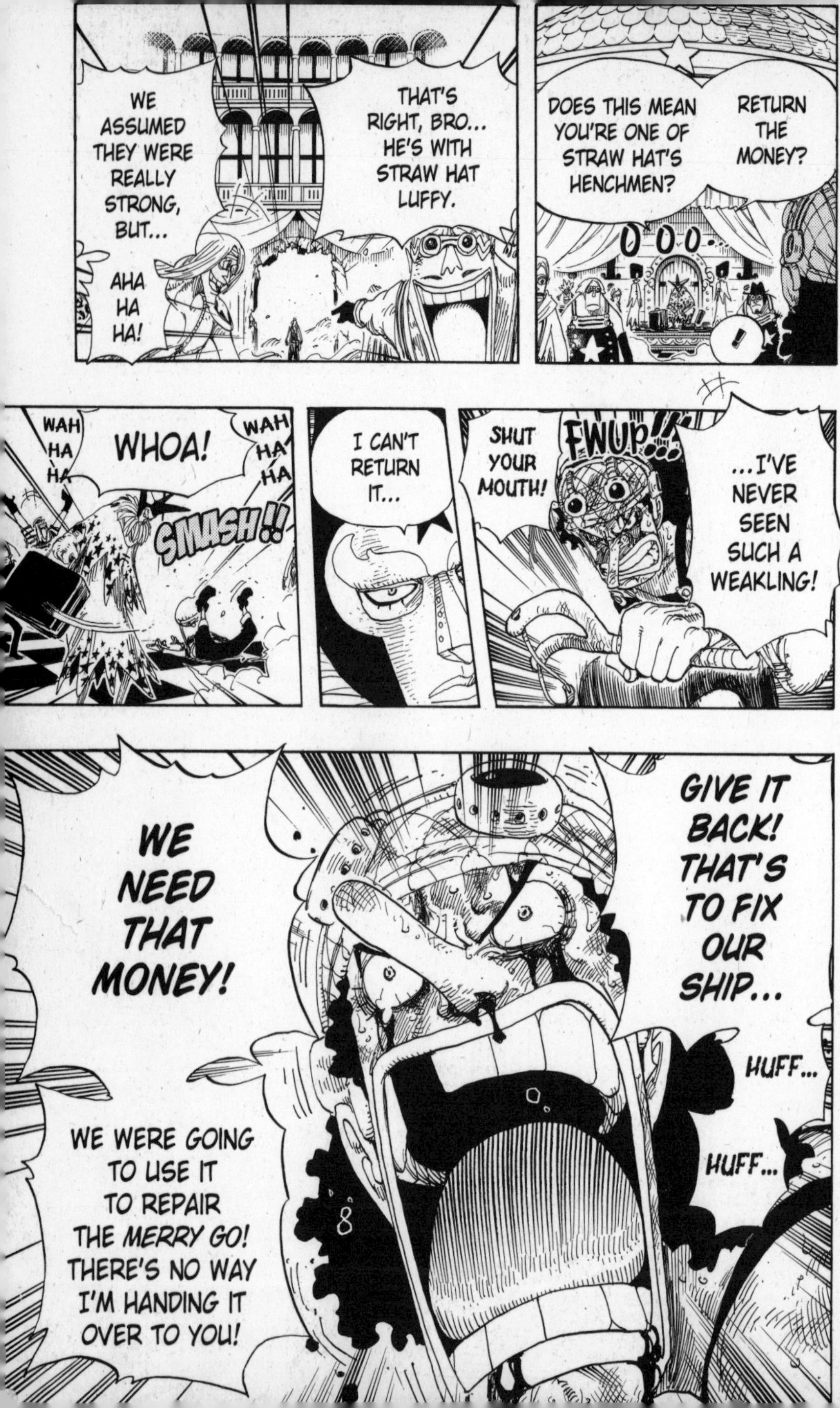
RETURN THE MONEY?
DOES THIS MEAN YOU'RE ONE OF STRAW HAT'S HENCHMEN?
!
THAT'S RIGHT, BRO... HE'S WITH STRAW HAT LUFFY.
WE ASSUMED THEY WERE REALLY STRONG, BUT...
AHA HA HA!
...I'VE NEVER SEEN SUCH A WEAKLING!
FWUP!!
SHUT YOUR MOUTH!
I CAN'T RETURN IT...
WAH HA HA
WHOA!
WAH HA HA
SMASH!!
GIVE IT BACK! THAT'S TO FIX OUR SHIP...
HUFF...
HUFF...
WE NEED THAT MONEY!
WE WERE GOING TO USE IT TO REPAIR THE MERRY GO! THERE'S NO WAY I'M HANDING IT OVER TO YOU!

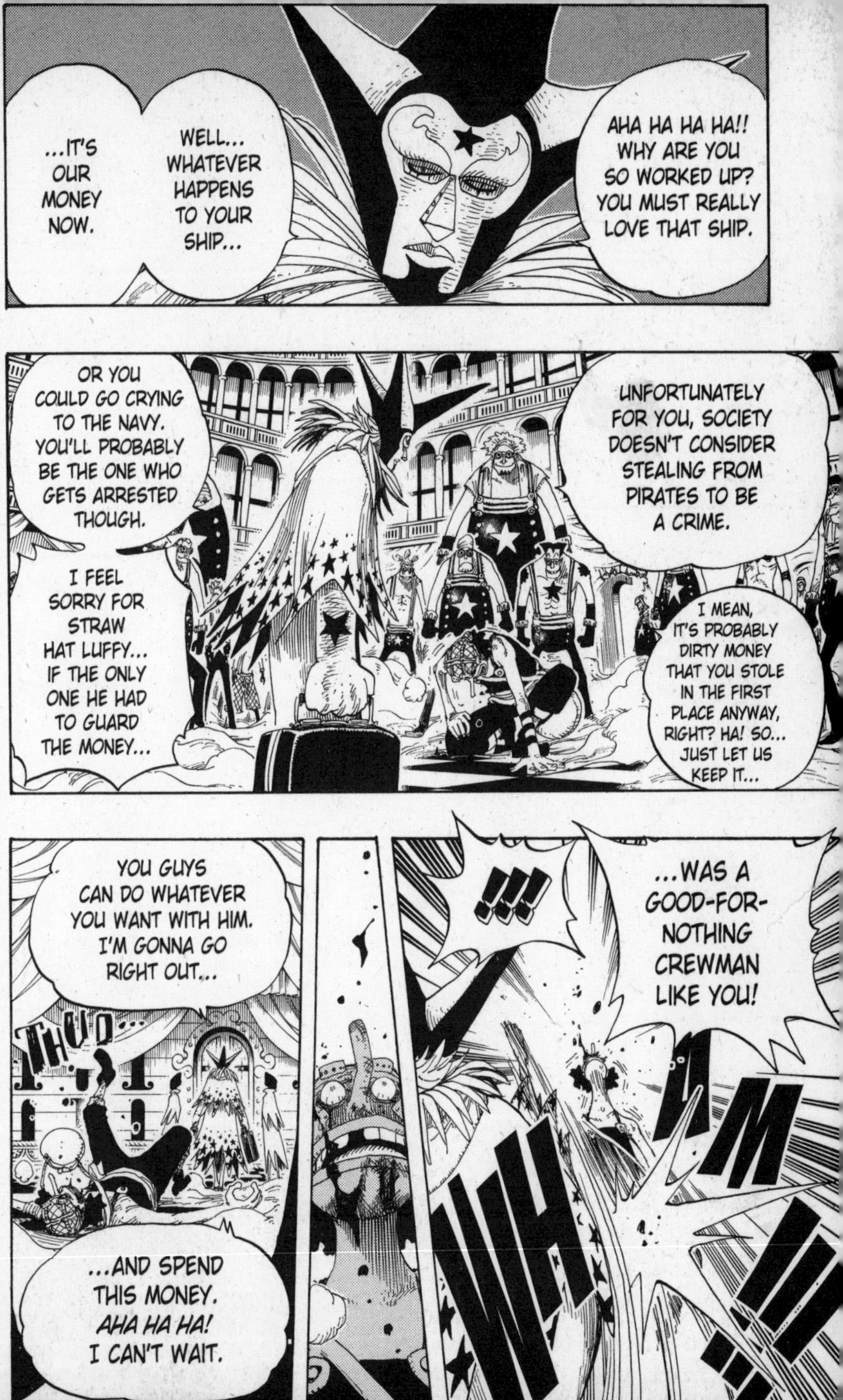
AHA HA HA HA!! WHY ARE YOU SO WORKED UP? YOU MUST REALLY LOVE THAT SHIP.
WELL... WHATEVER HAPPENS TO YOUR SHIP...
...IT'S OUR MONEY NOW.
UNFORTUNATELY FOR YOU, SOCIETY DOESN'T CONSIDER STEALING FROM PIRATES TO BE A CRIME.
I MEAN, IT'S PROBABLY DIRTY MONEY THAT YOU STOLE IN THE FIRST PLACE ANYWAY, RIGHT? HA! SO... JUST LET US KEEP IT...
OR YOU COULD GO CRYING TO THE NAVY. YOU'LL PROBABLY BE THE ONE WHO GETS ARRESTED THOUGH.
I FEEL SORRY FOR STRAW HAT LUFFY... IF THE ONLY ONE HE HAD TO GUARD THE MONEY...
!!!
...WAS A GOOD-FOR-NOTHING CREWMAN LIKE YOU!
WHAMM!!!
YOU GUYS CAN DO WHATEVER YOU WANT WITH HIM. I'M GONNA GO RIGHT OUT...
THUD
...AND SPEND THIS MONEY. AHA HA HA! I CAN'T WAIT.

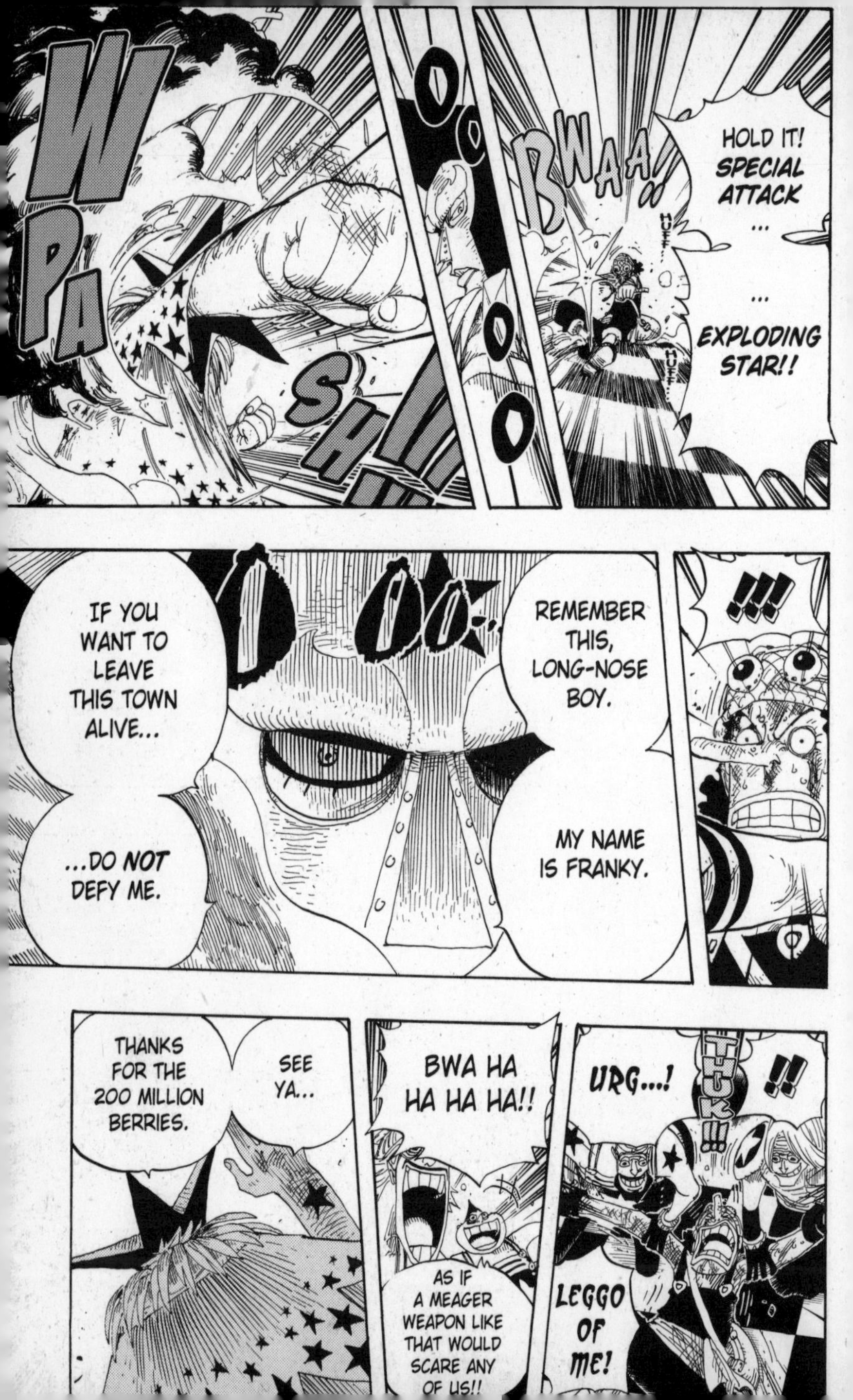
HOLD IT! SPECIAL ATTACK ... ... EXPLODING STAR!!
BWAA!!
HUFF...
HUFF...
SHH
WPA
!!!
REMEMBER THIS, LONG-NOSE BOY.
MY NAME IS FRANKY.
IF YOU WANT TO LEAVE THIS TOWN ALIVE...
...DO NOT DEFY ME.
!!
THUK!!
URG...!
LEGGO OF ME!
BWA HA HA HA HA!!
AS IF A MEAGER WEAPON LIKE THAT WOULD SCARE ANY OF US!!
THANKS FOR THE 200 MILLION BERRIES.
SEE YA...

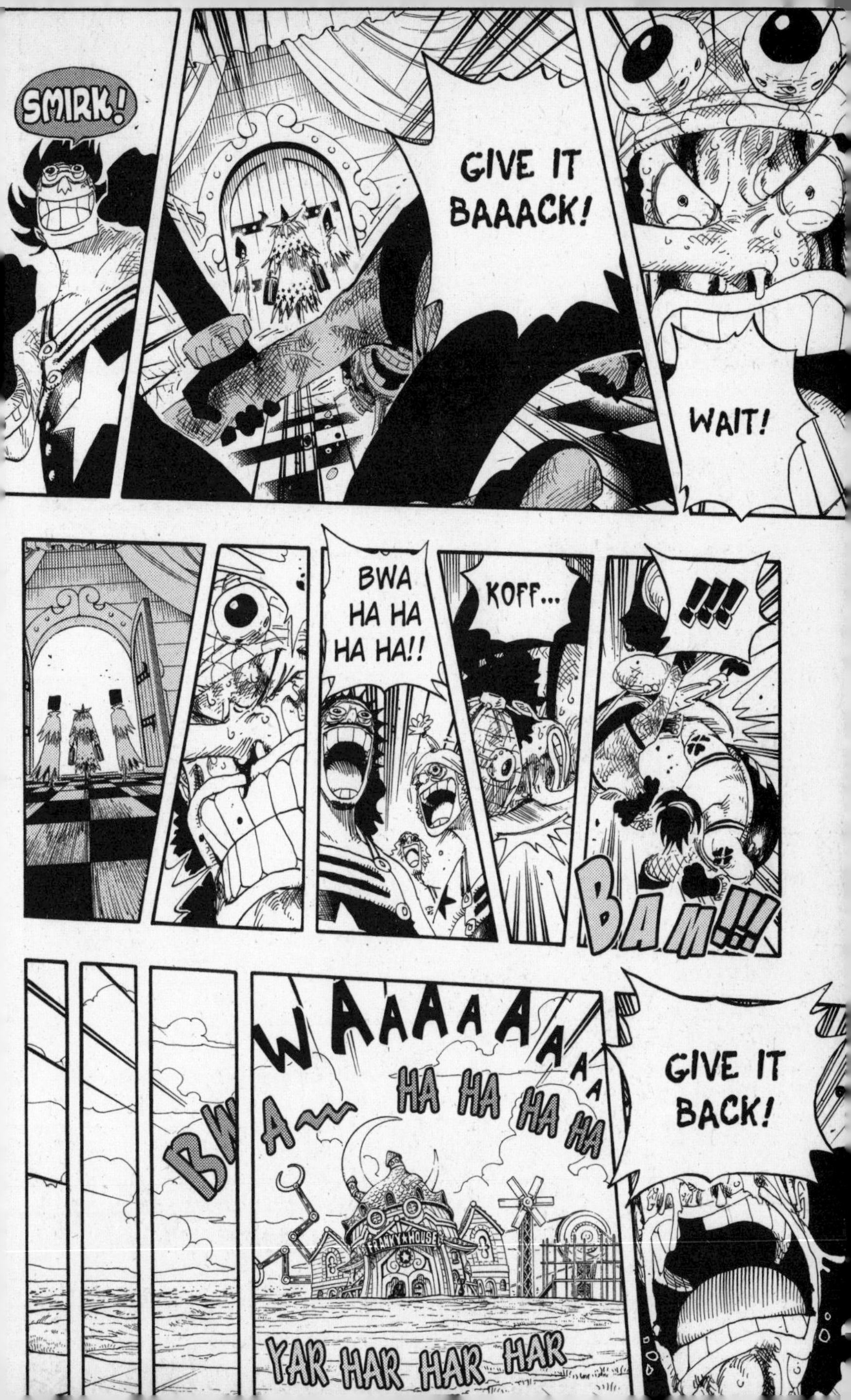
WAIT!
GIVE IT BAAACK!
SMIRK!
!!!
BAM!!!
KOFF...
BWA HA HA HA HA!!
GIVE IT BACK!
BWAAAAAAAAAA~
HA HA HA HA
YAR HAR HAR HAR

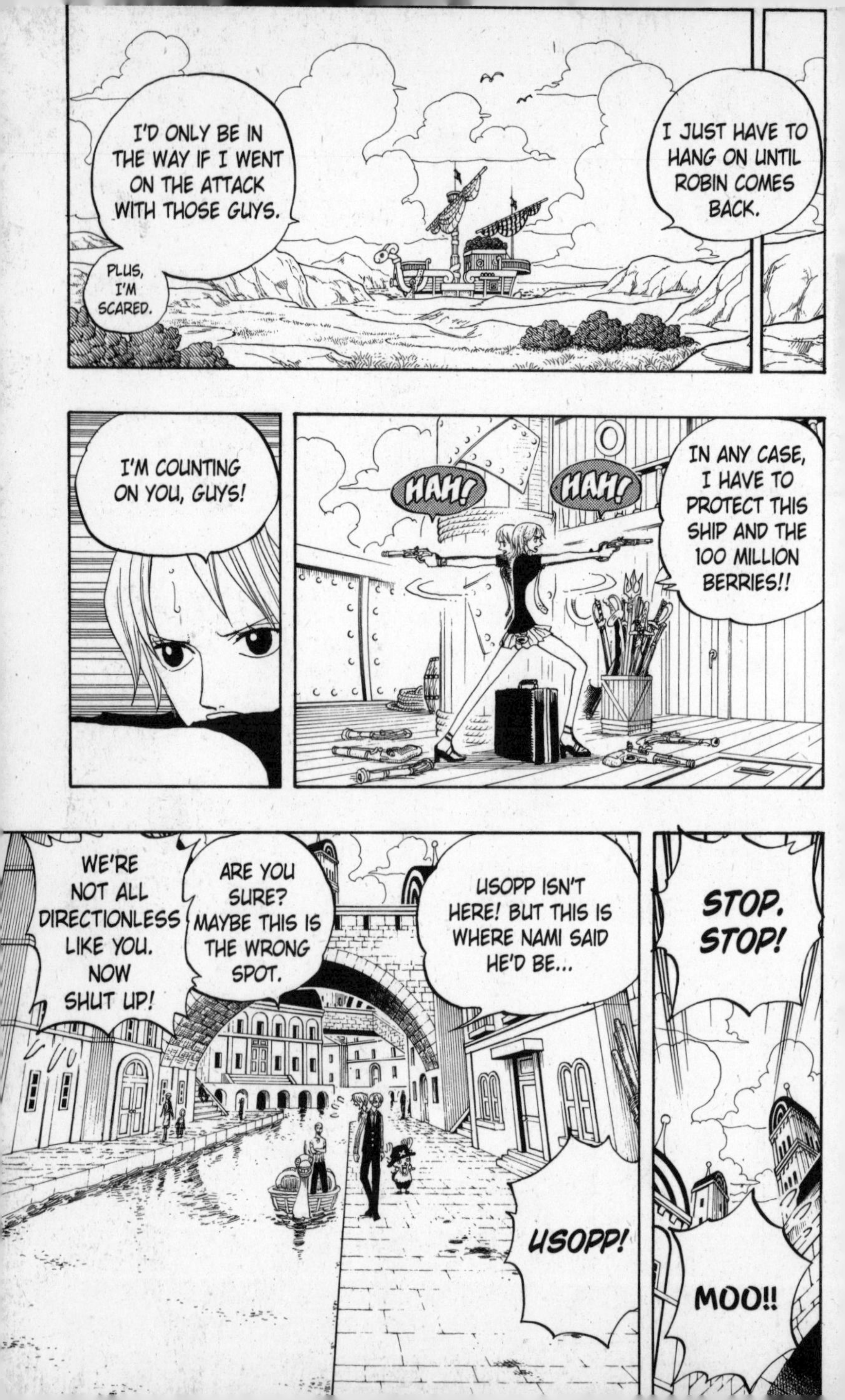
I JUST HAVE TO HANG ON UNTIL ROBIN COMES BACK.
I'D ONLY BE IN THE WAY IF I WENT ON THE ATTACK WITH THOSE GUYS.
PLUS, I'M SCARED.
IN ANY CASE, I HAVE TO PROTECT THIS SHIP AND THE 100 MILLION BERRIES!!
HAH!
HAH!
I'M COUNTING ON YOU, GUYS!
STOP. STOP!
MOO!!
USOPP ISN'T HERE! BUT THIS IS WHERE NAMI SAID HE'D BE...
ARE YOU SURE? MAYBE THIS IS THE WRONG SPOT.
WE'RE NOT ALL DIRECTIONLESS LIKE YOU. NOW SHUT UP!
USOPP!

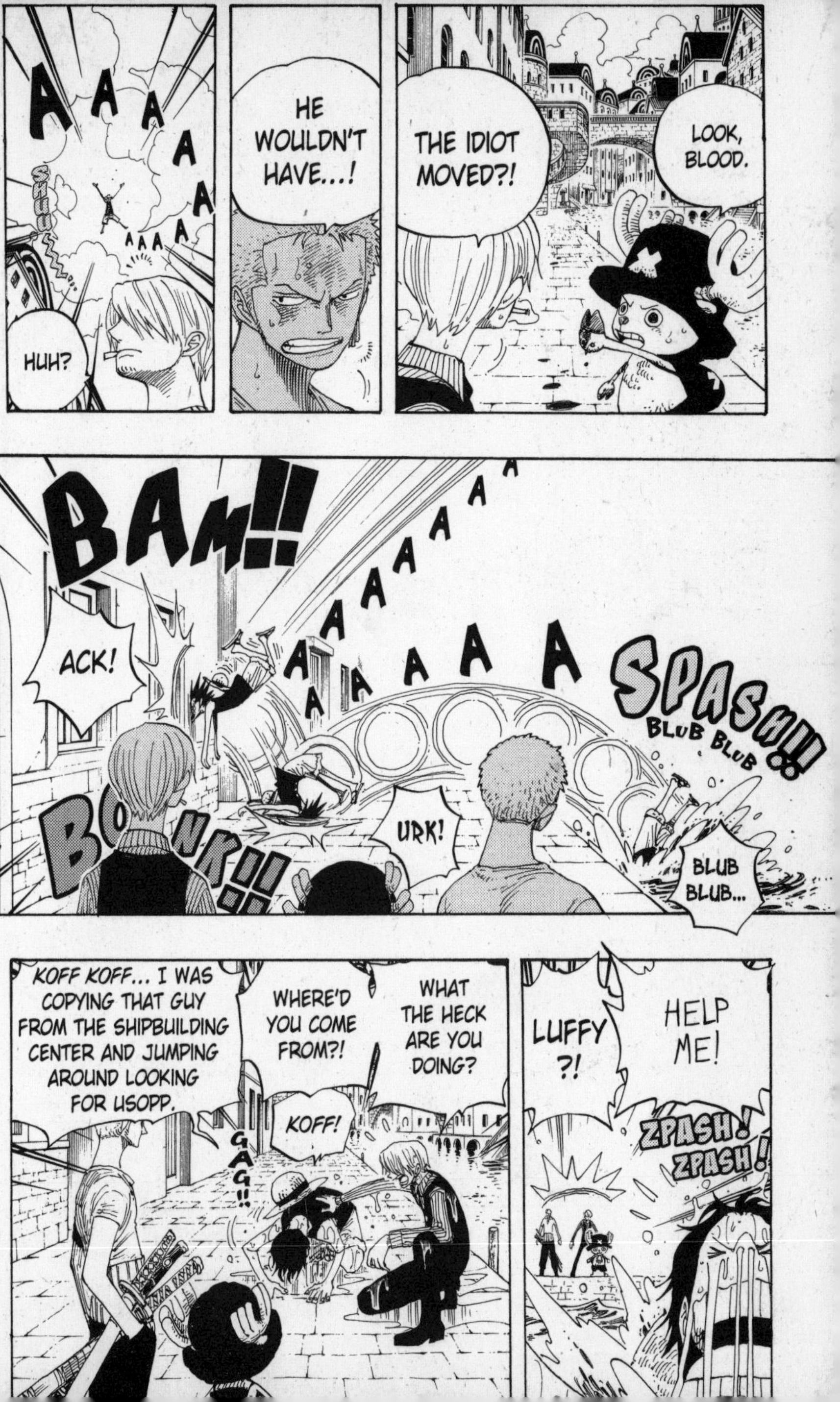
LOOK, BLOOD.
THE IDIOT MOVED?!
HE WOULDN'T HAVE...!
AAAAAAAAA
SHUU
HUH?
SPASH!!
BLUB BLUB
BLUB BLUB...
URK!
AAAAAAAAAAAAAAA
BAM!!
ACK!
BONK!!
HELP ME!
LUFFY ?!
ZPASH! ZPASH!
WHAT THE HECK ARE YOU DOING?
WHERE'D YOU COME FROM?!
KOFF KOFF... I WAS COPYING THAT GUY FROM THE SHIPBUILDING CENTER AND JUMPING AROUND LOOKING FOR USOPP.
KOFF!
GAG!!

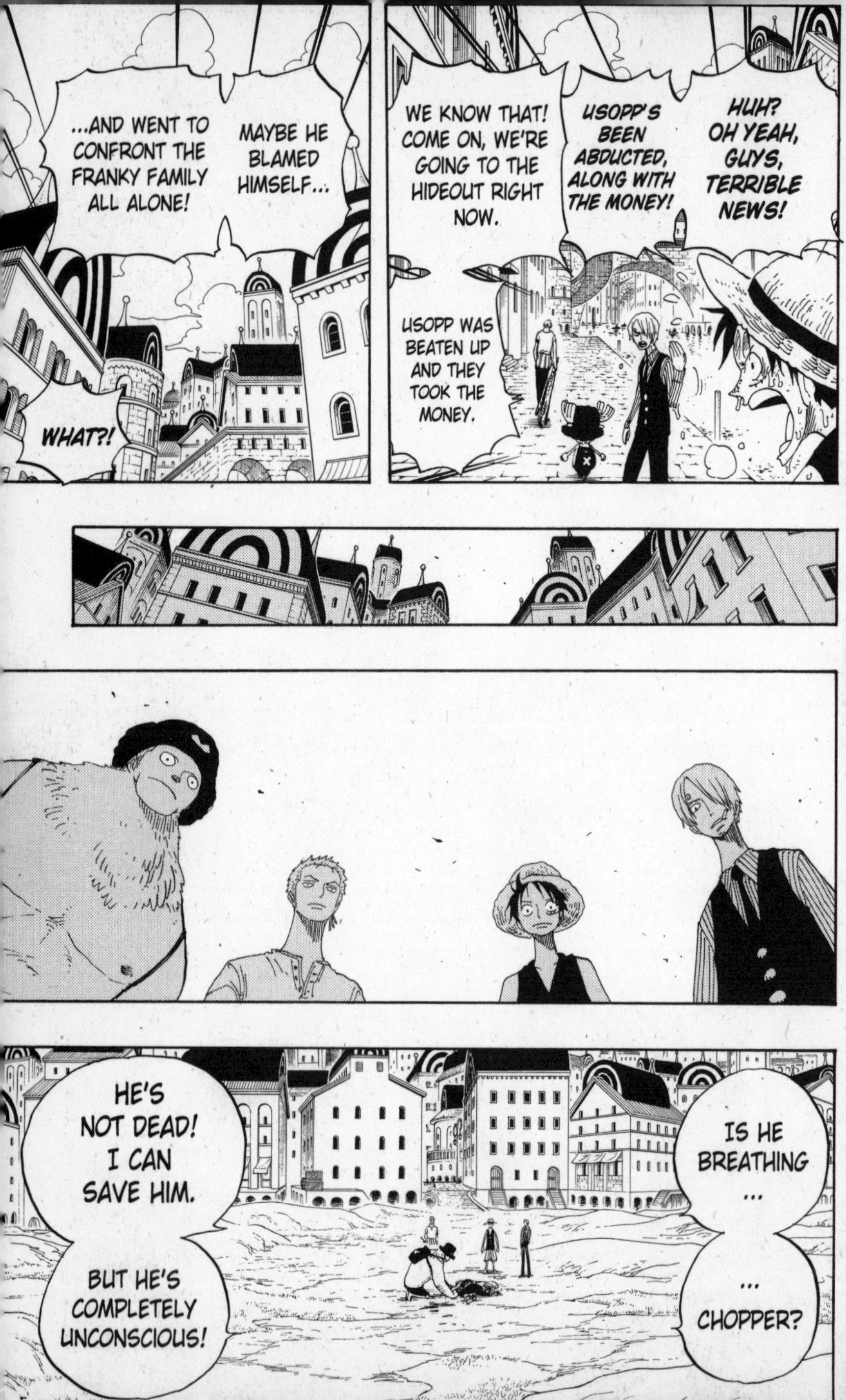
HUH? OH YEAH, GUYS, TERRIBLE NEWS!
USOPP'S BEEN ABDUCTED, ALONG WITH THE MONEY!
WE KNOW THAT! COME ON, WE'RE GOING TO THE HIDEOUT RIGHT NOW.
USOPP WAS BEATEN UP AND THEY TOOK THE MONEY.
MAYBE HE BLAMED HIMSELF...
...AND WENT TO CONFRONT THE FRANKY FAMILY ALL ALONE!
WHAT?!
IS HE BREATHING ...
... CHOPPER?
HE'S NOT DEAD! I CAN SAVE HIM.
BUT HE'S COMPLETELY UNCONSCIOUS!

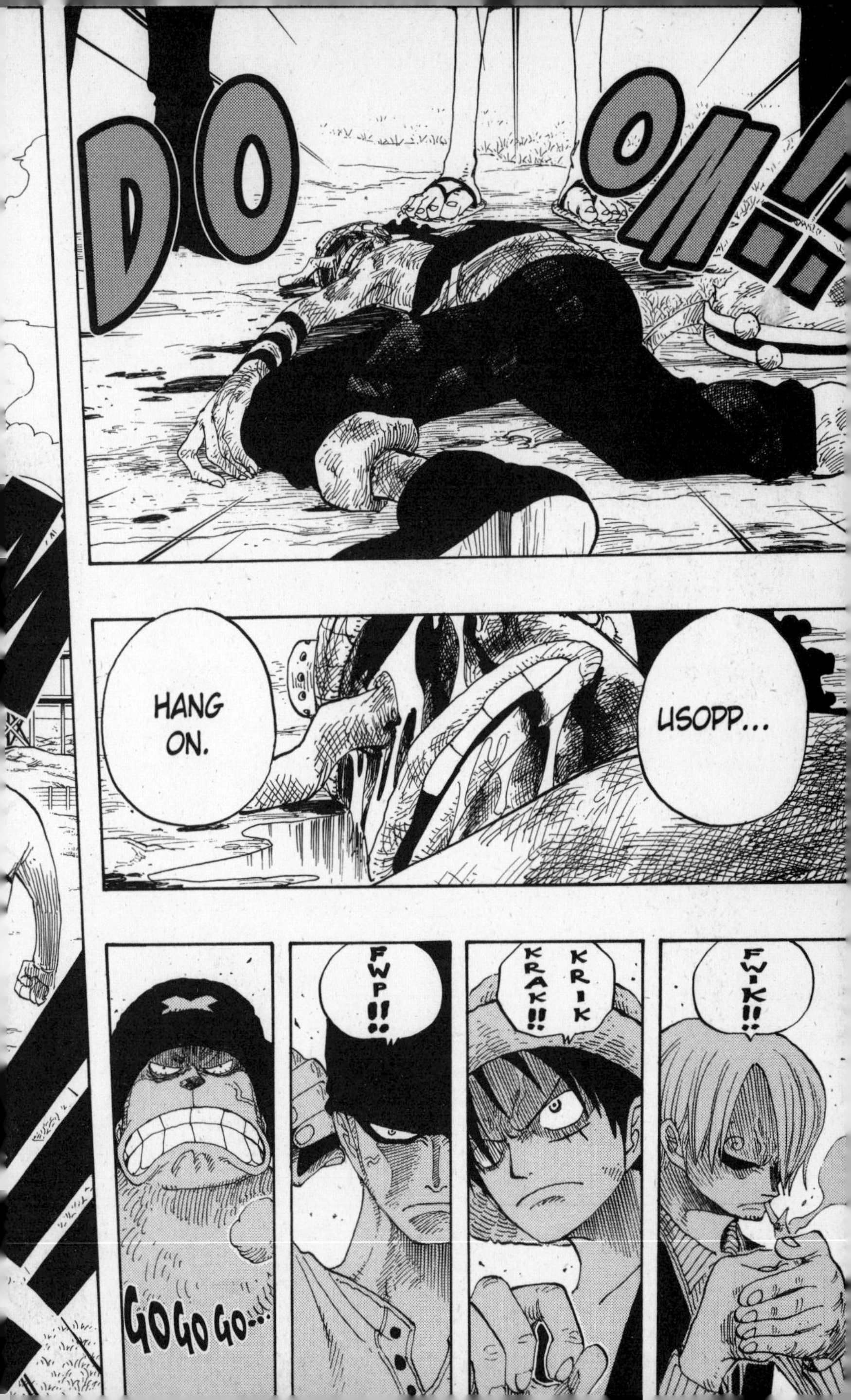
DOON!!
USOPP...
HANG ON.
FWIK!!
KRIK KRAK!!
FWP!!
GO GO GO...

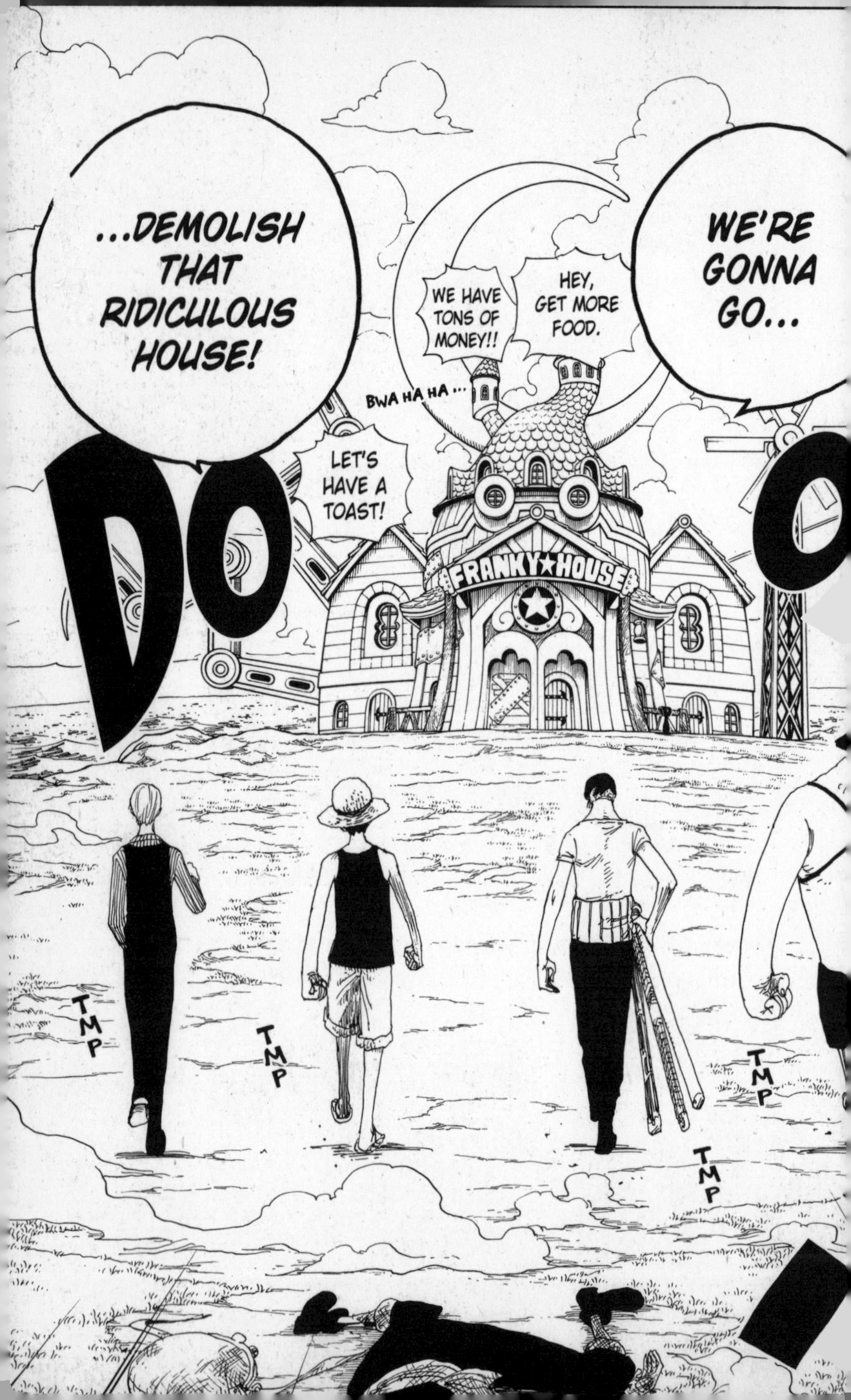
WE'RE GONNA GO...
HEY, GET MORE FOOD.
WE HAVE TONS OF MONEY!!
BWA HA HA...
LET'S HAVE A TOAST!
...DEMOLISH THAT RIDICULOUS HOUSE!
FRANKY★HOUSE
DO
TMP
TMP
TMP
TMP

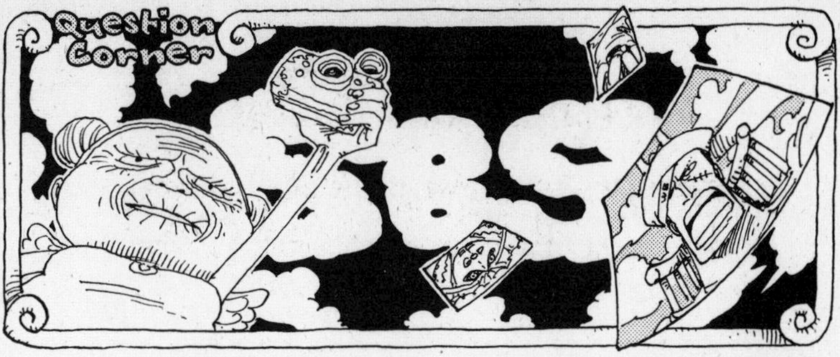
Question Corner
SBS

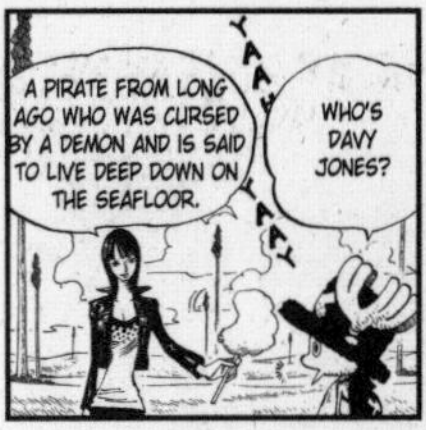
WHO'S DAVY JONES?
A PIRATE FROM LONG AGO WHO WAS CURSED BY A DEMON AND IS SAID TO LIVE DEEP DOWN ON THE SEAFLOOR.

Q: There's something I'd like to ask you, Odacchi. It's regarding vol. 33, page 21, panel 1: Why did Robin give Chopper the cotton candy that she had just taken a bite of? Wouldn't that be equivalent to an indirect kiss? And besides, if she was not going to finish it, she shouldn't have taken a bite at all!

--I want to have a figure like Robin's!

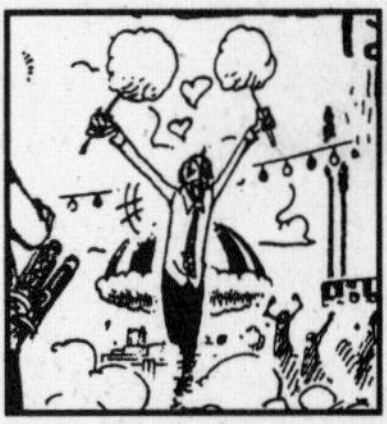

A: Please flip back two pages. Sanji says, "Nami, they're selling cotton candy! ♡" and has purchased two of them. Naturally, he bought them for Nami and Robin. For Robin to take it, and then turn around and give it immediately to Chopper would be rude from a grown-up woman's point of view. And so, although she didn't really want the cotton candy, she takes a little bite and then gives it away. That is Robin's way of being polite to Sanji.

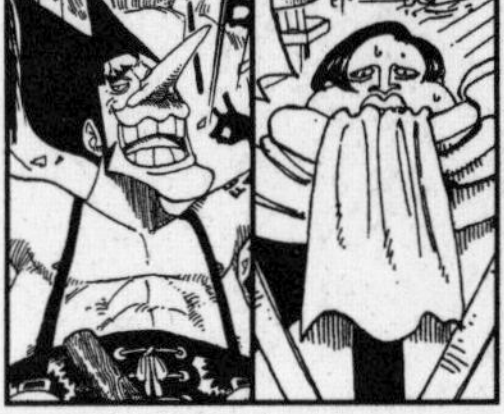

Q: Oda Sensei-sama. Please listen to my question. I had this thought recently…

What happens if Mr. 4 is bombarded by the Slow-Slow Beam?

--Chobi

A: Okay then, let's try it. I'll pretend to be Mr. 4 just after being hit by the Slow-Slow Beam. So I'll say, "Oh no!!" Ready...

OO...→

(Due to lack of space on the page, the answer has been cut)

Chapter 330:
IT'S DECIDED

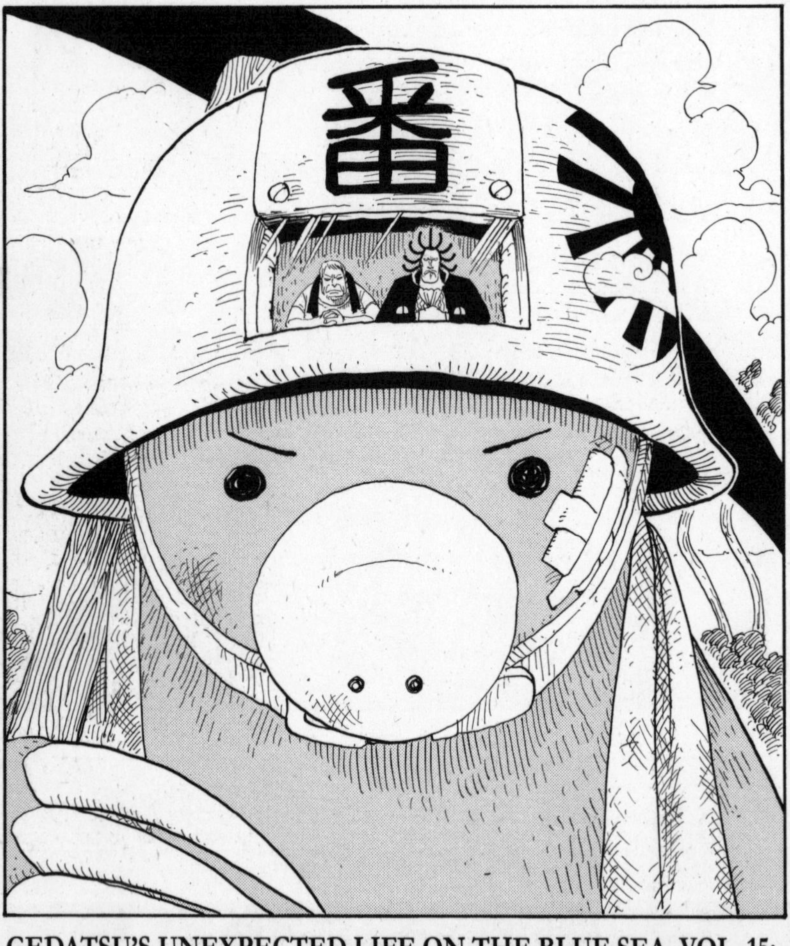
番

GEDATSU'S UNEXPECTED LIFE ON THE BLUE SEA, VOL. 15:
"I MADE IT MY SLAVE AND
UNEXPECTEDLY ALTERED ITS HELMET"

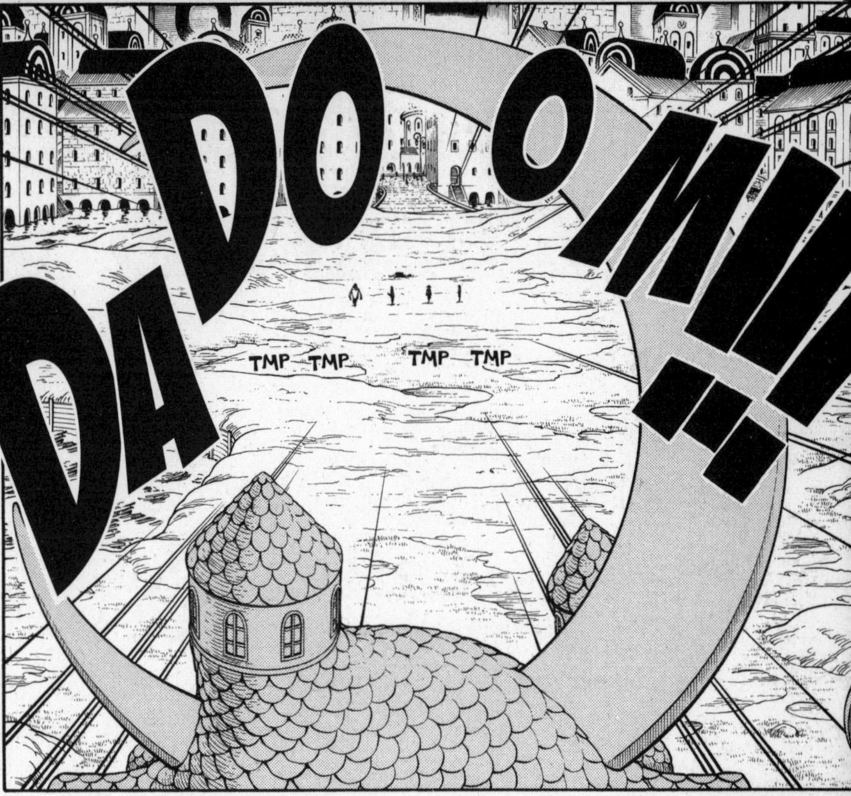
DADOOM!!
TMP TMP TMP TMP
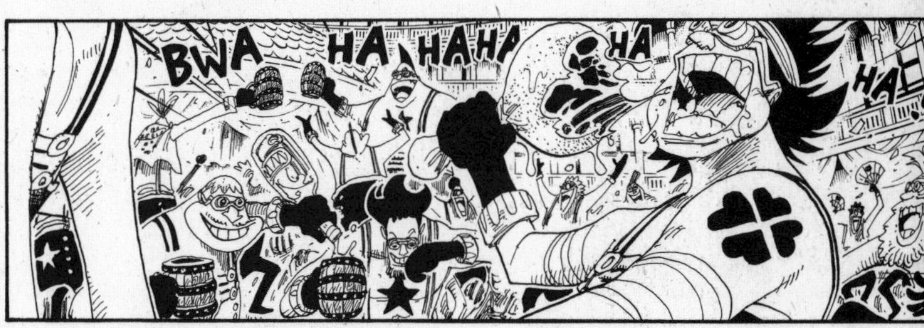
BWA HA HAHA HA
HA
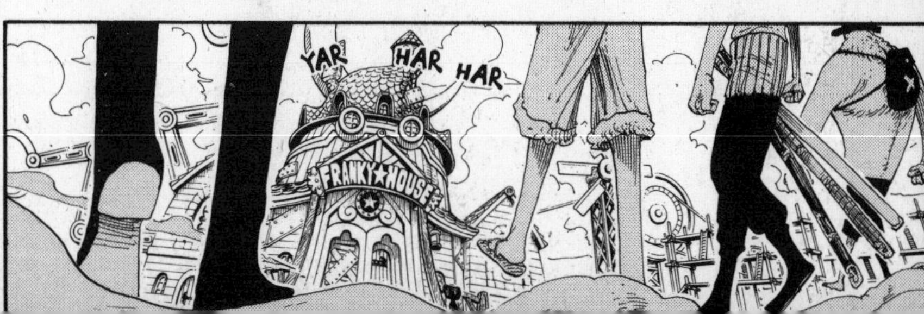
YAR HAR HAR
FRANKY★HOUSE

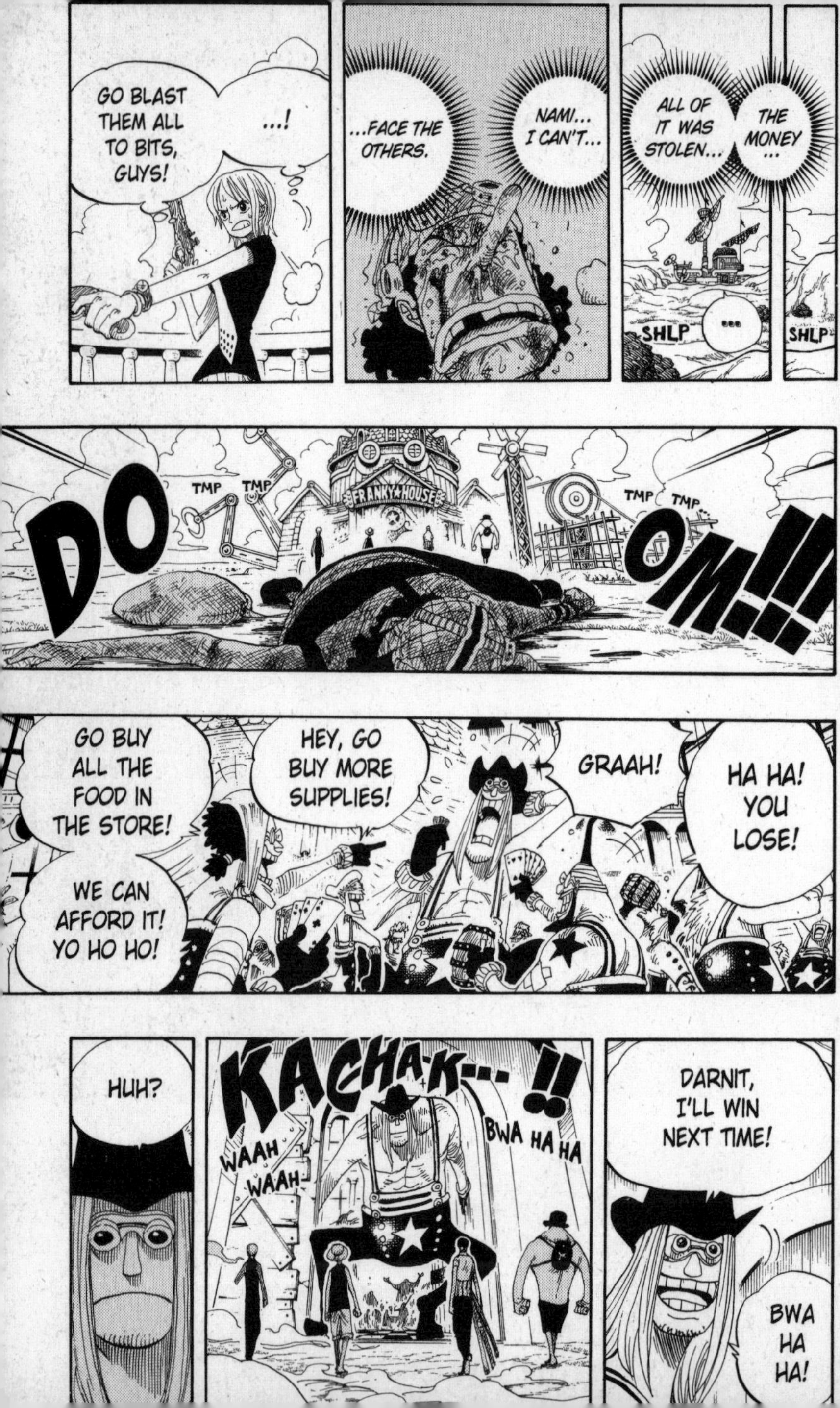
THE MONEY ...
SHLP
ALL OF IT WAS STOLEN...
...
SHLP
NAMI... I CAN'T...
...FACE THE OTHERS.
...!
GO BLAST THEM ALL TO BITS, GUYS!
DO
TMP TMP...
TMP TMP
OM!!!
HA HA! YOU LOSE!
GRAAH!
HEY, GO BUY MORE SUPPLIES!
GO BUY ALL THE FOOD IN THE STORE!
WE CAN AFFORD IT! YO HO HO!
DARNIT, I'LL WIN NEXT TIME!
BWA HA HA!
KACHA-K...!!
BWA HA HA
WAAH WAAH
HUH?

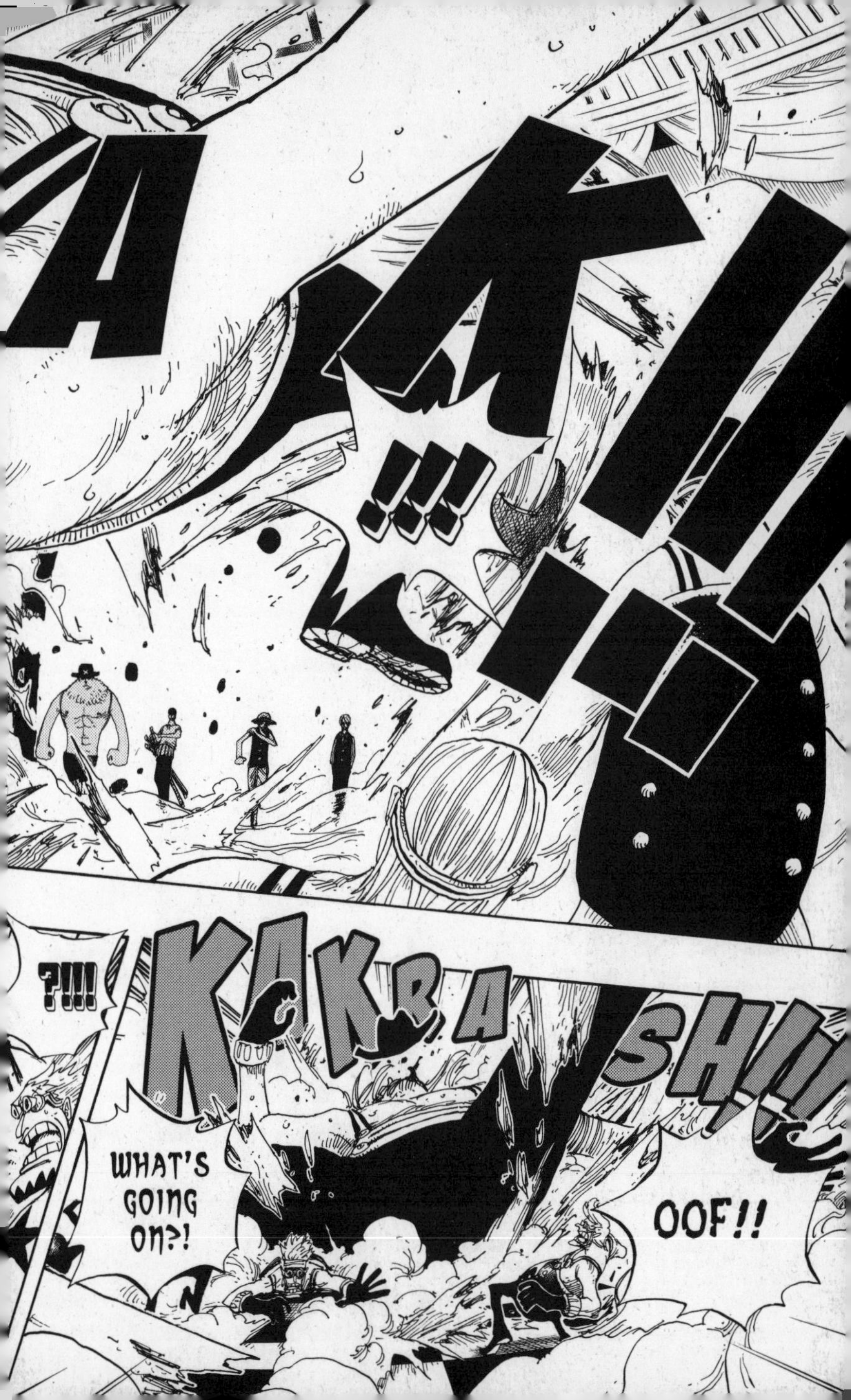

AA!!!
KACRASH!!
OOF!!
WHAT'S GOING ON?!
?!!!

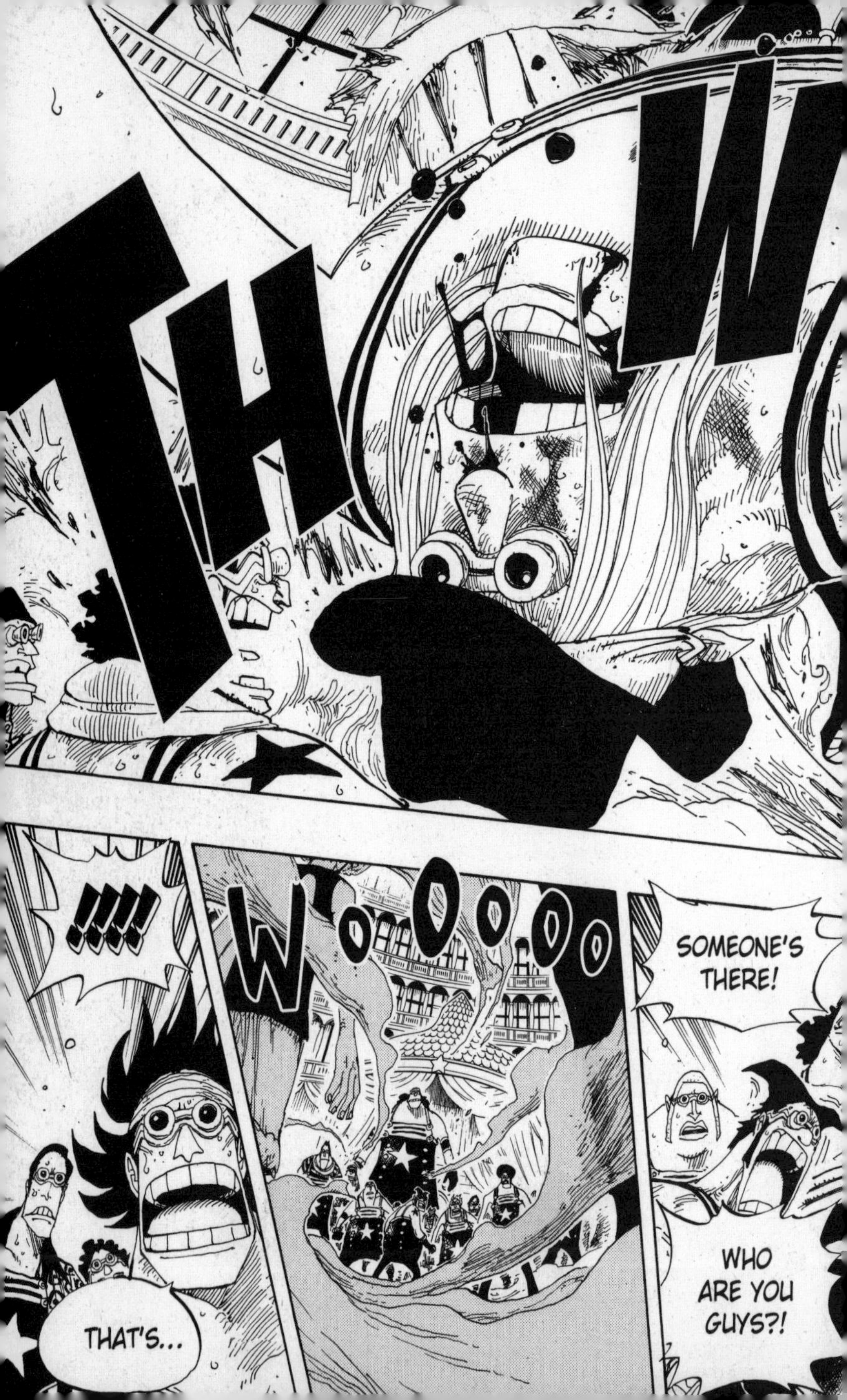
THW
SOMEONE'S THERE!
WHO ARE YOU GUYS?!
WOOOOO
!!!!
THAT'S...

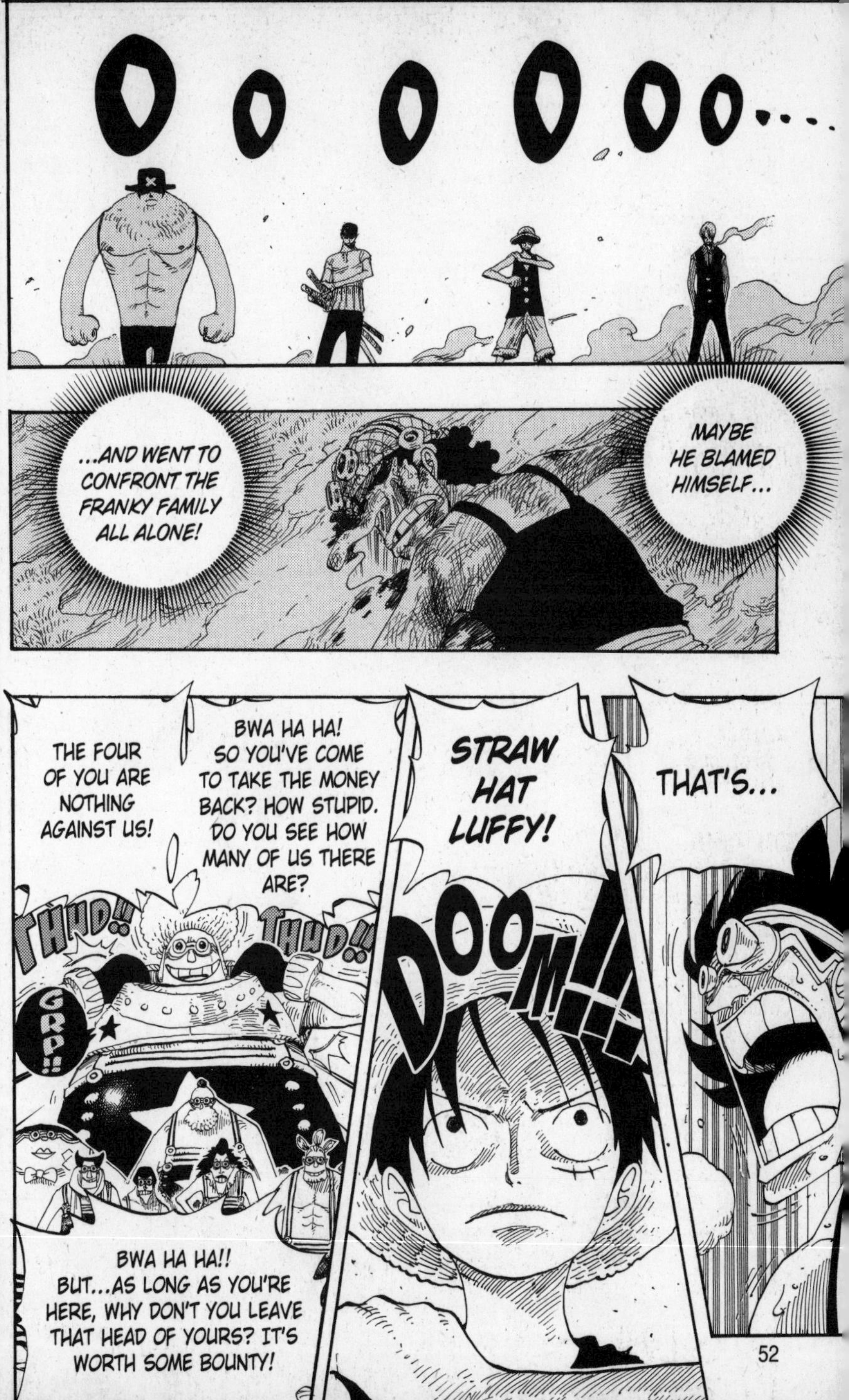
OOOOOO...
MAYBE HE BLAMED HIMSELF...
...AND WENT TO CONFRONT THE FRANKY FAMILY ALL ALONE!
THAT'S...
STRAW HAT LUFFY!
DOOM!!!
BWA HA HA! SO YOU'VE COME TO TAKE THE MONEY BACK? HOW STUPID. DO YOU SEE HOW MANY OF US THERE ARE?
THE FOUR OF YOU ARE NOTHING AGAINST US!
THUD!!
THUD!!
GRP!!
BWA HA HA!! BUT...AS LONG AS YOU'RE HERE, WHY DON'T YOU LEAVE THAT HEAD OF YOURS? IT'S WORTH SOME BOUNTY!

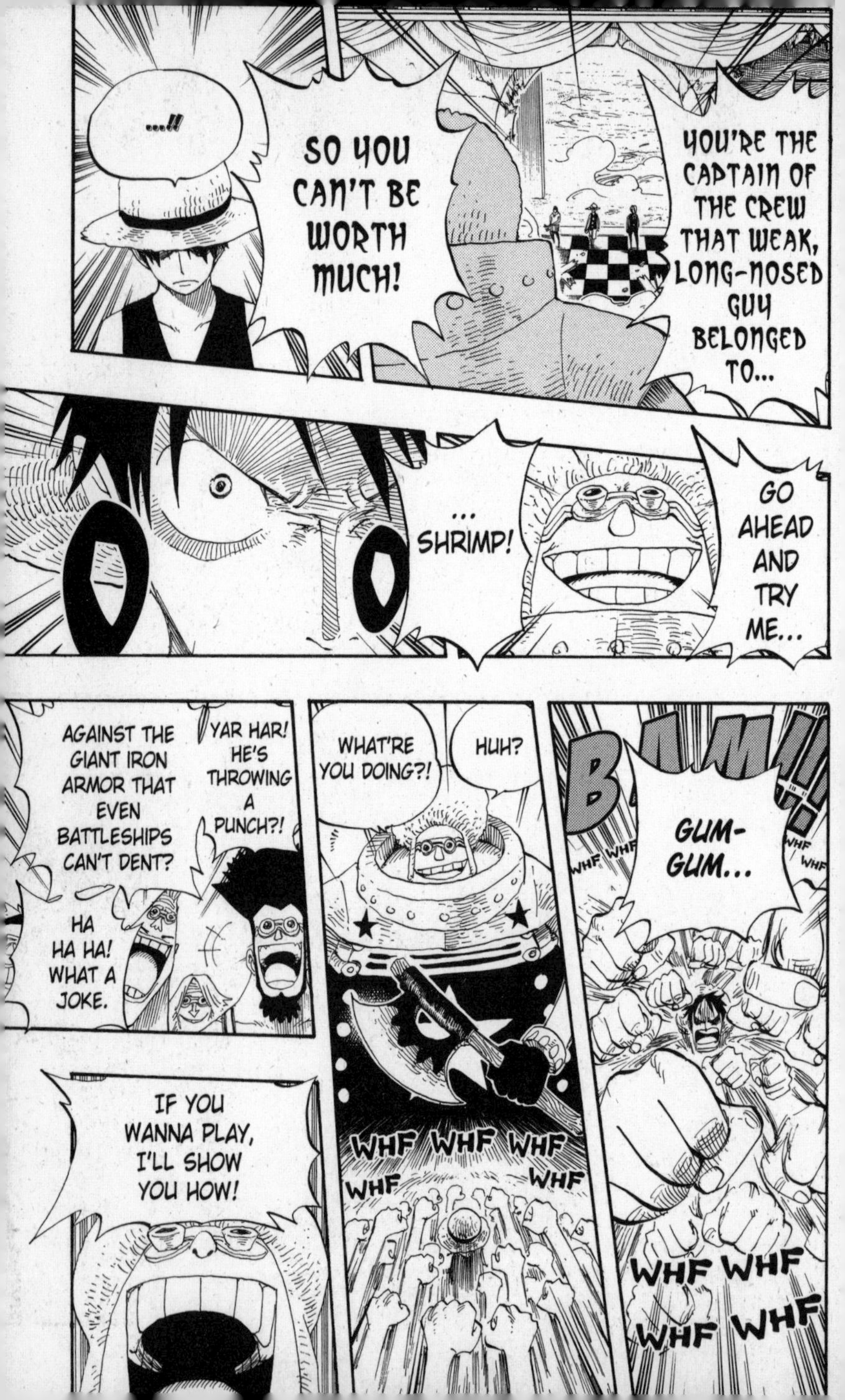
YOU'RE THE CAPTAIN OF THE CREW THAT WEAK, LONG-NOSED GUY BELONGED TO...
SO YOU CAN'T BE WORTH MUCH!
...!!
GO AHEAD AND TRY ME...
... SHRIMP!
BAM!!!
WHF
WHF
WHF WHF
GUM-GUM...
WHF WHF
WHF WHF
HUH?
WHAT'RE YOU DOING?!
WHF WHF WHF
WHF
WHF
YAR HAR! HE'S THROWING A PUNCH?!
AGAINST THE GIANT IRON ARMOR THAT EVEN BATTLESHIPS CAN'T DENT?
HA HA HA! WHAT A JOKE.
IF YOU WANNA PLAY, I'LL SHOW YOU HOW!

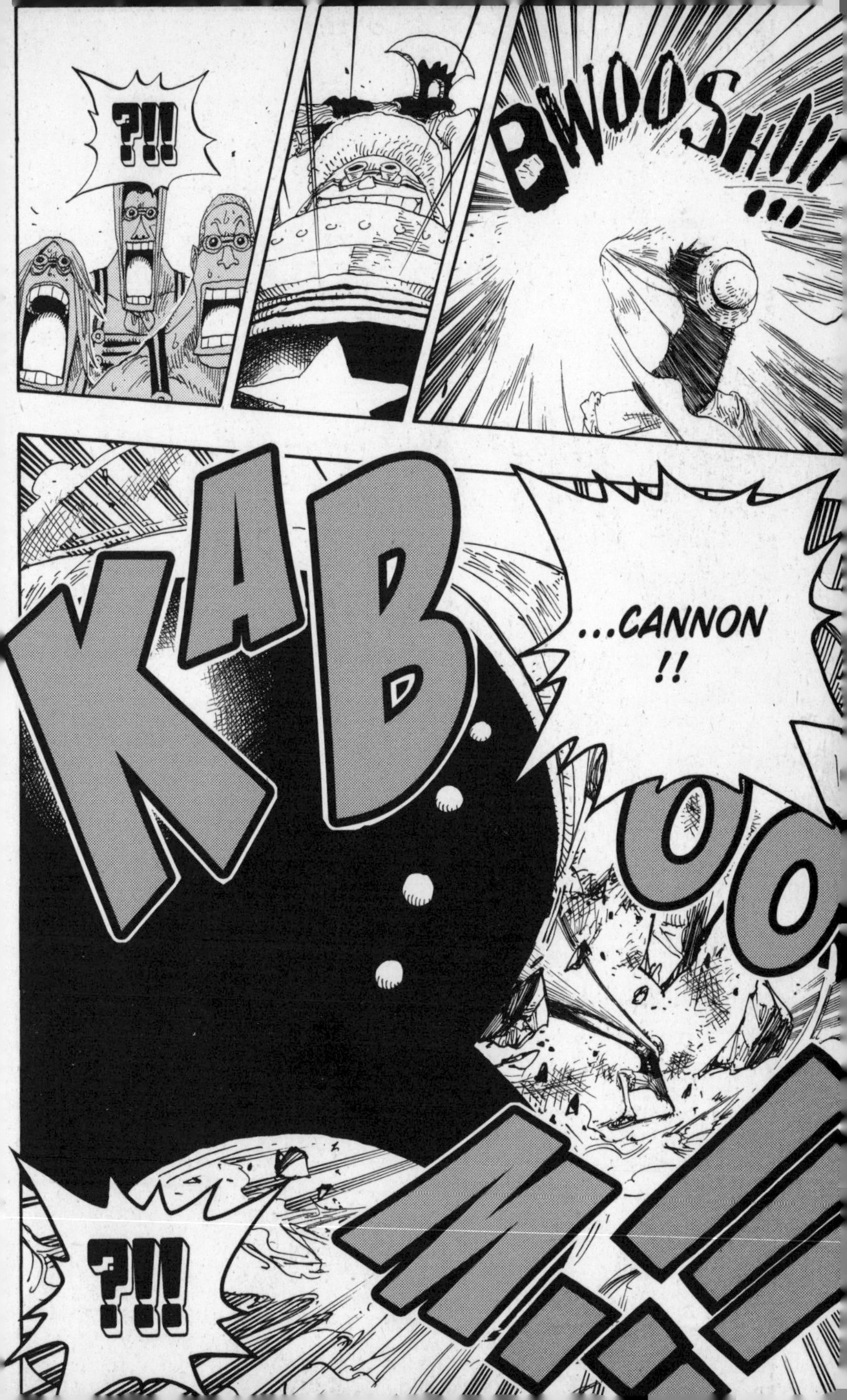
BWOOSH!!!...
?!!
...CANNON !!
KABOOM!!
?!!

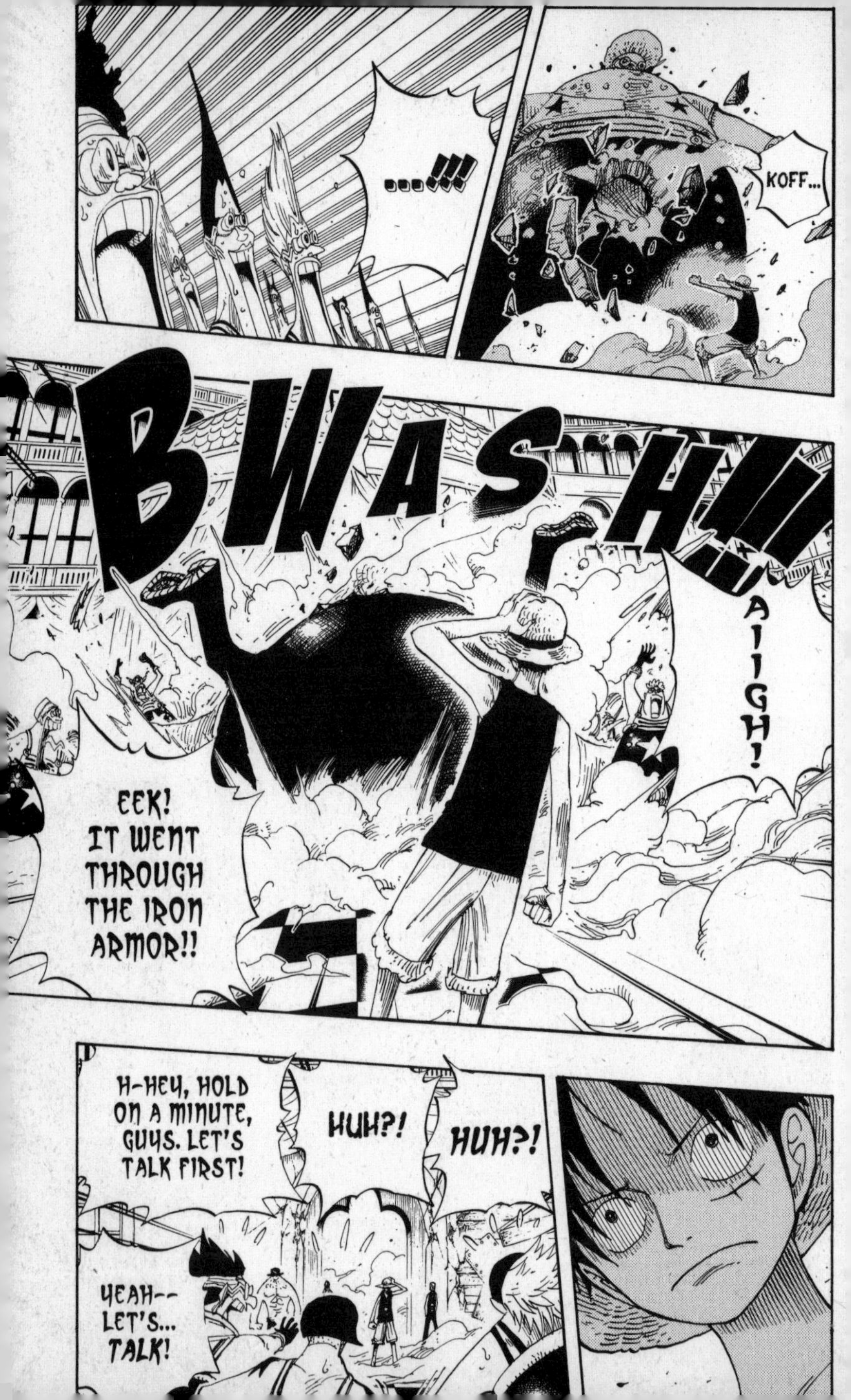
KOFF...
...!!!
BWASH!!
AIIGH!
EEK! IT WENT THROUGH THE IRON ARMOR!!
HUH?!
HUH?!
H-HEY, HOLD ON A MINUTE, GUYS. LET'S TALK FIRST!
YEAH-- LET'S... TALK!

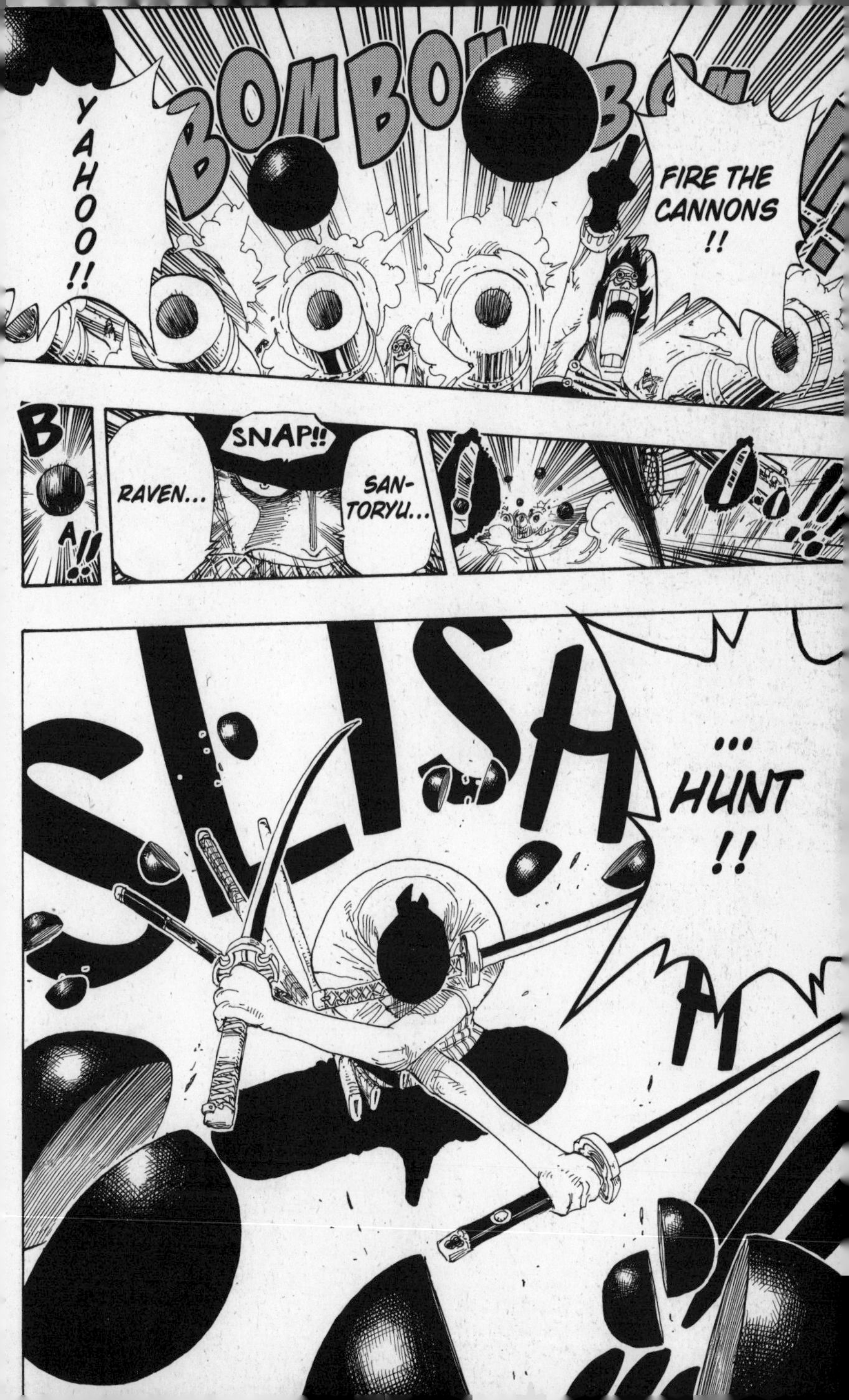

FIRE THE CANNONS !!
BOM BO
YAHOO!!
!!
SNAP!!
SAN-TORYU...
RAVEN...
BA!!
...HUNT !!
SLISH

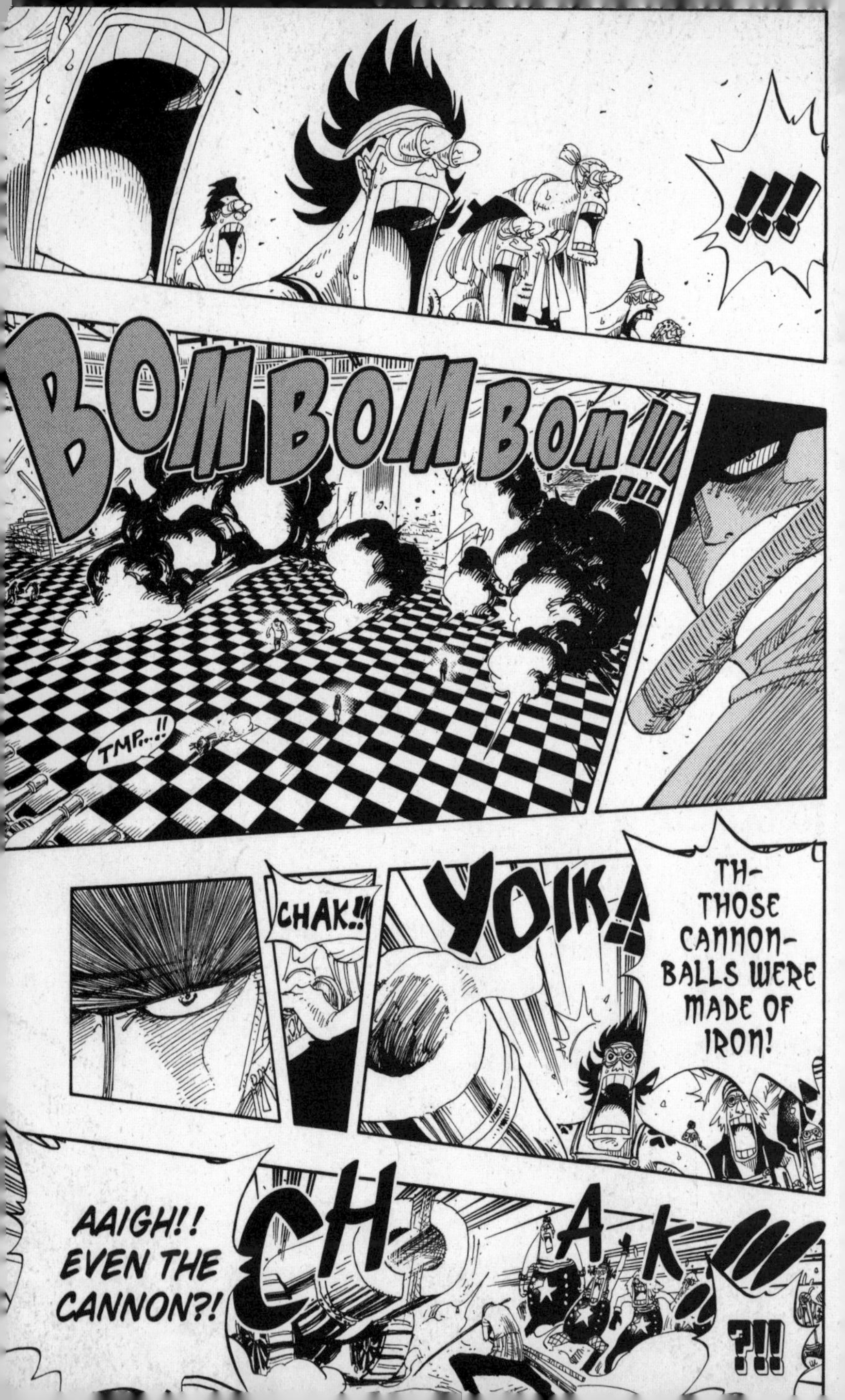
!!!
BOM BOM BOM!!!
TMP...!!
TH-THOSE CANNONBALLS WERE MADE OF IRON!
YOIK!!
CHAK!!
CHAK!!!
?!!
AAIGH!! EVEN THE CANNON?!

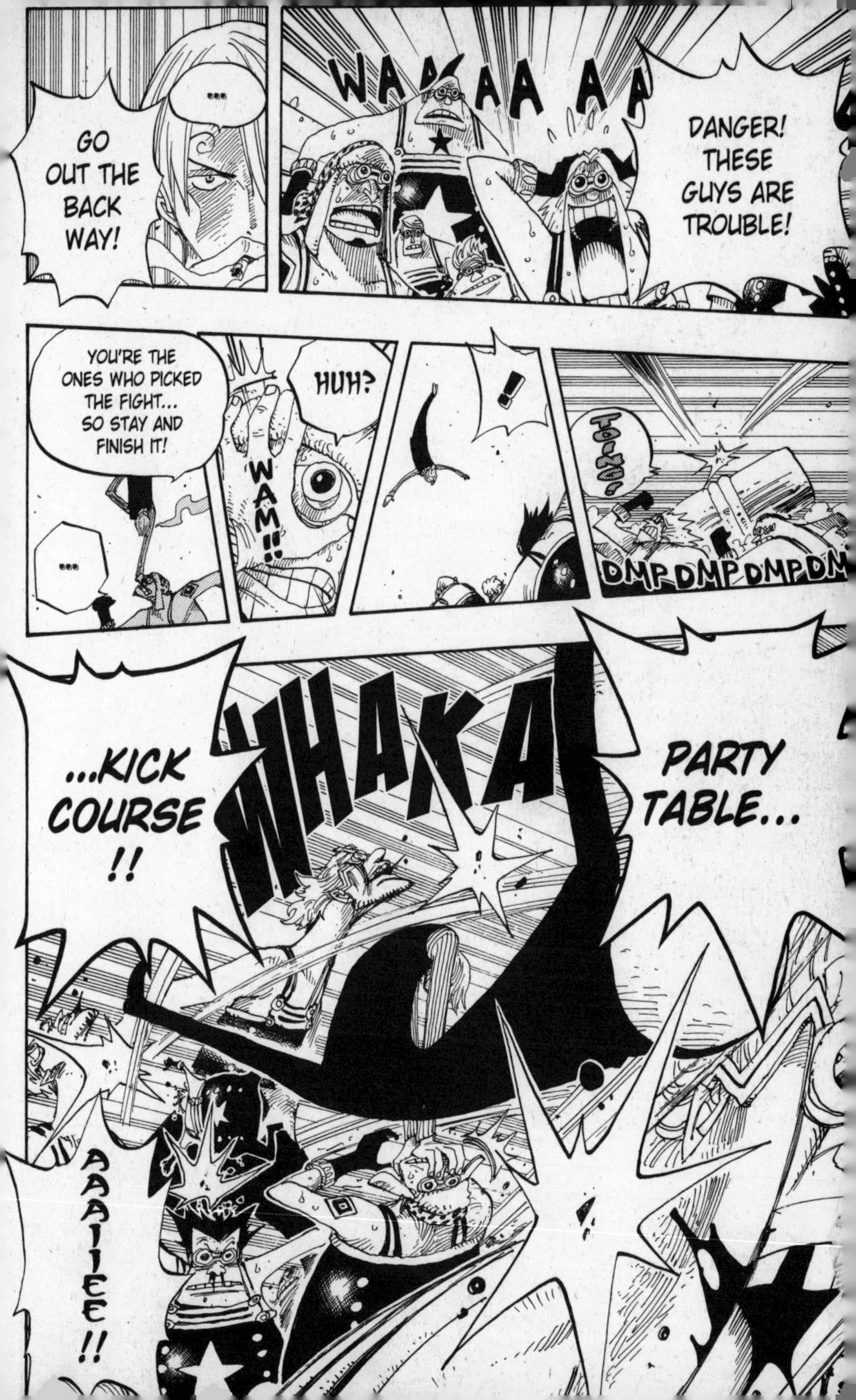

WAAAAA
DANGER! THESE GUYS ARE TROUBLE!
...
GO OUT THE BACK WAY!
TOING!
DMP DMP DMP DM
!
HUH?
WAM!!
YOU'RE THE ONES WHO PICKED THE FIGHT... SO STAY AND FINISH IT!
...
WHAKA
PARTY TABLE...
...KICK COURSE!!
AAAIIEE!!

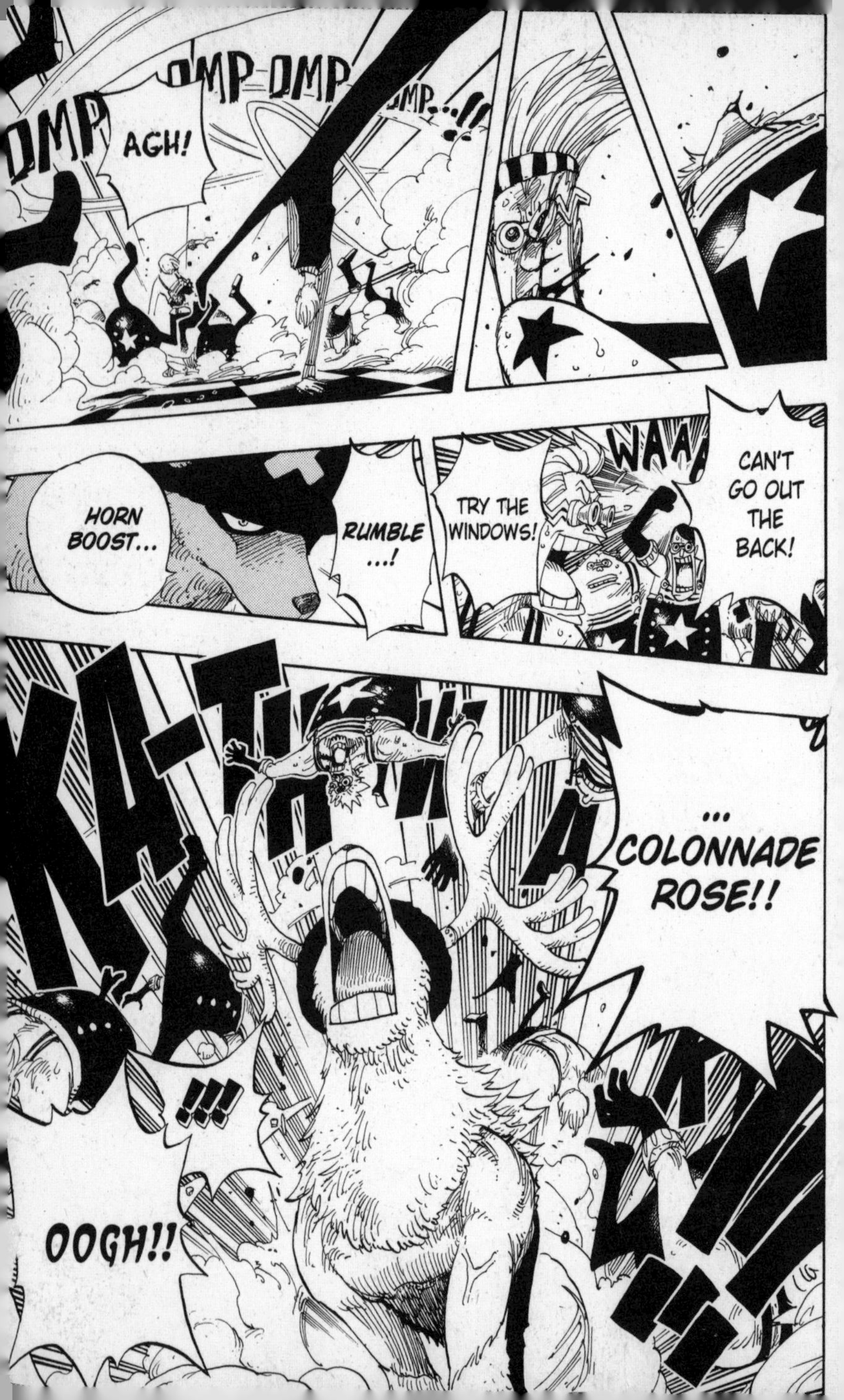

DMP...!!
DMP-DMP
DMP
AGH!
WAA
CAN'T GO OUT THE BACK!
TRY THE WINDOWS!
RUMBLE ...!
HORN BOOST...
... COLONNADE ROSE!!
!!!
OOGH!!

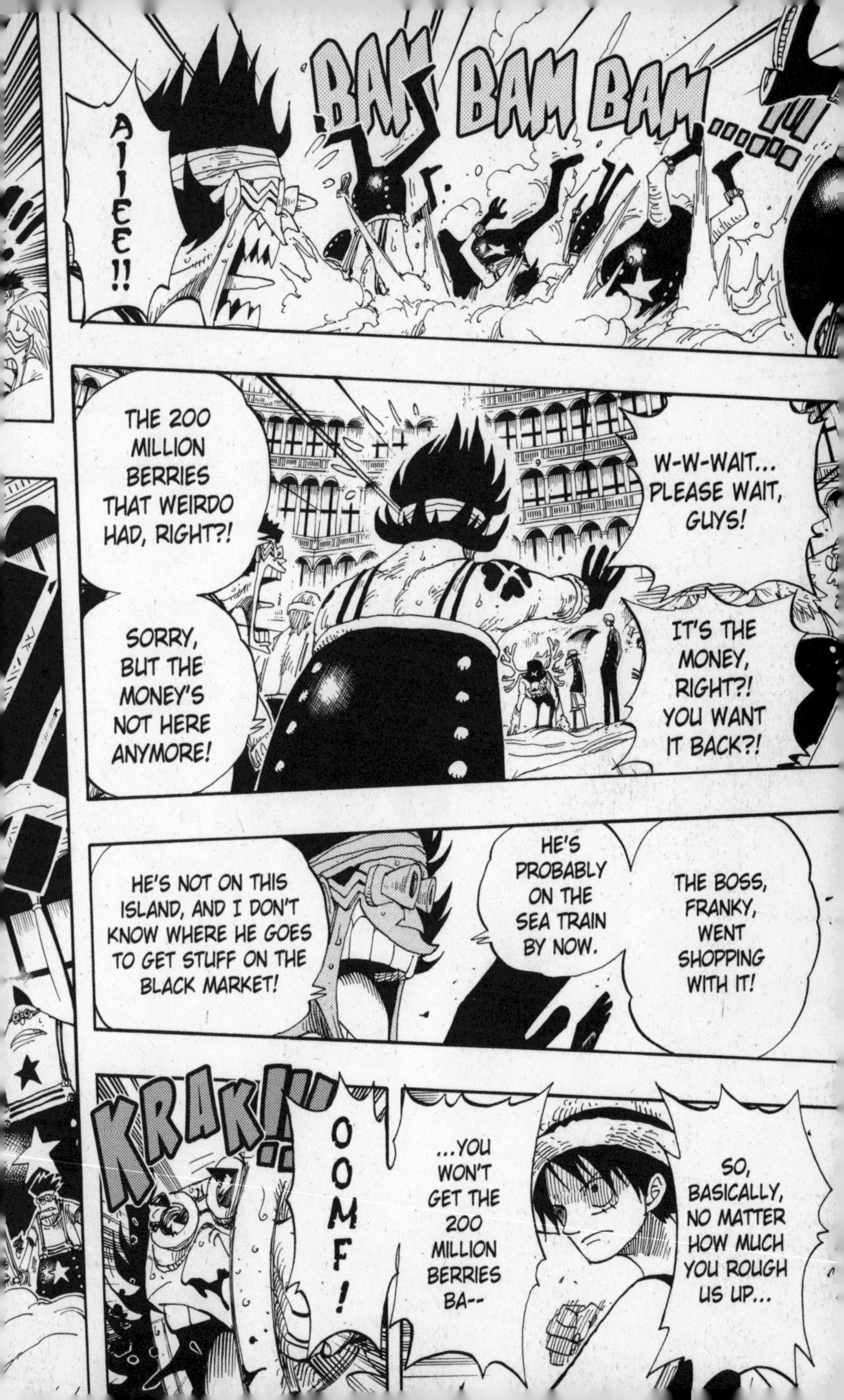
BAM BAM BAM...
AIIIEE!!
W-W-WAIT... PLEASE WAIT, GUYS!
IT'S THE MONEY, RIGHT?! YOU WANT IT BACK?!
THE 200 MILLION BERRIES THAT WEIRDO HAD, RIGHT?!
SORRY, BUT THE MONEY'S NOT HERE ANYMORE!
THE BOSS, FRANKY, WENT SHOPPING WITH IT!
HE'S PROBABLY ON THE SEA TRAIN BY NOW.
HE'S NOT ON THIS ISLAND, AND I DON'T KNOW WHERE HE GOES TO GET STUFF ON THE BLACK MARKET!
SO, BASICALLY, NO MATTER HOW MUCH YOU ROUGH US UP...
...YOU WON'T GET THE 200 MILLION BERRIES BA--
OOMF!
KRAK!!

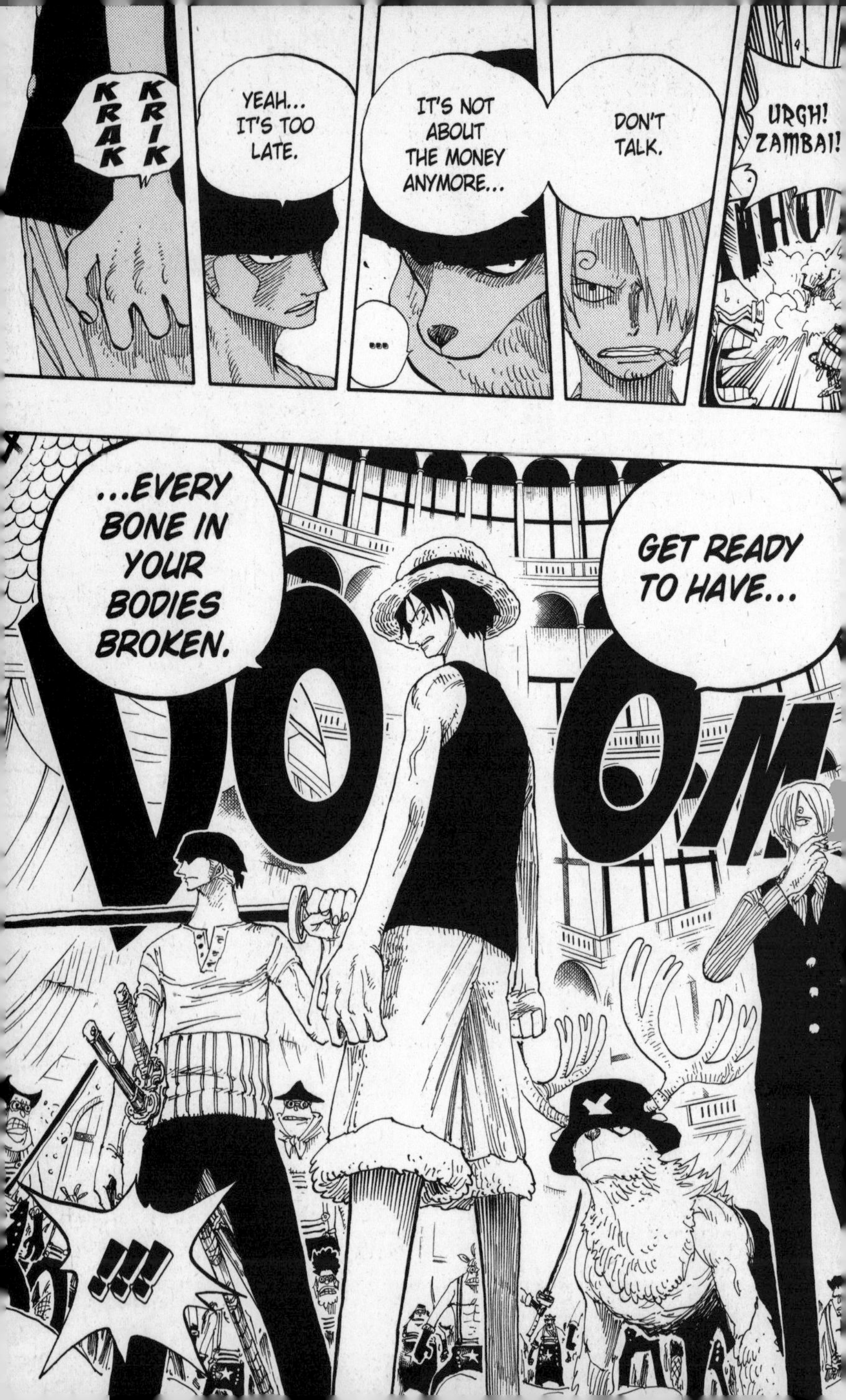
URGH! ZAMBAI!
DON'T TALK.
IT'S NOT ABOUT THE MONEY ANYMORE...
...
YEAH... IT'S TOO LATE.
KRIK KRIK
KRAK KRAK
GET READY TO HAVE...
...EVERY BONE IN YOUR BODIES BROKEN.
VOOM
!!!

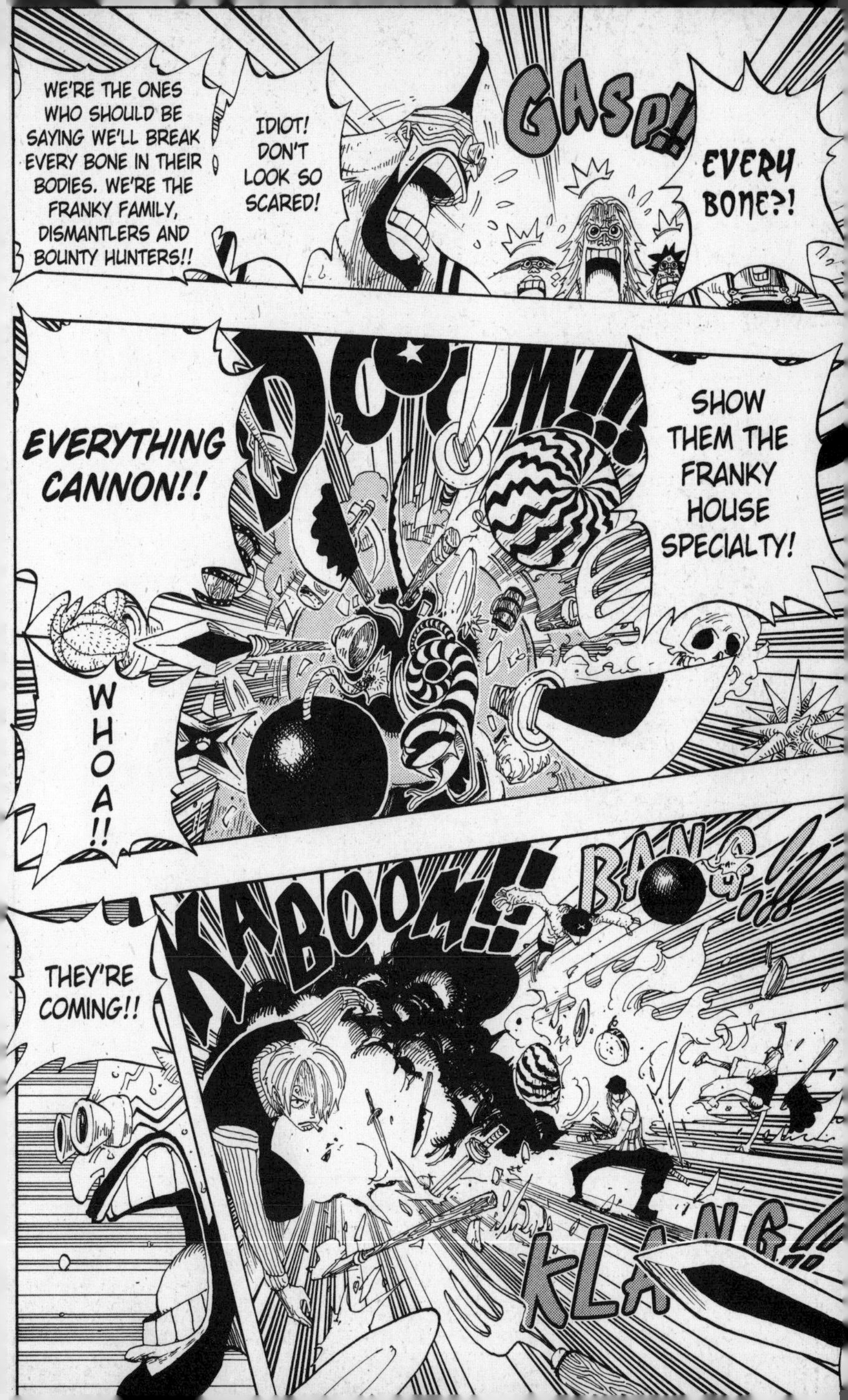
EVERY BONE?!
GASP!!
IDIOT! DON'T LOOK SO SCARED!
WE'RE THE ONES WHO SHOULD BE SAYING WE'LL BREAK EVERY BONE IN THEIR BODIES. WE'RE THE FRANKY FAMILY, DISMANTLERS AND BOUNTY HUNTERS!!
SHOW THEM THE FRANKY HOUSE SPECIALTY!
DOOM!!
EVERYTHING CANNON!!
WHOA!!
BANG!!
KABOOM!!
THEY'RE COMING!!
KLANG!!

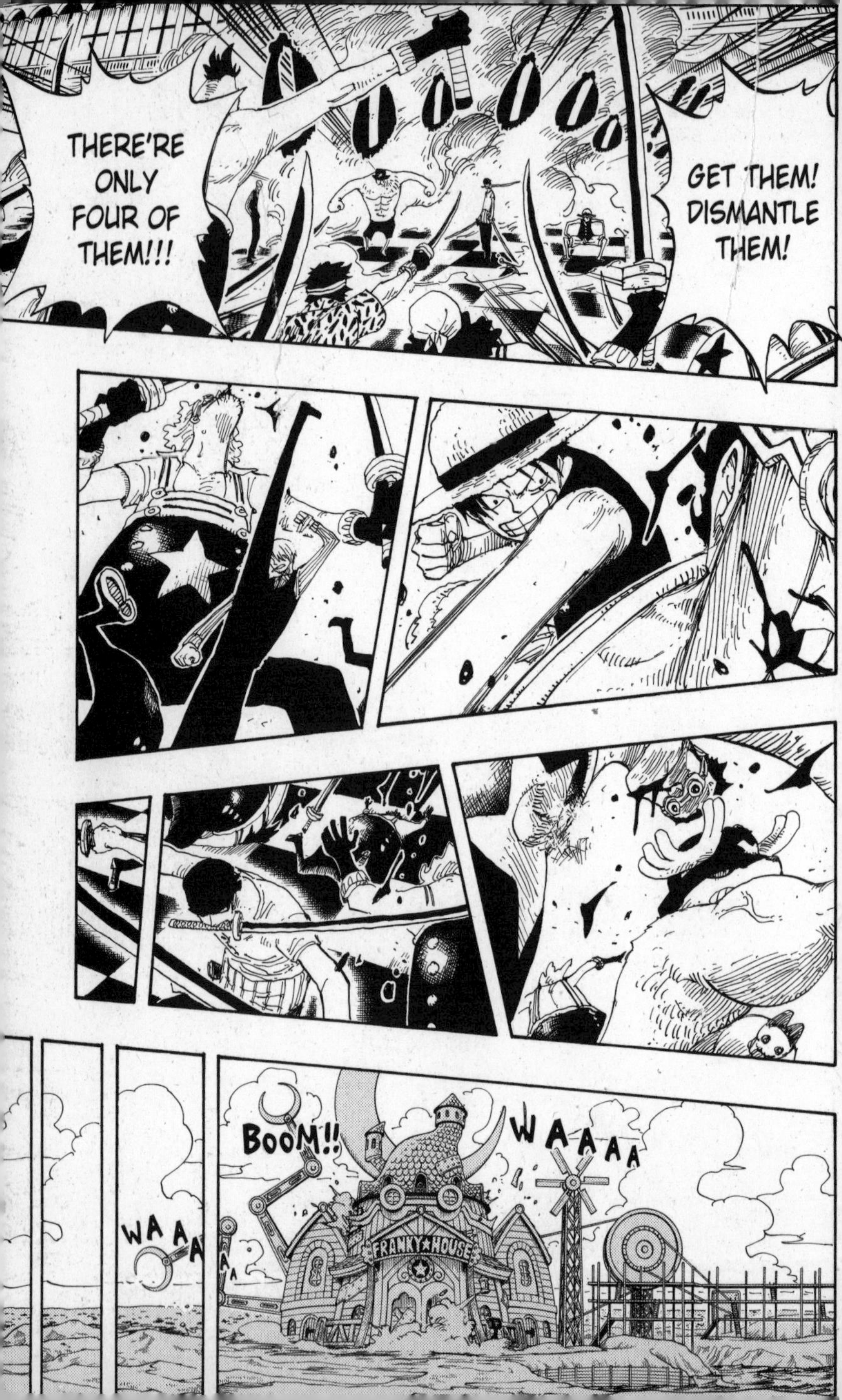
GET THEM! DISMANTLE THEM!
OOOOOO!!
THERE'RE ONLY FOUR OF THEM!!!
WAAAA
FRANKY★HOUSE
BOOM!!
WAAAA

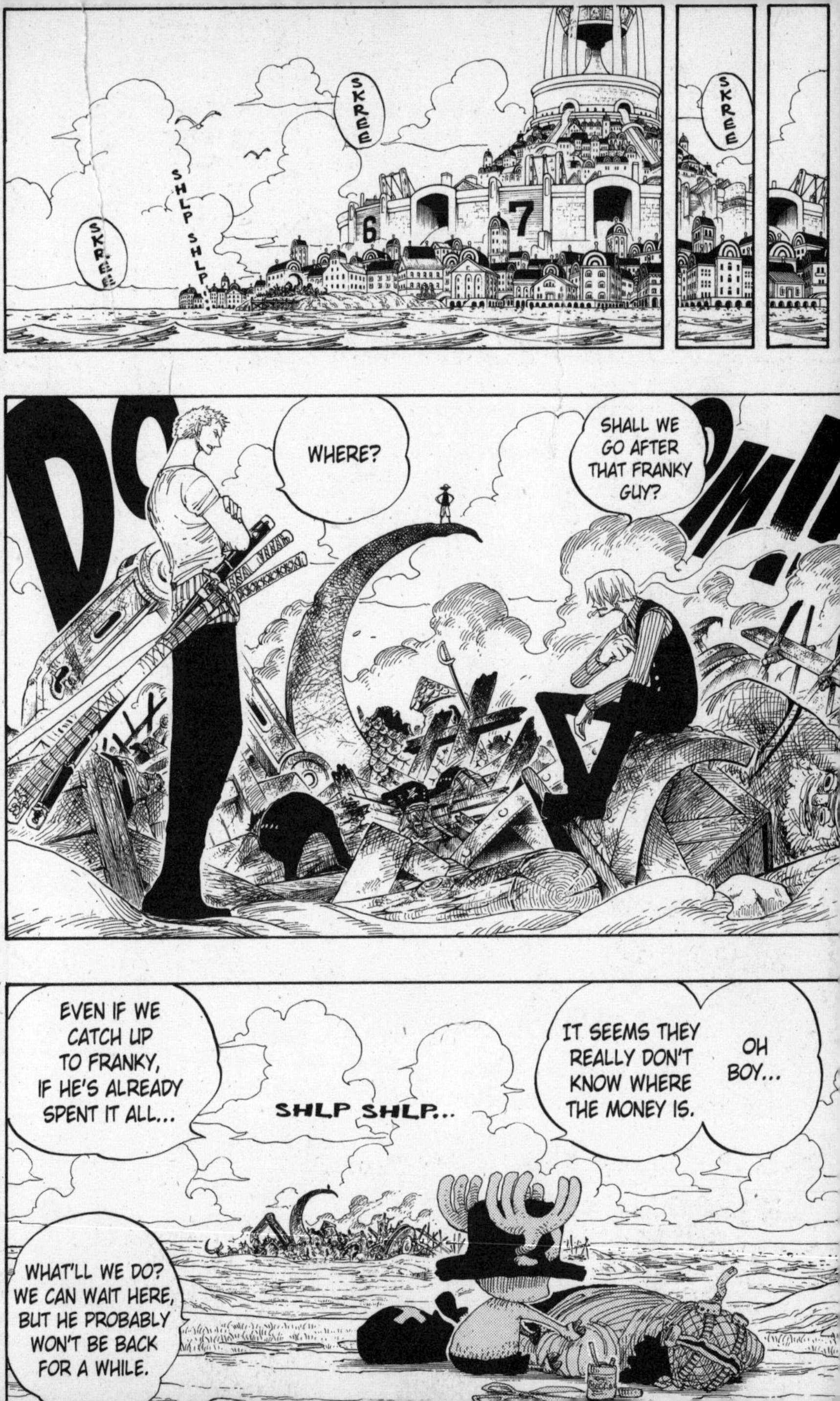
SKREE
SKREE
SHLP SHLP...
SKREE
SHALL WE GO AFTER THAT FRANKY GUY?
WHERE?
OH BOY...
IT SEEMS THEY REALLY DON'T KNOW WHERE THE MONEY IS.
SHLP SHLP...
EVEN IF WE CATCH UP TO FRANKY, IF HE'S ALREADY SPENT IT ALL...
WHAT'LL WE DO? WE CAN WAIT HERE, BUT HE PROBABLY WON'T BE BACK FOR A WHILE.

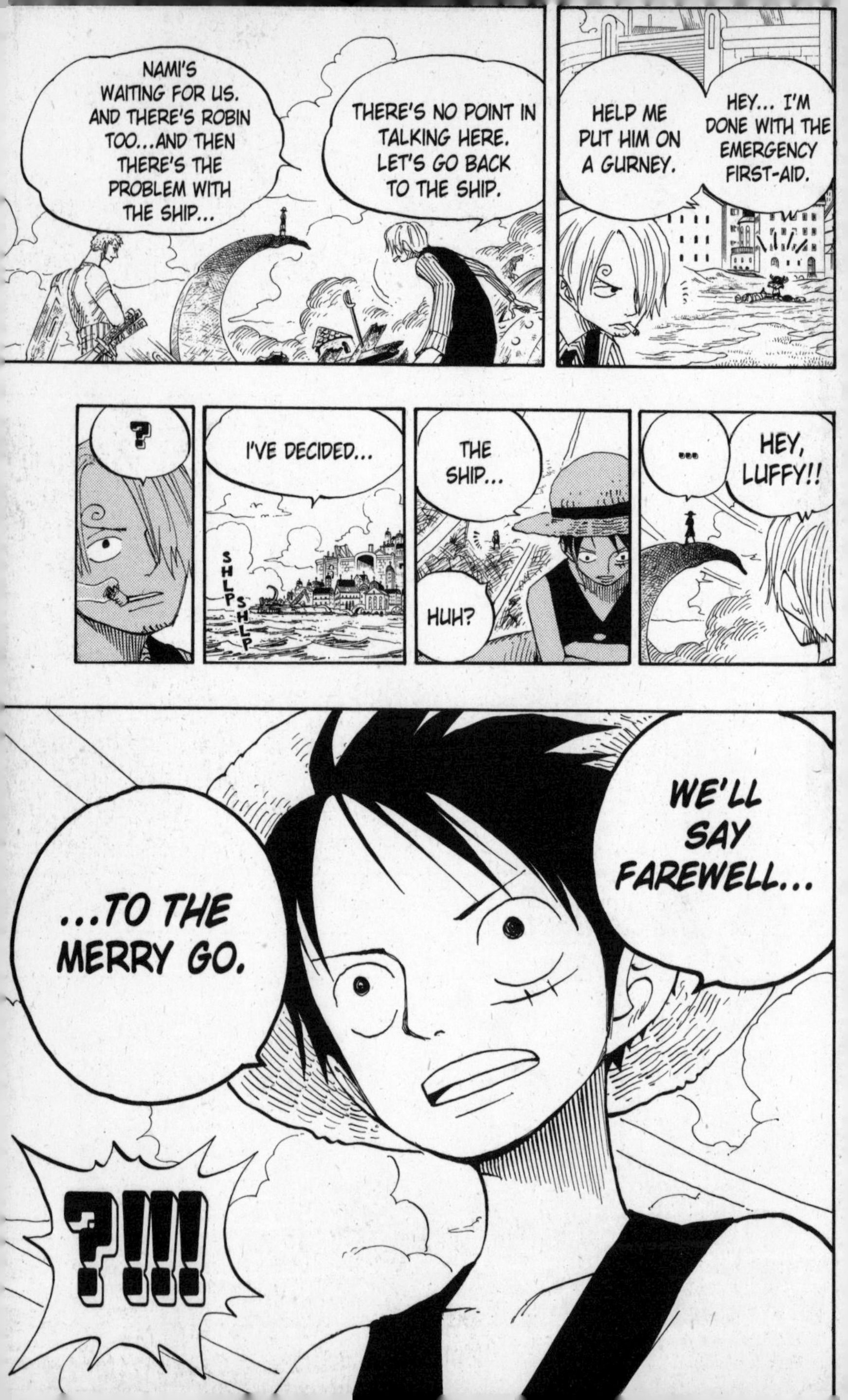

HEY... I'M DONE WITH THE EMERGENCY FIRST-AID.
HELP ME PUT HIM ON A GURNEY.
THERE'S NO POINT IN TALKING HERE. LET'S GO BACK TO THE SHIP.
NAMI'S WAITING FOR US. AND THERE'S ROBIN TOO...AND THEN THERE'S THE PROBLEM WITH THE SHIP...
HEY, LUFFY!!
...
THE SHIP...
HUH?
I'VE DECIDED...
SHLP SHLP
?
WE'LL SAY FAREWELL...
...TO THE MERRY GO.
?!!!

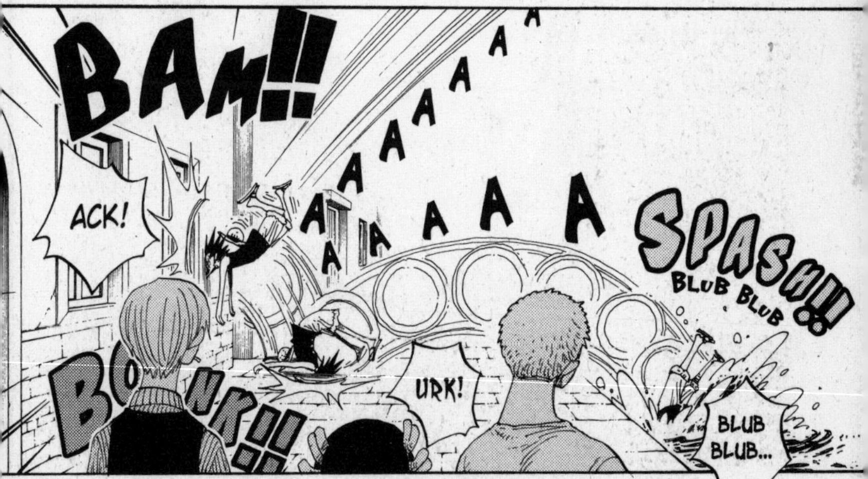
AAAAAAAAAAAAAA
BAM!!
SPASH!!
BLUB BLUB
ACK!
URK!
BLUB BLUB...
BONK!!

Chapter 331:
THE BIG ARGUMENT

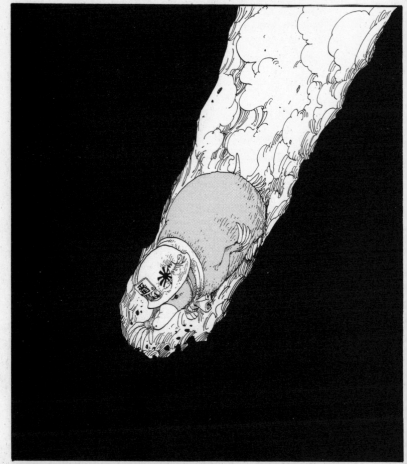

GEDATSU'S UNEXPECTED LIFE ON THE BLUE SEA, VOL. 16:
"DIG, DIG, EARTH BOSS"

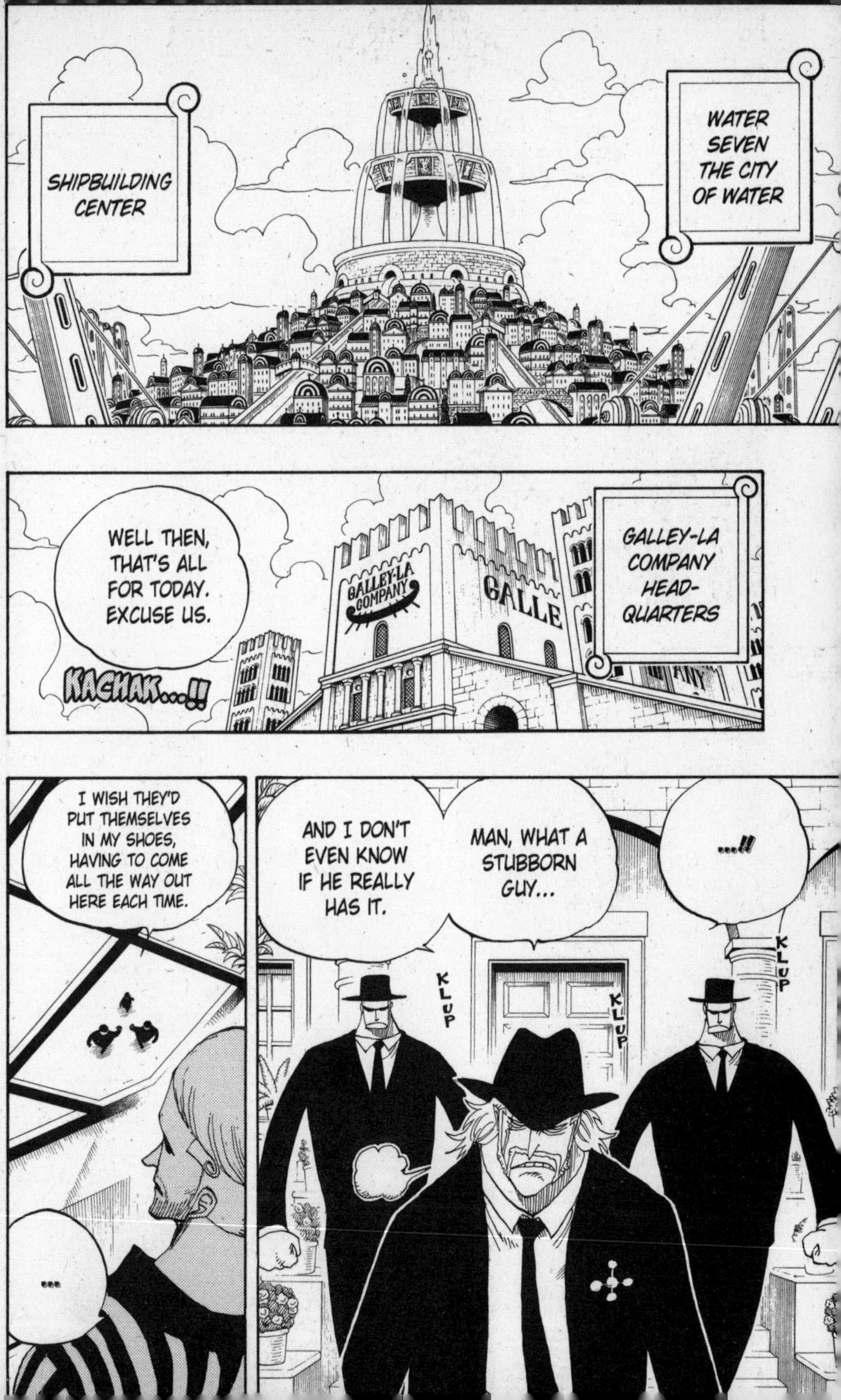
WATER SEVEN THE CITY OF WATER
SHIPBUILDING CENTER
GALLEY-LA COMPANY HEAD-QUARTERS
GALLEY-LA COMPANY
GALLE
WELL THEN, THAT'S ALL FOR TODAY. EXCUSE US.
KACHAK...!!
...!!
KLUP
MAN, WHAT A STUBBORN GUY...
KLUP
AND I DON'T EVEN KNOW IF HE REALLY HAS IT.
KLUP
I WISH THEY'D PUT THEMSELVES IN MY SHOES, HAVING TO COME ALL THE WAY OUT HERE EACH TIME.
...

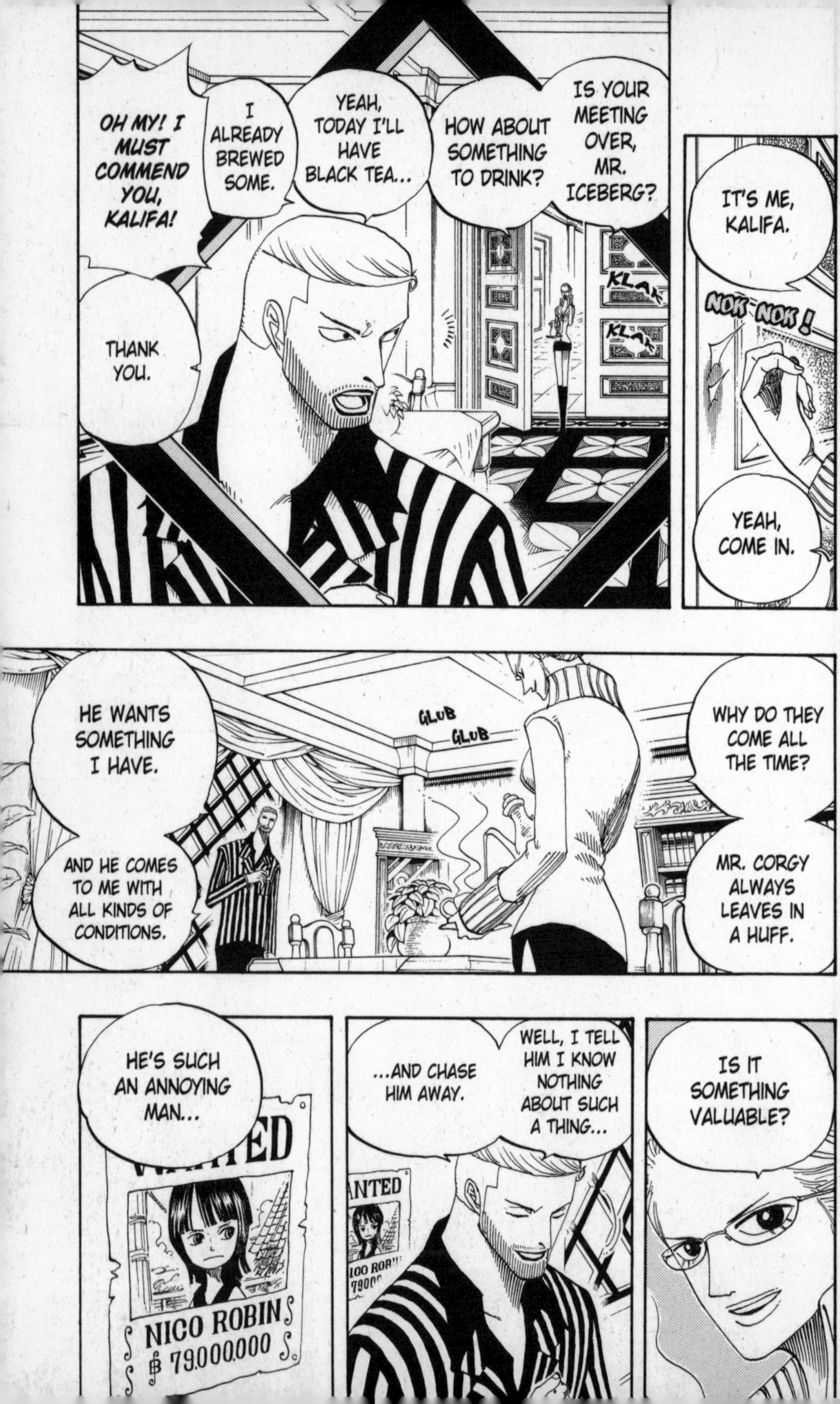
IT'S ME, KALIFA.
NOK NOK!
YEAH, COME IN.
KLAK
KLAK
IS YOUR MEETING OVER, MR. ICEBERG?
HOW ABOUT SOMETHING TO DRINK?
YEAH, TODAY I'LL HAVE BLACK TEA...
I ALREADY BREWED SOME.
OH MY! I MUST COMMEND YOU, KALIFA!
THANK YOU.
WHY DO THEY COME ALL THE TIME?
MR. CORGY ALWAYS LEAVES IN A HUFF.
GLUB
GLUB
HE WANTS SOMETHING I HAVE.
AND HE COMES TO ME WITH ALL KINDS OF CONDITIONS.
IS IT SOMETHING VALUABLE?
WELL, I TELL HIM I KNOW NOTHING ABOUT SUCH A THING...
...AND CHASE HIM AWAY.
HE'S SUCH AN ANNOYING MAN...
NICO ROBIN
฿ 79.000.000

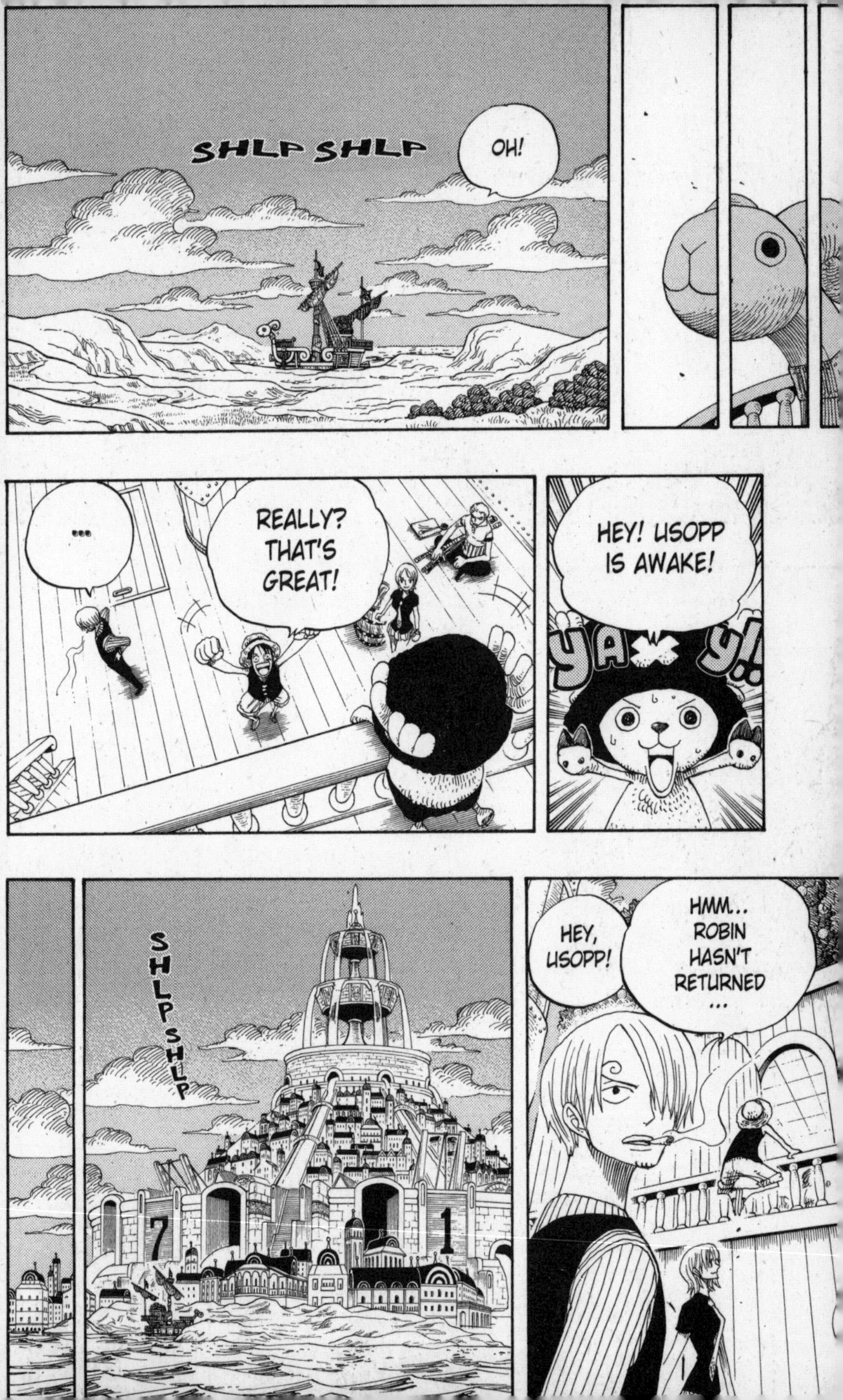
SHLP SHLP
OH!
HEY! USOPP IS AWAKE!
YA Y!!
REALLY? THAT'S GREAT!
...
HMM.. ROBIN HASN'T RETURNED ...
HEY, USOPP!
SHLP SHLP
7
1

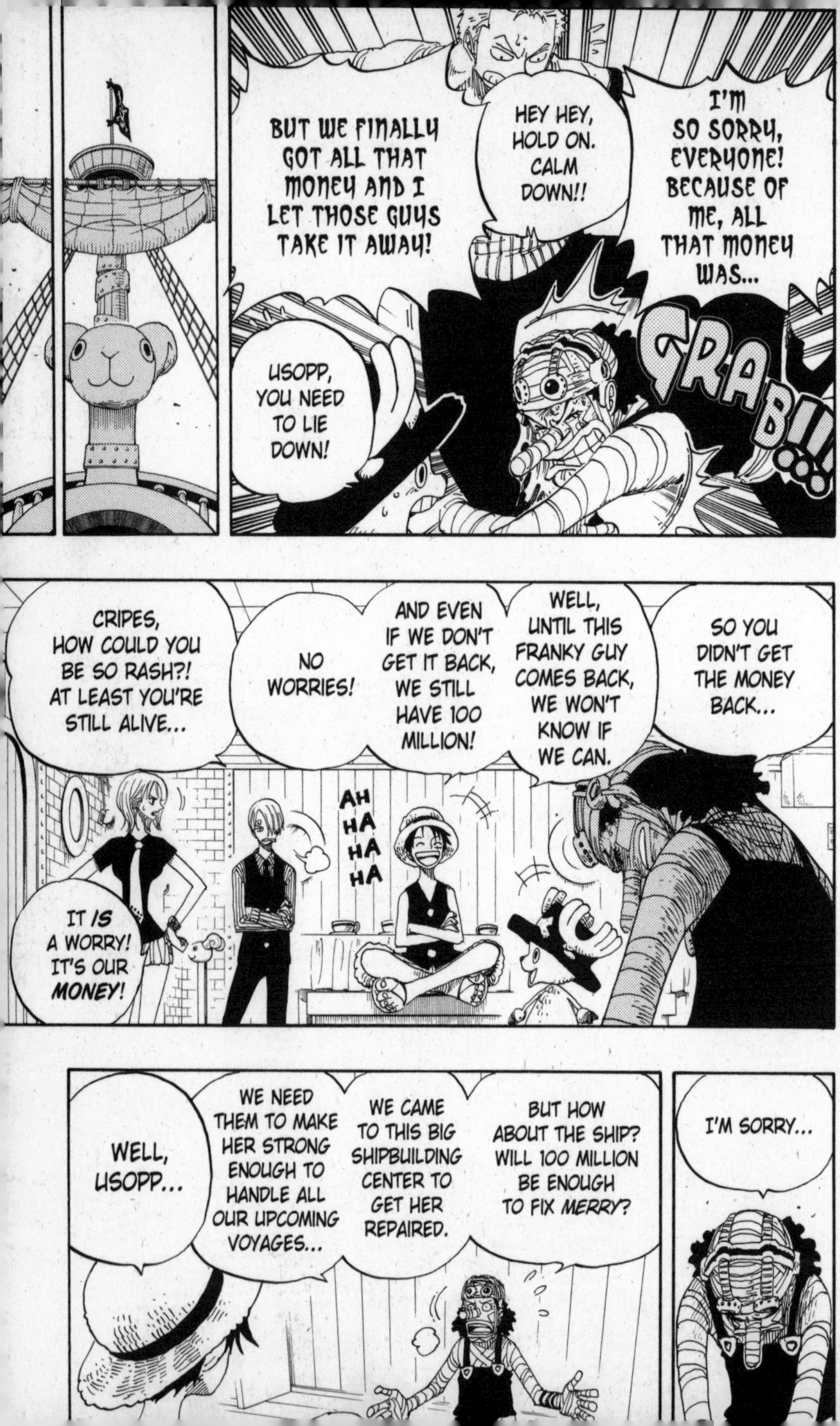
I'M SO SORRY, EVERYONE! BECAUSE OF ME, ALL THAT MONEY WAS...
HEY HEY, HOLD ON. CALM DOWN!!
BUT WE FINALLY GOT ALL THAT MONEY AND I LET THOSE GUYS TAKE IT AWAY!
GRAB!!...
USOPP, YOU NEED TO LIE DOWN!
SO YOU DIDN'T GET THE MONEY BACK...
WELL, UNTIL THIS FRANKY GUY COMES BACK, WE WON'T KNOW IF WE CAN.
AND EVEN IF WE DON'T GET IT BACK, WE STILL HAVE 100 MILLION!
NO WORRIES!
AH HA HA HA
CRIPES, HOW COULD YOU BE SO RASH?! AT LEAST YOU'RE STILL ALIVE...
IT *IS* A WORRY! IT'S OUR *MONEY*!
I'M SORRY...
BUT HOW ABOUT THE SHIP? WILL 100 MILLION BE ENOUGH TO FIX *MERRY*?
WE CAME TO THIS BIG SHIPBUILDING CENTER TO GET HER REPAIRED.
WE NEED THEM TO MAKE HER STRONG ENOUGH TO HANDLE ALL OUR UPCOMING VOYAGES...
WELL, USOPP...

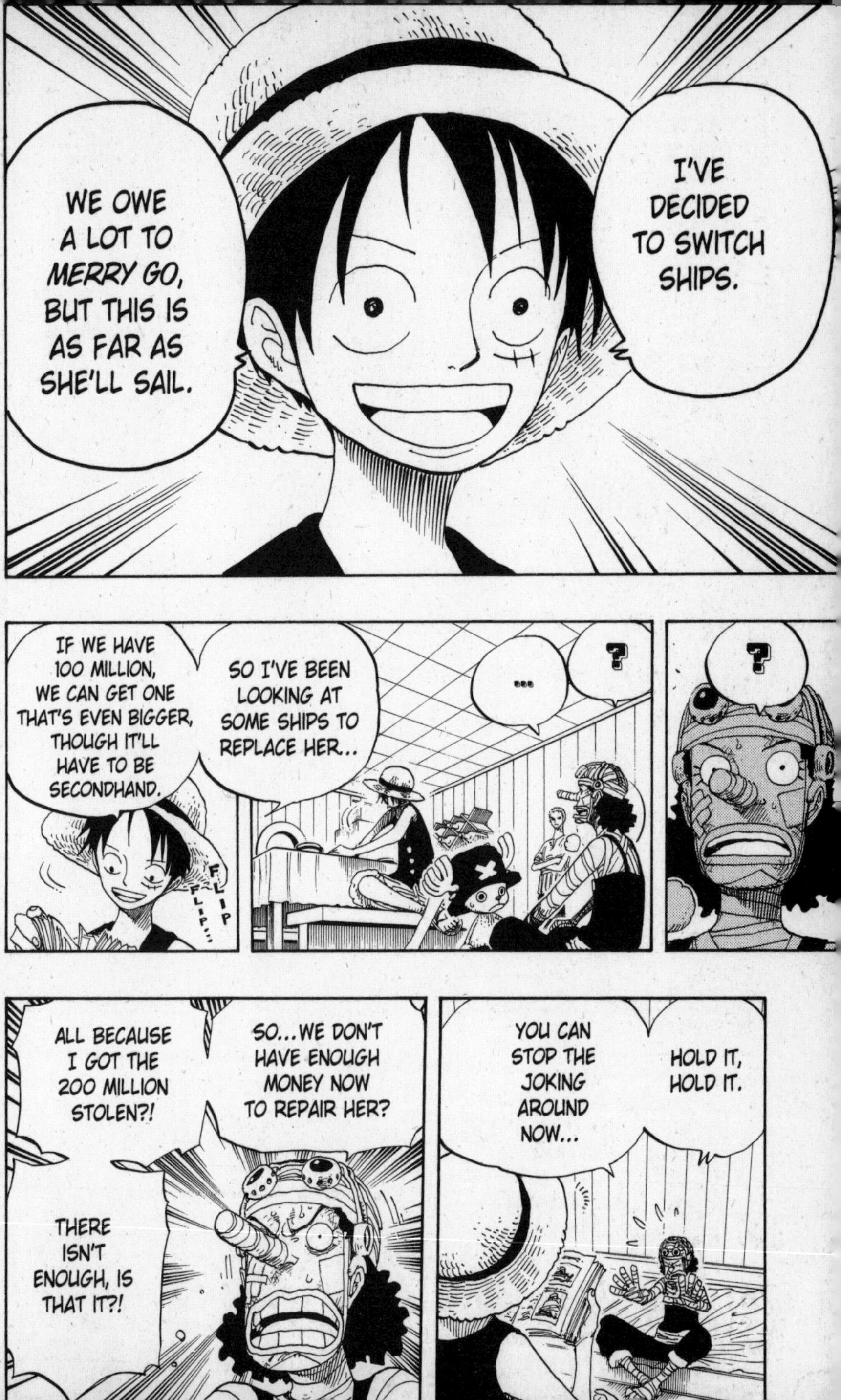
I'VE DECIDED TO SWITCH SHIPS.
WE OWE A LOT TO MERRY GO, BUT THIS IS AS FAR AS SHE'LL SAIL.
?
?
...
SO I'VE BEEN LOOKING AT SOME SHIPS TO REPLACE HER...
IF WE HAVE 100 MILLION, WE CAN GET ONE THAT'S EVEN BIGGER, THOUGH IT'LL HAVE TO BE SECONDHAND.
FLIP FLIP...
HOLD IT, HOLD IT.
YOU CAN STOP THE JOKING AROUND NOW...
SO...WE DON'T HAVE ENOUGH MONEY NOW TO REPAIR HER?
ALL BECAUSE I GOT THE 200 MILLION STOLEN?!
THERE ISN'T ENOUGH, IS THAT IT?!

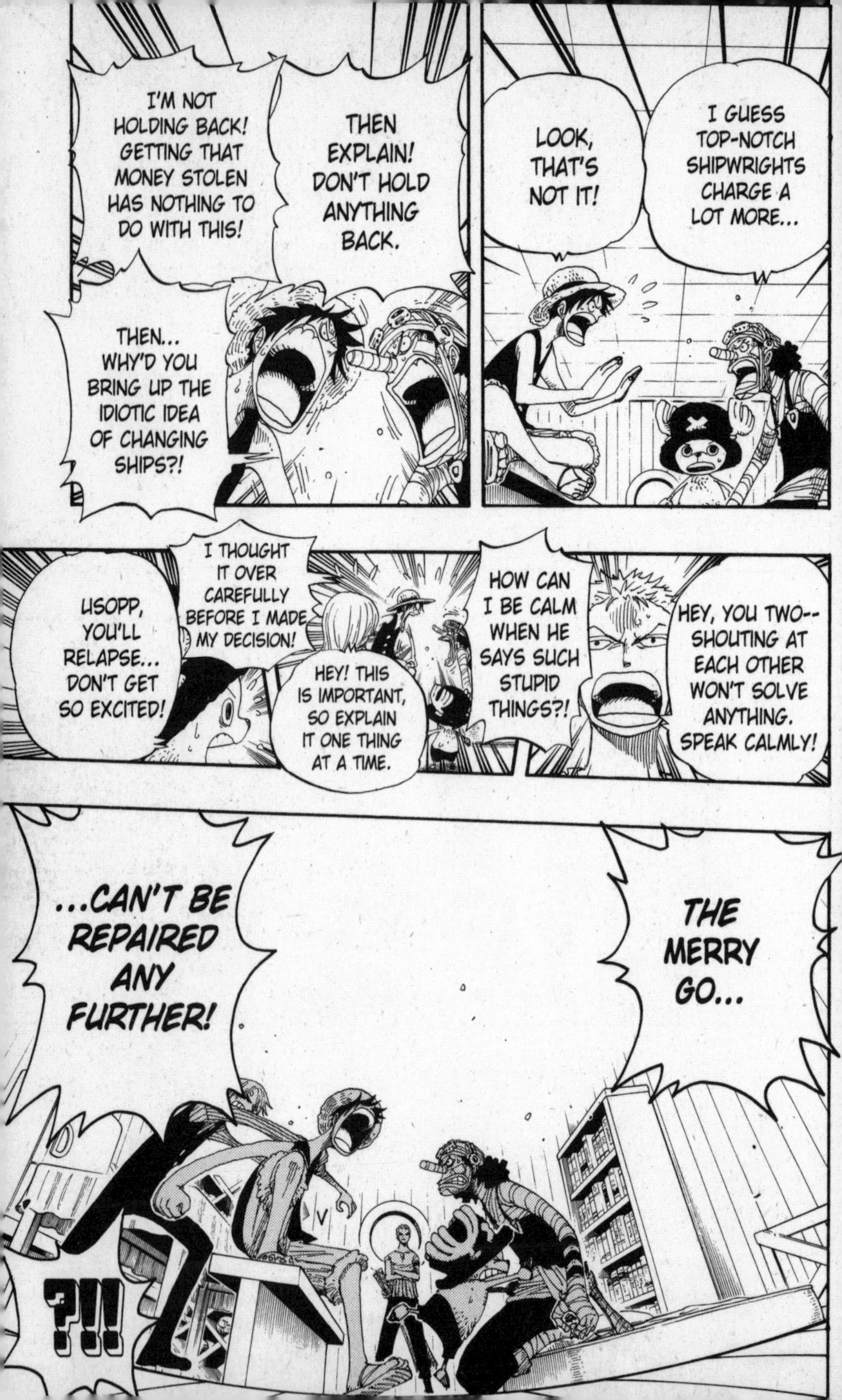
I GUESS TOP-NOTCH SHIPWRIGHTS CHARGE A LOT MORE...
LOOK, THAT'S NOT IT!
THEN EXPLAIN! DON'T HOLD ANYTHING BACK.
I'M NOT HOLDING BACK! GETTING THAT MONEY STOLEN HAS NOTHING TO DO WITH THIS!
THEN... WHY'D YOU BRING UP THE IDIOTIC IDEA OF CHANGING SHIPS?!
HEY, YOU TWO-- SHOUTING AT EACH OTHER WON'T SOLVE ANYTHING. SPEAK CALMLY!
HOW CAN I BE CALM WHEN HE SAYS SUCH STUPID THINGS?!
I THOUGHT IT OVER CAREFULLY BEFORE I MADE MY DECISION!
HEY! THIS IS IMPORTANT, SO EXPLAIN IT ONE THING AT A TIME.
USOPP, YOU'LL RELAPSE... DON'T GET SO EXCITED!
THE MERRY GO...
...CAN'T BE REPAIRED ANY FURTHER!
?!!

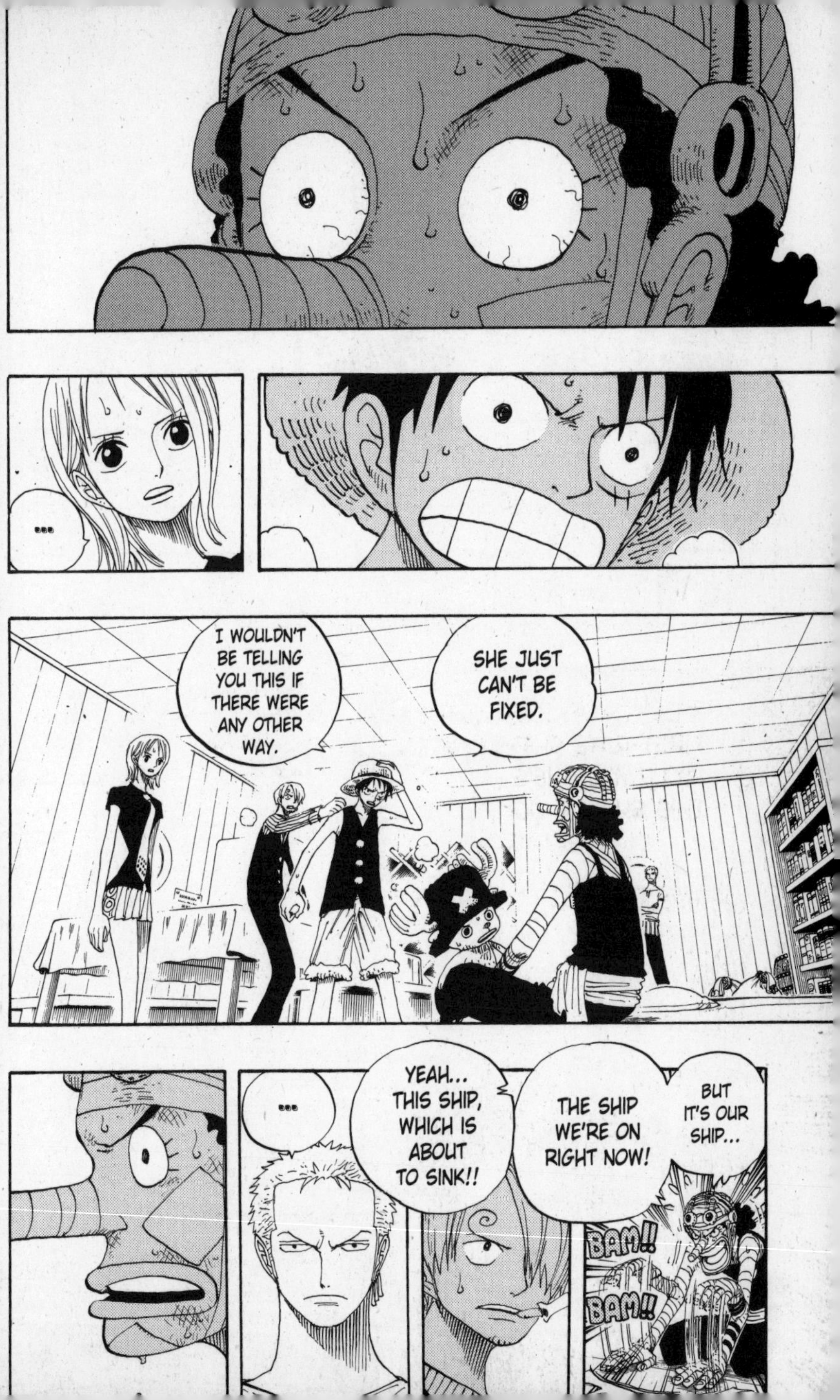
...
SHE JUST CAN'T BE FIXED.
I WOULDN'T BE TELLING YOU THIS IF THERE WERE ANY OTHER WAY.
BUT IT'S OUR SHIP...
BAM!!
BAM!!
THE SHIP WE'RE ON RIGHT NOW!
YEAH... THIS SHIP, WHICH IS ABOUT TO SINK!!
...

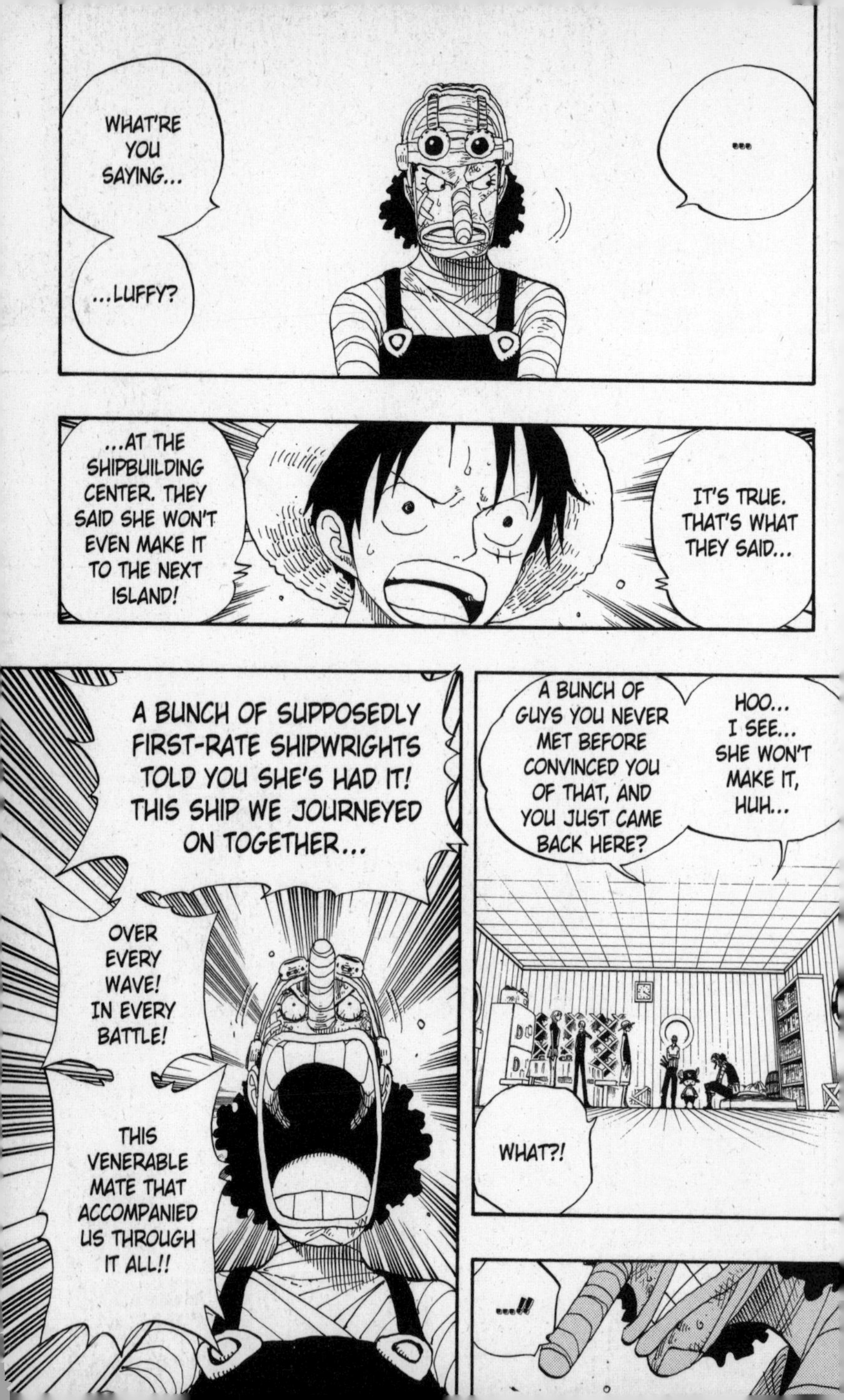
...
WHAT'RE YOU SAYING...
...LUFFY?
IT'S TRUE. THAT'S WHAT THEY SAID...
...AT THE SHIPBUILDING CENTER. THEY SAID SHE WON'T EVEN MAKE IT TO THE NEXT ISLAND!
HOO... I SEE... SHE WON'T MAKE IT, HUH...
A BUNCH OF GUYS YOU NEVER MET BEFORE CONVINCED YOU OF THAT, AND YOU JUST CAME BACK HERE?
WHAT?!
...!!
A BUNCH OF SUPPOSEDLY FIRST-RATE SHIPWRIGHTS TOLD YOU SHE'S HAD IT! THIS SHIP WE JOURNEYED ON TOGETHER...
OVER EVERY WAVE! IN EVERY BATTLE!
THIS VENERABLE MATE THAT ACCOMPANIED US THROUGH IT ALL!!

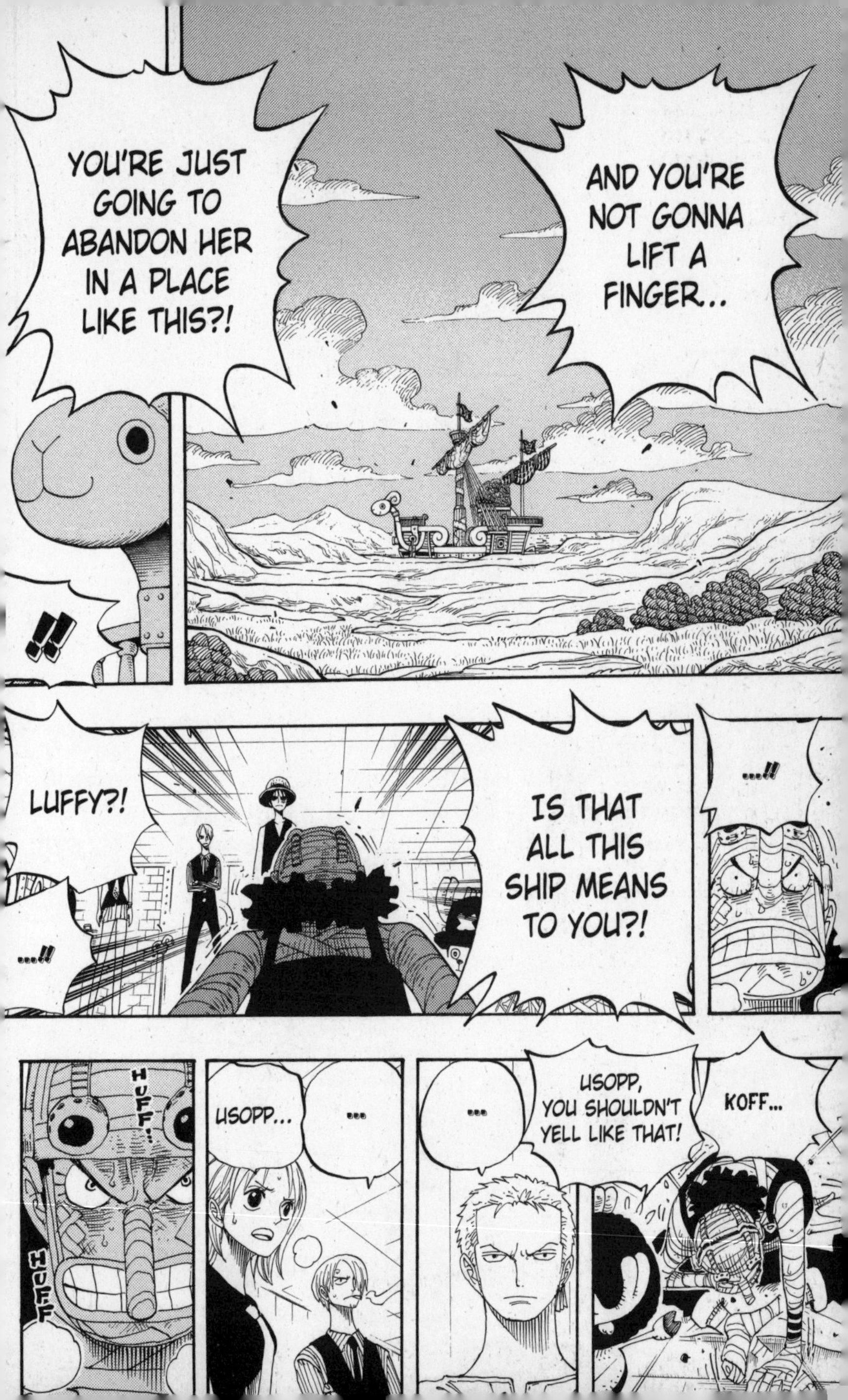
AND YOU'RE NOT GONNA LIFT A FINGER...
YOU'RE JUST GOING TO ABANDON HER IN A PLACE LIKE THIS?!
!!
...!!
IS THAT ALL THIS SHIP MEANS TO YOU?!
LUFFY?!
...!!
KOFF...
USOPP, YOU SHOULDN'T YELL LIKE THAT!
...
...
USOPP...
HUFF!!
HUFF

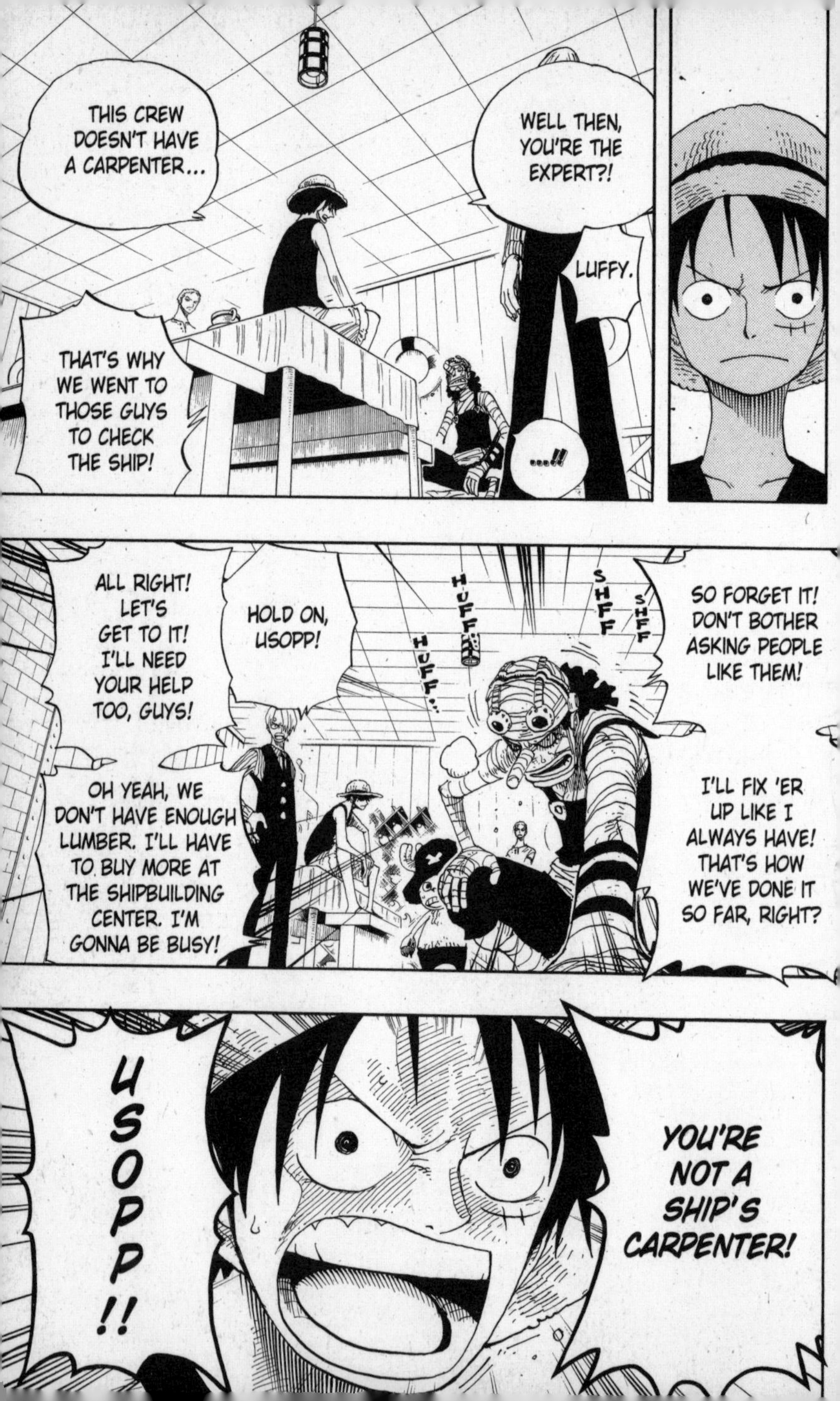
WELL THEN, YOU'RE THE EXPERT?!
THIS CREW DOESN'T HAVE A CARPENTER...
LUFFY.
...!!
THAT'S WHY WE WENT TO THOSE GUYS TO CHECK THE SHIP!
SO FORGET IT! DON'T BOTHER ASKING PEOPLE LIKE THEM!
SHFF
SHFF
I'LL FIX 'ER UP LIKE I ALWAYS HAVE! THAT'S HOW WE'VE DONE IT SO FAR, RIGHT?
HUFF...
HUFF...
HOLD ON, USOPP!
ALL RIGHT! LET'S GET TO IT! I'LL NEED YOUR HELP TOO, GUYS!
OH YEAH, WE DON'T HAVE ENOUGH LUMBER. I'LL HAVE TO BUY MORE AT THE SHIPBUILDING CENTER. I'M GONNA BE BUSY!
YOU'RE NOT A SHIP'S CARPENTER!
USOPP!!

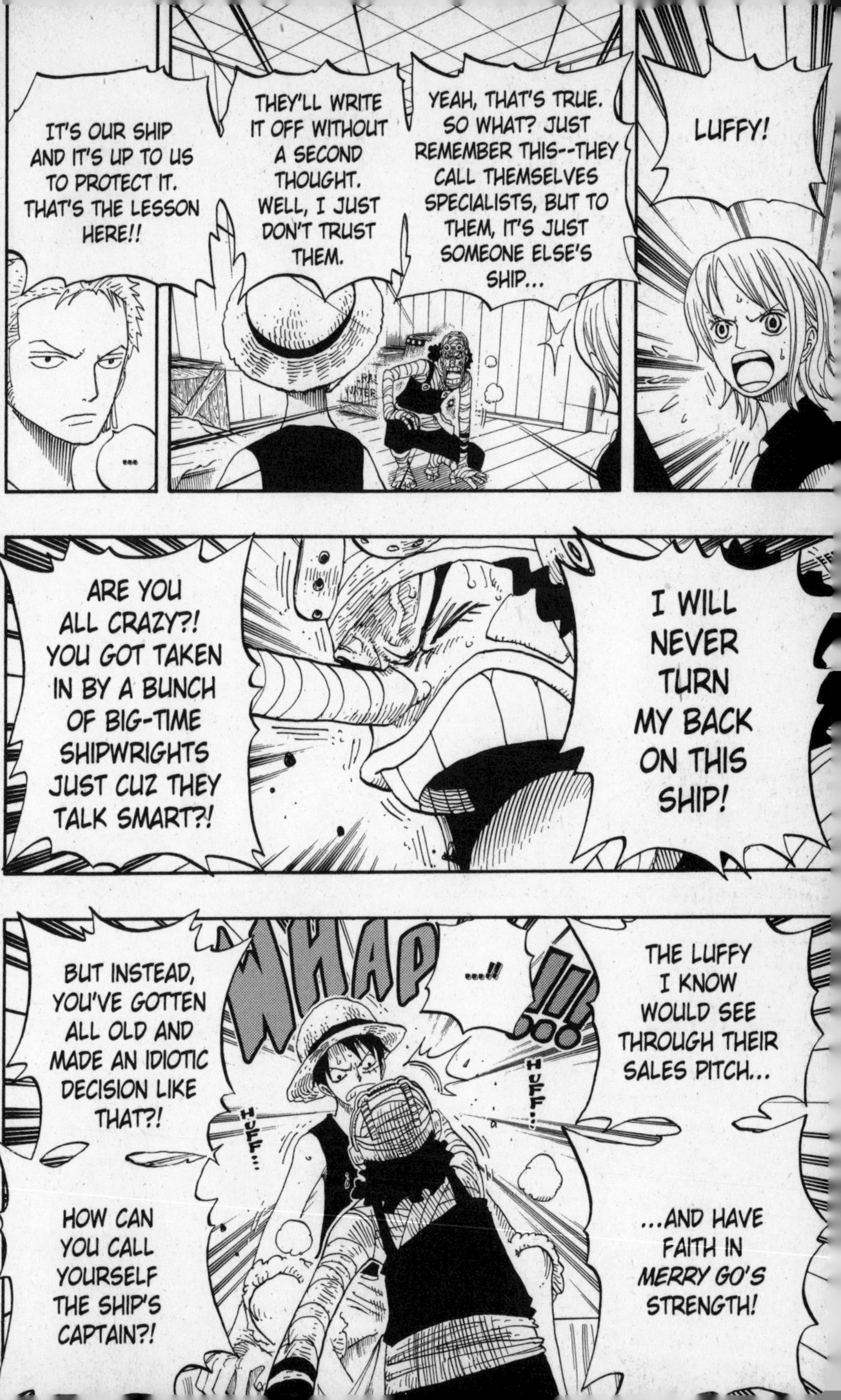
LUFFY!
YEAH, THAT'S TRUE. SO WHAT? JUST REMEMBER THIS--THEY CALL THEMSELVES SPECIALISTS, BUT TO THEM, IT'S JUST SOMEONE ELSE'S SHIP...
THEY'LL WRITE IT OFF WITHOUT A SECOND THOUGHT. WELL, I JUST DON'T TRUST THEM.
IT'S OUR SHIP AND IT'S UP TO US TO PROTECT IT. THAT'S THE LESSON HERE!!
...
I WILL NEVER TURN MY BACK ON THIS SHIP!
ARE YOU ALL CRAZY?! YOU GOT TAKEN IN BY A BUNCH OF BIG-TIME SHIPWRIGHTS JUST CUZ THEY TALK SMART?!
THE LUFFY I KNOW WOULD SEE THROUGH THEIR SALES PITCH...
...AND HAVE FAITH IN *MERRY GO'S* STRENGTH!
!!
HUFF...
...!!
WHAP
HUFF...
BUT INSTEAD, YOU'VE GOTTEN ALL OLD AND MADE AN IDIOTIC DECISION LIKE THAT?!
HOW CAN YOU CALL YOURSELF THE SHIP'S CAPTAIN?!

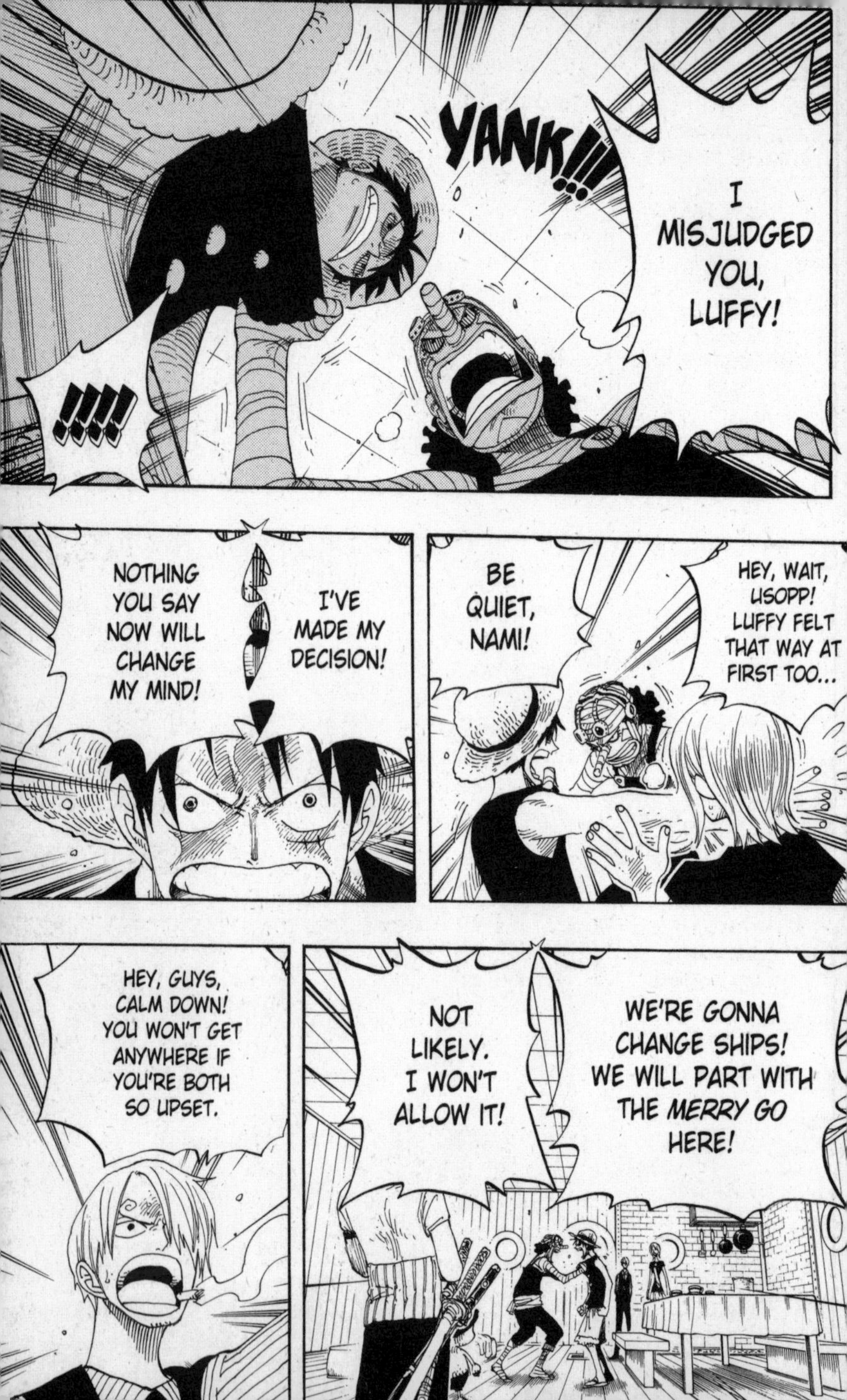

I MISJUDGED YOU, LUFFY!
YANK!!!
!!!!
HEY, WAIT, USOPP! LUFFY FELT THAT WAY AT FIRST TOO...
BE QUIET, NAMI!
I'VE MADE MY DECISION!
NOTHING YOU SAY NOW WILL CHANGE MY MIND!
WE'RE GONNA CHANGE SHIPS! WE WILL PART WITH THE *MERRY GO* HERE!
NOT LIKELY. I WON'T ALLOW IT!
HEY, GUYS, CALM DOWN! YOU WON'T GET ANYWHERE IF YOU'RE BOTH SO UPSET.

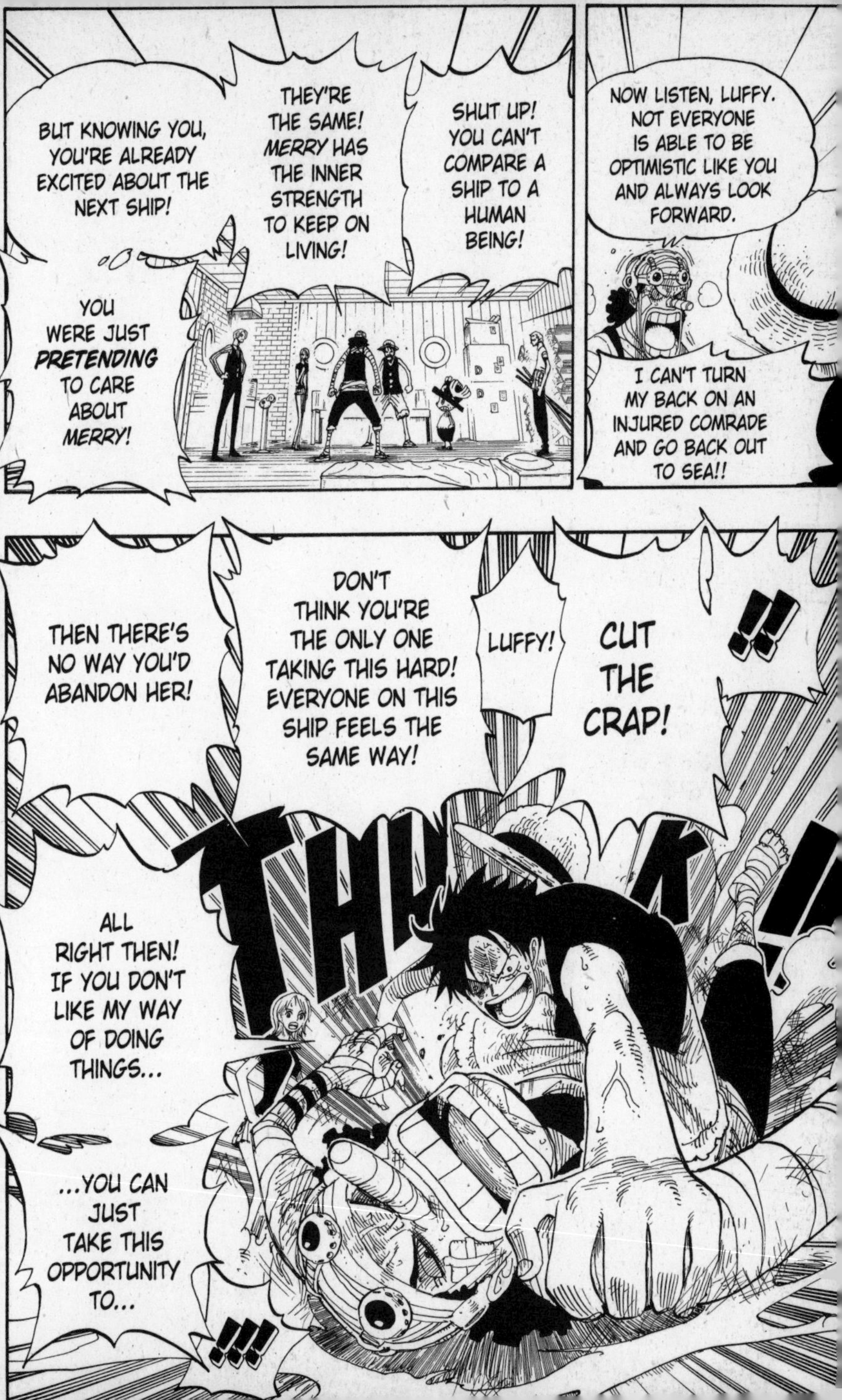
NOW LISTEN, LUFFY. NOT EVERYONE IS ABLE TO BE OPTIMISTIC LIKE YOU AND ALWAYS LOOK FORWARD.
I CAN'T TURN MY BACK ON AN INJURED COMRADE AND GO BACK OUT TO SEA!!
SHUT UP! YOU CAN'T COMPARE A SHIP TO A HUMAN BEING!
THEY'RE THE SAME! *MERRY* HAS THE INNER STRENGTH TO KEEP ON LIVING!
BUT KNOWING YOU, YOU'RE ALREADY EXCITED ABOUT THE NEXT SHIP!
YOU WERE JUST ***PRETENDING*** TO CARE ABOUT *MERRY*!
CUT THE CRAP!!
LUFFY!
DON'T THINK YOU'RE THE ONLY ONE TAKING THIS HARD! EVERYONE ON THIS SHIP FEELS THE SAME WAY!
THEN THERE'S NO WAY YOU'D ABANDON HER!
ALL RIGHT THEN! IF YOU DON'T LIKE MY WAY OF DOING THINGS...
...YOU CAN JUST TAKE THIS OPPORTUNITY TO...

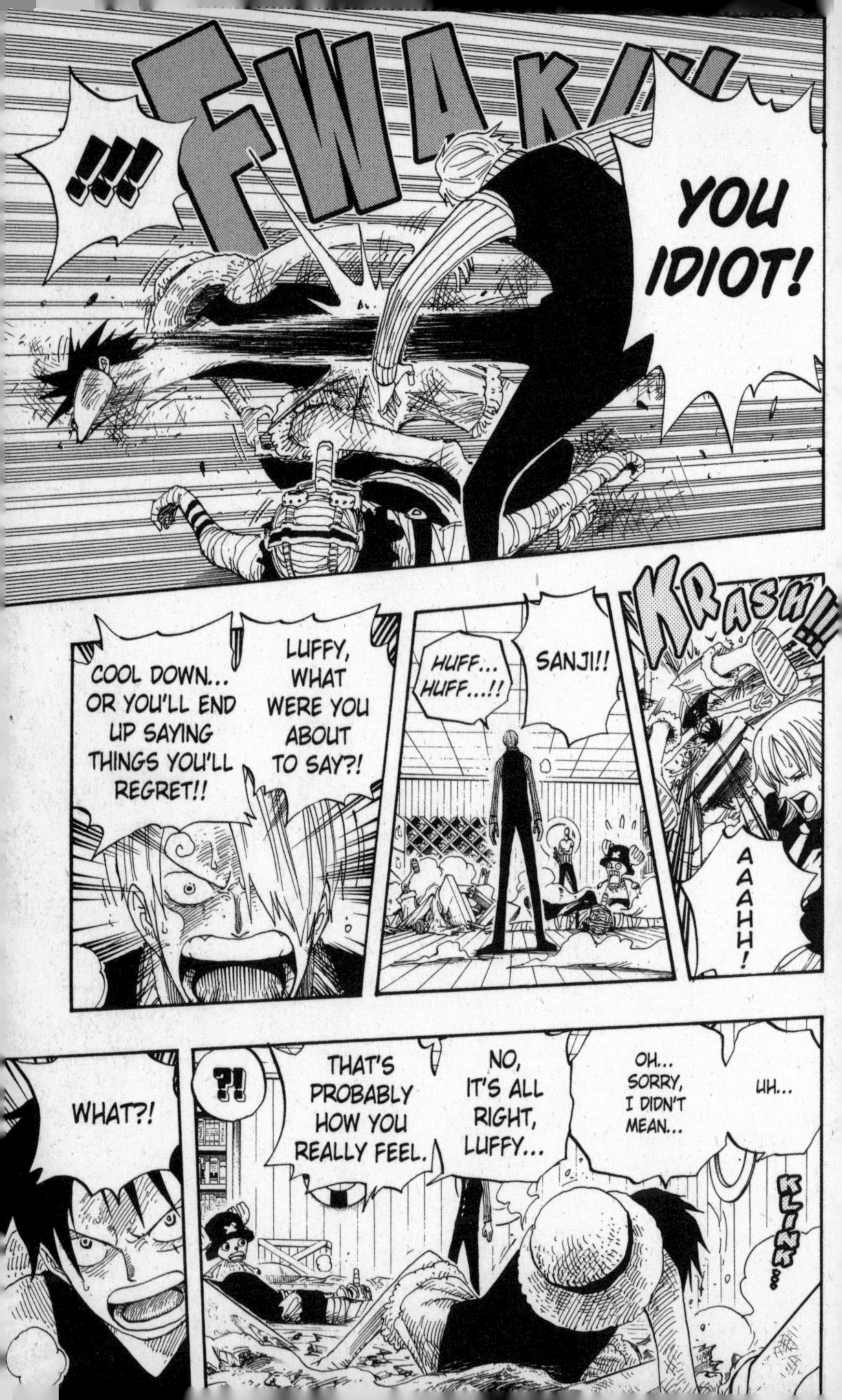
YOU IDIOT!
FWAKK
!!!
KRASH!!!
AAAAHH!
SANJI!!
HUFF... HUFF...!!
LUFFY, WHAT WERE YOU ABOUT TO SAY?!
COOL DOWN... OR YOU'LL END UP SAYING THINGS YOU'LL REGRET!!
UH...
OH... SORRY, I DIDN'T MEAN...
KLINK...
NO, IT'S ALL RIGHT, LUFFY...
THAT'S PROBABLY HOW YOU REALLY FEEL.
?!
WHAT?!

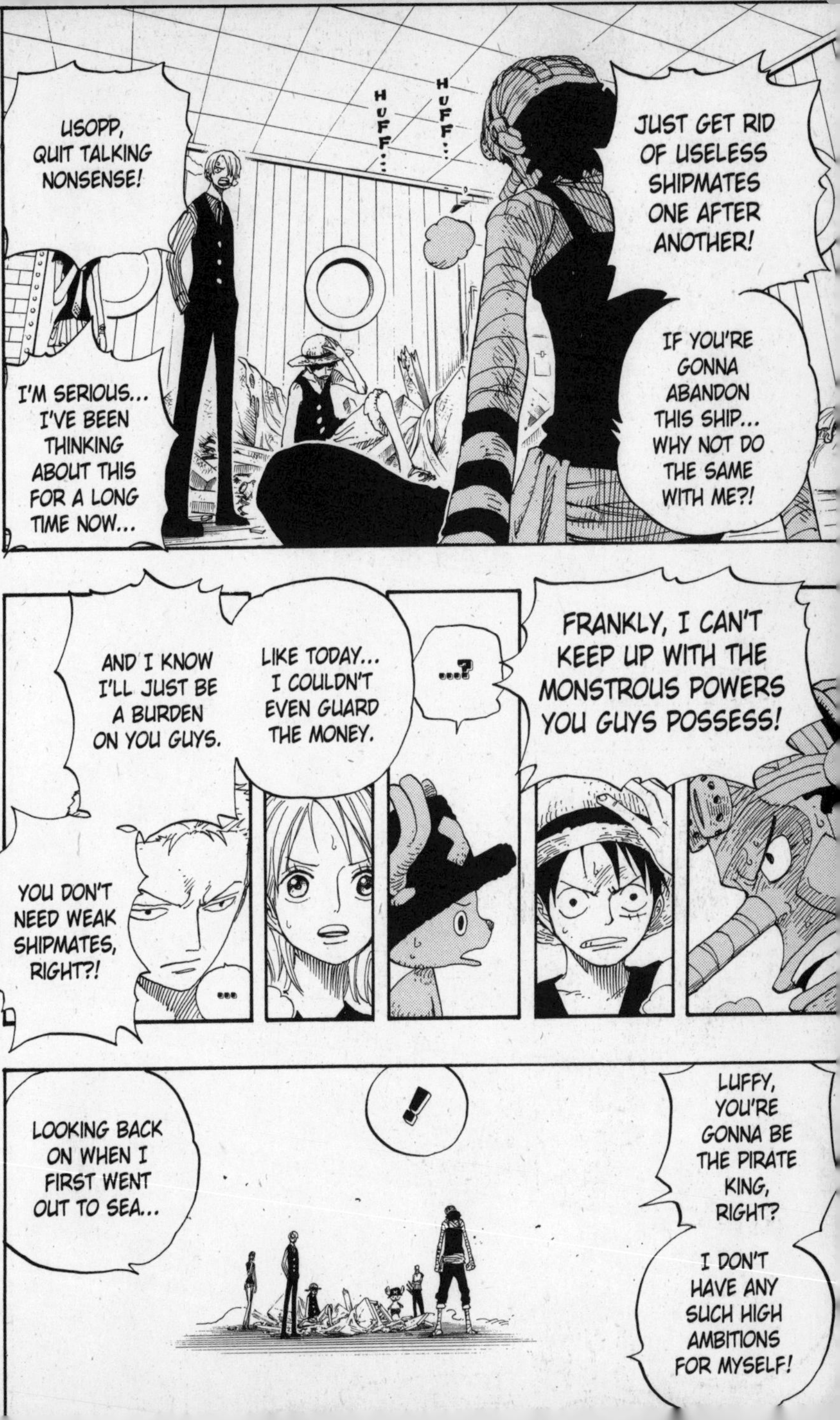
JUST GET RID OF USELESS SHIPMATES ONE AFTER ANOTHER!
HUFF...
HUFF...
USOPP, QUIT TALKING NONSENSE!
IF YOU'RE GONNA ABANDON THIS SHIP... WHY NOT DO THE SAME WITH ME?!
I'M SERIOUS... I'VE BEEN THINKING ABOUT THIS FOR A LONG TIME NOW...
FRANKLY, I CAN'T KEEP UP WITH THE MONSTROUS POWERS YOU GUYS POSSESS!
...?
LIKE TODAY... I COULDN'T EVEN GUARD THE MONEY.
AND I KNOW I'LL JUST BE A BURDEN ON YOU GUYS.
YOU DON'T NEED WEAK SHIPMATES, RIGHT?!
...
LUFFY, YOU'RE GONNA BE THE PIRATE KING, RIGHT?
I DON'T HAVE ANY SUCH HIGH AMBITIONS FOR MYSELF!
!
LOOKING BACK ON WHEN I FIRST WENT OUT TO SEA...

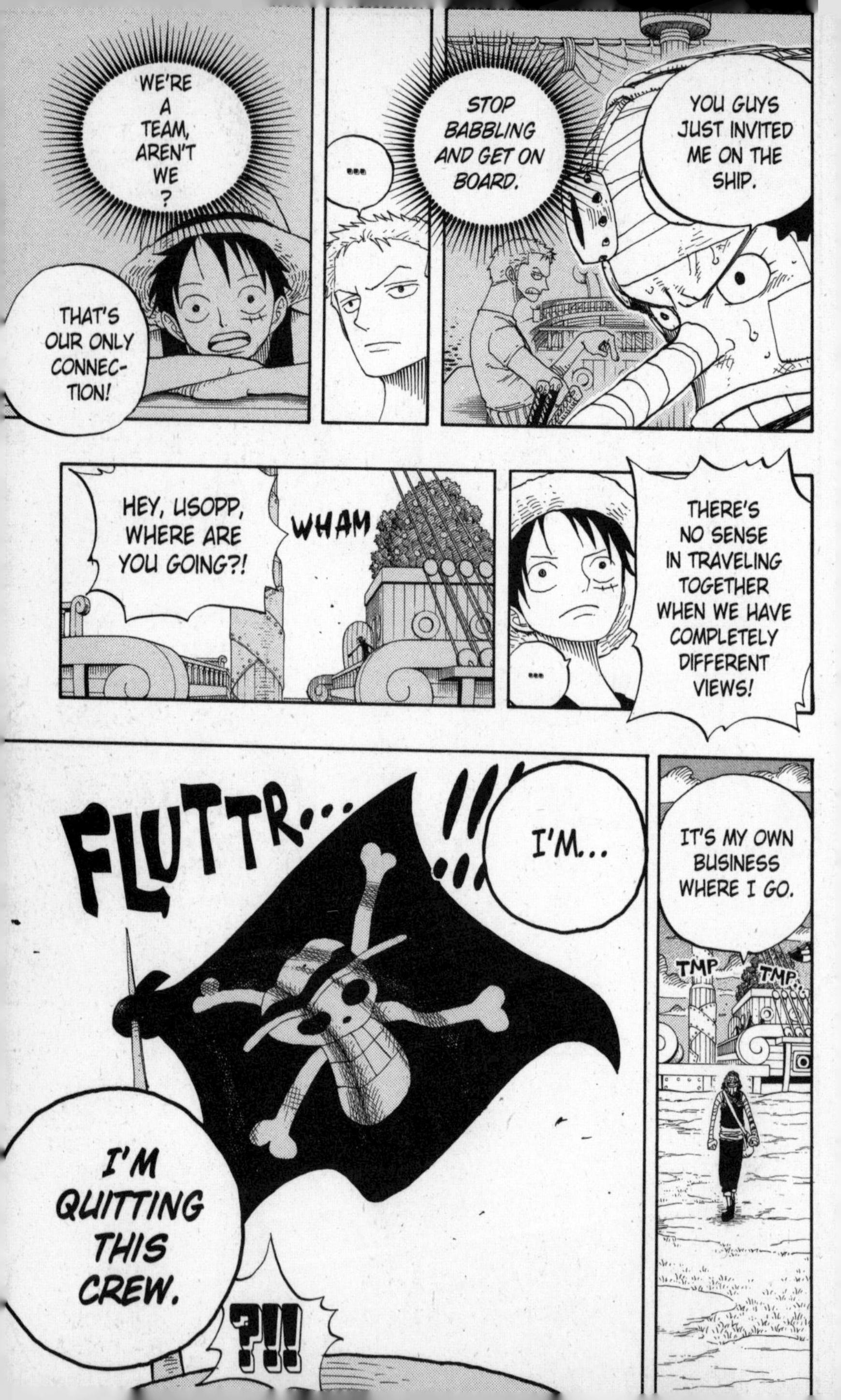

YOU GUYS JUST INVITED ME ON THE SHIP.
STOP BABBLING AND GET ON BOARD.
...
WE'RE A TEAM, AREN'T WE?
THAT'S OUR ONLY CONNECTION!
THERE'S NO SENSE IN TRAVELING TOGETHER WHEN WE HAVE COMPLETELY DIFFERENT VIEWS!
...
HEY, USOPP, WHERE ARE YOU GOING?!
WHAM
IT'S MY OWN BUSINESS WHERE I GO.
TMP
TMP...
I'M...
!!!
FLUTTR...
I'M QUITTING THIS CREW.
?!!

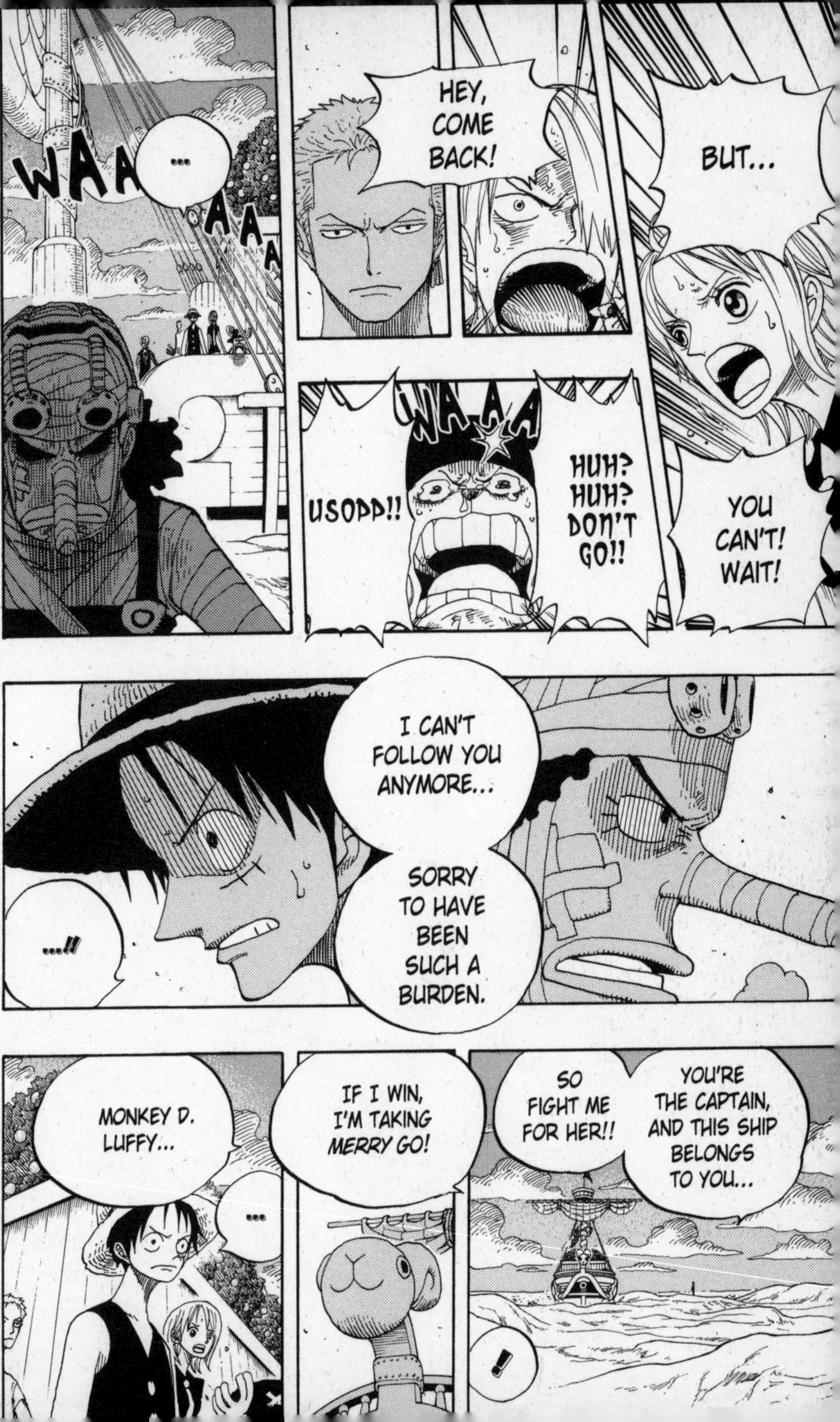
BUT...
YOU CAN'T! WAIT!
HEY, COME BACK!
WAAA
HUH? HUH? DON'T GO!!
USOPP!!
...
WAAAAA
I CAN'T FOLLOW YOU ANYMORE...
SORRY TO HAVE BEEN SUCH A BURDEN.
...!!
YOU'RE THE CAPTAIN, AND THIS SHIP BELONGS TO YOU...
SO FIGHT ME FOR HER!!
!
IF I WIN, I'M TAKING *MERRY GO*!
MONKEY D. LUFFY...
...

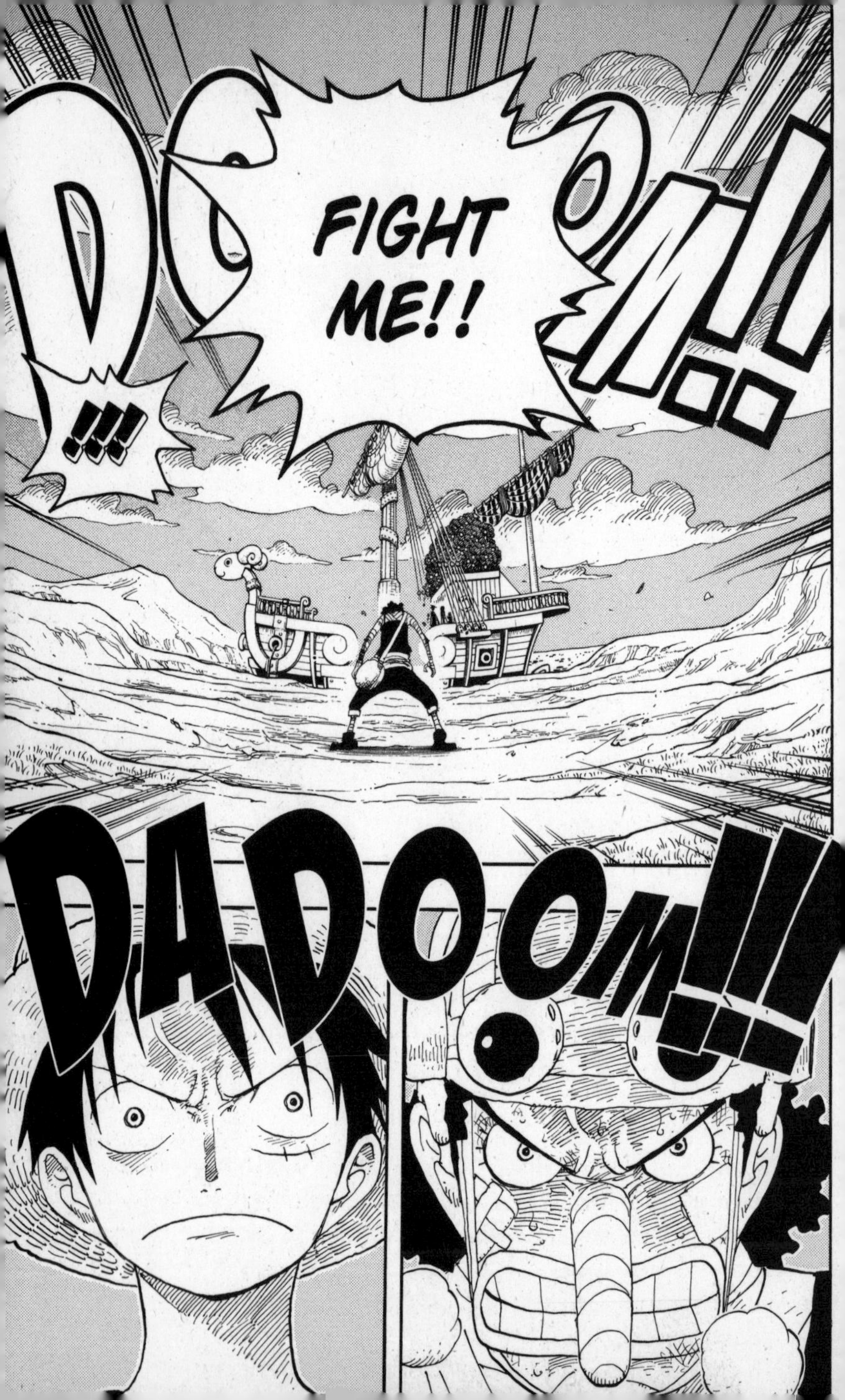
FIGHT ME!!
DADOOM!!!

Q: In The Question Corner in volume 29, page 148, we saw the "Daytime Rider." Today, I'd like to introduce you to his friend, "Morning Clown"!

Daytime Rider

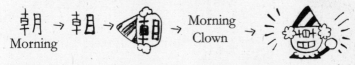

朝月 → 卓月 → Morning Clown →

Morning

He's Buggy's teacher and Daytime Rider's friend.

--Husky

A: Hm, interesting... "Morning Clown." The "Daytime Rider" in vol. 29 was strangely well received by the readers—they'd often scribble it in the corner of their fan letters (laugh). And so, here's another one that anybody can draw: つる三八〇〇ムシ (tsu-ru-mi-ha-o-o-mu-shi-jiisan)!

Here you go →

Yo.

Q: Oda Sensei!! Good morning. ★ I'm an aspiring manga artist, and from the day I first picked up my pen, I've had this strange question. Please hear me out. ★

Why can't I draw with a ballpoint pen?!

--One who admires Oda Sensei

A: Huh? Sure you can. You can draw with anything. There's no set rule. Just use whichever supplies you prefer. As long as you're having fun, anything works. However... It's best not to use things that don't print well or are difficult to use on manuscripts (like crayons).
There are even some pros who use markers.

Chapter 332:
LUFFY VS. USOPP

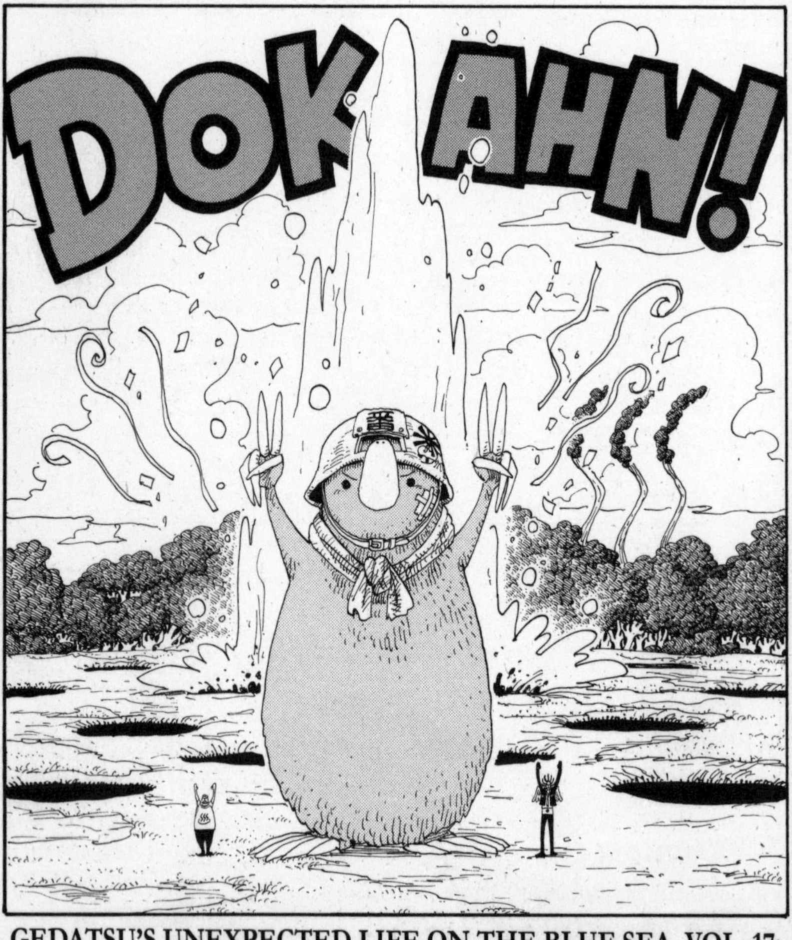
DOKAHN!
GEDATSU'S UNEXPECTED LIFE ON THE BLUE SEA, VOL. 17:
"WE HIT PAYDIRT--HURRAH!"

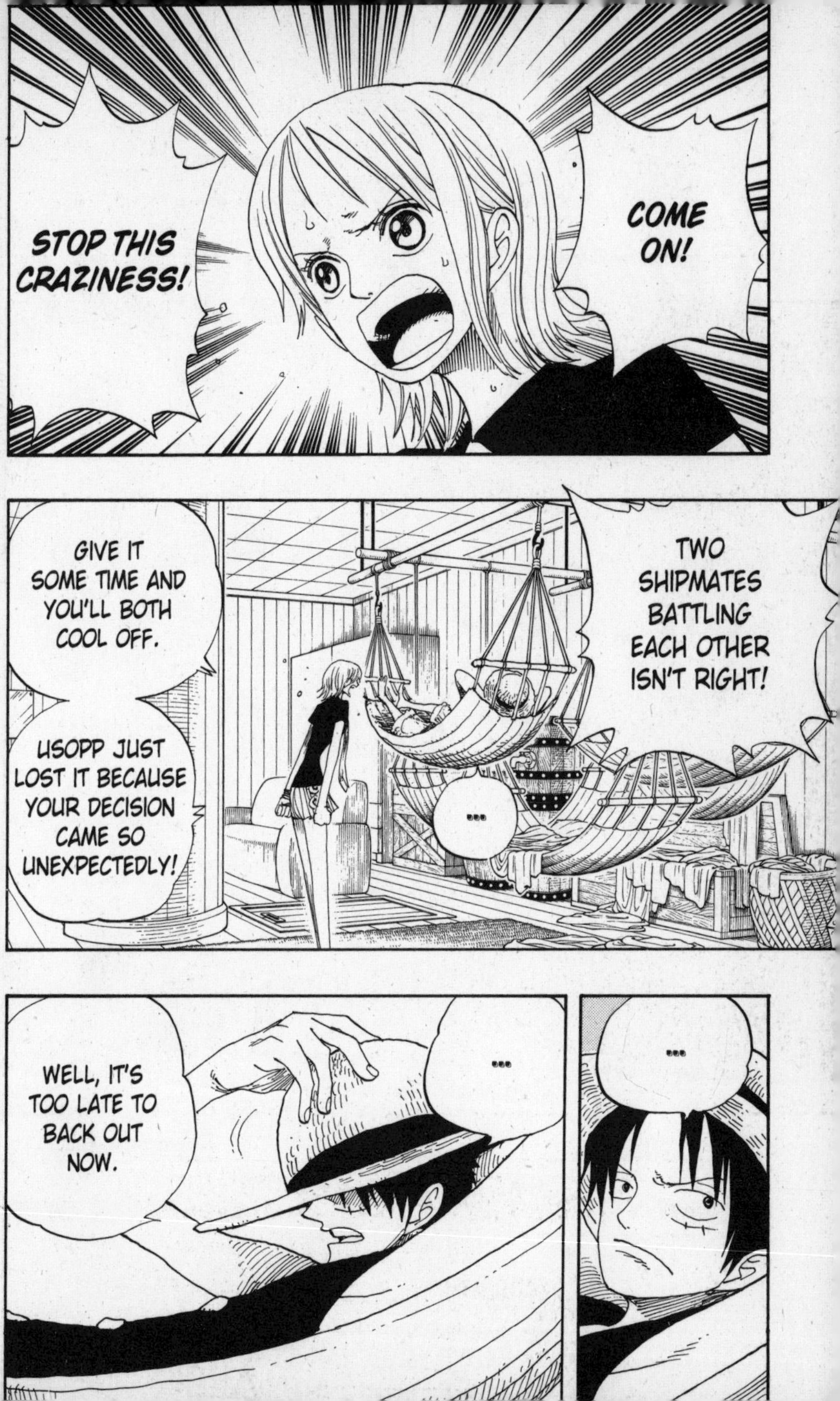
COME ON!
STOP THIS CRAZINESS!
TWO SHIPMATES BATTLING EACH OTHER ISN'T RIGHT!
GIVE IT SOME TIME AND YOU'LL BOTH COOL OFF.
USOPP JUST LOST IT BECAUSE YOUR DECISION CAME SO UNEXPECTEDLY!
...
...
...
WELL, IT'S TOO LATE TO BACK OUT NOW.

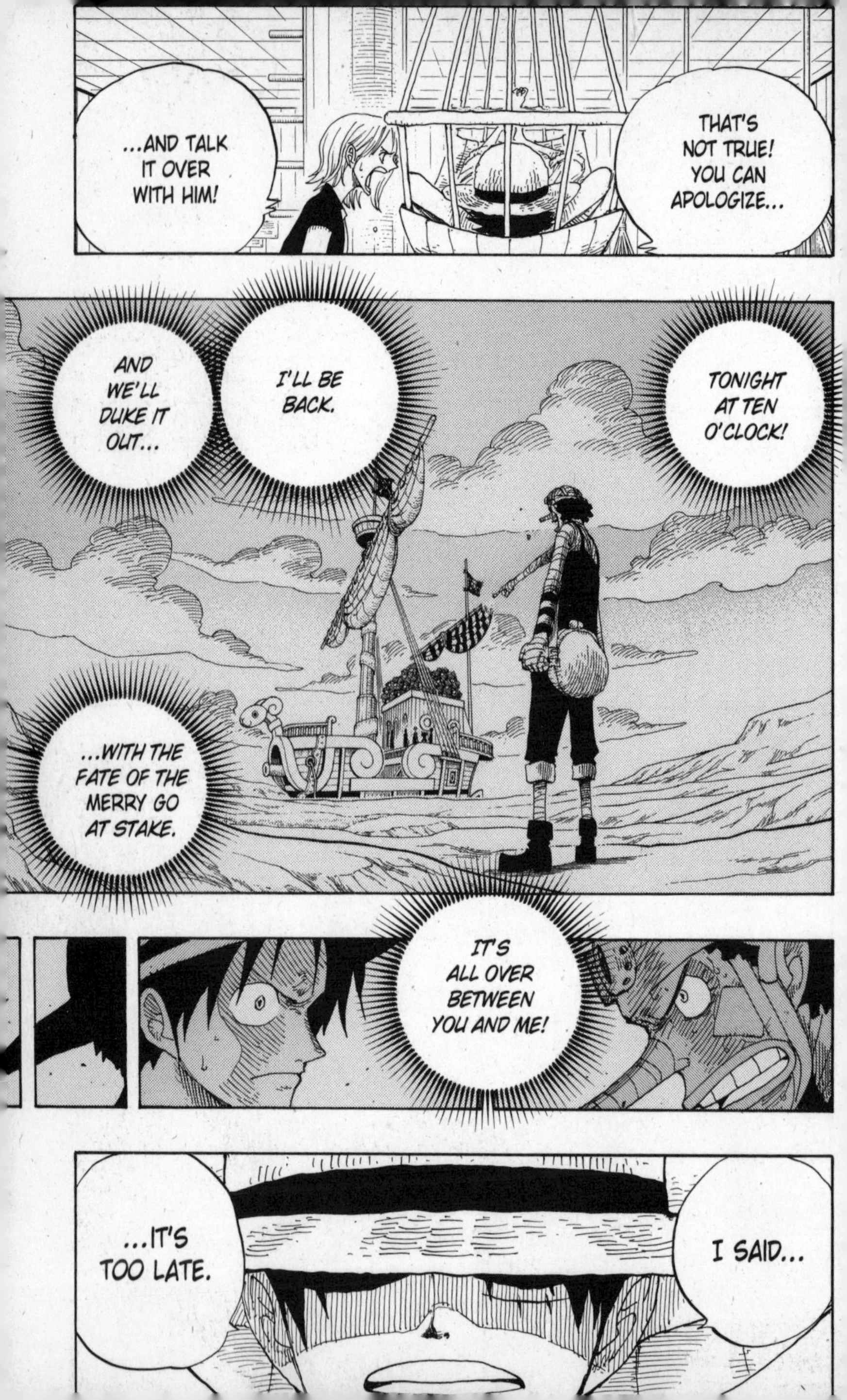
THAT'S NOT TRUE! YOU CAN APOLOGIZE...
...AND TALK IT OVER WITH HIM!
TONIGHT AT TEN O'CLOCK!
I'LL BE BACK.
AND WE'LL DUKE IT OUT...
...WITH THE FATE OF THE MERRY GO AT STAKE.
IT'S ALL OVER BETWEEN YOU AND ME!
I SAID...
...IT'S TOO LATE.

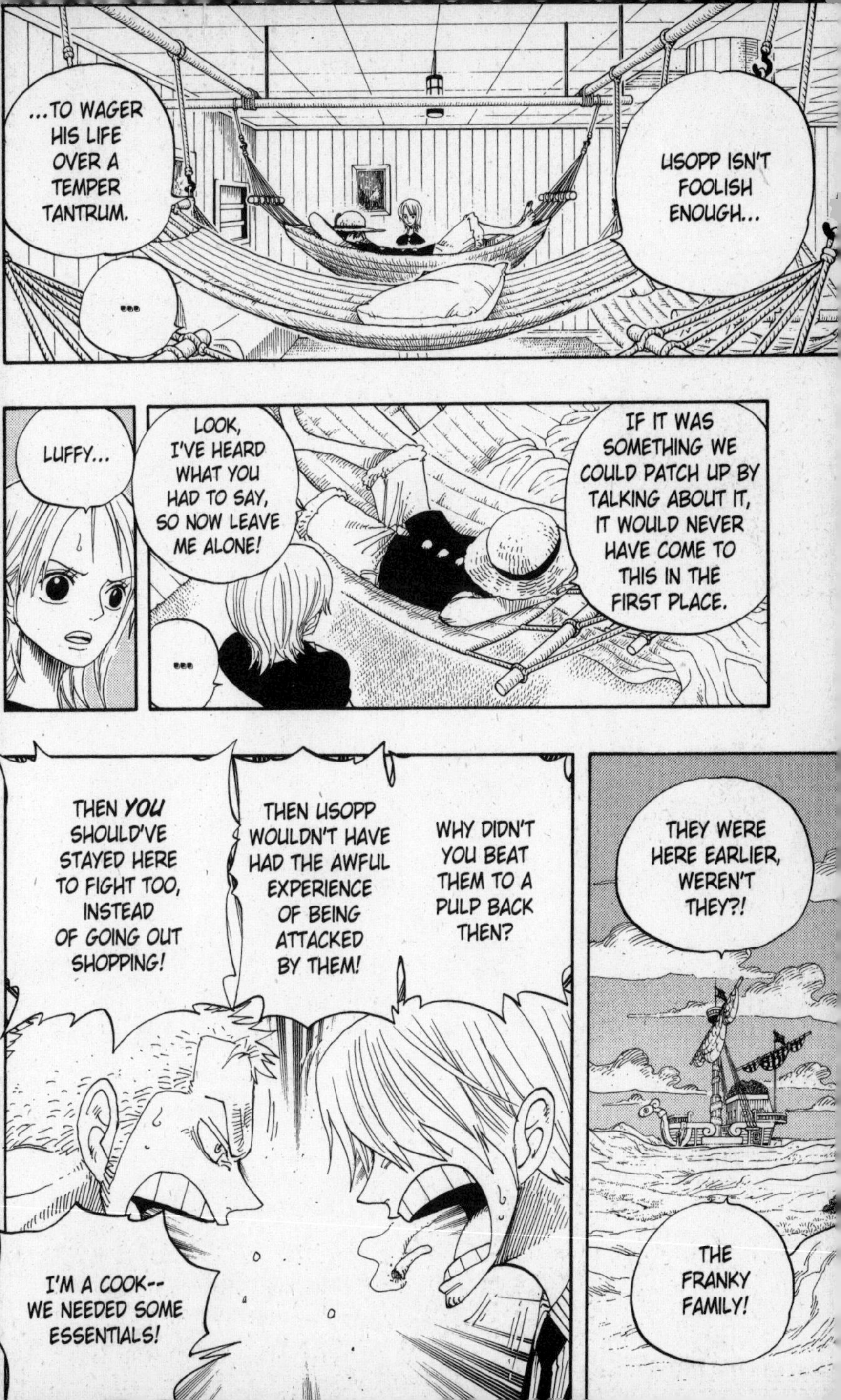
USOPP ISN'T FOOLISH ENOUGH...
...TO WAGER HIS LIFE OVER A TEMPER TANTRUM.
...
IF IT WAS SOMETHING WE COULD PATCH UP BY TALKING ABOUT IT, IT WOULD NEVER HAVE COME TO THIS IN THE FIRST PLACE.
LOOK, I'VE HEARD WHAT YOU HAD TO SAY, SO NOW LEAVE ME ALONE!
...
LUFFY...
THEY WERE HERE EARLIER, WEREN'T THEY?!
THE FRANKY FAMILY!
WHY DIDN'T YOU BEAT THEM TO A PULP BACK THEN?
THEN USOPP WOULDN'T HAVE HAD THE AWFUL EXPERIENCE OF BEING ATTACKED BY THEM!
THEN *YOU* SHOULD'VE STAYED HERE TO FIGHT TOO, INSTEAD OF GOING OUT SHOPPING!
I'M A COOK-- WE NEEDED SOME ESSENTIALS!

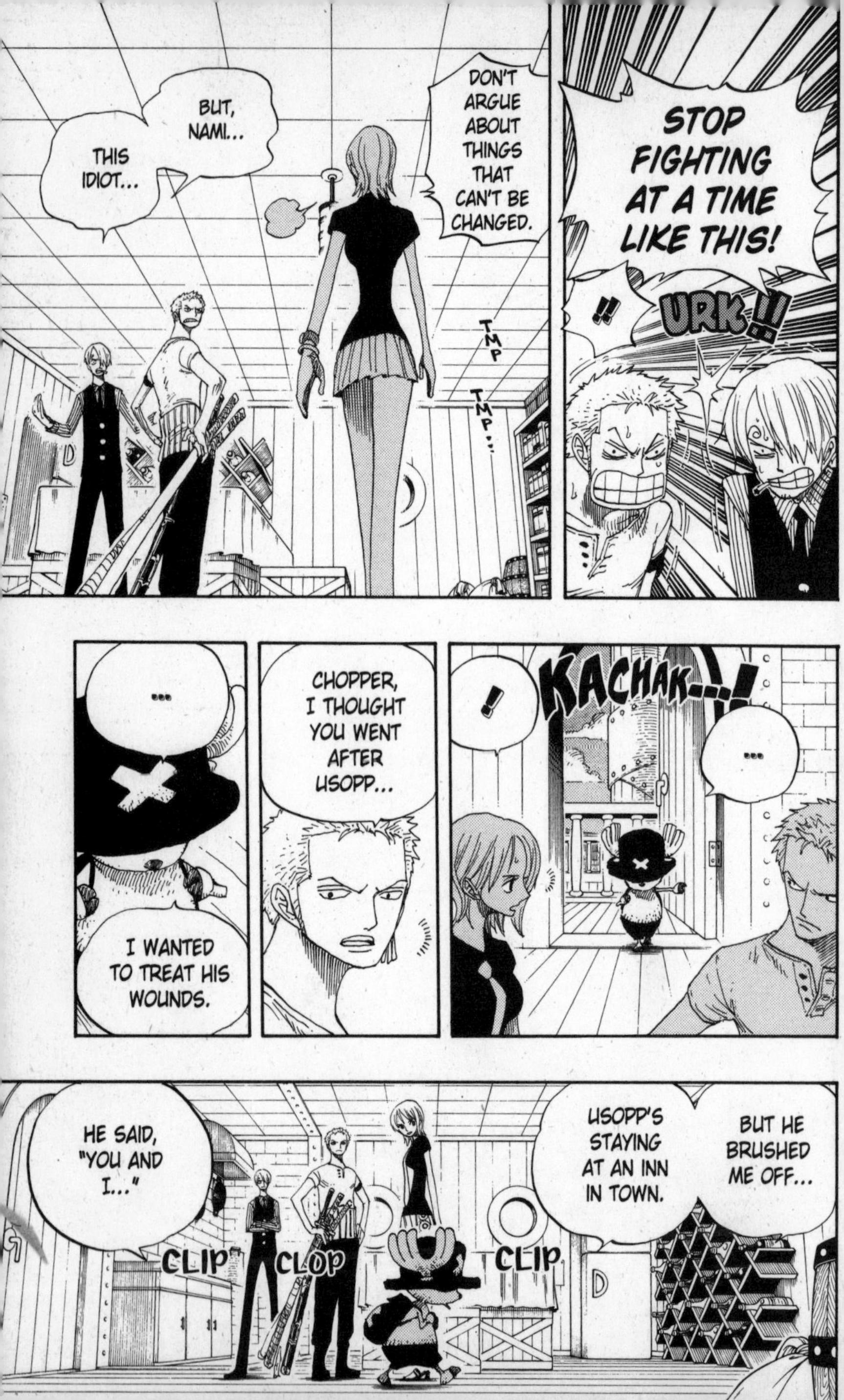
STOP FIGHTING AT A TIME LIKE THIS!
!!
URK!!
DON'T ARGUE ABOUT THINGS THAT CAN'T BE CHANGED.
TMP
TMP...
BUT, NAMI...
THIS IDIOT...
KACHAK...!
...
!
CHOPPER, I THOUGHT YOU WENT AFTER USOPP...
...
I WANTED TO TREAT HIS WOUNDS.
BUT HE BRUSHED ME OFF...
USOPP'S STAYING AT AN INN IN TOWN.
CLIP
CLOP
CLIP
HE SAID, "YOU AND I..."

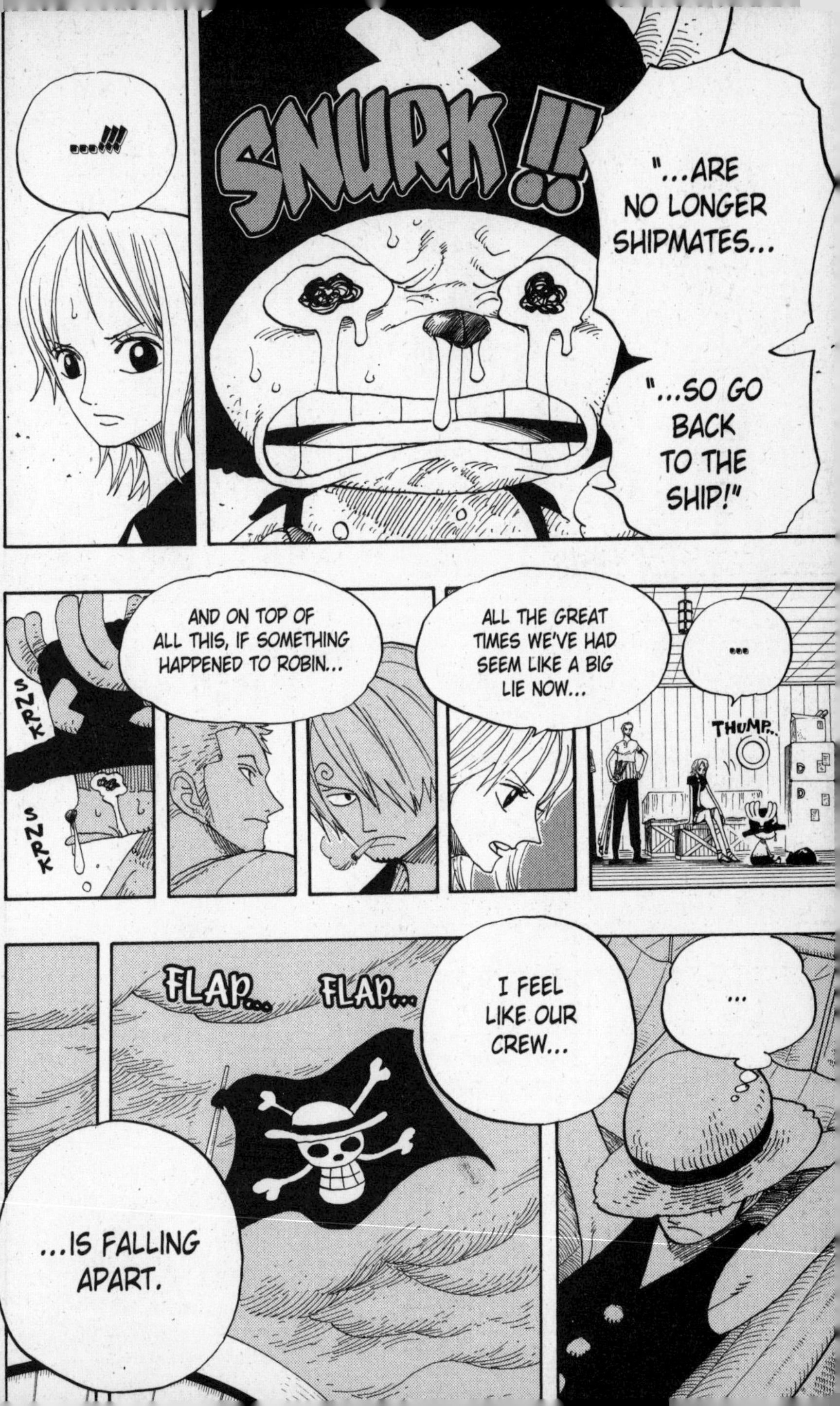
SNURK!!
"...ARE NO LONGER SHIPMATES...
"...SO GO BACK TO THE SHIP!"
...!!!
...
THUMP...
ALL THE GREAT TIMES WE'VE HAD SEEM LIKE A BIG LIE NOW...
AND ON TOP OF ALL THIS, IF SOMETHING HAPPENED TO ROBIN...
SNRK
SNRK
...
I FEEL LIKE OUR CREW...
FLAP... FLAP...
...IS FALLING APART.

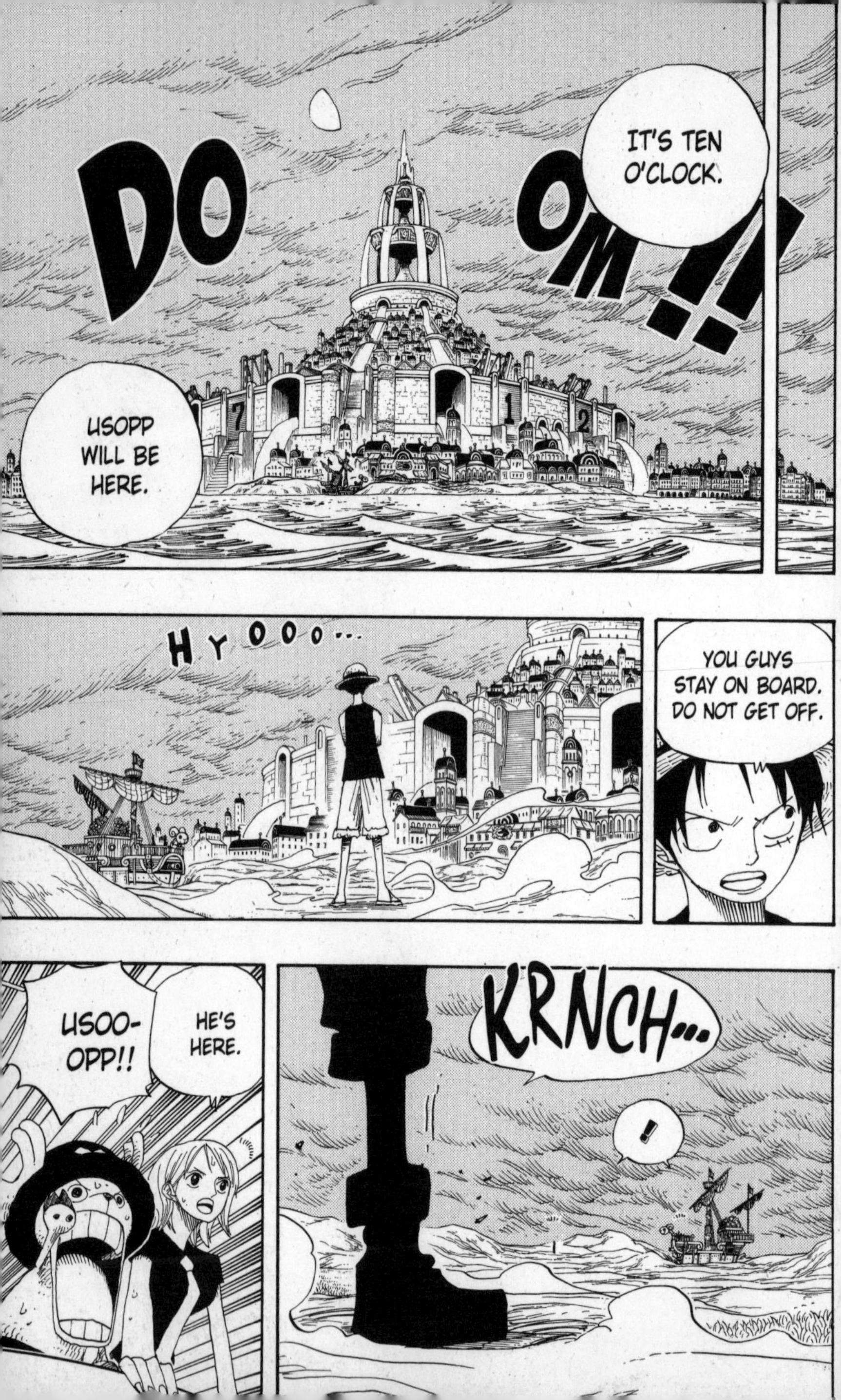
IT'S TEN O'CLOCK.
DOOM!!
USOPP WILL BE HERE.
YOU GUYS STAY ON BOARD. DO NOT GET OFF.
HYOOO...
KRNCH...
!
HE'S HERE.
USOO-OPP!!

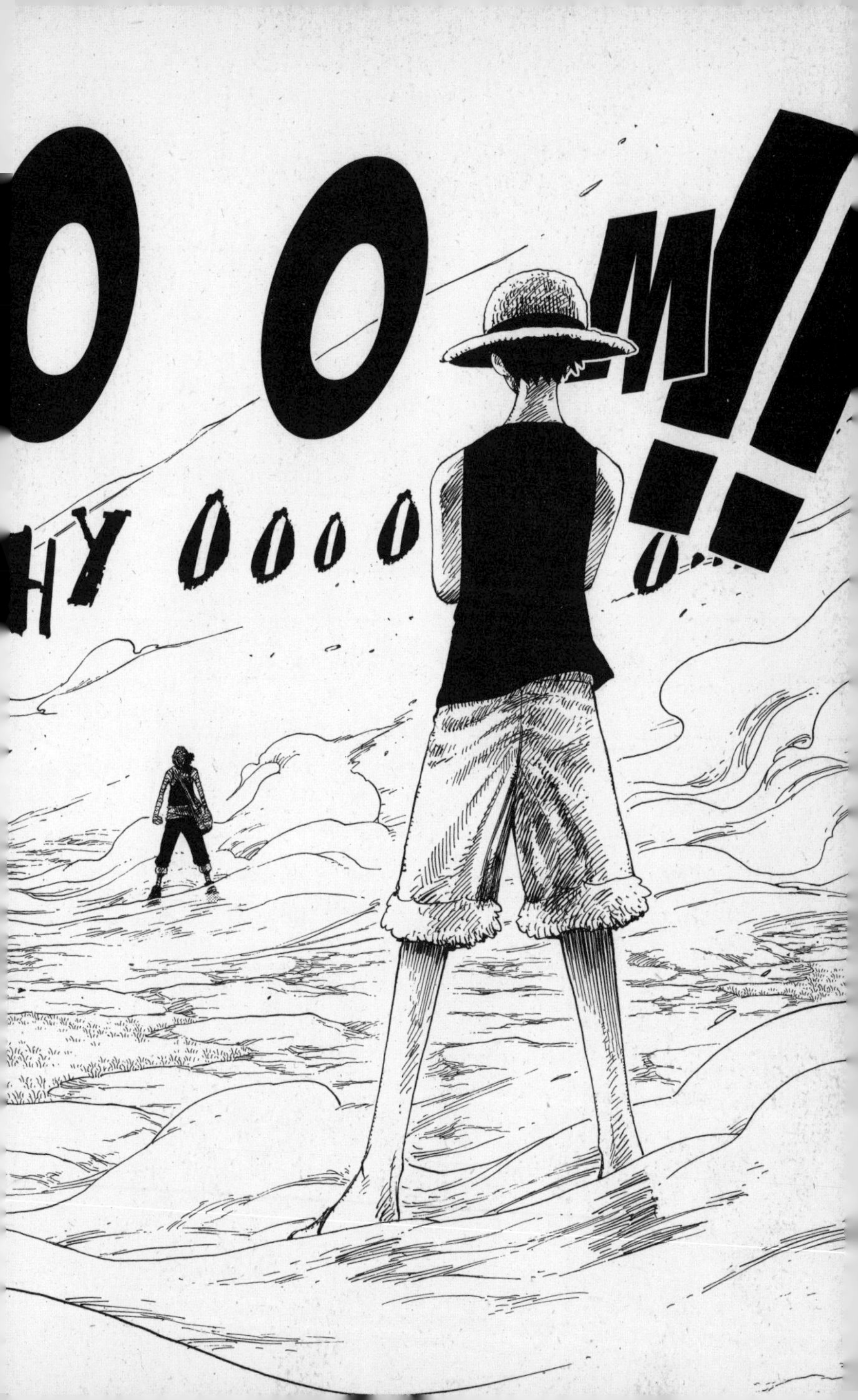
OOM!!
HYOOOOO...

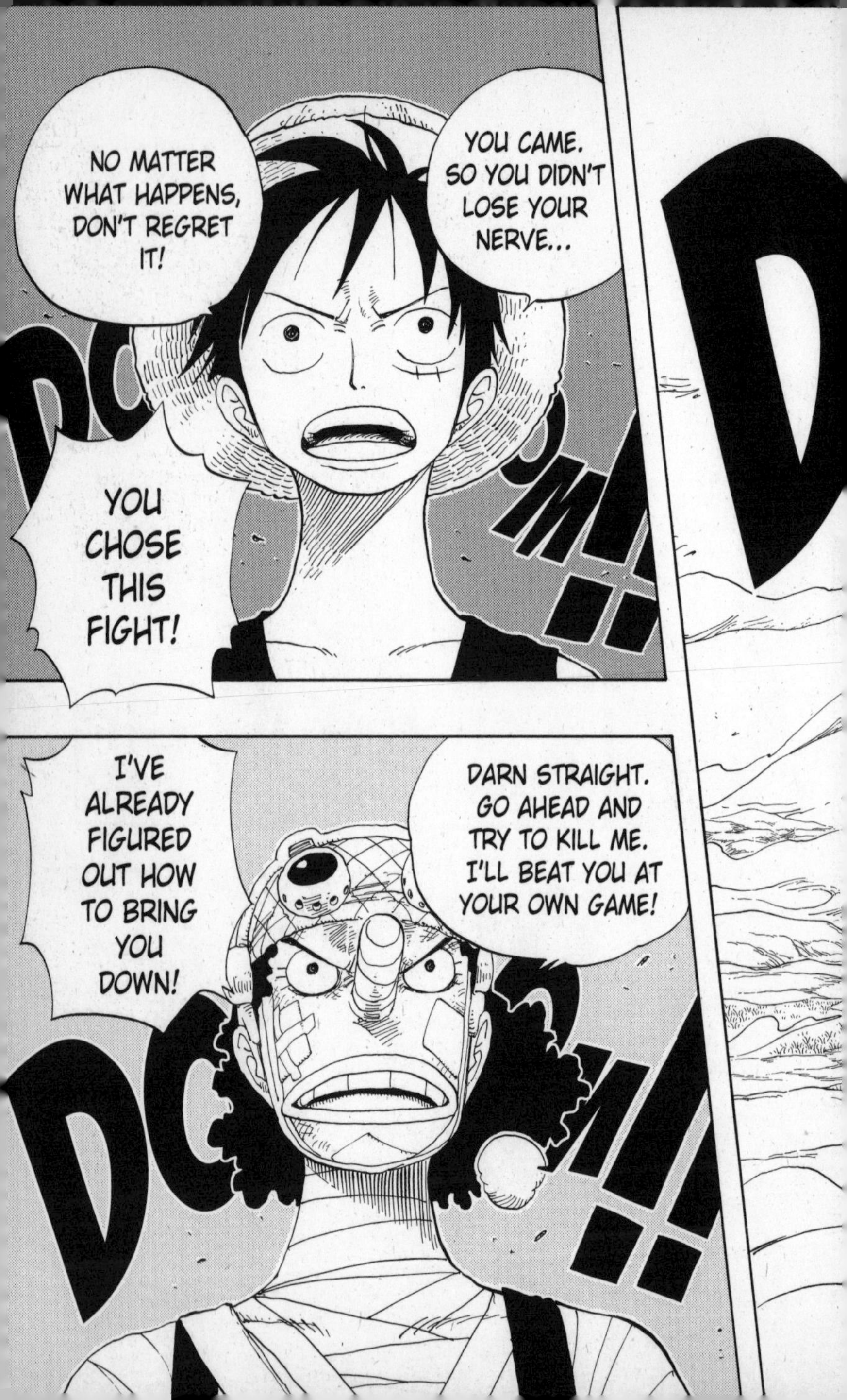
YOU CAME. SO YOU DIDN'T LOSE YOUR NERVE...
NO MATTER WHAT HAPPENS, DON'T REGRET IT!
YOU CHOSE THIS FIGHT!
DARN STRAIGHT. GO AHEAD AND TRY TO KILL ME. I'LL BEAT YOU AT YOUR OWN GAME!
I'VE ALREADY FIGURED OUT HOW TO BRING YOU DOWN!

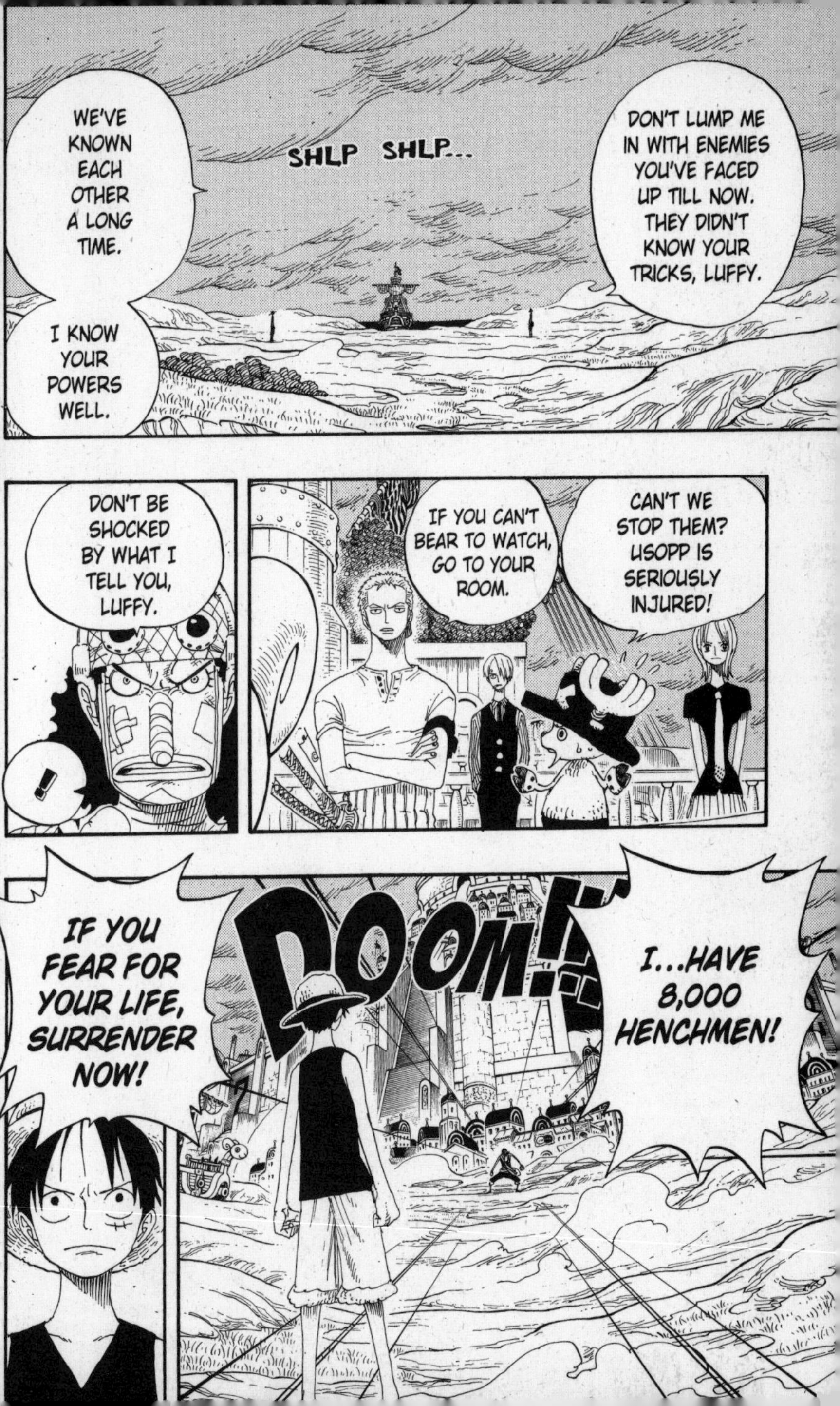
DON'T LUMP ME IN WITH ENEMIES YOU'VE FACED UP TILL NOW. THEY DIDN'T KNOW YOUR TRICKS, LUFFY.
SHLP SHLP...
WE'VE KNOWN EACH OTHER A LONG TIME.
I KNOW YOUR POWERS WELL.
CAN'T WE STOP THEM? USOPP IS SERIOUSLY INJURED!
IF YOU CAN'T BEAR TO WATCH, GO TO YOUR ROOM.
DON'T BE SHOCKED BY WHAT I TELL YOU, LUFFY.
!
I...HAVE 8,000 HENCHMEN!
DOOM!!
IF YOU FEAR FOR YOUR LIFE, SURRENDER NOW!

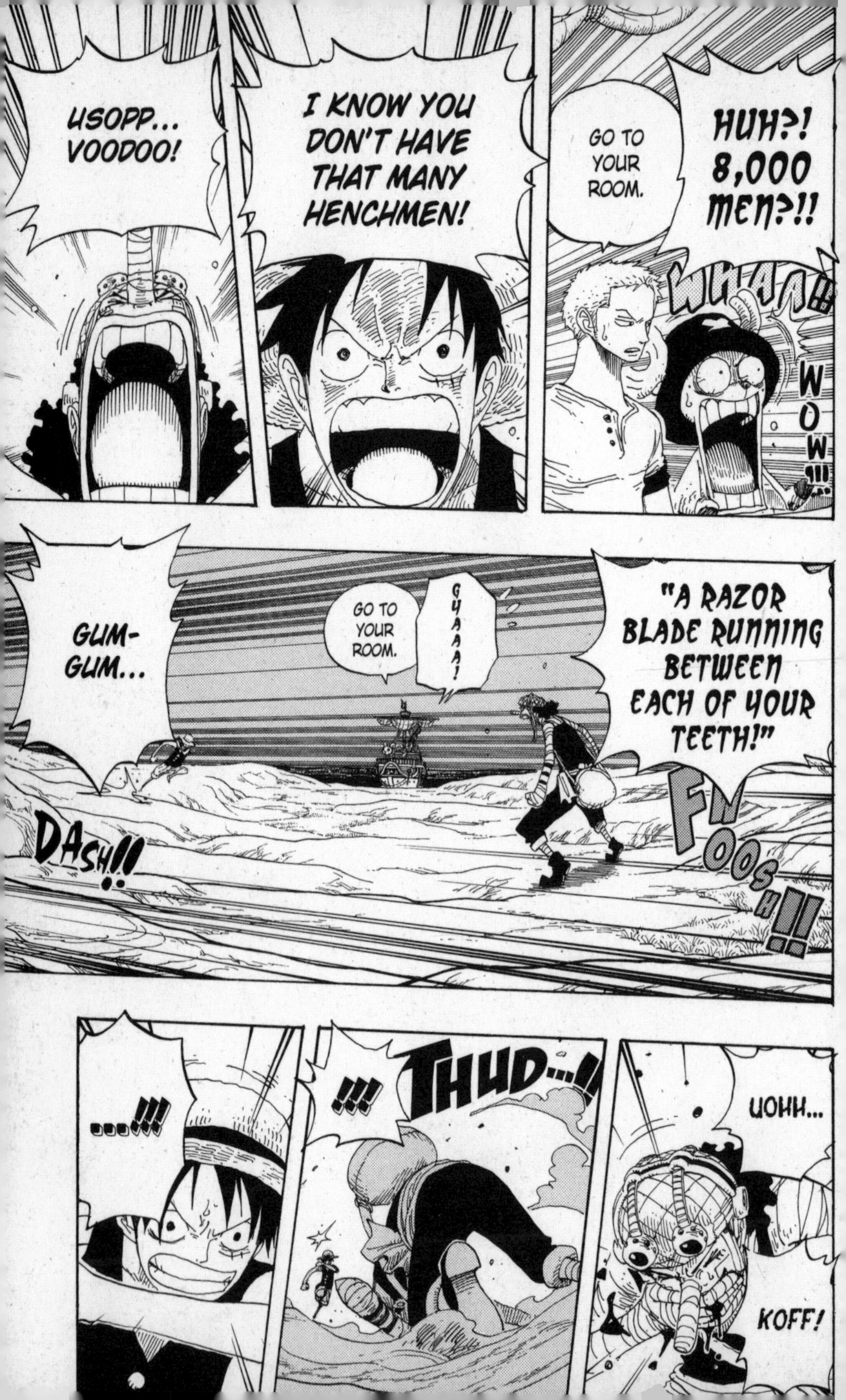

HUH?! 8,000 MEN?!!
GO TO YOUR ROOM.
WHAA!!
WOW!!!...
I KNOW YOU DON'T HAVE THAT MANY HENCHMEN!
USOPP... VOODOO!
"A RAZOR BLADE RUNNING BETWEEN EACH OF YOUR TEETH!"
GUAAAA!
GO TO YOUR ROOM.
GUM-GUM...
FWOOSH!!
DASH!!
UOHH...
KOFF!
THUD...!!
!!!
...!!!

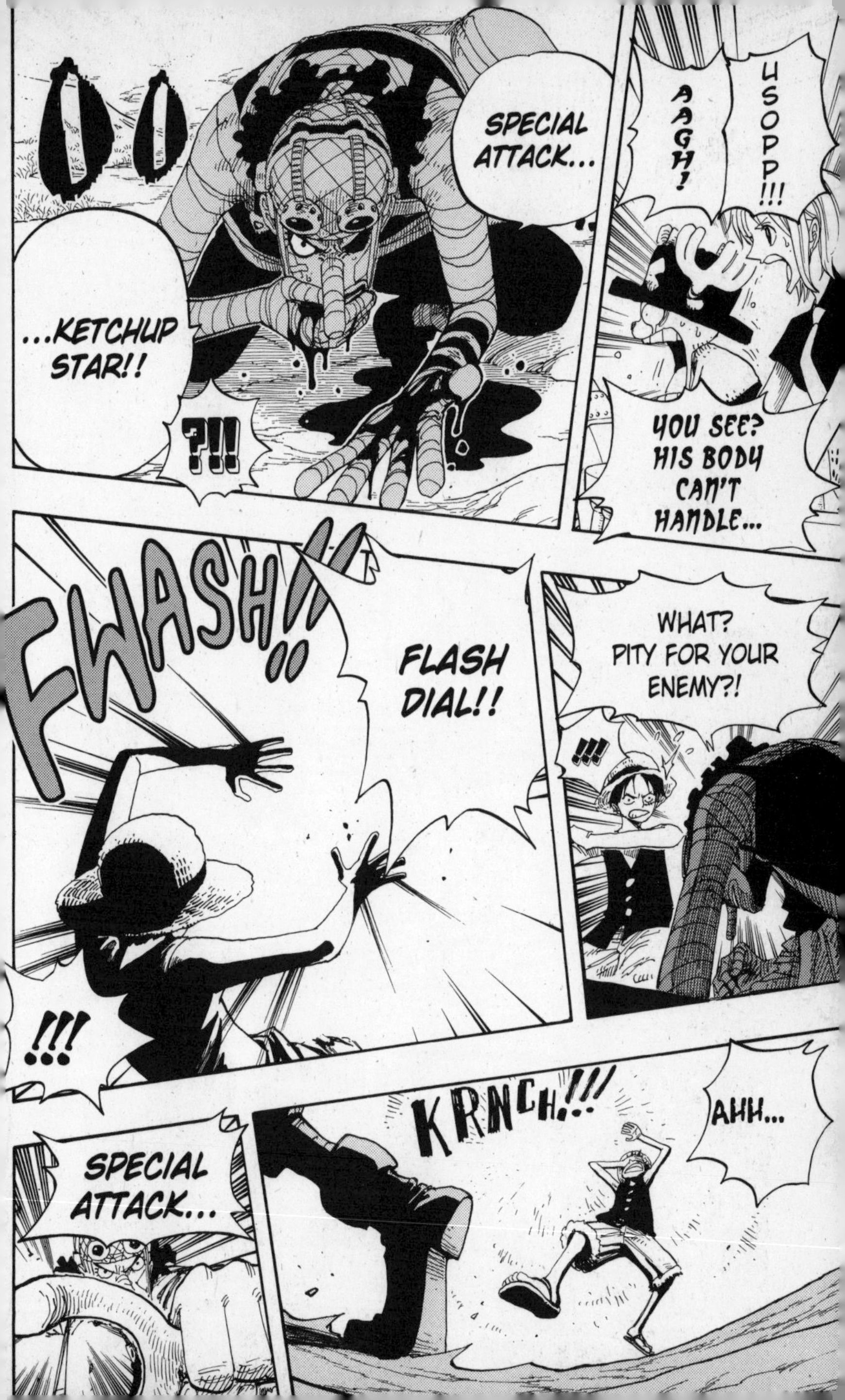

USOPP!!!
AAGH!
YOU SEE? HIS BODY CAN'T HANDLE...
SPECIAL ATTACK...
...KETCHUP STAR!!
?!!
WHAT? PITY FOR YOUR ENEMY?!
!!!
FLASH DIAL!!
FWASH!!
!!!
AHH...
KRNCH!!!
SPECIAL ATTACK...

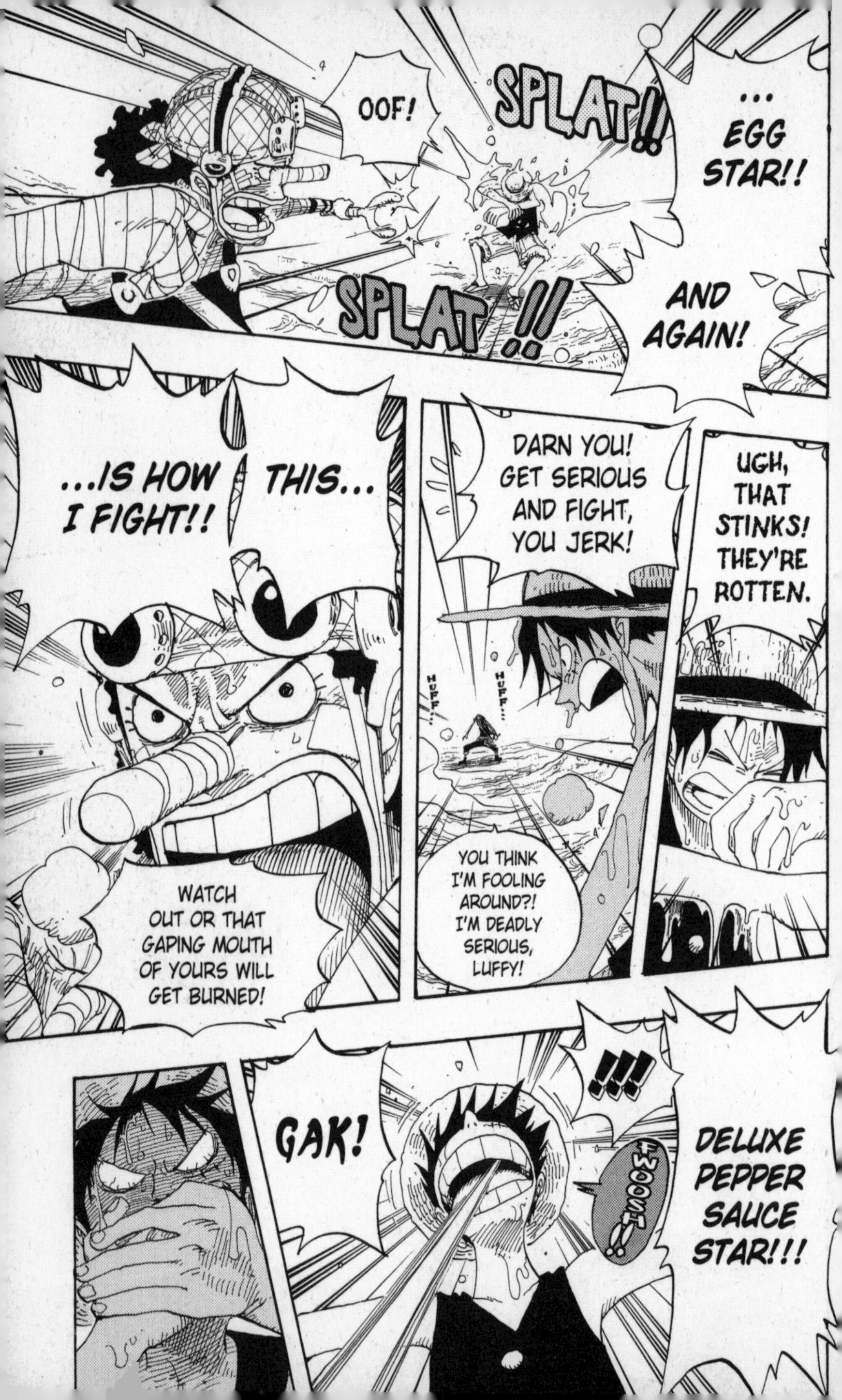
...EGG STAR!!
SPLAT!!
OOF!
AND AGAIN!
SPLAT!!
UGH, THAT STINKS! THEY'RE ROTTEN.
DARN YOU! GET SERIOUS AND FIGHT, YOU JERK!
HUFF...
HUFF...
YOU THINK I'M FOOLING AROUND?! I'M DEADLY SERIOUS, LUFFY!
THIS...
...IS HOW I FIGHT!!
WATCH OUT OR THAT GAPING MOUTH OF YOURS WILL GET BURNED!
DELUXE PEPPER SAUCE STAR!!!
FWOOSH!!
!!!
GAK!

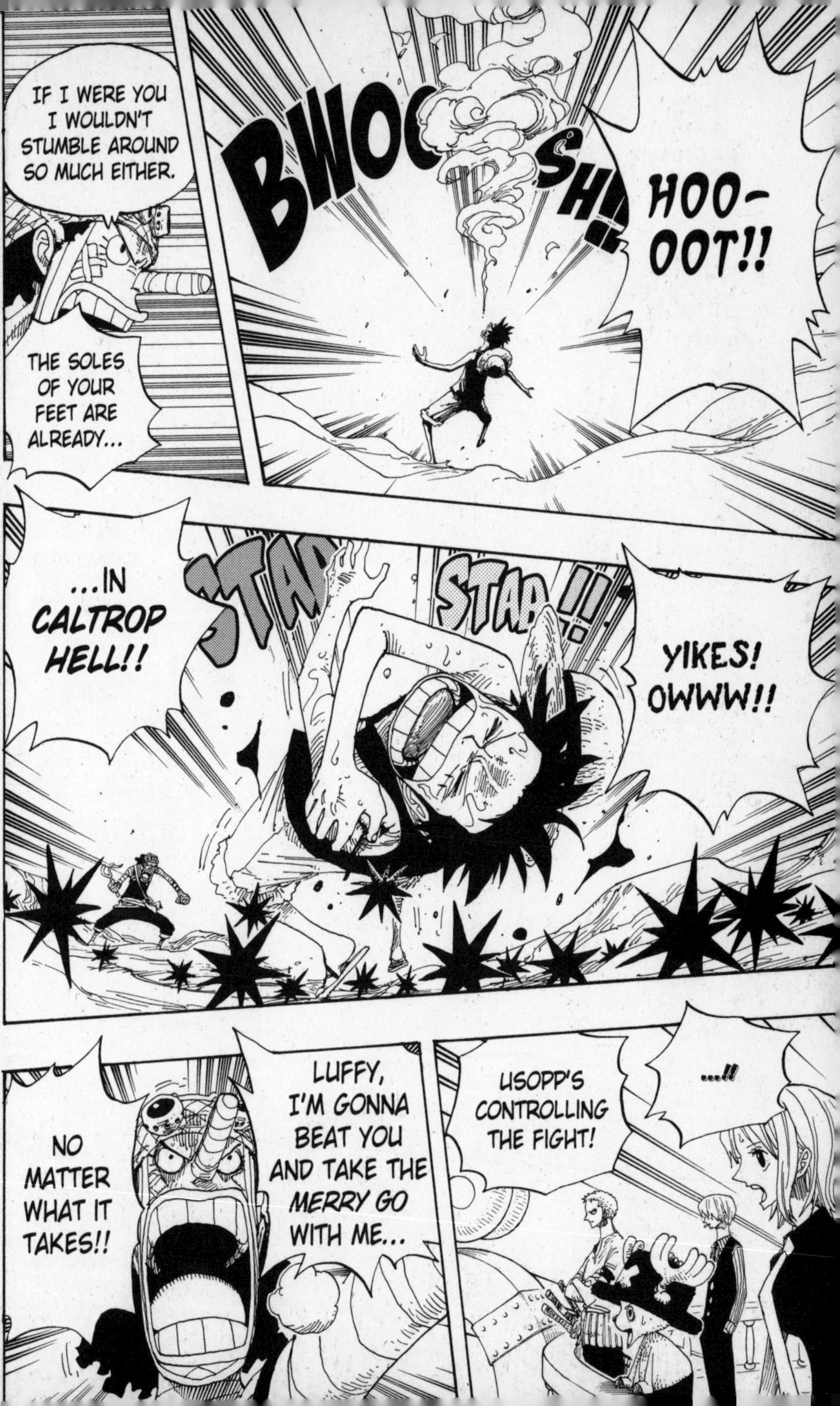
BWOOSH!!
HOO-OOT!!
IF I WERE YOU I WOULDN'T STUMBLE AROUND SO MUCH EITHER.
THE SOLES OF YOUR FEET ARE ALREADY...
YIKES! OWWW!!
STAB!!
STAB
...IN *CALTROP HELL!!*
...!!
USOPP'S CONTROLLING THE FIGHT!
LUFFY, I'M GONNA BEAT YOU AND TAKE THE *MERRY GO* WITH ME...
NO MATTER WHAT IT TAKES!!

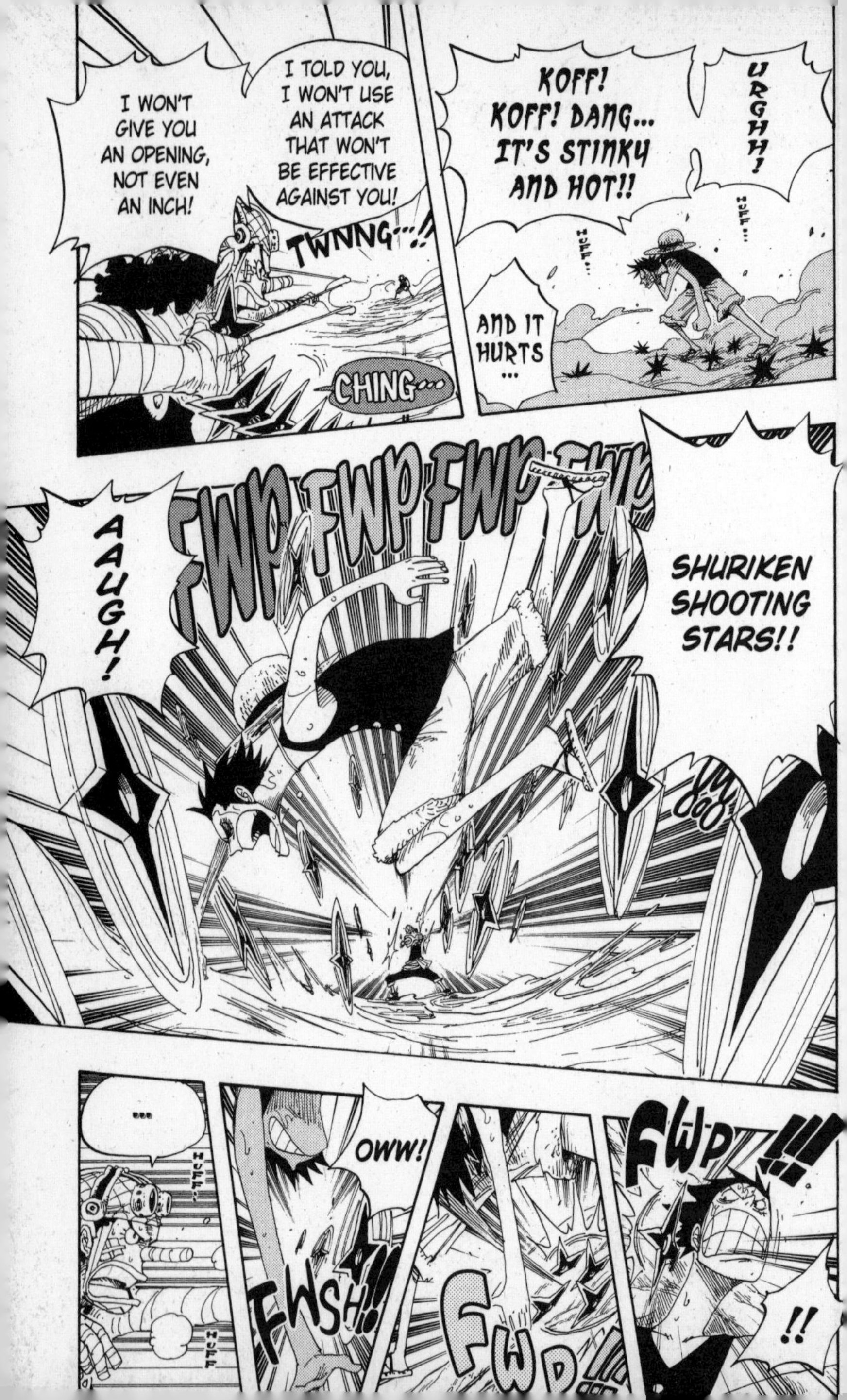
URGHH!
KOFF! KOFF! DANG... IT'S STINKY AND HOT!!
HUFF...
HUFF...
AND IT HURTS...
I TOLD YOU, I WON'T USE AN ATTACK THAT WON'T BE EFFECTIVE AGAINST YOU!
I WON'T GIVE YOU AN OPENING, NOT EVEN AN INCH!
TWNNG...!!
CHING...
SHURIKEN SHOOTING STARS!!
FWP FWP FWP FWP
AAUGH!
FWPZ!!!
!!
FWD!!!
OWW!
FWSH!!
...
HUFF
HUFF

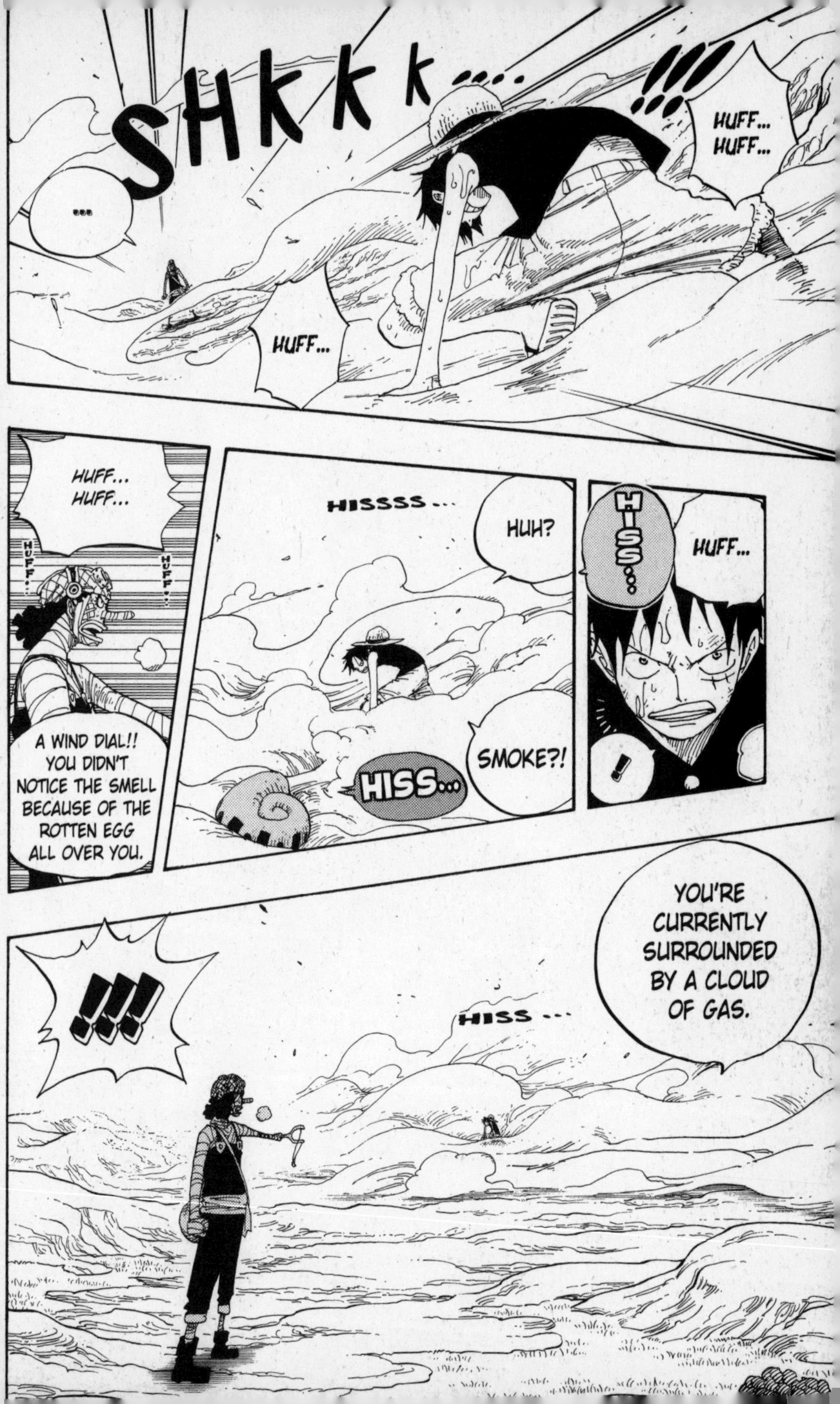
HUFF... HUFF...
!!!
SHKKK....
...
HUFF...
HUFF...
HISS...
!
HUH?
HISSSS...
SMOKE?!
HISS...
HUFF... HUFF...
HUFF...
HUFF...
A WIND DIAL!! YOU DIDN'T NOTICE THE SMELL BECAUSE OF THE ROTTEN EGG ALL OVER YOU.
YOU'RE CURRENTLY SURROUNDED BY A CLOUD OF GAS.
HISS...
!!!

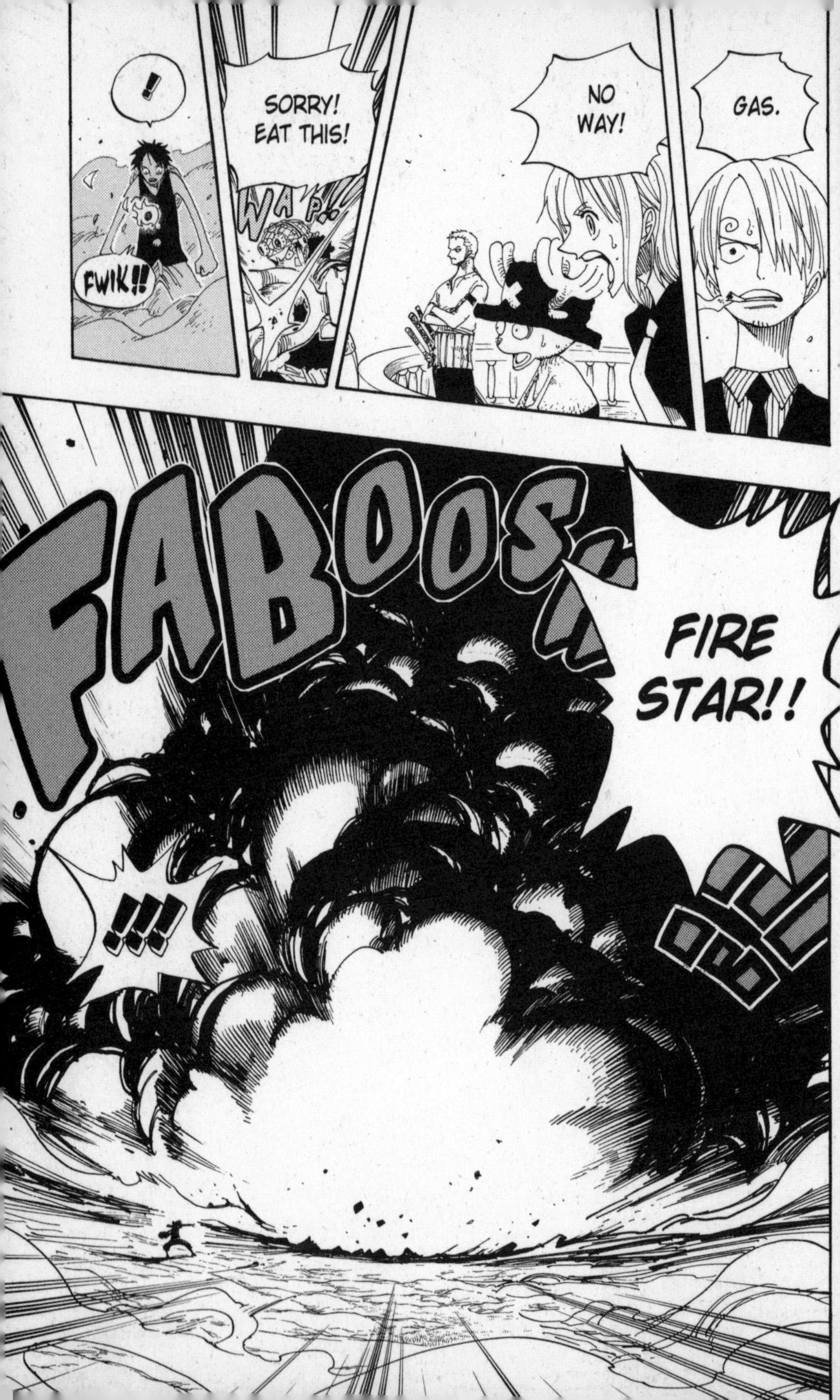
GAS.
NO WAY!
SORRY! EAT THIS!
WAP!!
!
FWIK!!
FIRE STAR!!
FABOOS
!!!

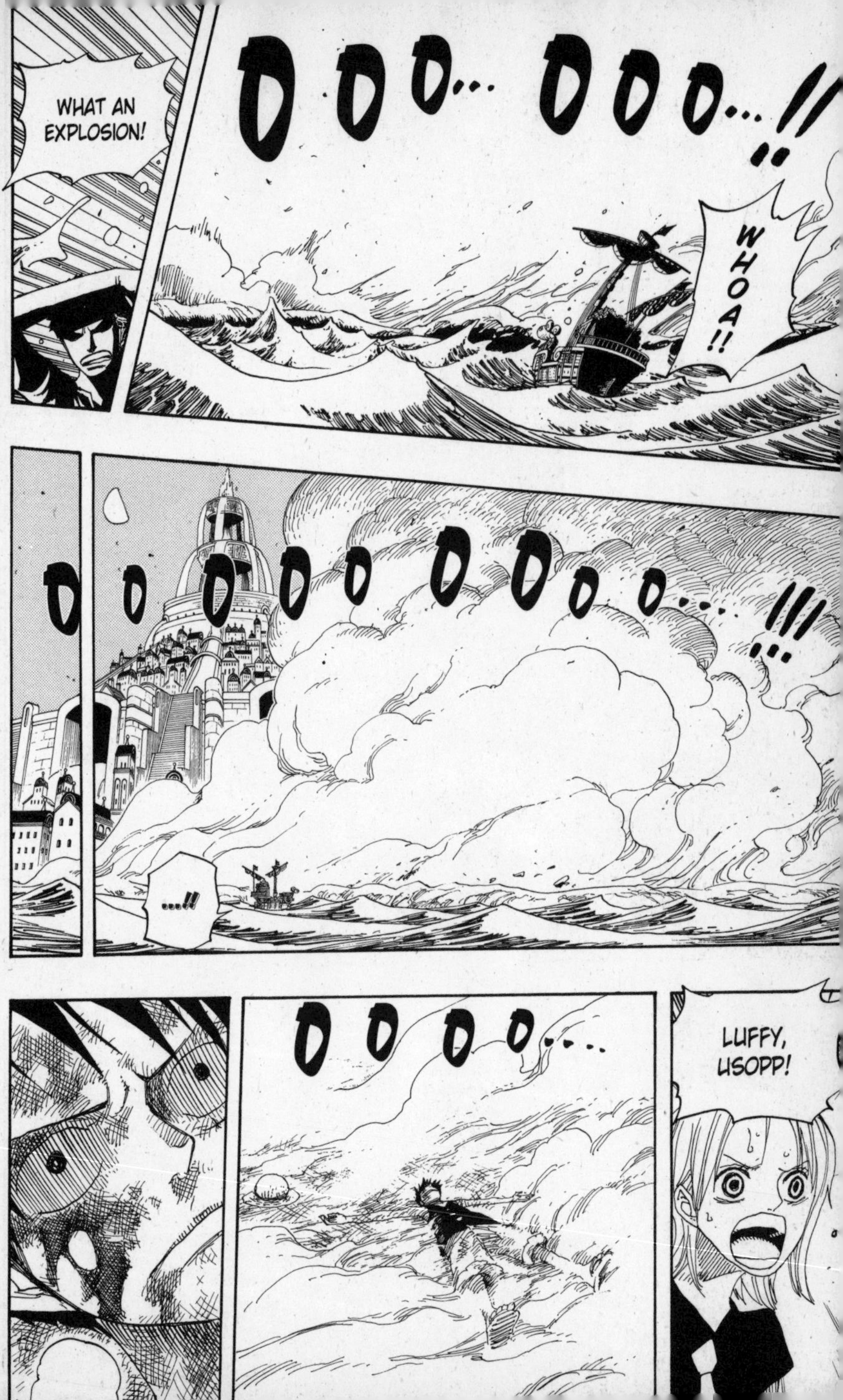
DOOO... DOOO...!!
WHOA!!
WHAT AN EXPLOSION!
DDDDDDDDDDD...!!!
...!!
LUFFY, USOPP!
DDDD...

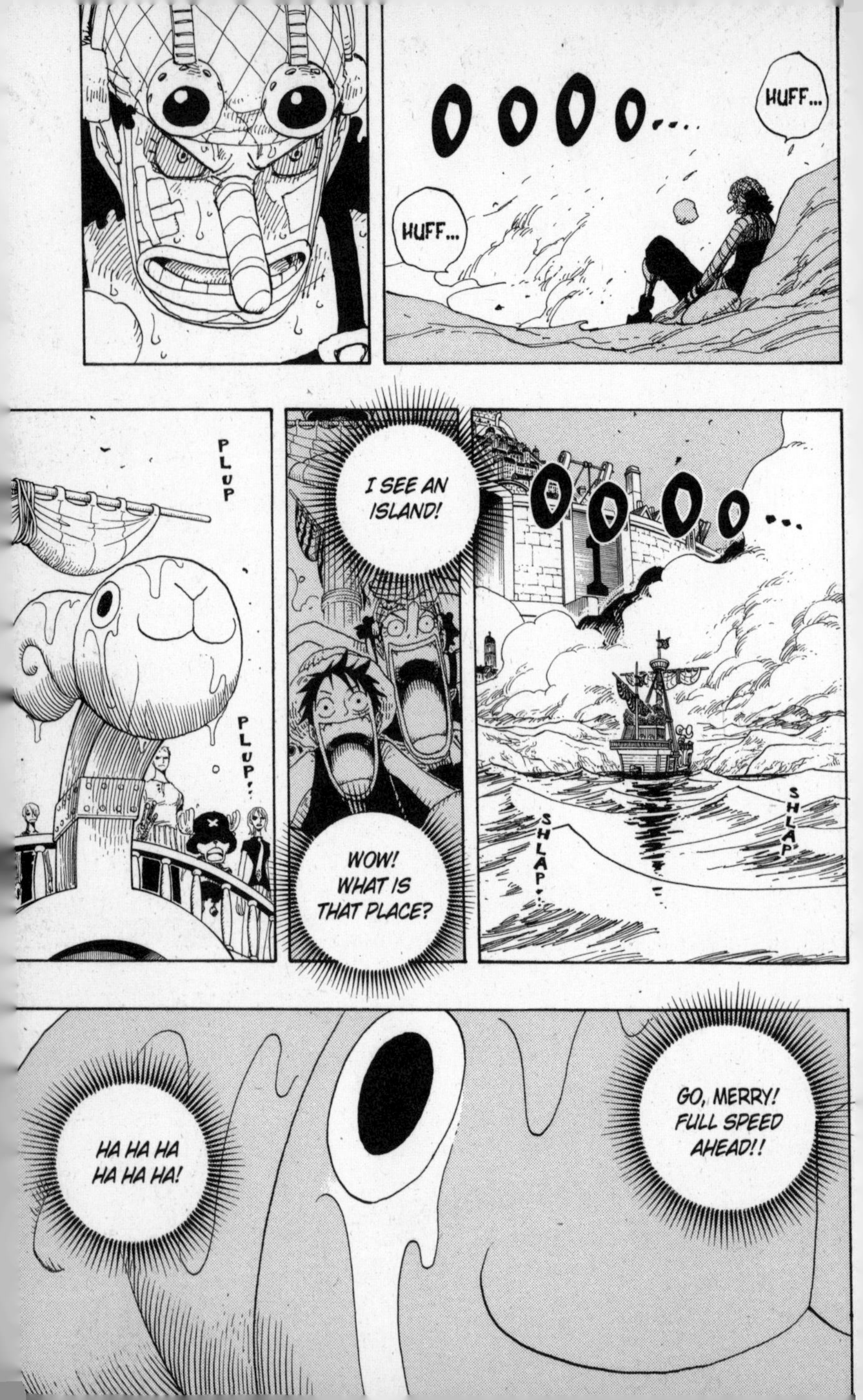
HUFF...
OOOO....
HUFF...
OOOO....
SHLAP
SHLAP...
I SEE AN ISLAND!
WOW! WHAT IS THAT PLACE?
PLUP
PLUP...
GO, MERRY! FULL SPEED AHEAD!!
HA HA HA HA HA HA!

Chapter 333:
CAPTAIN

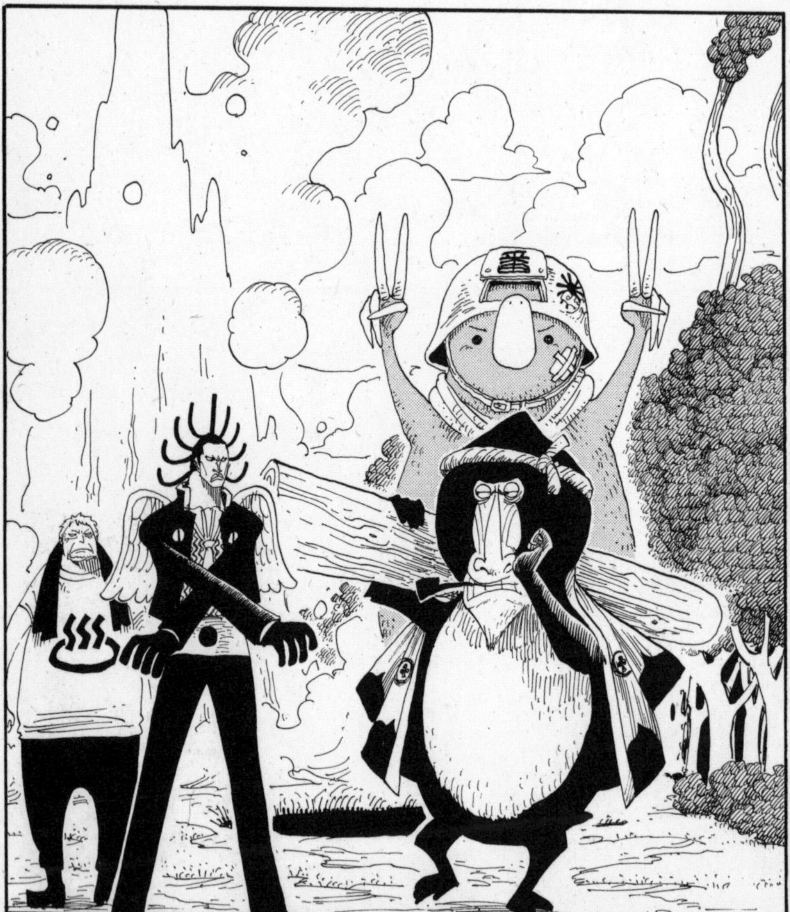

GEDATSU'S UNEXPECTED LIFE ON THE BLUE SEA, VOL. 18:
"THE EXPLOSION BRINGS OUT THE FOREST BOSS"

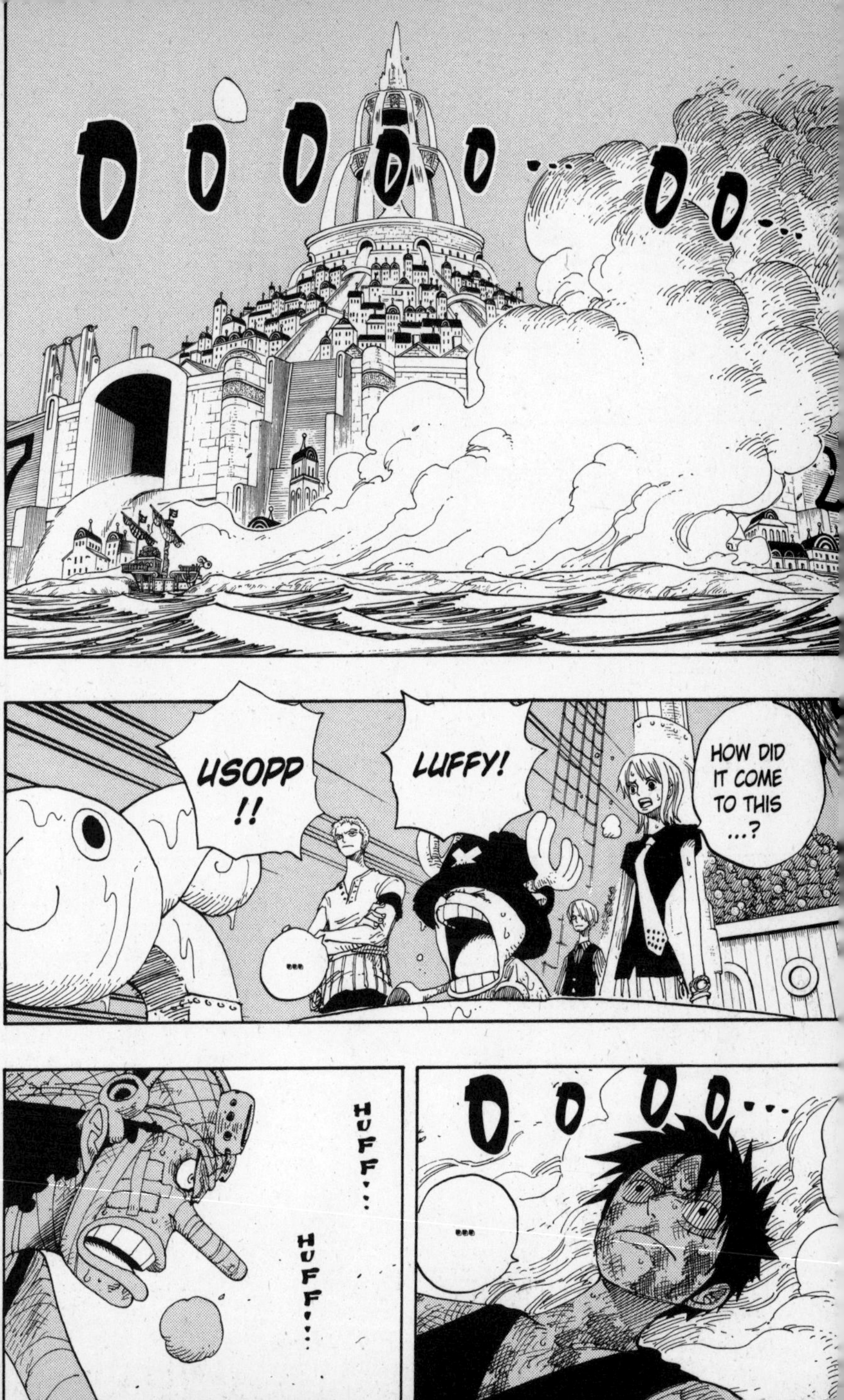
DOOOO...OO...
HOW DID IT COME TO THIS ...?
LUFFY!
USOPP !!
...
DOOO...
...
HUFF..
HUFF..

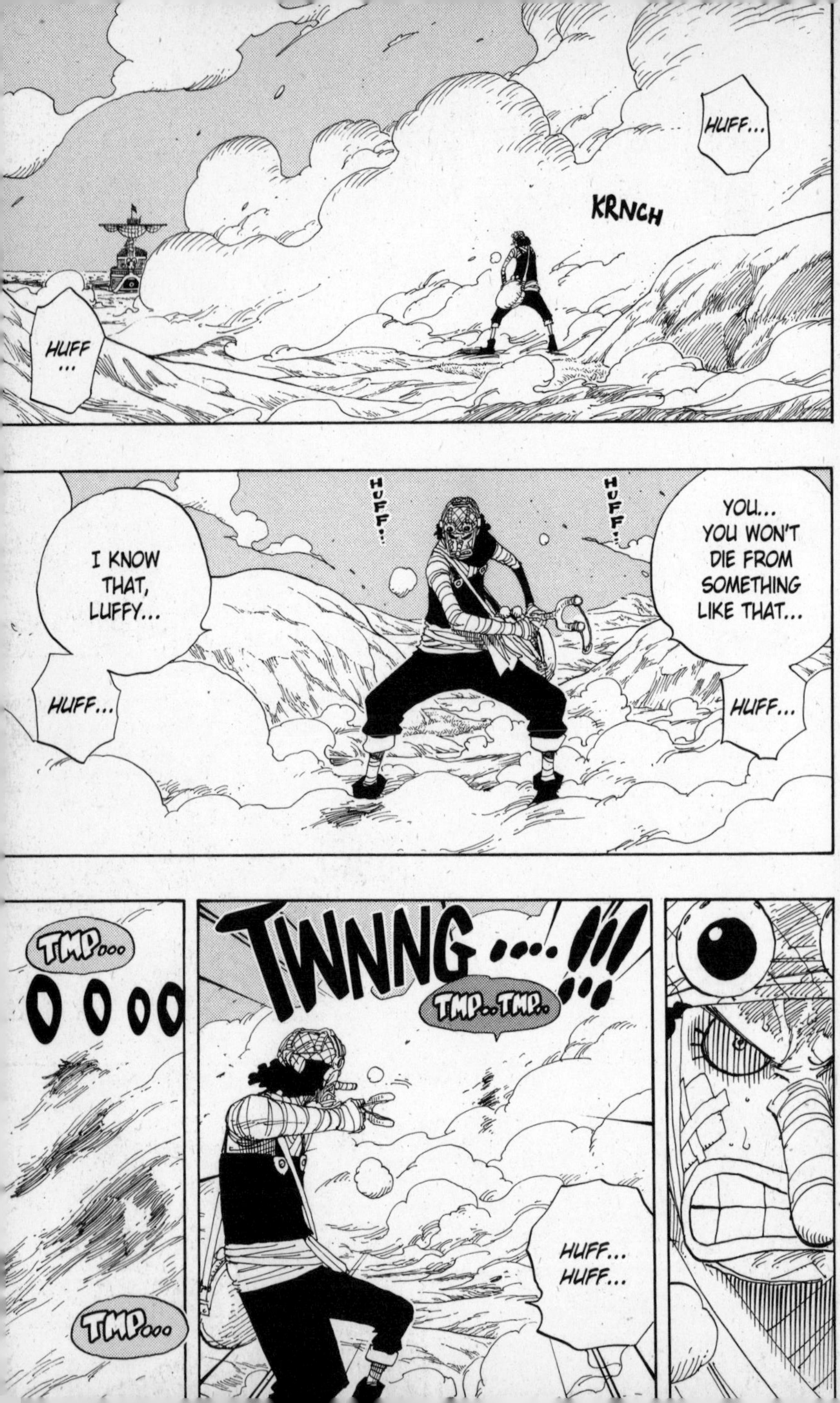
HUFF...
KRNCH
HUFF ...
YOU... YOU WON'T DIE FROM SOMETHING LIKE THAT...
HUFF...
HUFF!
HUFF!
I KNOW THAT, LUFFY...
HUFF...
TWNNG...!!!
TMP..TMP..
HUFF... HUFF...
TMP...
OOOO
TMP...

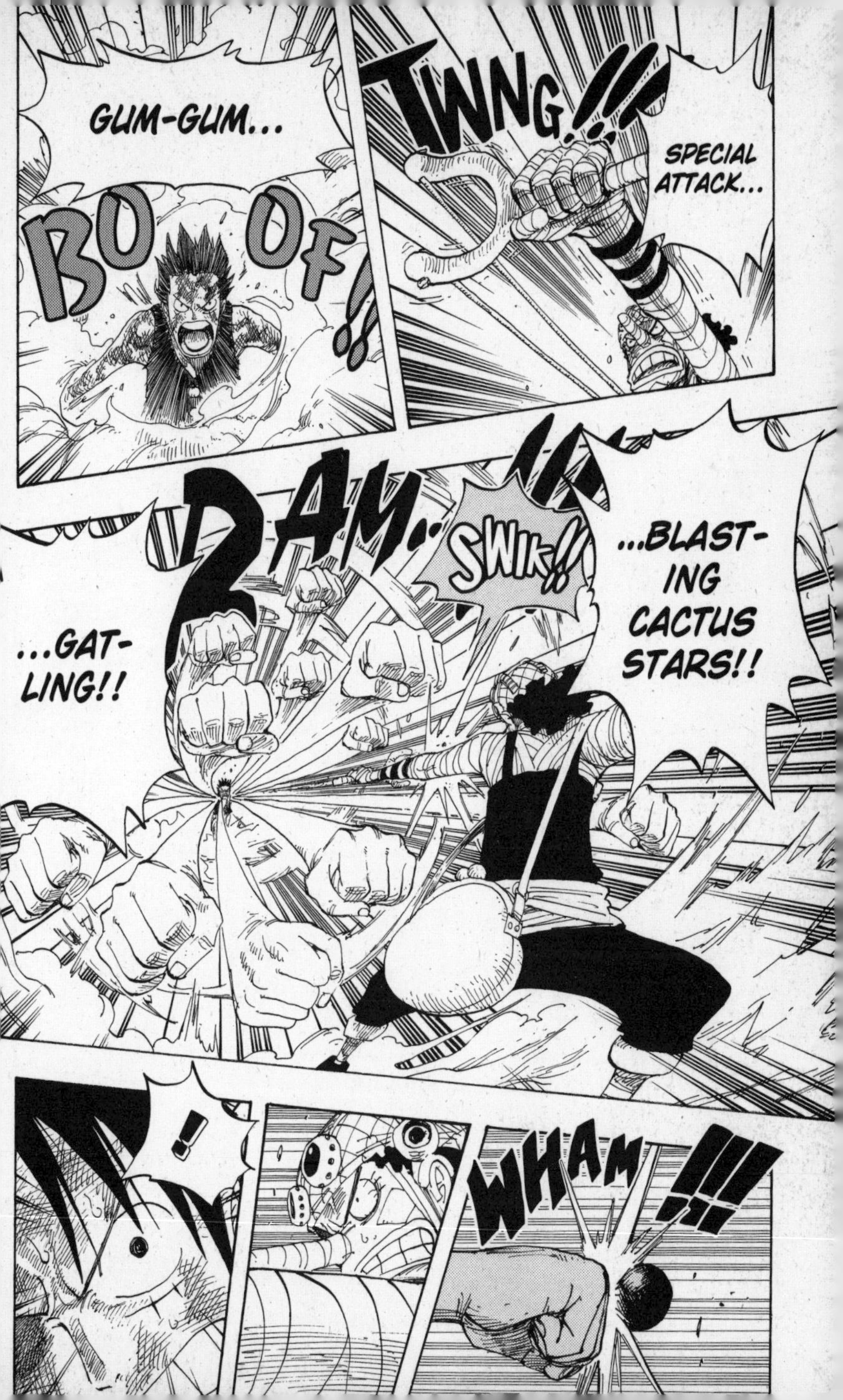
TWNG!!!
SPECIAL ATTACK...
GUM-GUM...
BOOF!!
...BLASTING CACTUS STARS!!
SWIK!!
ZAM!!
...GATLING!!
WHAM!!!
!

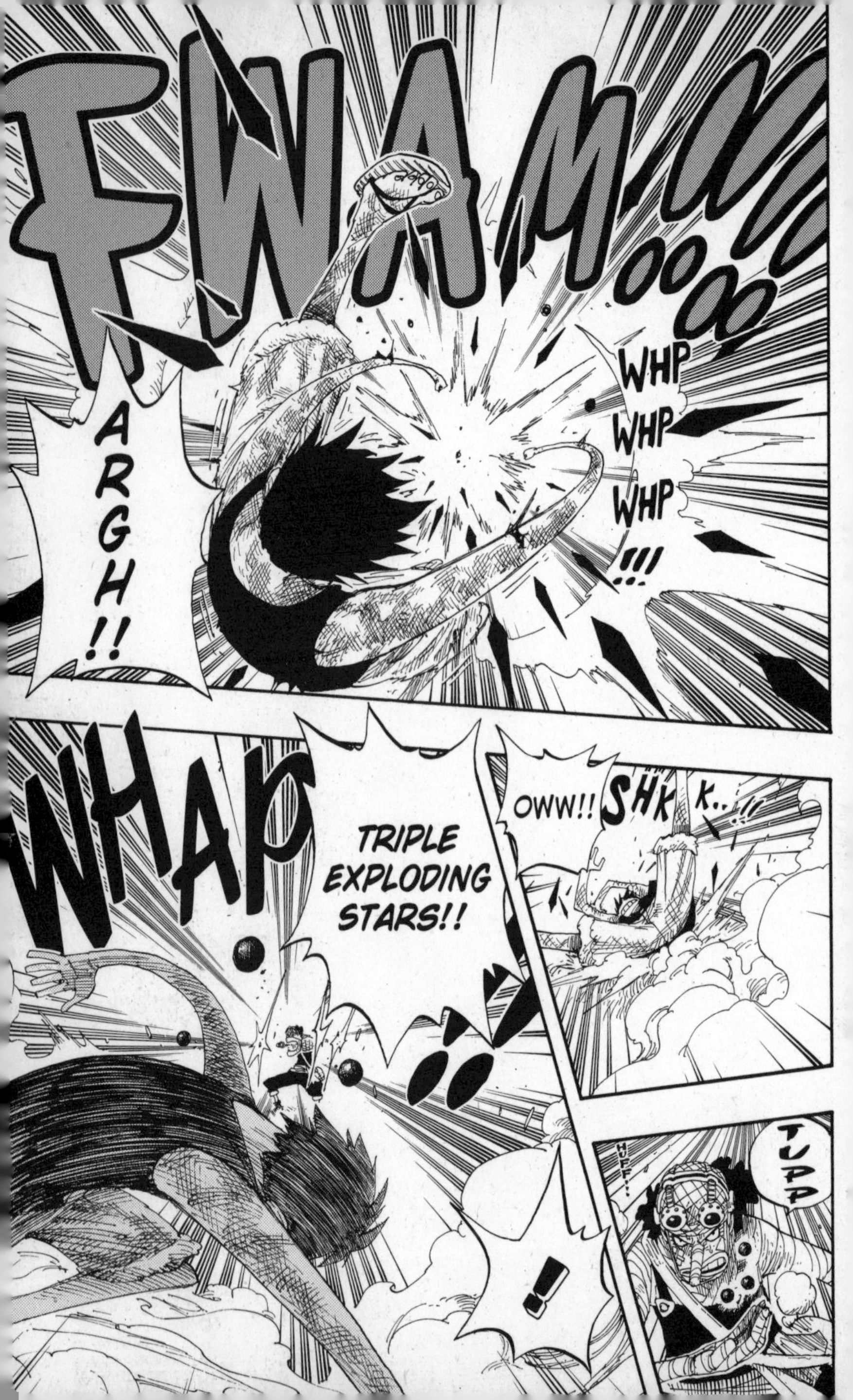
FWAMMM
WHP WHP WHP!!!
ARGH!!
OWW!!
SHK K..!!
HUFF...
TUPP
TRIPLE EXPLODING STARS!!
WHAP

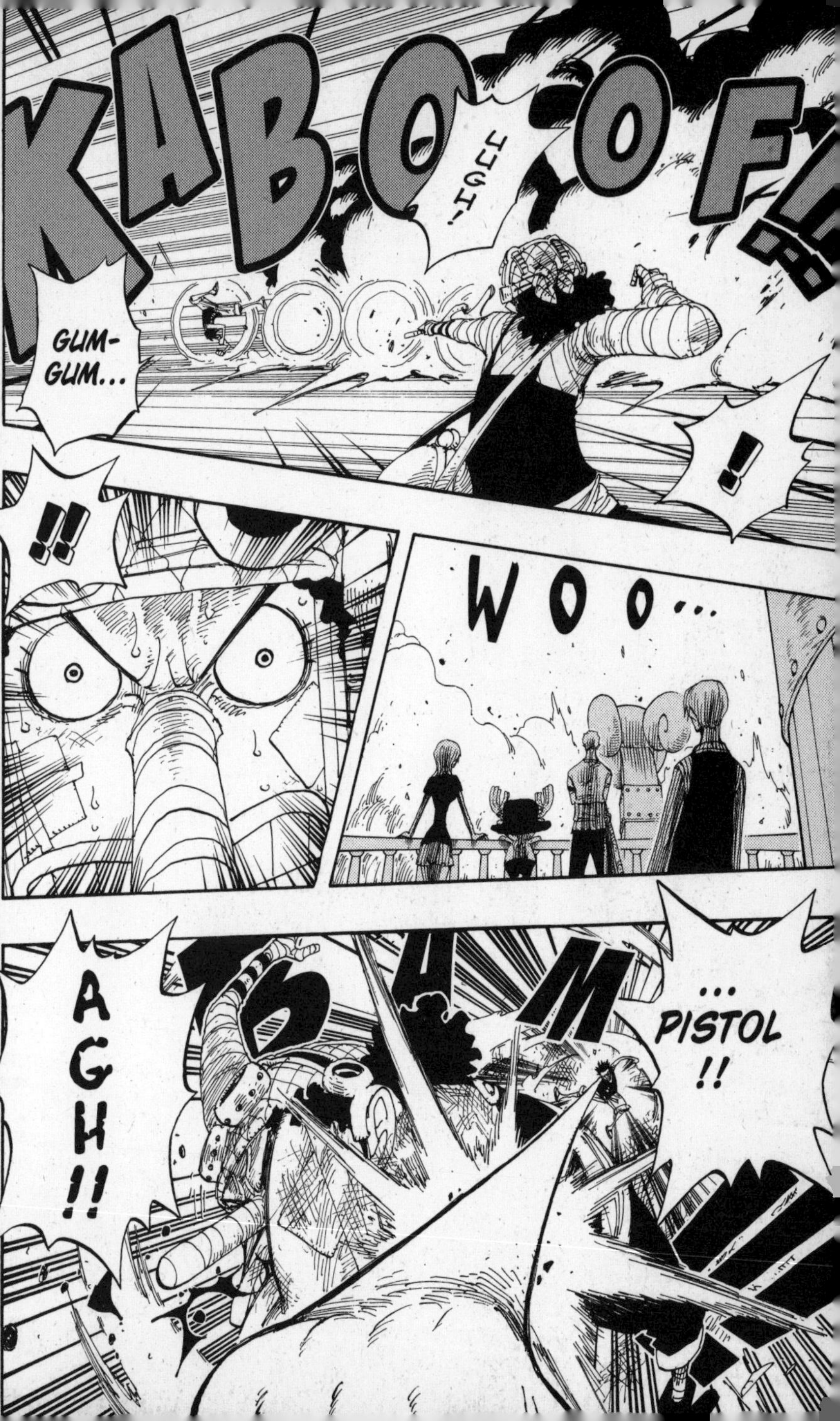
KABOOOF!!
UUGH!
GUM-GUM...
!
WOO...
!!
...PISTOL!!
BAM
AGH!!

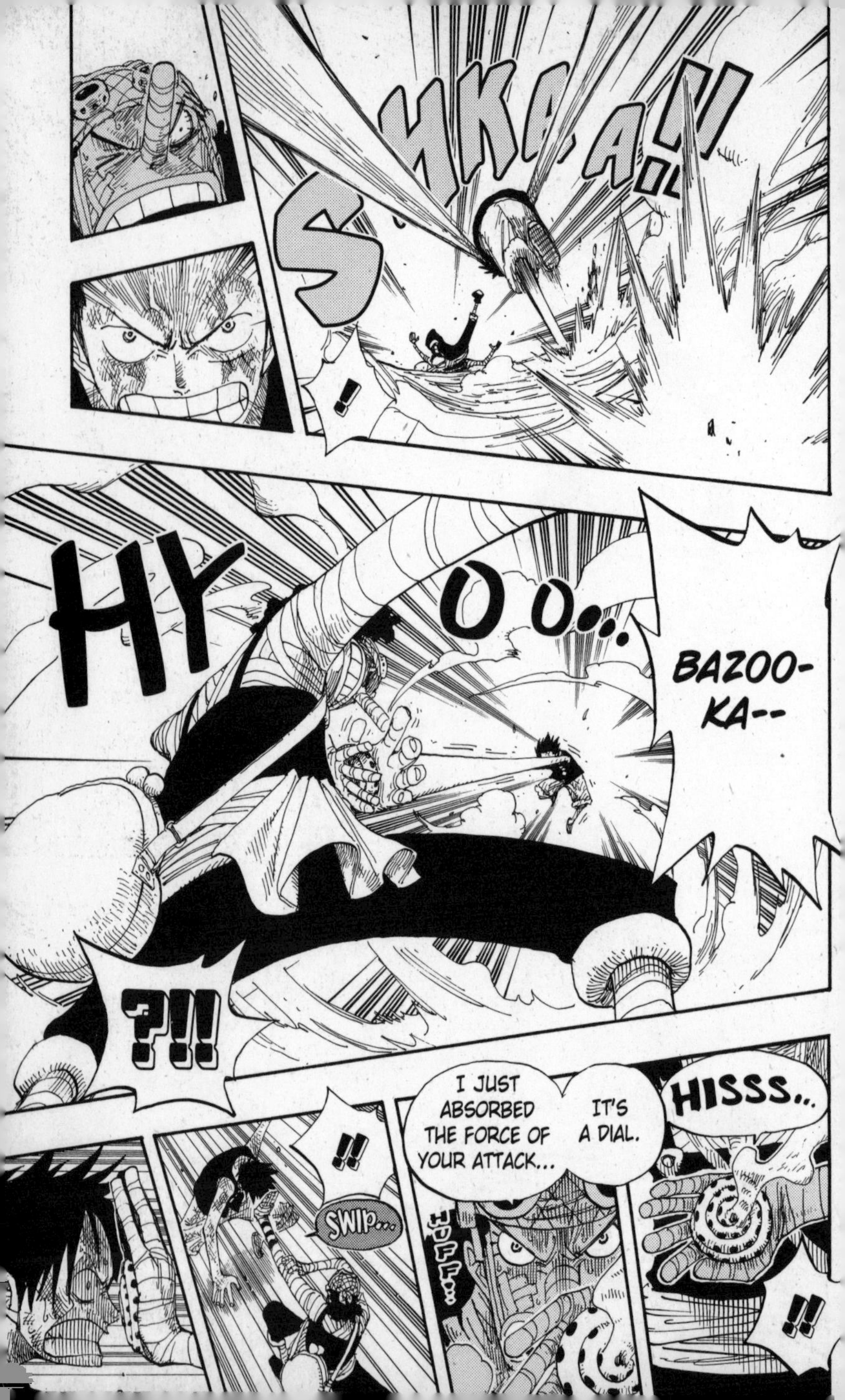
SHKAA!!
!
HYOOO...
BAZOO-KA--
?!!
HISSS...
!!
IT'S A DIAL.
I JUST ABSORBED THE FORCE OF YOUR ATTACK...
HUFF...
!!
SWIP...

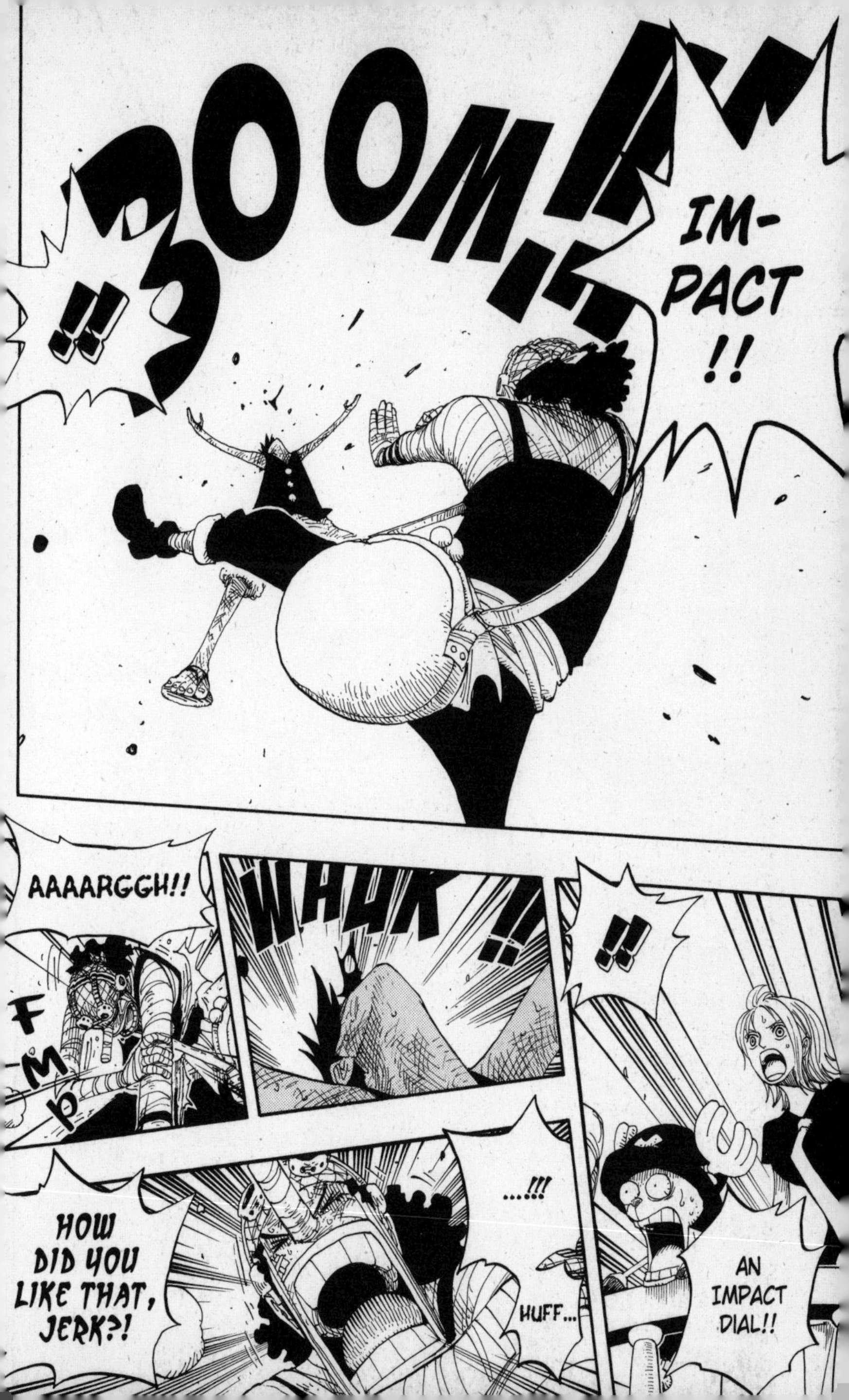
BOOM!!
IM-
PACT
!!
!!
WHUK!!
AAAARGGH!!
FMP
AN
IMPACT
DIAL!!
...!!!
HOW
DID YOU
LIKE THAT,
JERK?!
HUFF...

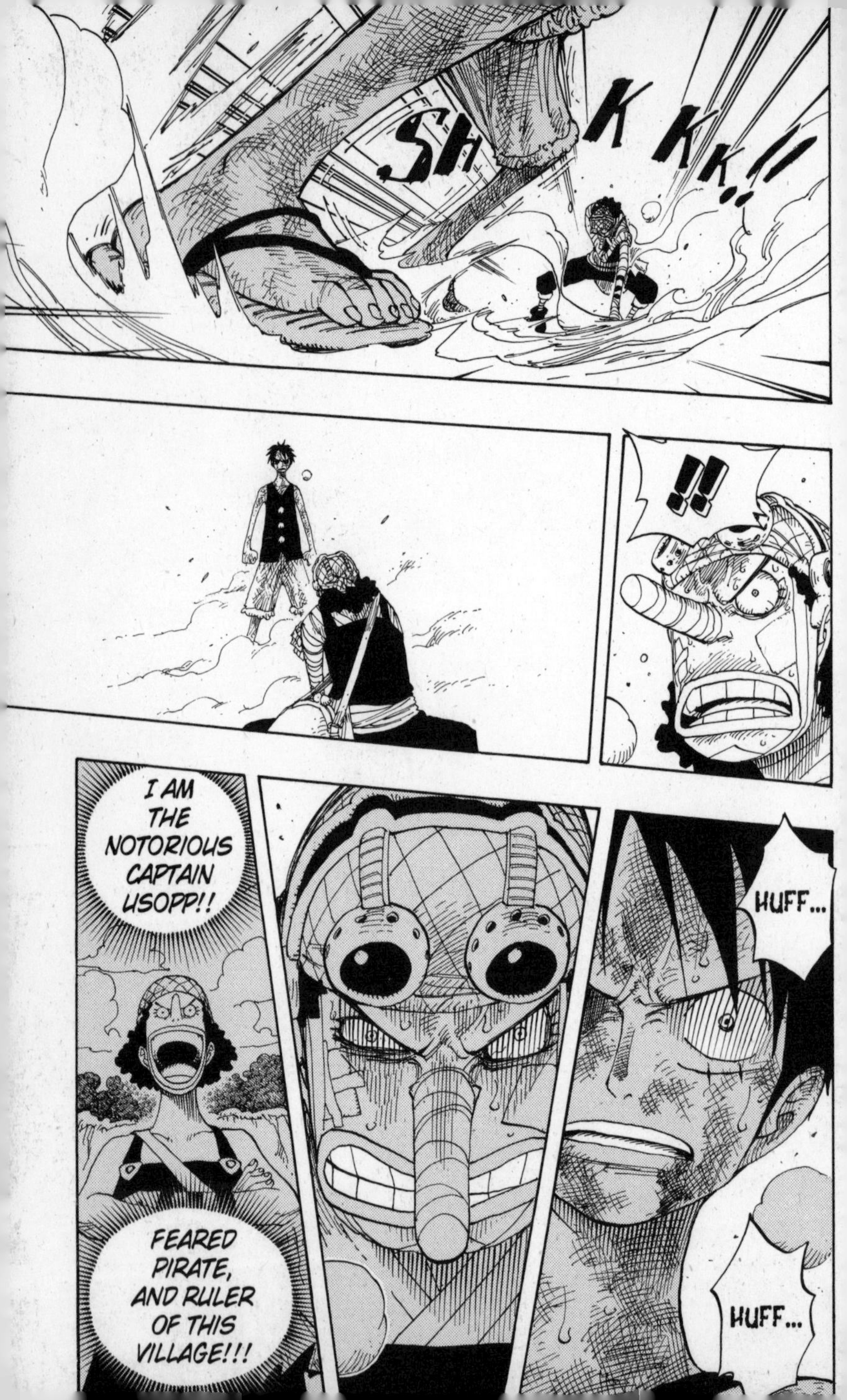
SHKKKK!!
!!
HUFF...
HUFF...
I AM THE NOTORIOUS CAPTAIN USOPP!!
FEARED PIRATE, AND RULER OF THIS VILLAGE!!!

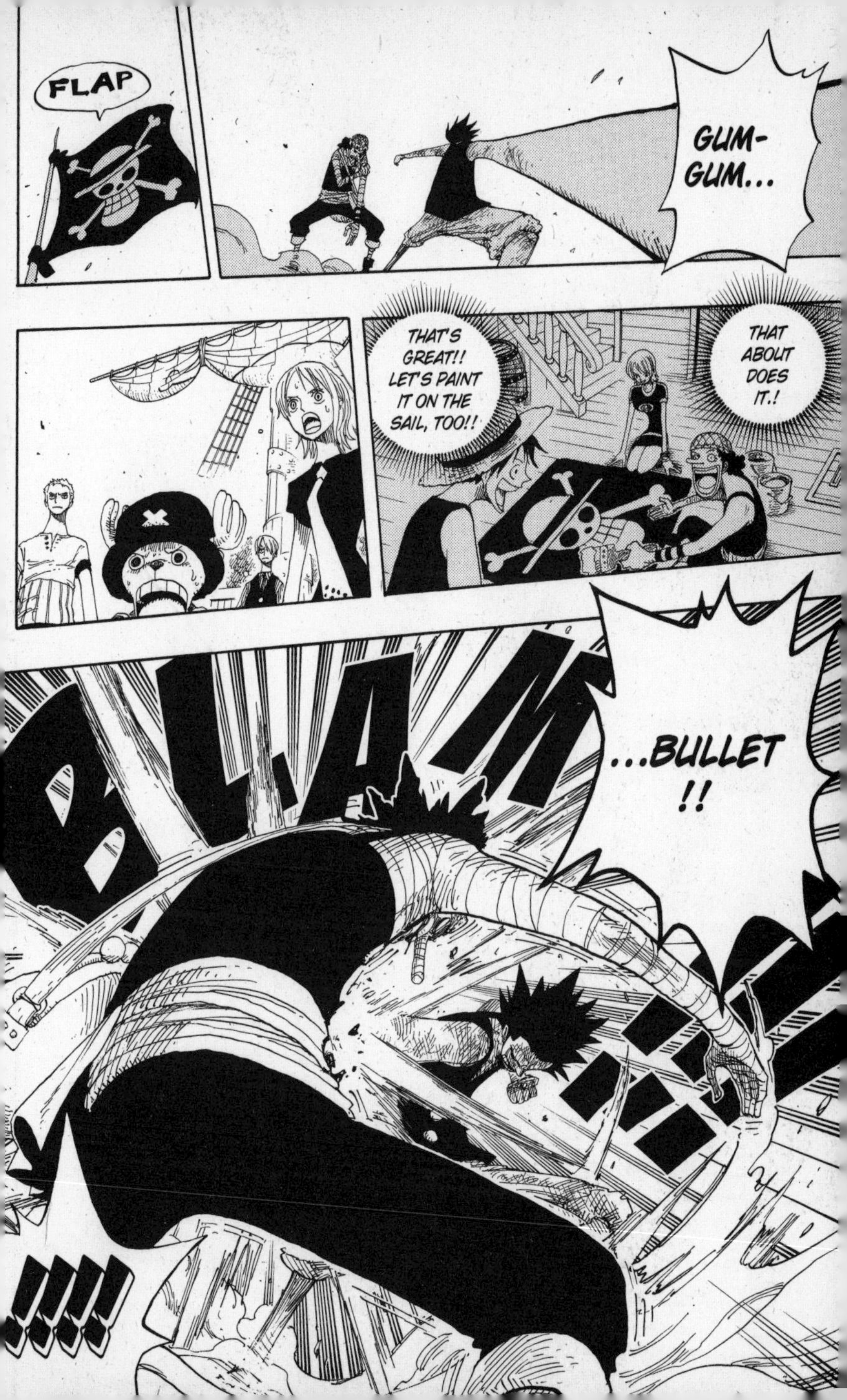
GUM-GUM...
FLAP
THAT ABOUT DOES IT.!
THAT'S GREAT!! LET'S PAINT IT ON THE SAIL, TOO!!
...BULLET !!
BLAM

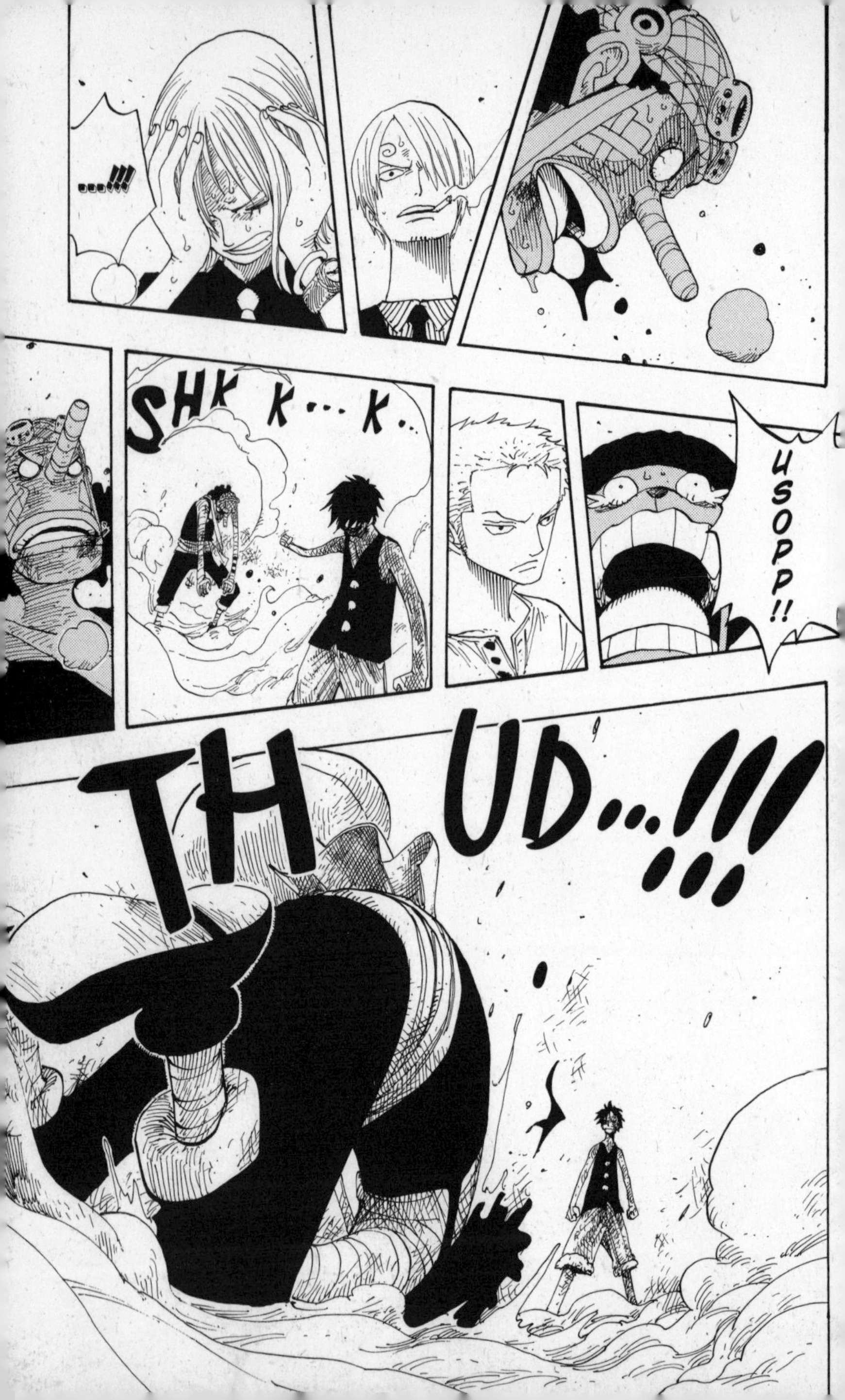
...!!!
USOPP!!
SHK K... K...
THUD...!!!

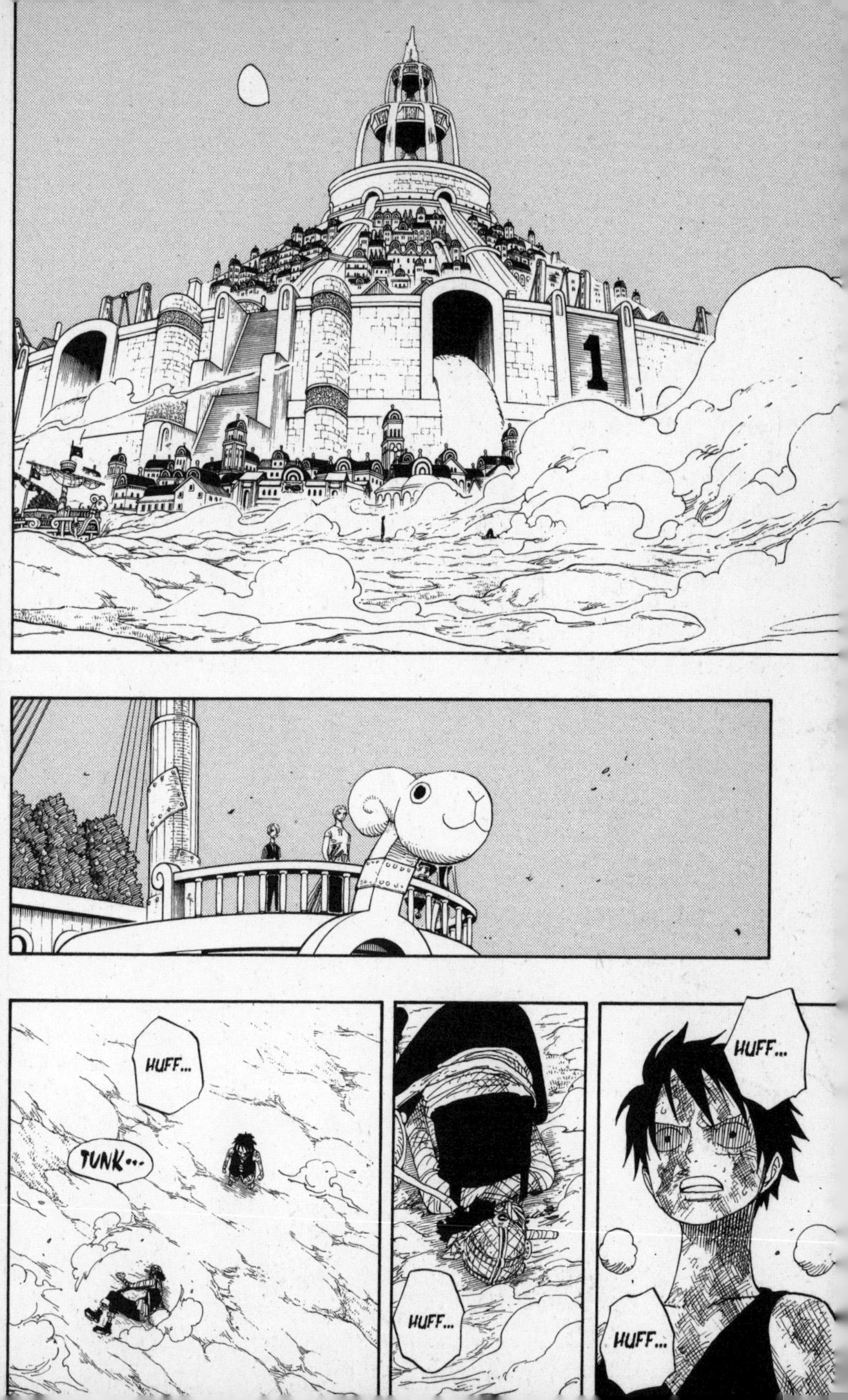
HUFF...
HUFF...
HUFF...
HUFF...
TUNK...

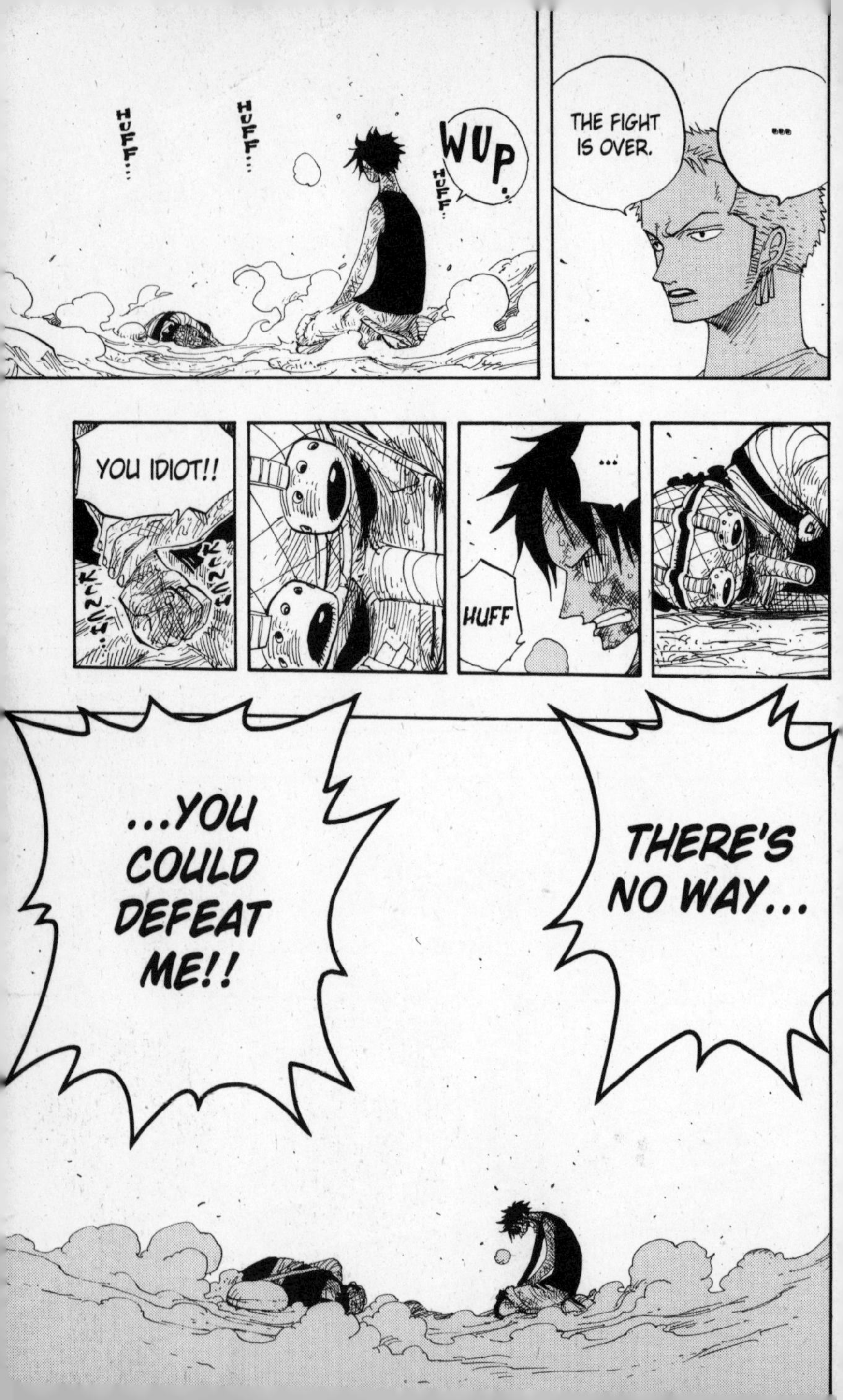
...
THE FIGHT IS OVER.
WUP.
HUFF...
HUFF...
HUFF...
...
HUFF
YOU IDIOT!!
KLINCH
KLINCH...
THERE'S NO WAY...
...YOU COULD DEFEAT ME!!

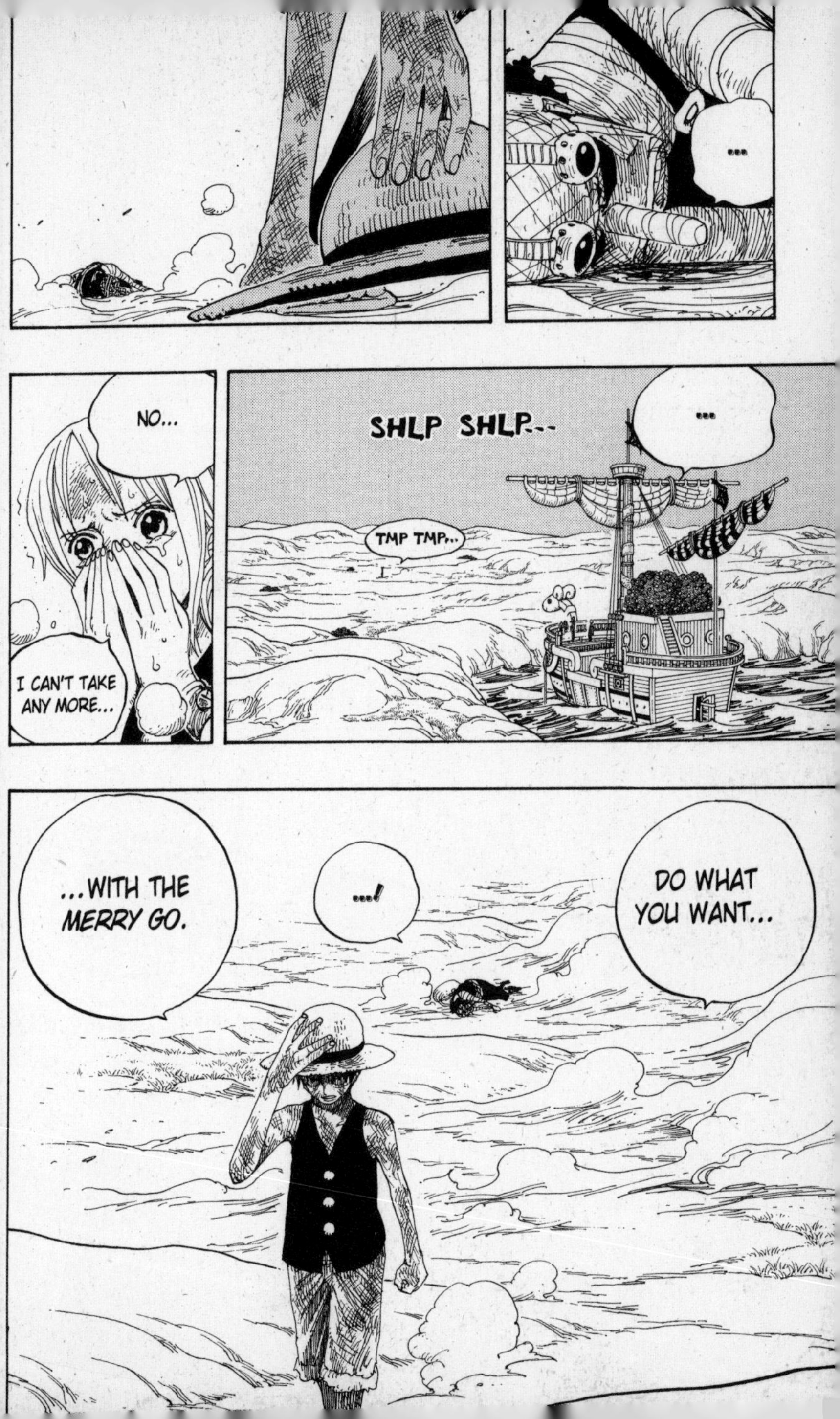
...
...
SHLP SHLP...
TMP TMP...
NO...
I CAN'T TAKE ANY MORE...
DO WHAT YOU WANT...
...!
...WITH THE *MERRY GO*.

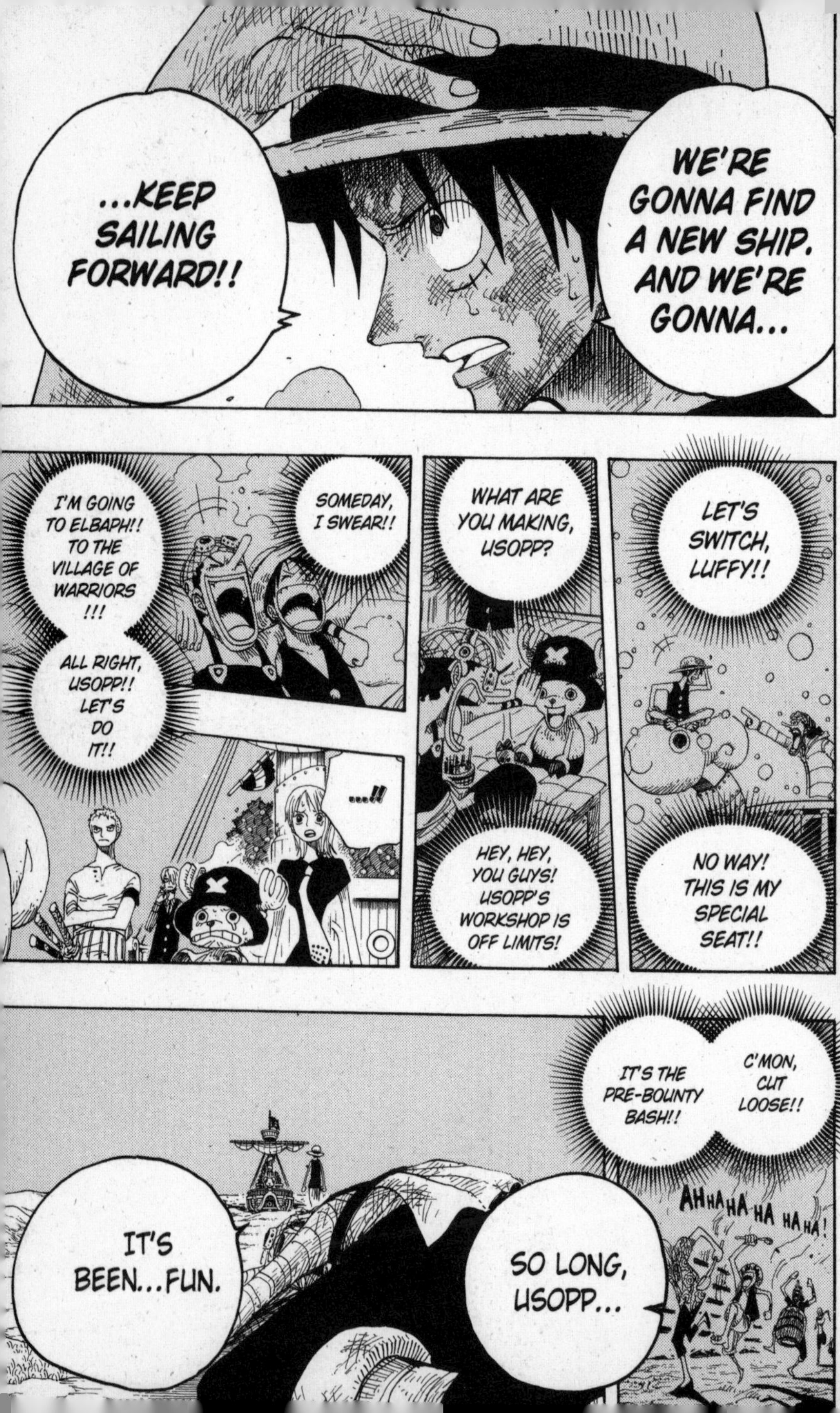

WE'RE GONNA FIND A NEW SHIP. AND WE'RE GONNA...
...KEEP SAILING FORWARD!!
LET'S SWITCH, LUFFY!!
NO WAY! THIS IS MY SPECIAL SEAT!!
WHAT ARE YOU MAKING, USOPP?
HEY, HEY, YOU GUYS! USOPP'S WORKSHOP IS OFF LIMITS!
SOMEDAY, I SWEAR!!
I'M GOING TO ELBAPH!! TO THE VILLAGE OF WARRIORS!!!
ALL RIGHT, USOPP!! LET'S DO IT!!
...!!
C'MON, CUT LOOSE!!
IT'S THE PRE-BOUNTY BASH!!
AHHAHA HA HA HAHA!
SO LONG, USOPP...
IT'S BEEN...FUN.

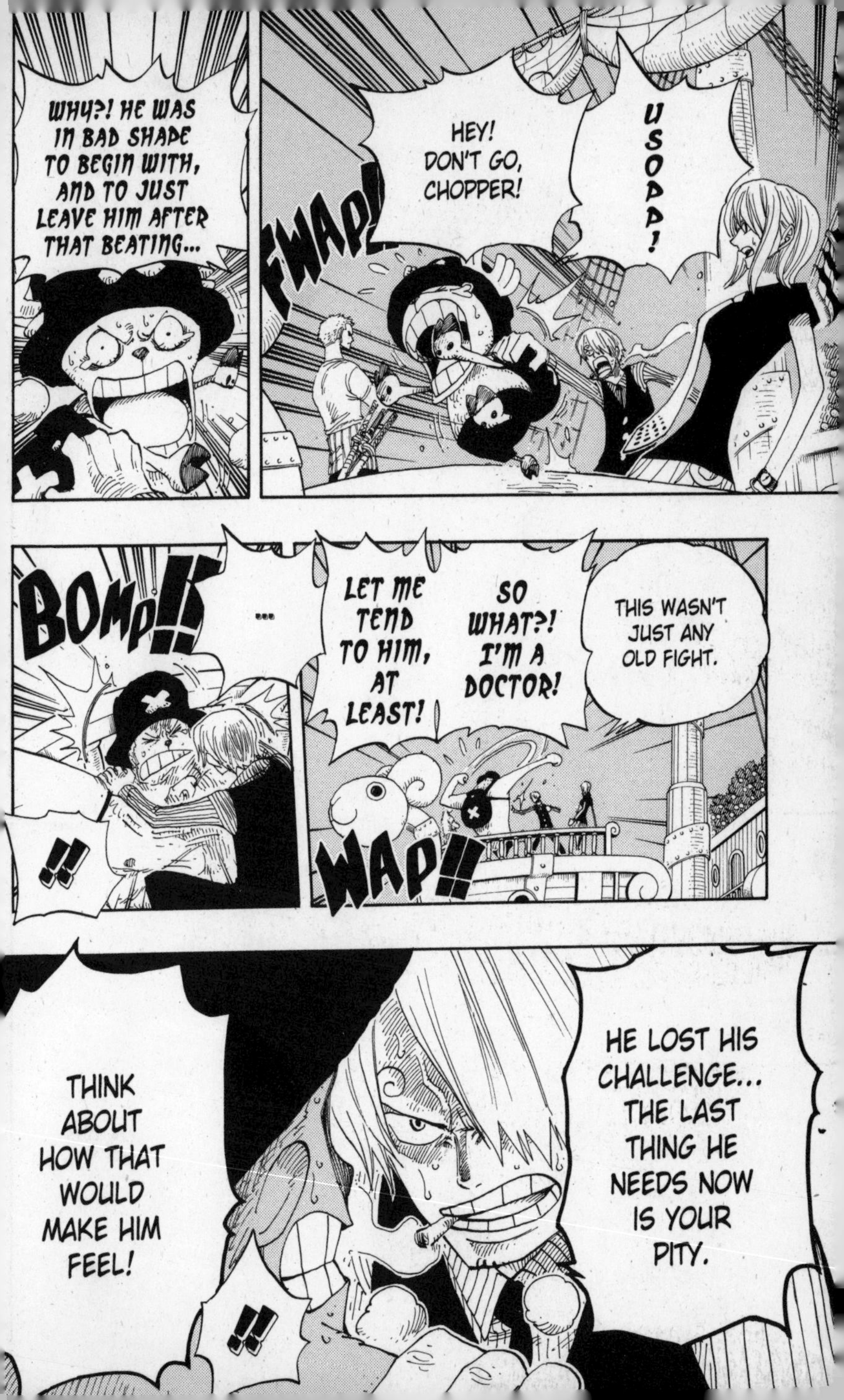
USOPP!
HEY! DON'T GO, CHOPPER!
FWAP!
WHY?! HE WAS IN BAD SHAPE TO BEGIN WITH, AND TO JUST LEAVE HIM AFTER THAT BEATING...
THIS WASN'T JUST ANY OLD FIGHT.
SO WHAT?! I'M A DOCTOR!
LET ME TEND TO HIM, AT LEAST!
WAP!!
...
BOMP!!
!!
HE LOST HIS CHALLENGE... THE LAST THING HE NEEDS NOW IS YOUR PITY.
THINK ABOUT HOW THAT WOULD MAKE HIM FEEL!
!!

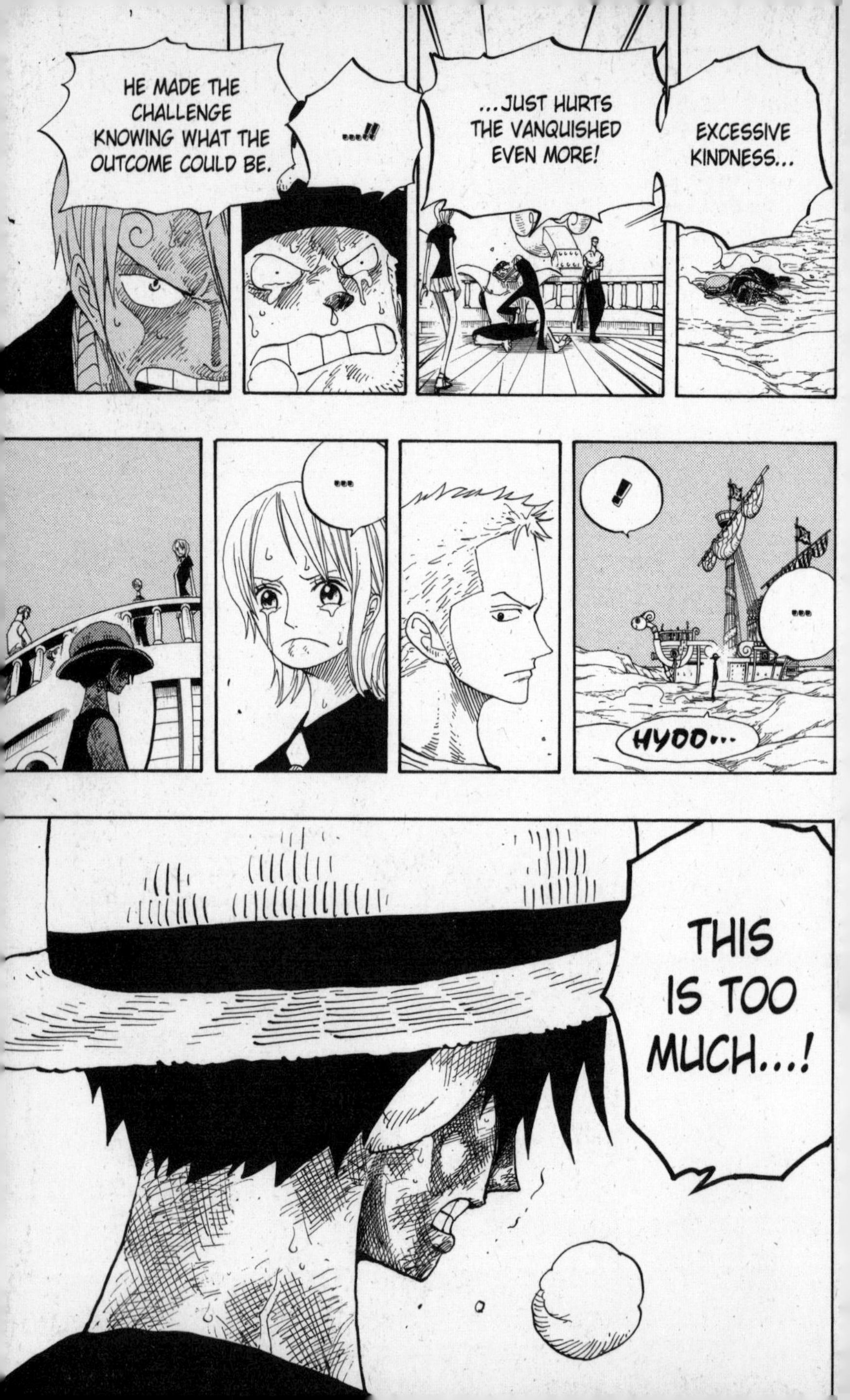
EXCESSIVE KINDNESS...
...JUST HURTS THE VANQUISHED EVEN MORE!
...!!
HE MADE THE CHALLENGE KNOWING WHAT THE OUTCOME COULD BE.
!
...
HYOO...
...
THIS IS TOO MUCH...!

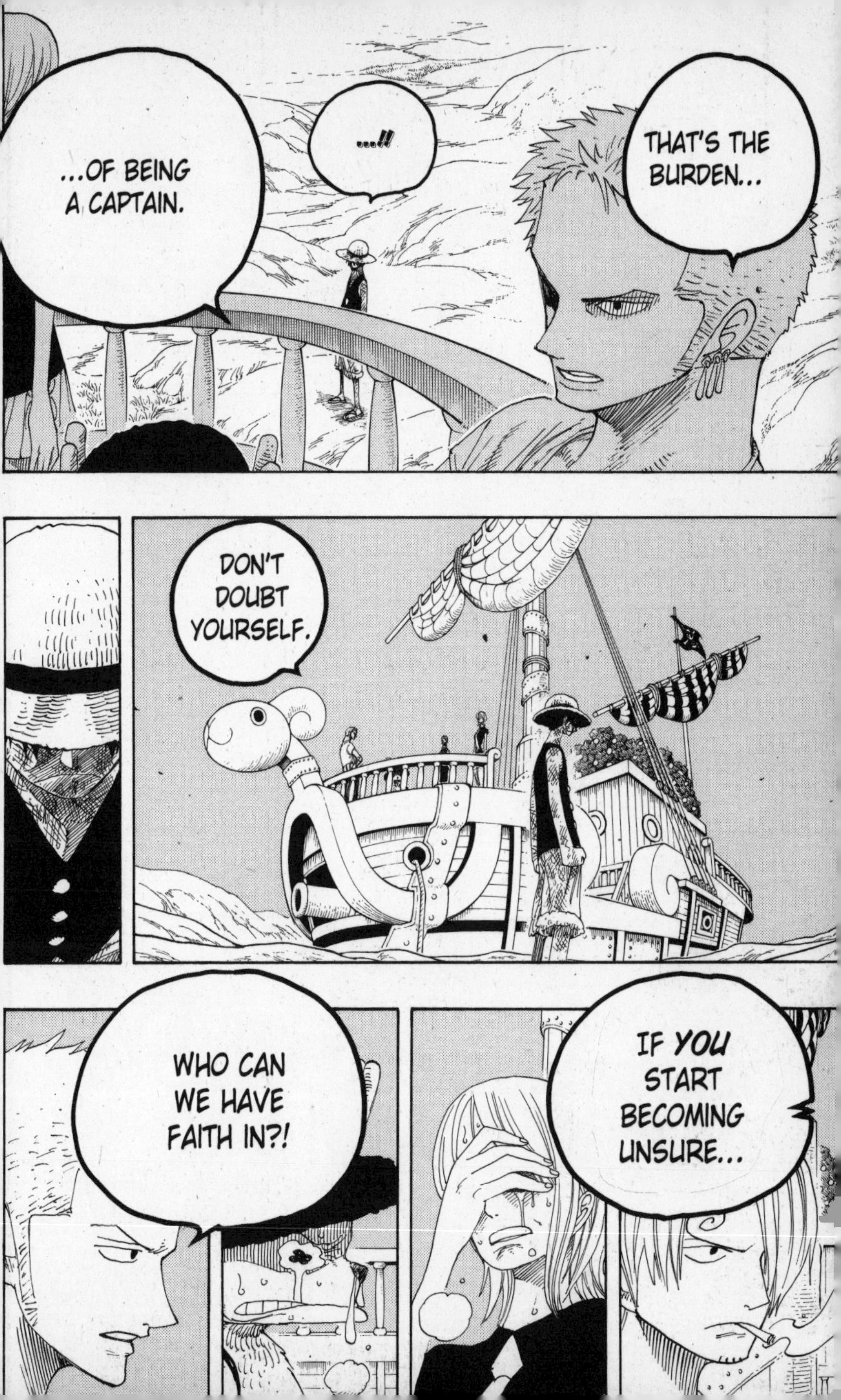
THAT'S THE BURDEN...
...!!
...OF BEING A CAPTAIN.
DON'T DOUBT YOURSELF.
IF *YOU* START BECOMING UNSURE...
WHO CAN WE HAVE FAITH IN?!

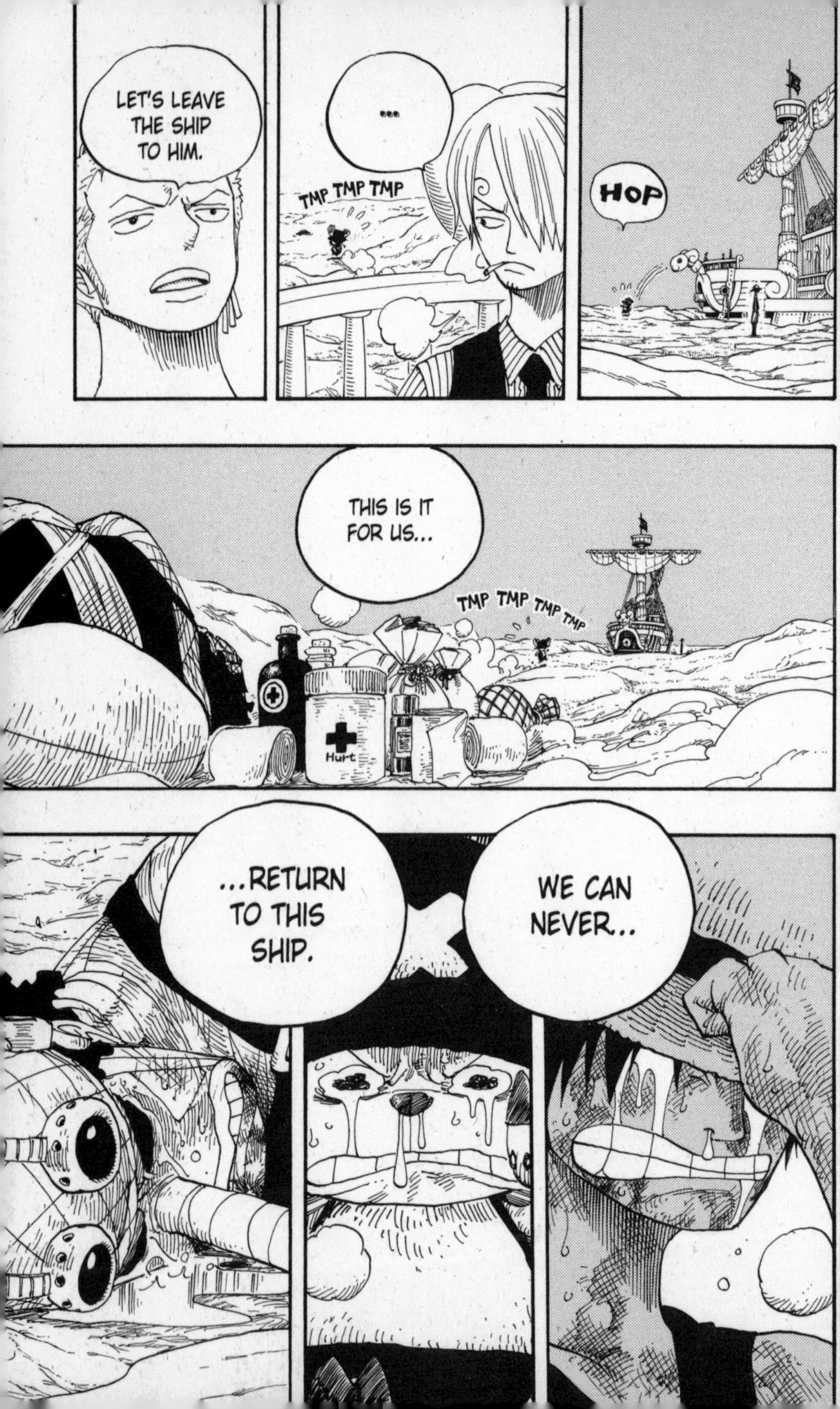
HOP
...
TMP TMP TMP
LET'S LEAVE THE SHIP TO HIM.
THIS IS IT FOR US...
TMP TMP TMP TMP TMP
Hurt
WE CAN NEVER...
...RETURN TO THIS SHIP.

N THE SECRET ROOM

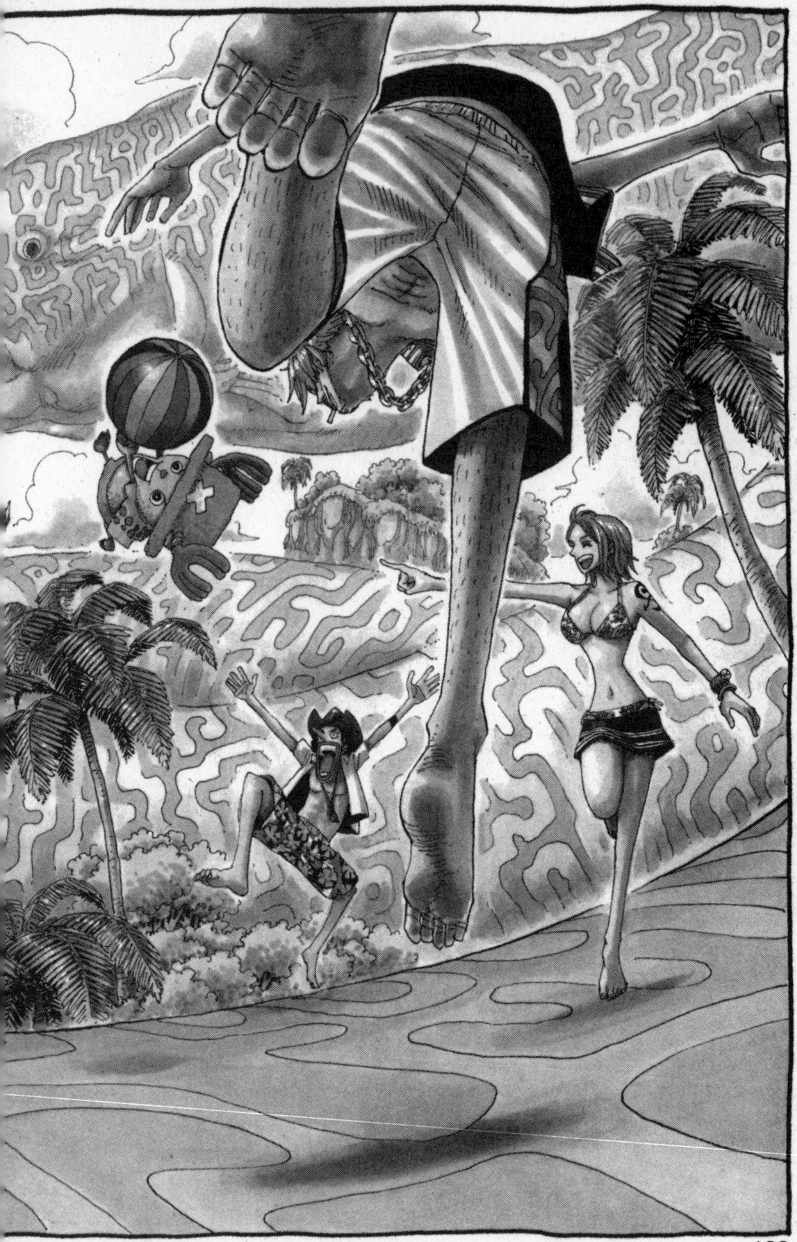

Chapter 334: BIG TROUBLE

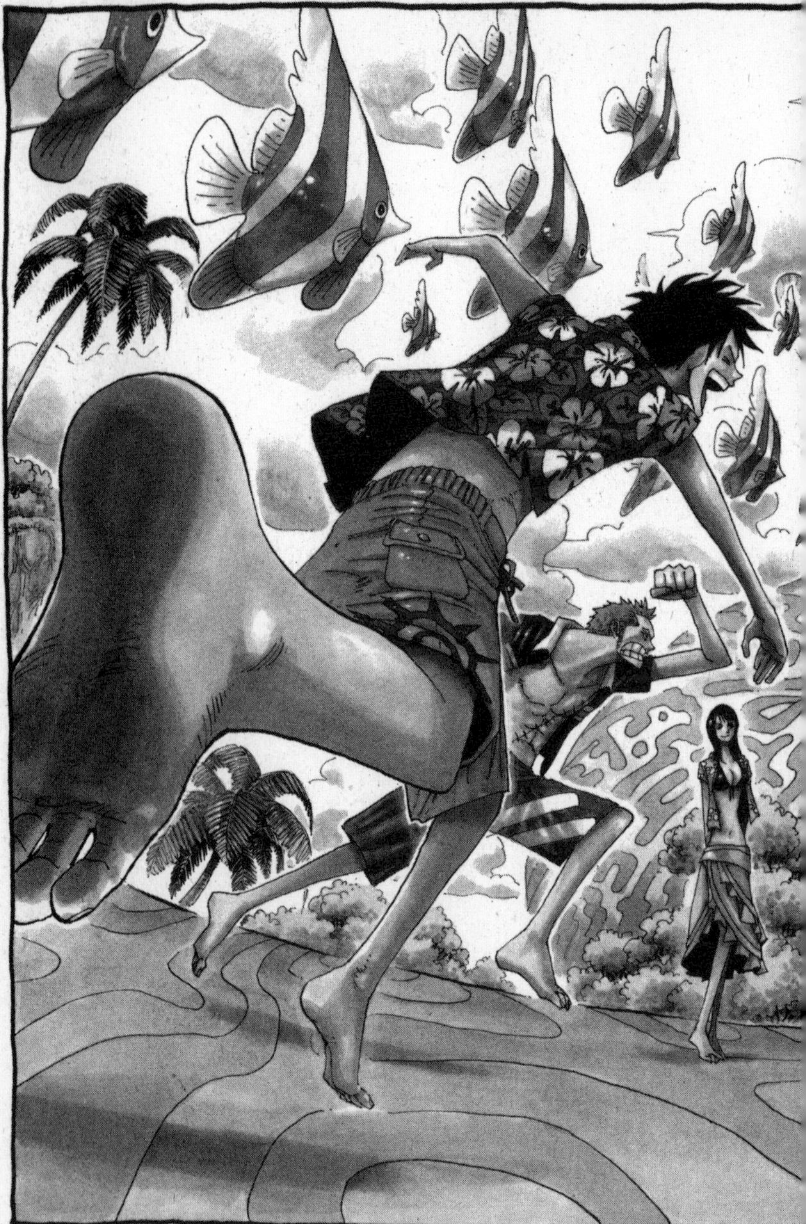

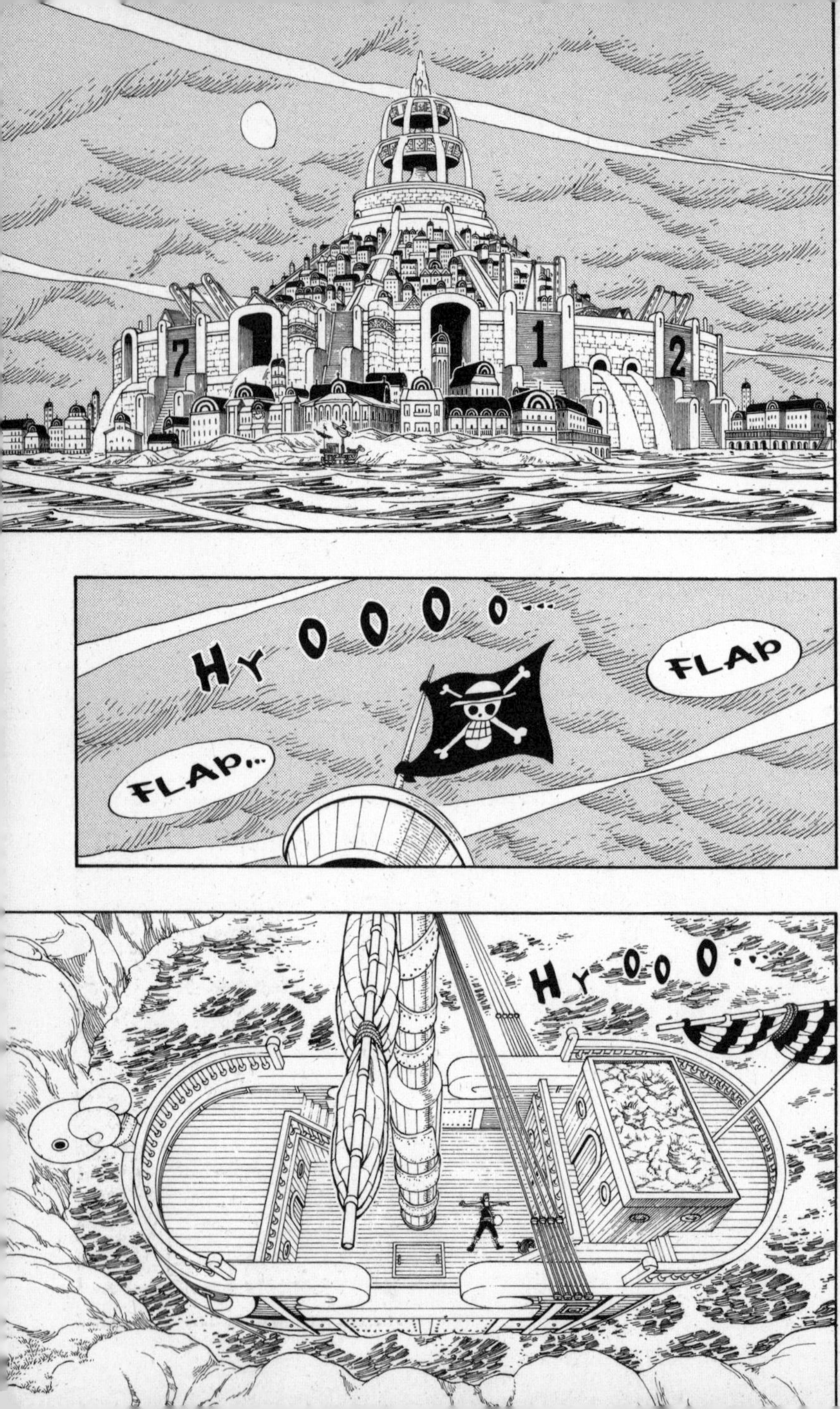
7
1
2
FLAP
HYOOOO...
FLAP...
HYOOO...

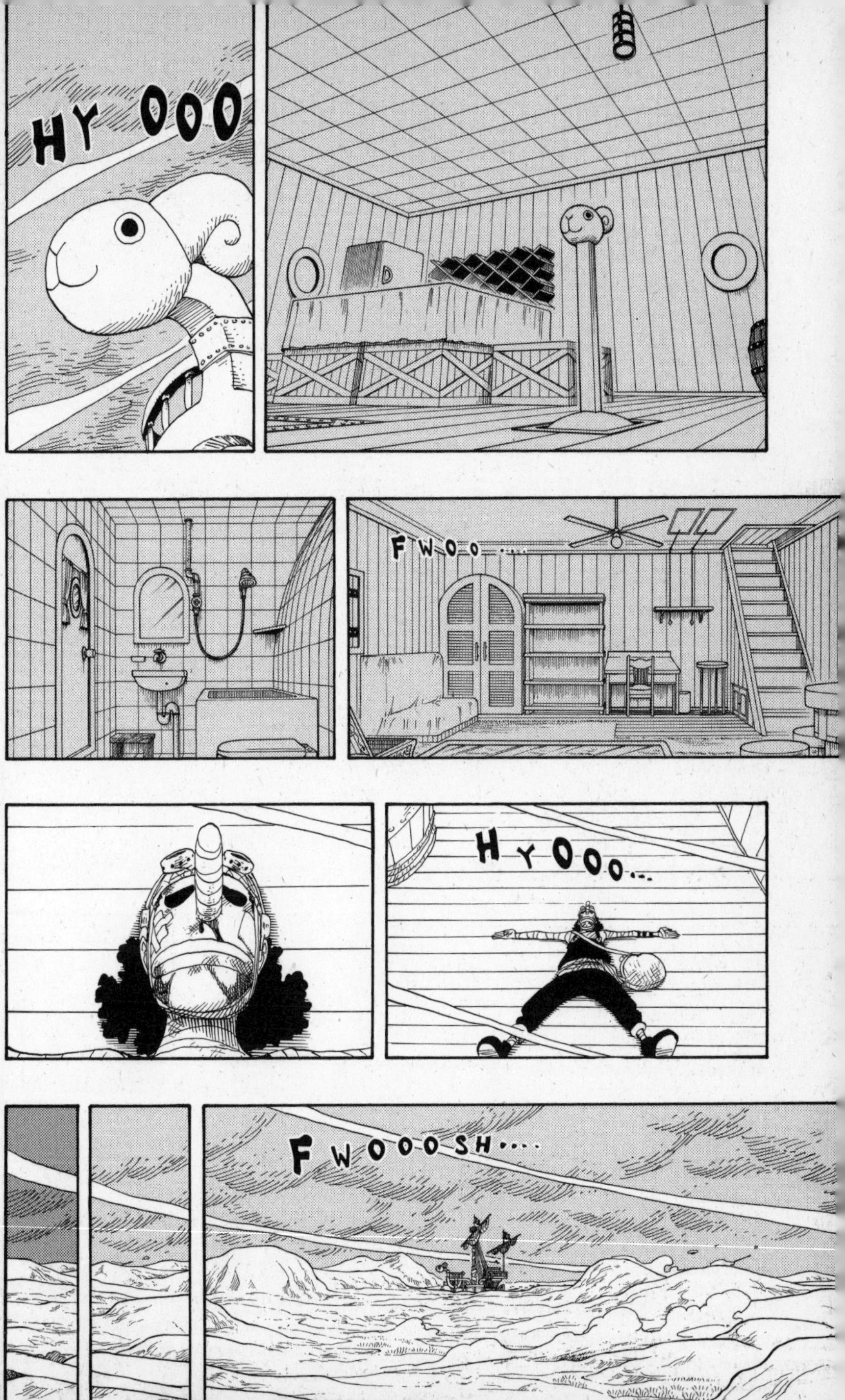
HYOOO
FWOO...
HYOOO...
FWOOOSH...

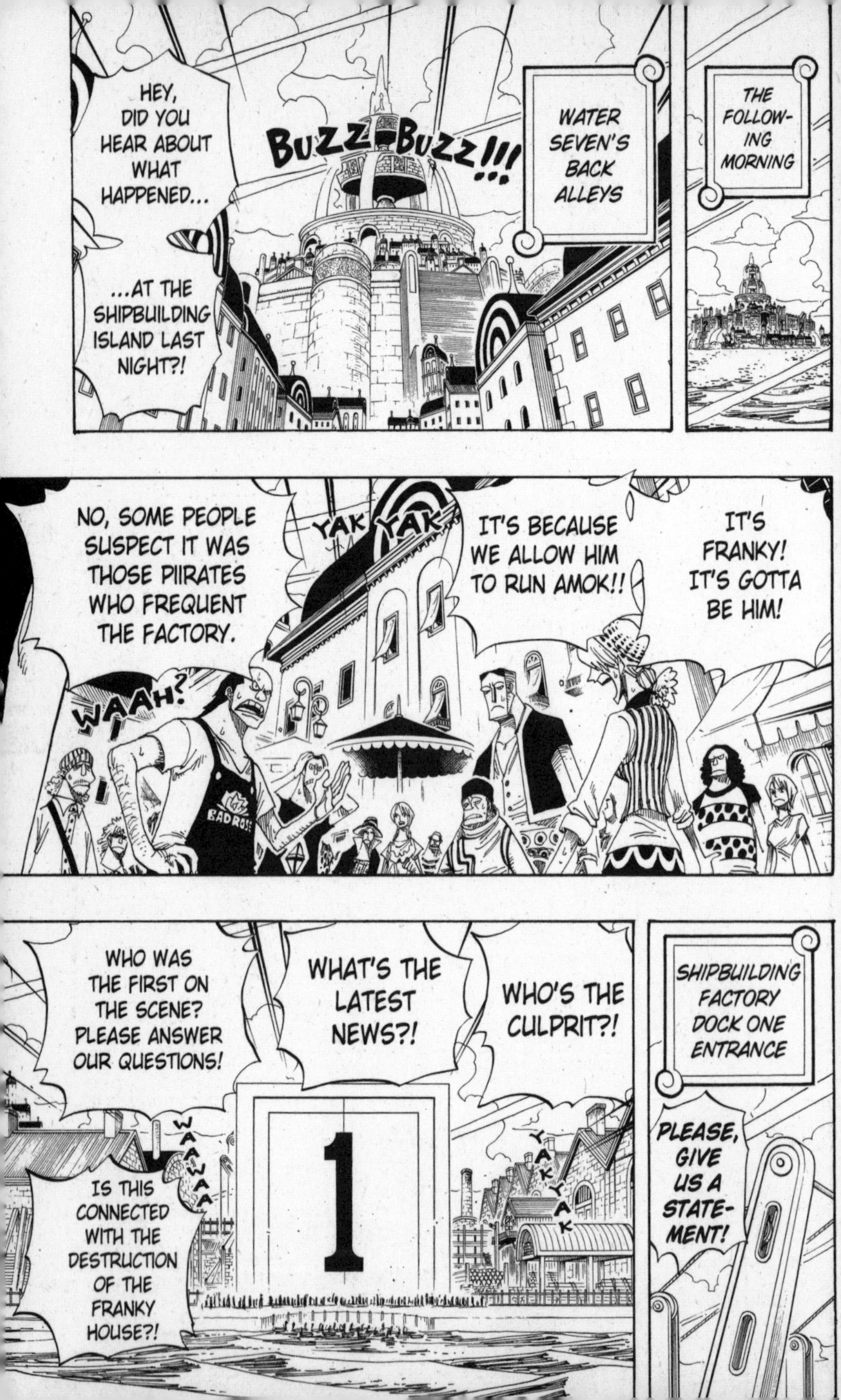
THE FOLLOWING MORNING
WATER SEVEN'S BACK ALLEYS
BUZZ BUZZ!!!
HEY, DID YOU HEAR ABOUT WHAT HAPPENED...
...AT THE SHIPBUILDING ISLAND LAST NIGHT?!
IT'S FRANKY! IT'S GOTTA BE HIM!
IT'S BECAUSE WE ALLOW HIM TO RUN AMOK!!
YAK YAK
NO, SOME PEOPLE SUSPECT IT WAS THOSE PIIRATES WHO FREQUENT THE FACTORY.
WAAH?
SHIPBUILDING FACTORY DOCK ONE ENTRANCE
PLEASE, GIVE US A STATEMENT!
WHO'S THE CULPRIT?!
YAK YAK
WHAT'S THE LATEST NEWS?!
1
WHO WAS THE FIRST ON THE SCENE? PLEASE ANSWER OUR QUESTIONS!
WAA WAA
IS THIS CONNECTED WITH THE DESTRUCTION OF THE FRANKY HOUSE?!

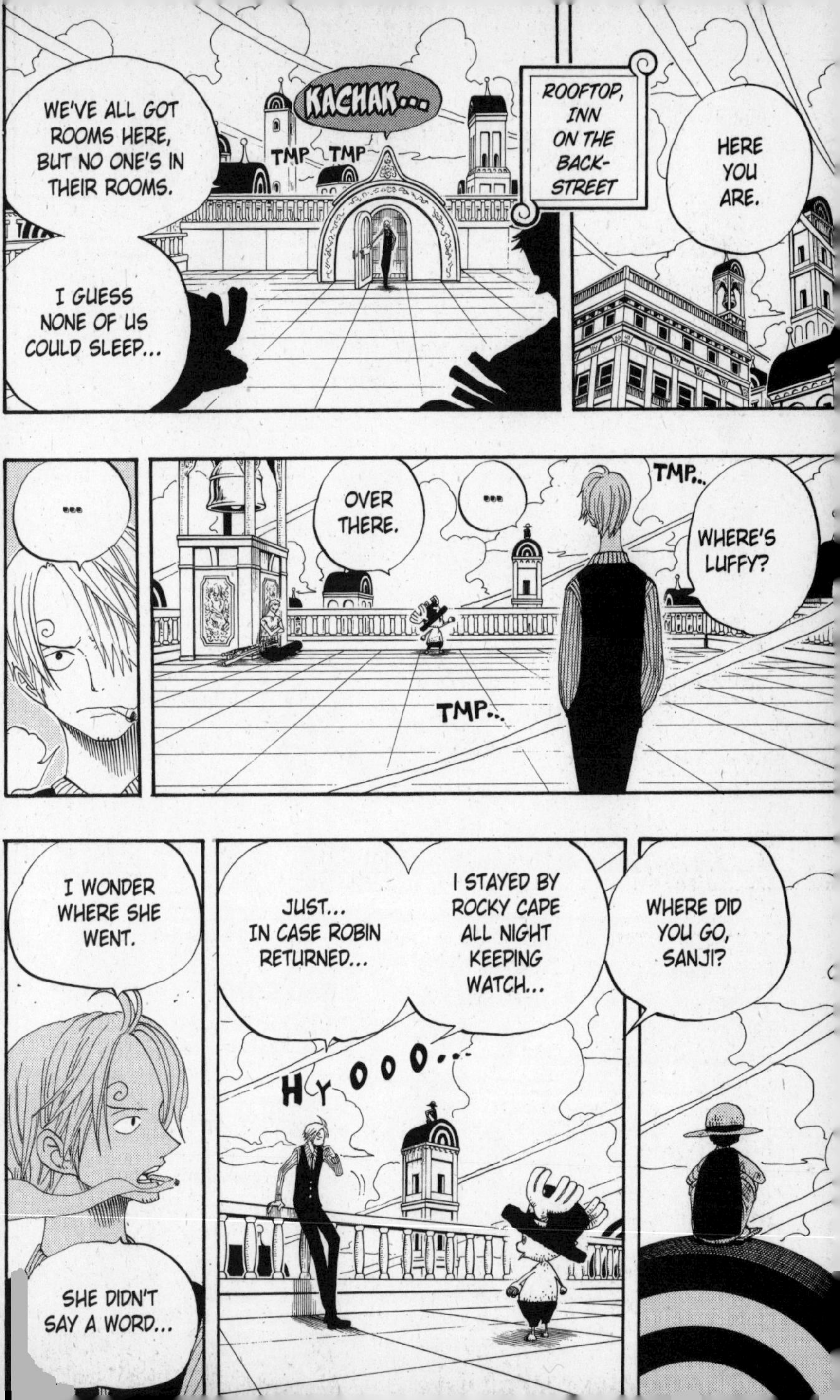
HERE YOU ARE.
ROOFTOP, INN ON THE BACK-STREET
KACHAK...
TMP TMP
WE'VE ALL GOT ROOMS HERE, BUT NO ONE'S IN THEIR ROOMS.
I GUESS NONE OF US COULD SLEEP...
TMP...
WHERE'S LUFFY?
...
OVER THERE.
TMP...
...
WHERE DID YOU GO, SANJI?
I STAYED BY ROCKY CAPE ALL NIGHT KEEPING WATCH...
JUST... IN CASE ROBIN RETURNED...
HYOOO...
I WONDER WHERE SHE WENT.
SHE DIDN'T SAY A WORD...

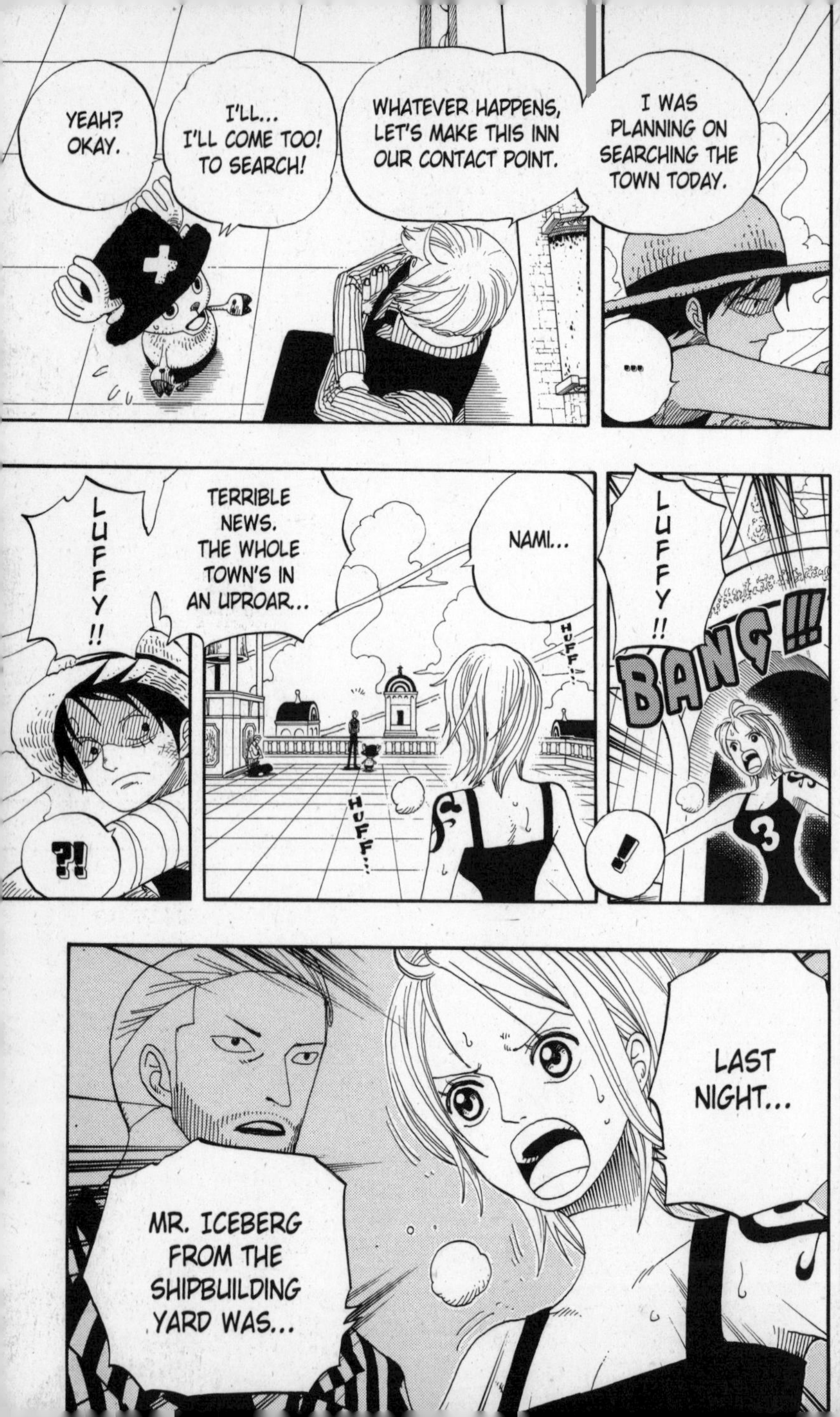
I WAS PLANNING ON SEARCHING THE TOWN TODAY.
...
WHATEVER HAPPENS, LET'S MAKE THIS INN OUR CONTACT POINT.
I'LL... I'LL COME TOO! TO SEARCH!
YEAH? OKAY.
LUFFY!!
BANG!!!
!
NAMI...
HUFF
TERRIBLE NEWS. THE WHOLE TOWN'S IN AN UPROAR...
HUFF
LUFFY!!
?!
LAST NIGHT...
MR. ICEBERG FROM THE SHIPBUILDING YARD WAS...

MR. ICEBERG WAS SHOT AT HIS HOME?!

HEY! DON'T KID AROUND. WAS HE KILLED?

HE DOESN'T HAVE A LOT OF ENEMIES...

HOLD ON. CALM DOWN AND LISTEN!

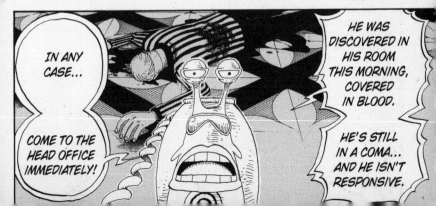

HE WAS DISCOVERED IN HIS ROOM THIS MORNING, COVERED IN BLOOD.

HE'S STILL IN A COMA... AND HE ISN'T RESPONSIVE.

IN ANY CASE...

COME TO THE HEAD OFFICE IMMEDIATELY!

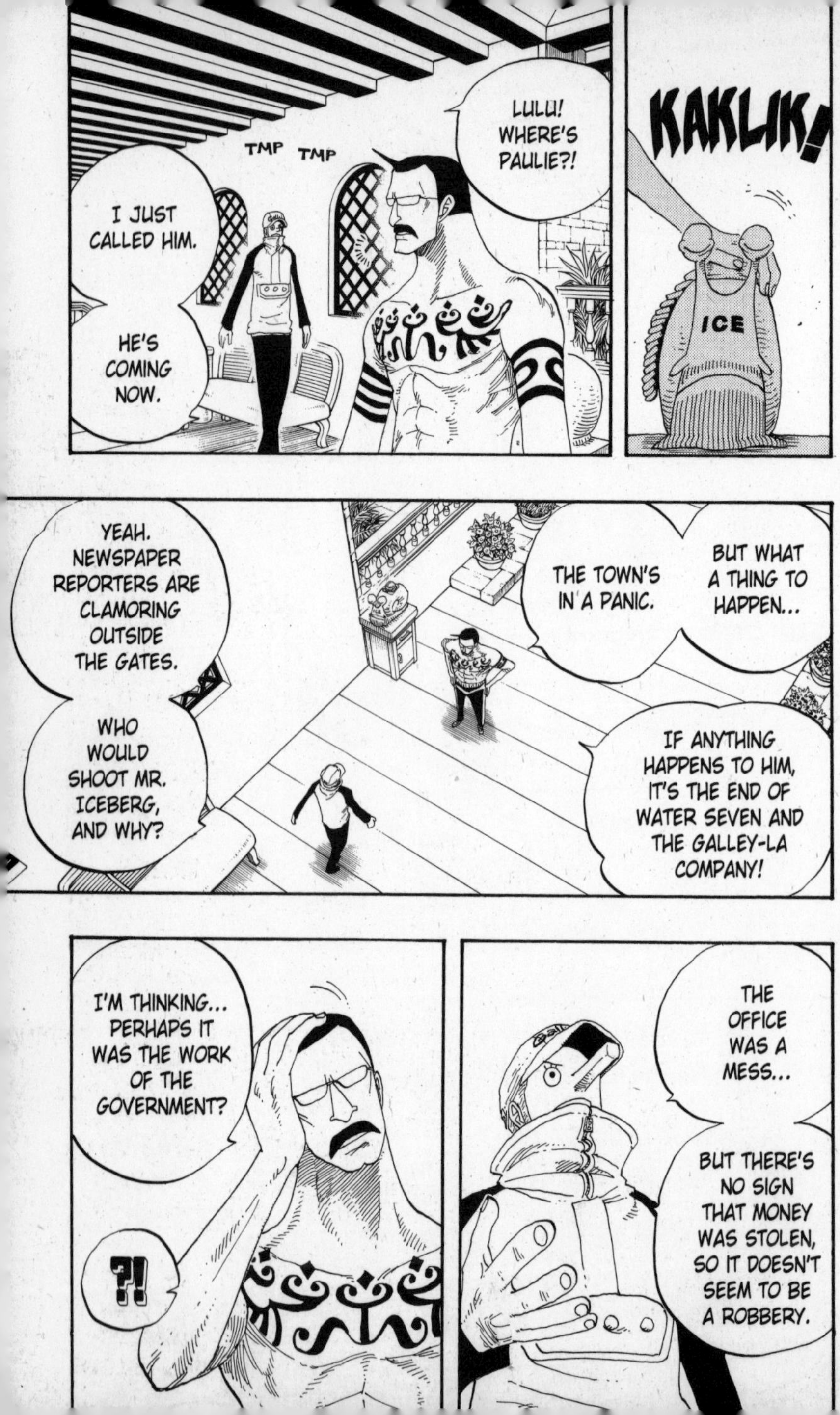
KAKLIK!
ICE
LULU! WHERE'S PAULIE?!
TMP TMP
I JUST CALLED HIM.
HE'S COMING NOW.
BUT WHAT A THING TO HAPPEN...
THE TOWN'S IN A PANIC.
IF ANYTHING HAPPENS TO HIM, IT'S THE END OF WATER SEVEN AND THE GALLEY-LA COMPANY!
YEAH. NEWSPAPER REPORTERS ARE CLAMORING OUTSIDE THE GATES.
WHO WOULD SHOOT MR. ICEBERG, AND WHY?
THE OFFICE WAS A MESS...
BUT THERE'S NO SIGN THAT MONEY WAS STOLEN, SO IT DOESN'T SEEM TO BE A ROBBERY.
I'M THINKING... PERHAPS IT WAS THE WORK OF THE GOVERNMENT?
?!

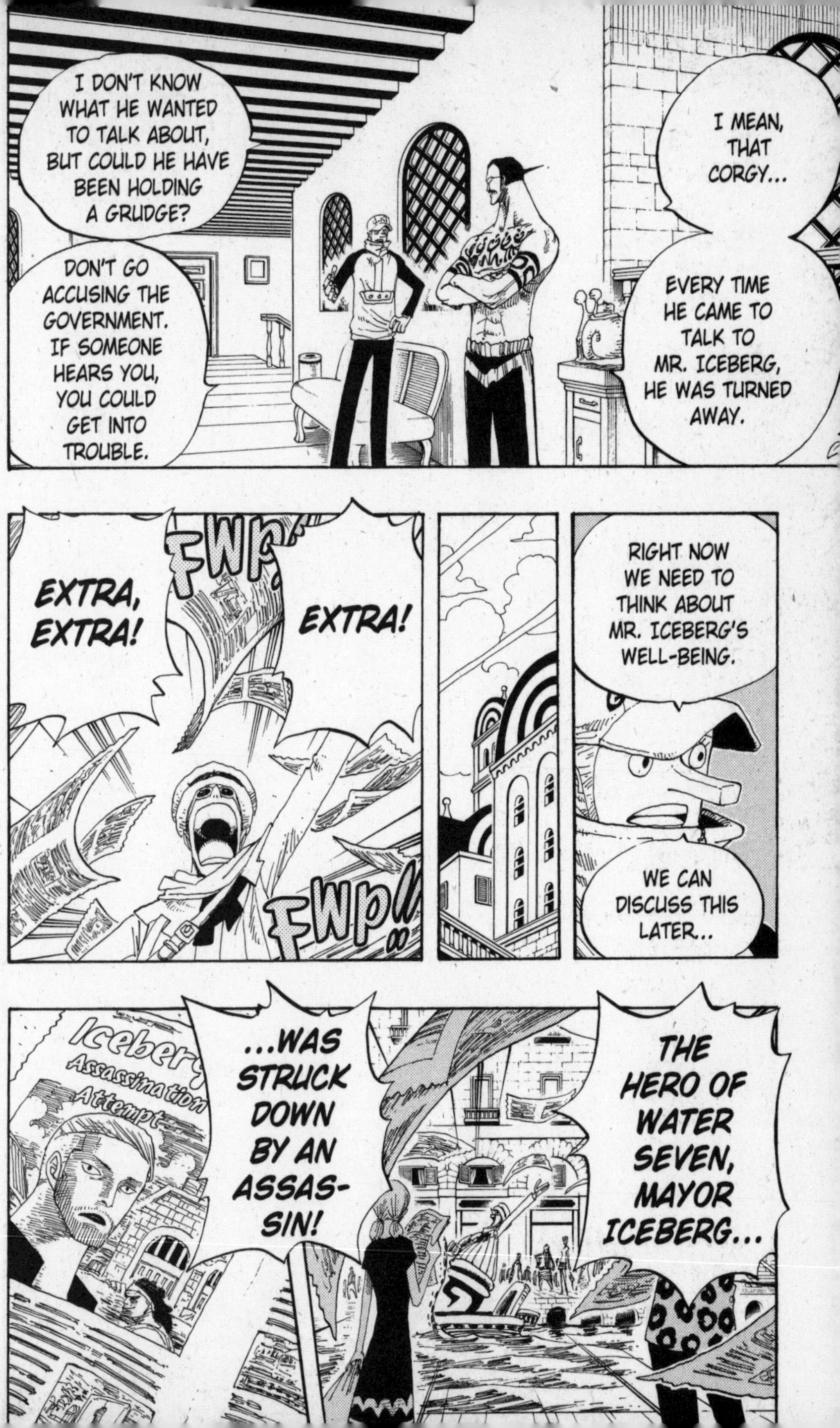
I MEAN, THAT CORGY...
EVERY TIME HE CAME TO TALK TO MR. ICEBERG, HE WAS TURNED AWAY.
I DON'T KNOW WHAT HE WANTED TO TALK ABOUT, BUT COULD HE HAVE BEEN HOLDING A GRUDGE?
DON'T GO ACCUSING THE GOVERNMENT. IF SOMEONE HEARS YOU, YOU COULD GET INTO TROUBLE.
RIGHT NOW WE NEED TO THINK ABOUT MR. ICEBERG'S WELL-BEING.
WE CAN DISCUSS THIS LATER...
EXTRA!
EXTRA, EXTRA!
FWP!!
THE HERO OF WATER SEVEN, MAYOR ICEBERG...
...WAS STRUCK DOWN BY AN ASSAS-SIN!
Assassination Attempt

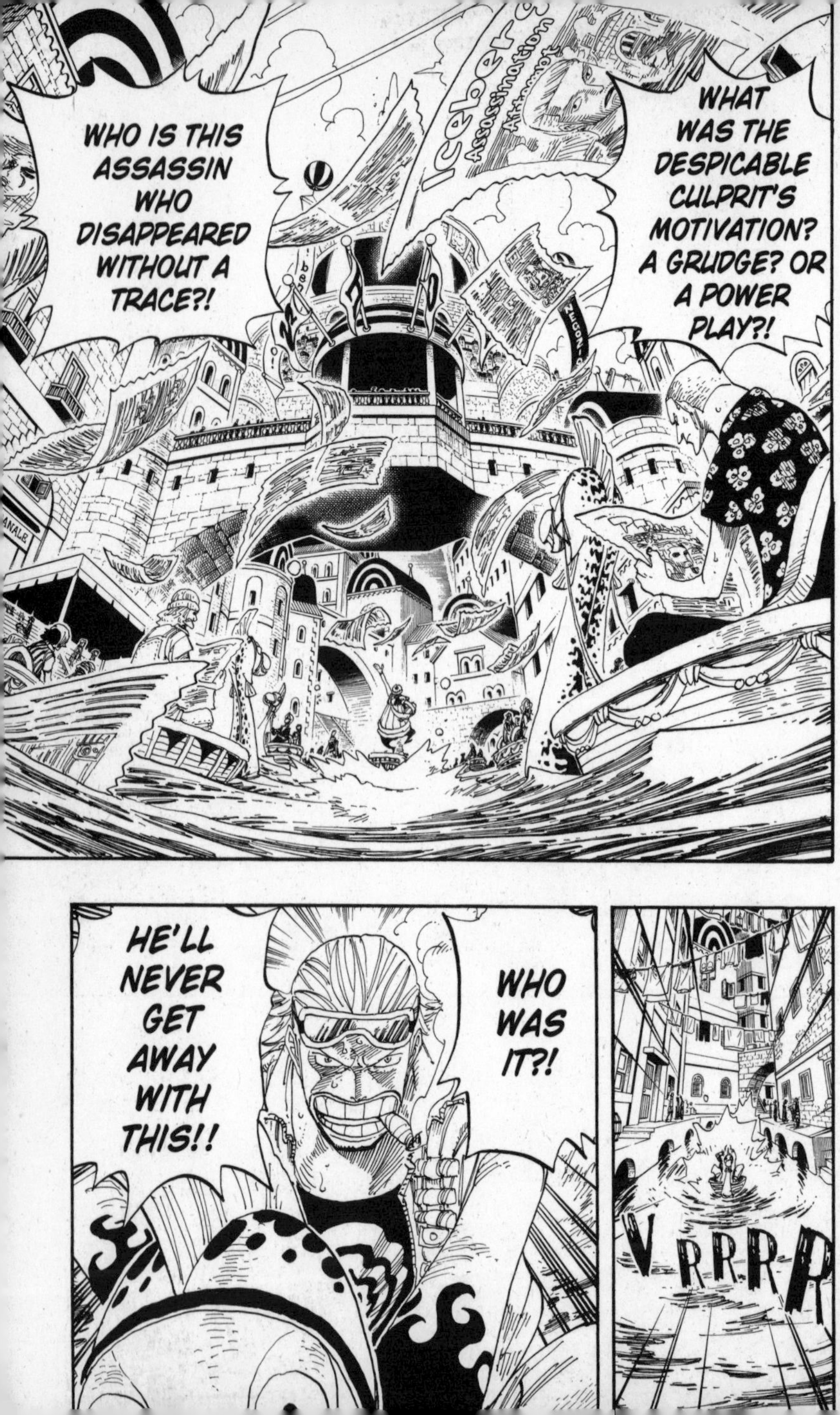
WHAT WAS THE DESPICABLE CULPRIT'S MOTIVATION? A GRUDGE? OR A POWER PLAY?!
WHO IS THIS ASSASSIN WHO DISAPPEARED WITHOUT A TRACE?!
VRRRR
WHO WAS IT?!
HE'LL NEVER GET AWAY WITH THIS!!

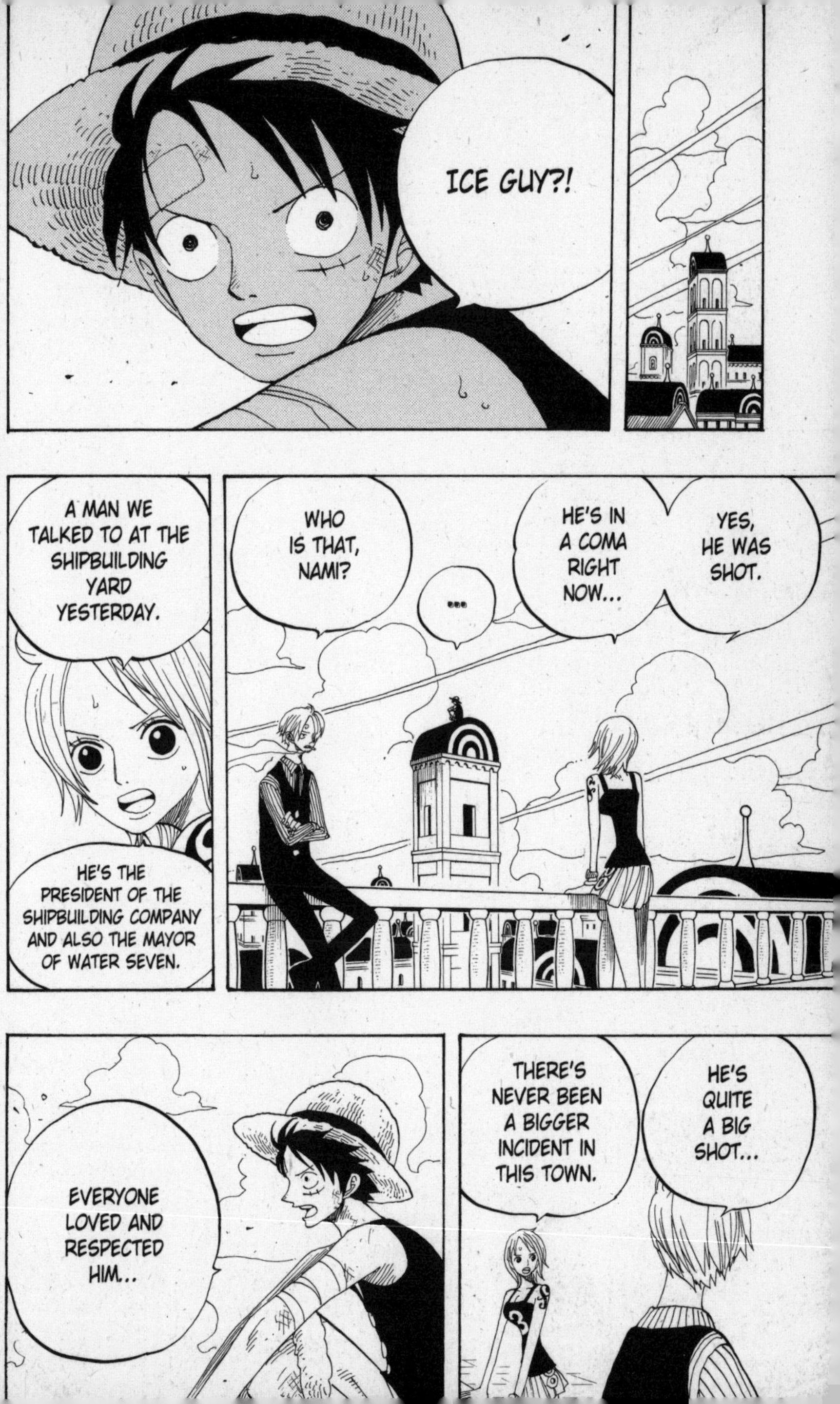
ICE GUY?!
YES, HE WAS SHOT.
HE'S IN A COMA RIGHT NOW...
...
WHO IS THAT, NAMI?
A MAN WE TALKED TO AT THE SHIPBUILDING YARD YESTERDAY.
HE'S THE PRESIDENT OF THE SHIPBUILDING COMPANY AND ALSO THE MAYOR OF WATER SEVEN.
HE'S QUITE A BIG SHOT...
THERE'S NEVER BEEN A BIGGER INCIDENT IN THIS TOWN.
EVERYONE LOVED AND RESPECTED HIM...

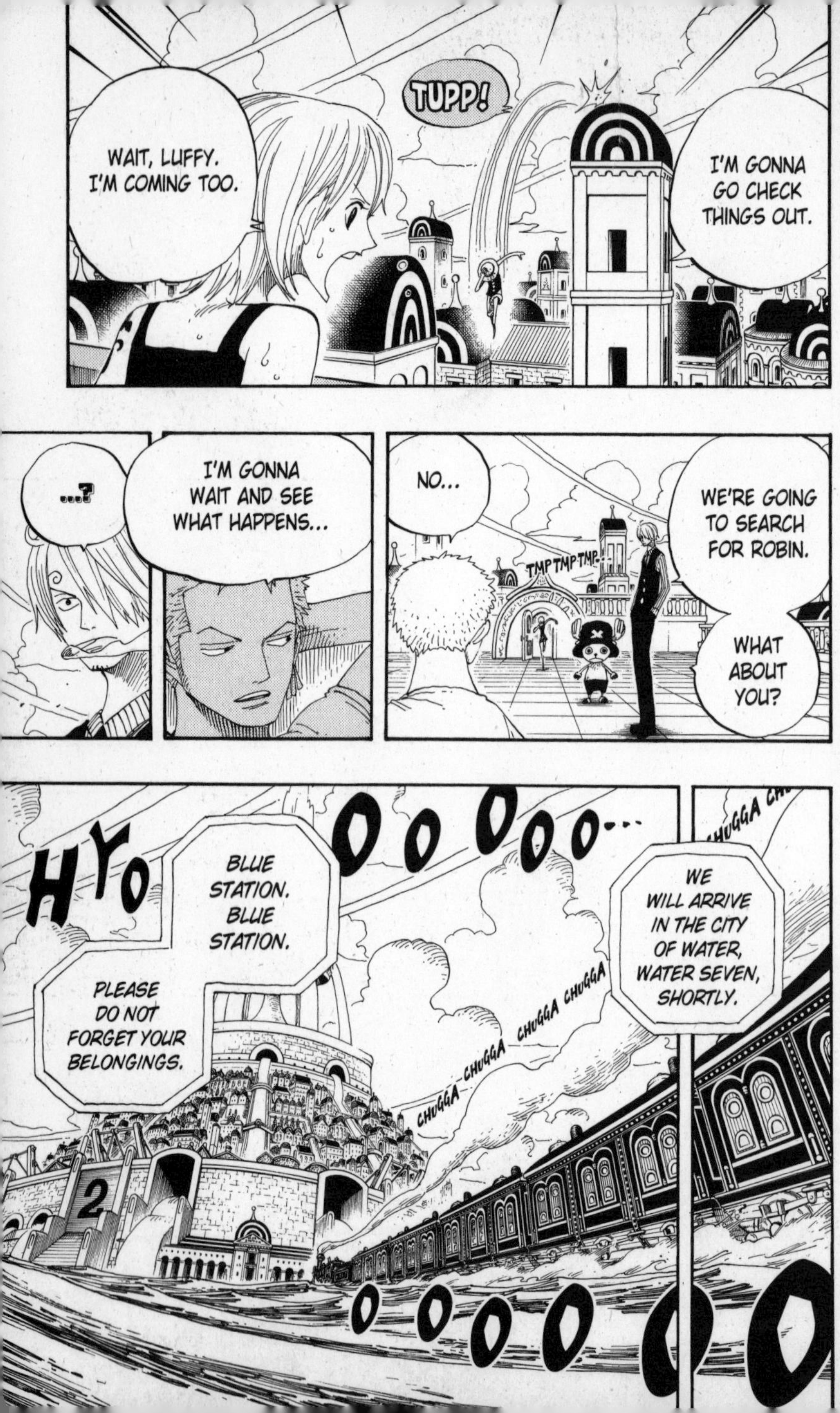
I'M GONNA GO CHECK THINGS OUT.
TUPP!
WAIT, LUFFY. I'M COMING TOO.
WE'RE GOING TO SEARCH FOR ROBIN.
WHAT ABOUT YOU?
NO...
TMP TMP TMP...
I'M GONNA WAIT AND SEE WHAT HAPPENS...
...?
CHUGGA CH
WE WILL ARRIVE IN THE CITY OF WATER, WATER SEVEN, SHORTLY.
HYO O O O O O...
BLUE STATION. BLUE STATION.
PLEASE DO NOT FORGET YOUR BELONGINGS.
CHUGGA CHUGGA CHUGGA CHUGGA
O O O O O O O O

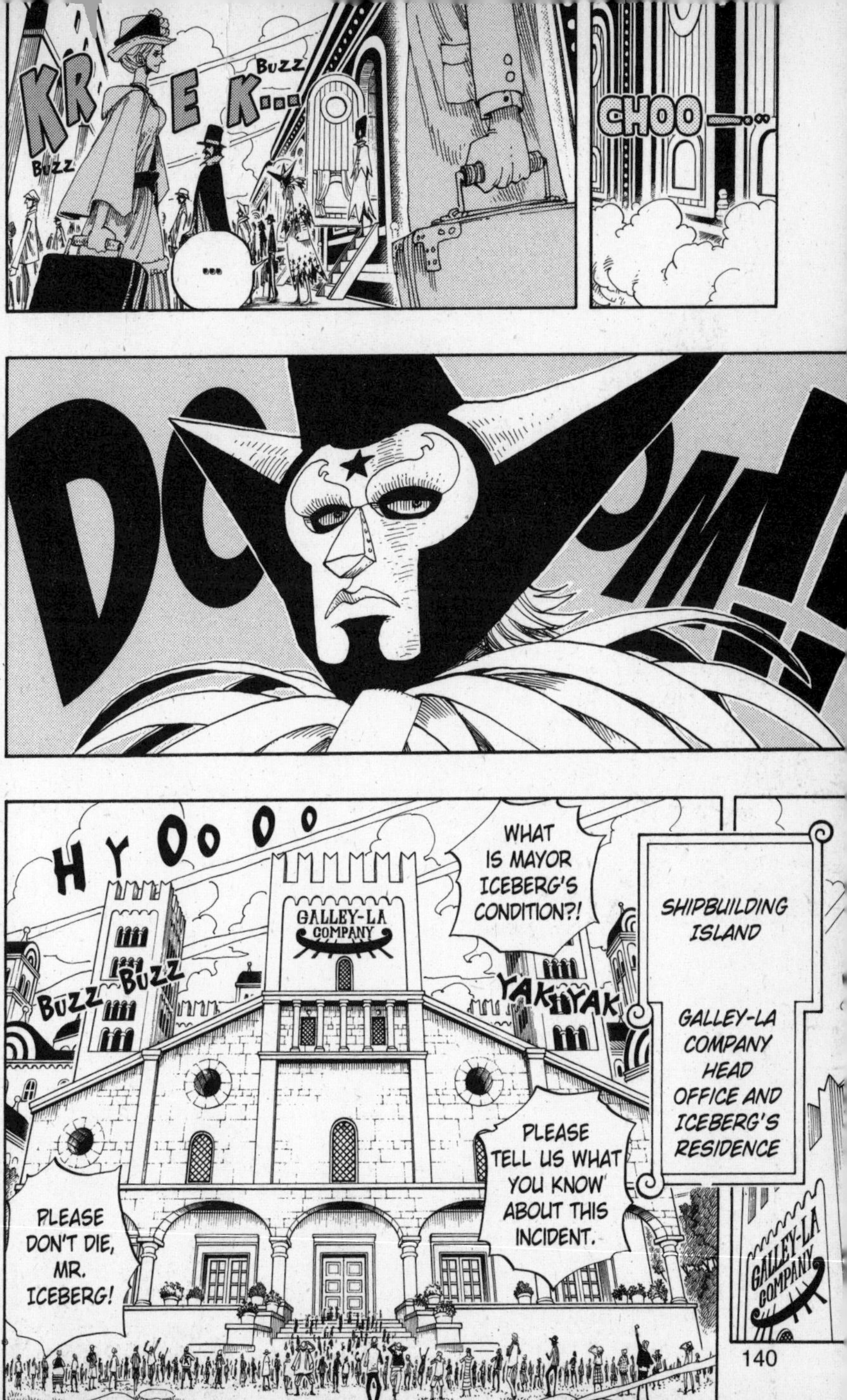
CHOO—…
KREK…
BUZZ
BUZZ
…
DO
OM!!
GALLEY-LA COMPANY
SHIPBUILDING ISLAND
GALLEY-LA COMPANY HEAD OFFICE AND ICEBERG'S RESIDENCE
WHAT IS MAYOR ICEBERG'S CONDITION?!
HYOOOO
GALLEY-LA COMPANY
YAK YAK
PLEASE TELL US WHAT YOU KNOW ABOUT THIS INCIDENT.
BUZZ BUZZ
PLEASE DON'T DIE, MR. ICEBERG!

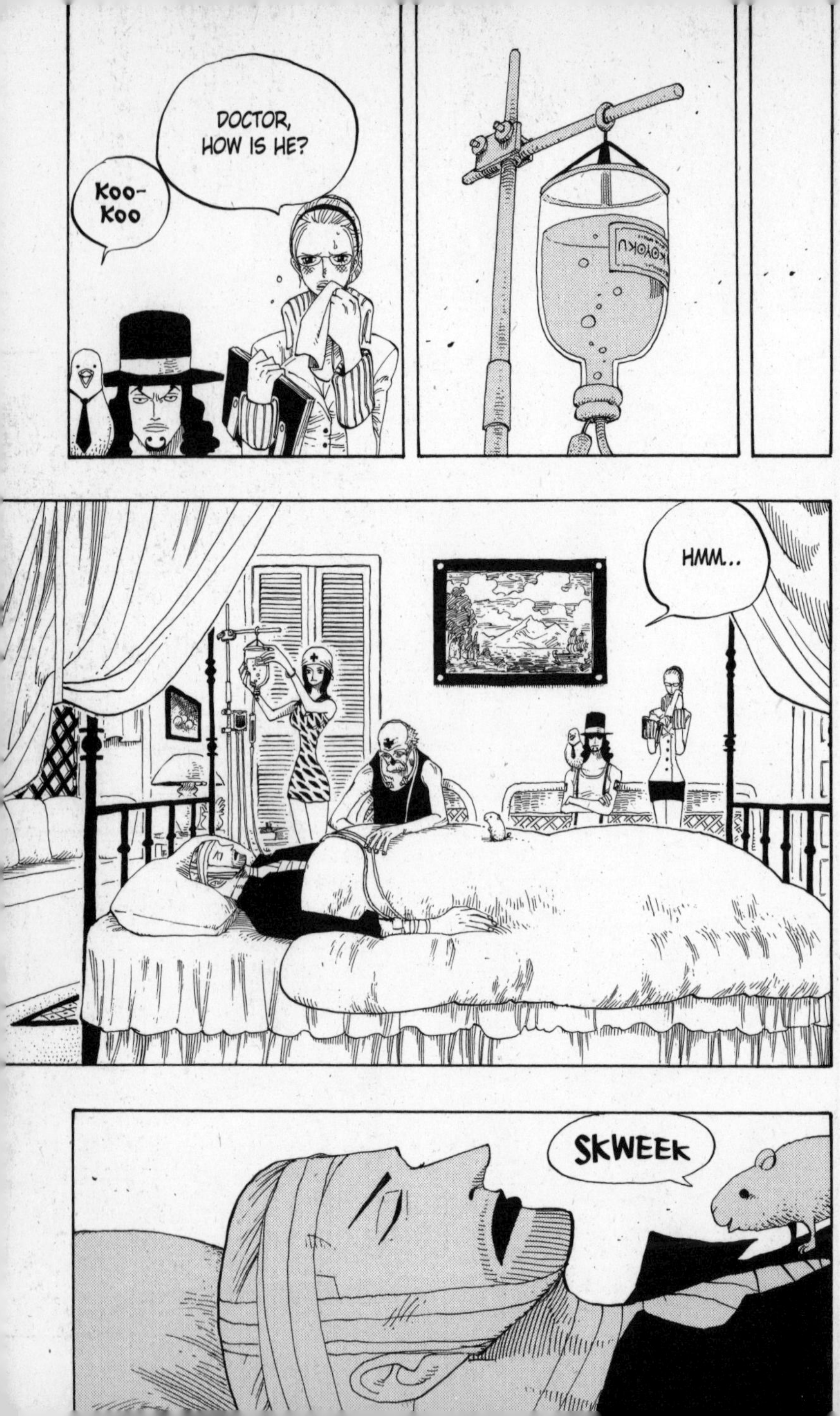
DOCTOR, HOW IS HE?
Koo-Koo
HMM...
SKWEEK

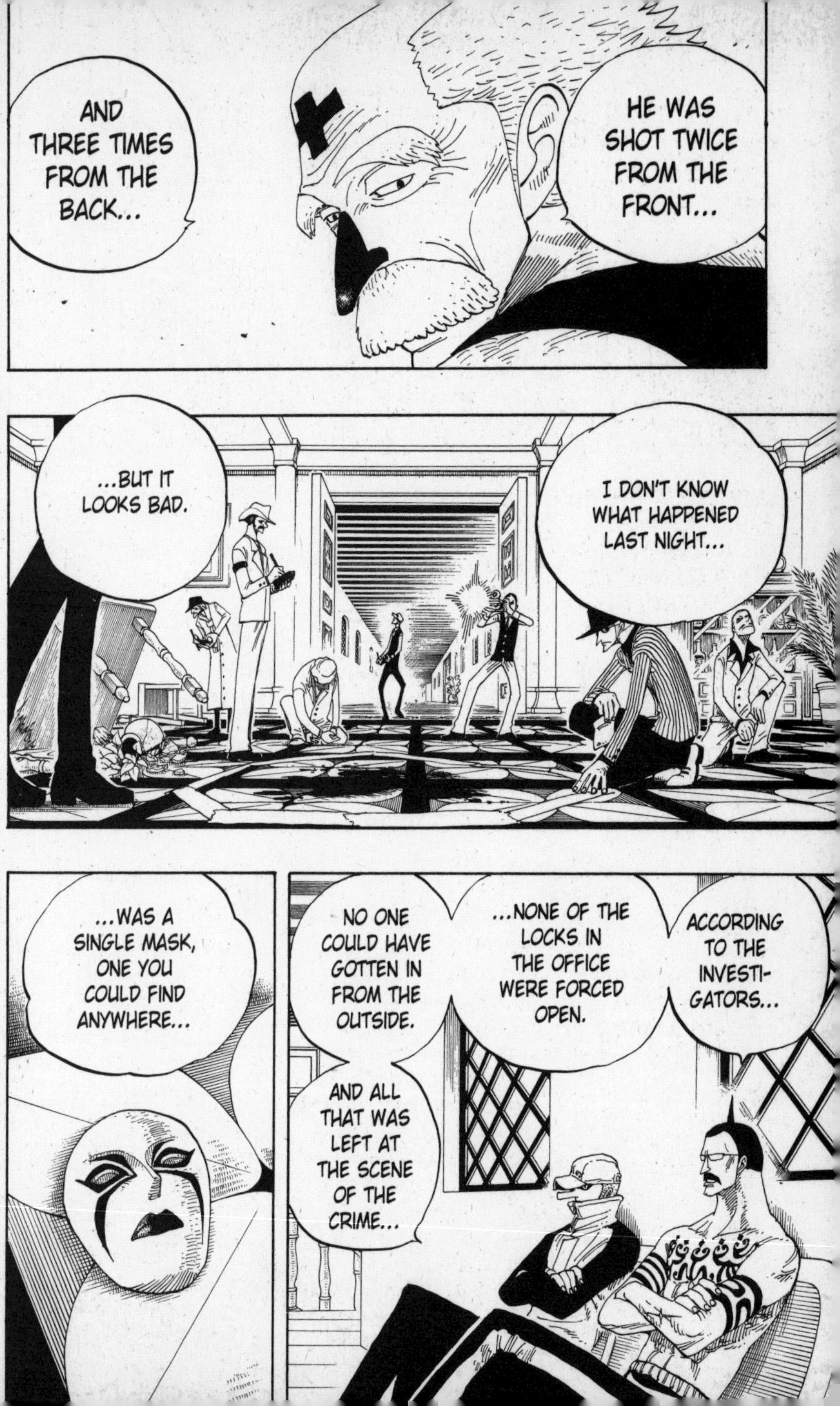
HE WAS SHOT TWICE FROM THE FRONT...
AND THREE TIMES FROM THE BACK...
I DON'T KNOW WHAT HAPPENED LAST NIGHT...
...BUT IT LOOKS BAD.
ACCORDING TO THE INVESTI- GATORS...
...NONE OF THE LOCKS IN THE OFFICE WERE FORCED OPEN.
NO ONE COULD HAVE GOTTEN IN FROM THE OUTSIDE.
AND ALL THAT WAS LEFT AT THE SCENE OF THE CRIME...
...WAS A SINGLE MASK, ONE YOU COULD FIND ANYWHERE...

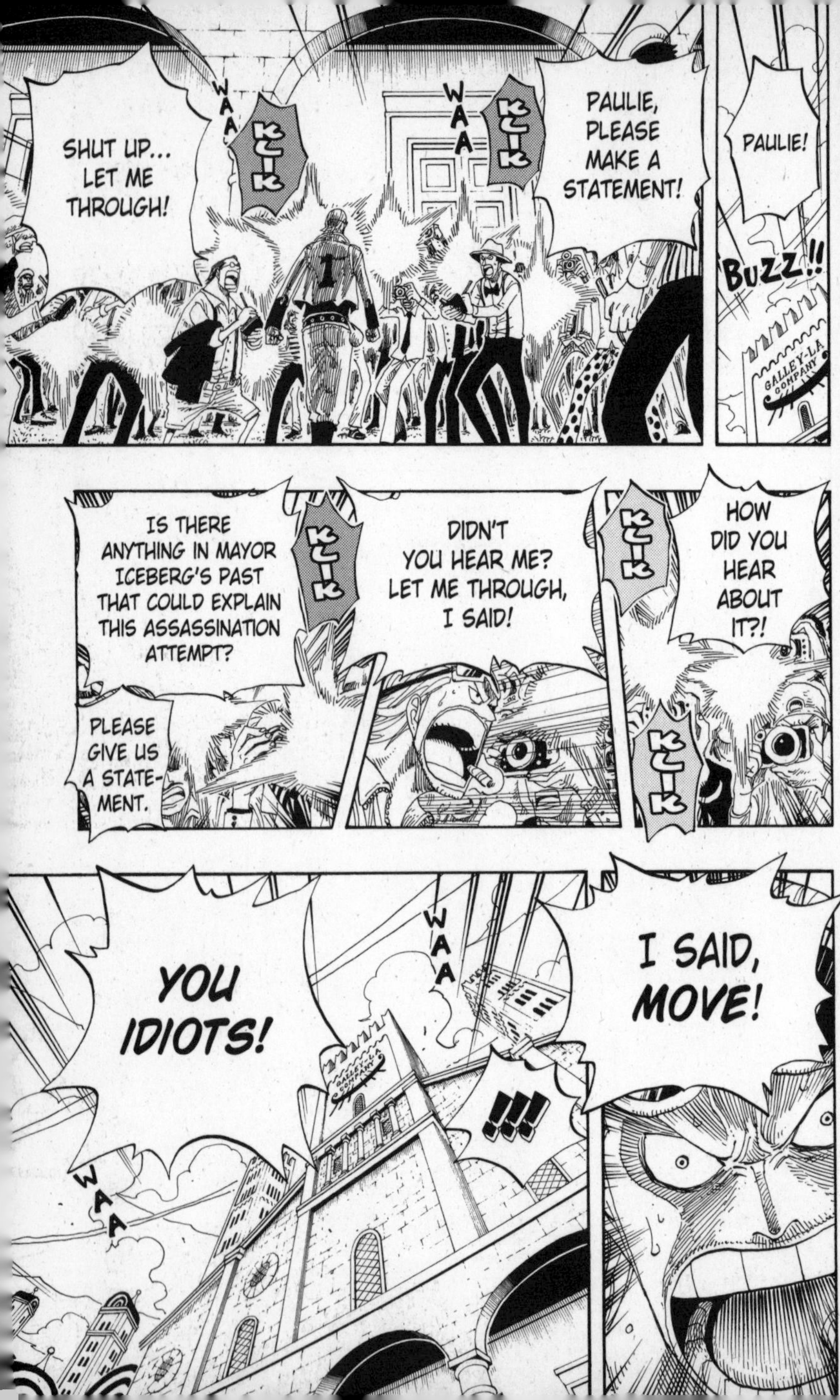
PAULIE!
BUZZ!!
GALLEY-LA COMPANY
PAULIE, PLEASE MAKE A STATEMENT!
KLIK
WAA
KLIK
WAA
SHUT UP... LET ME THROUGH!
HOW DID YOU HEAR ABOUT IT?!
KLIK
KLIK
DIDN'T YOU HEAR ME? LET ME THROUGH, I SAID!
KLIK
IS THERE ANYTHING IN MAYOR ICEBERG'S PAST THAT COULD EXPLAIN THIS ASSASSINATION ATTEMPT?
PLEASE GIVE US A STATE-MENT.
I SAID, MOVE!
!!!
WAA
GALLEY-LA COMPANY
YOU IDIOTS!
WAA

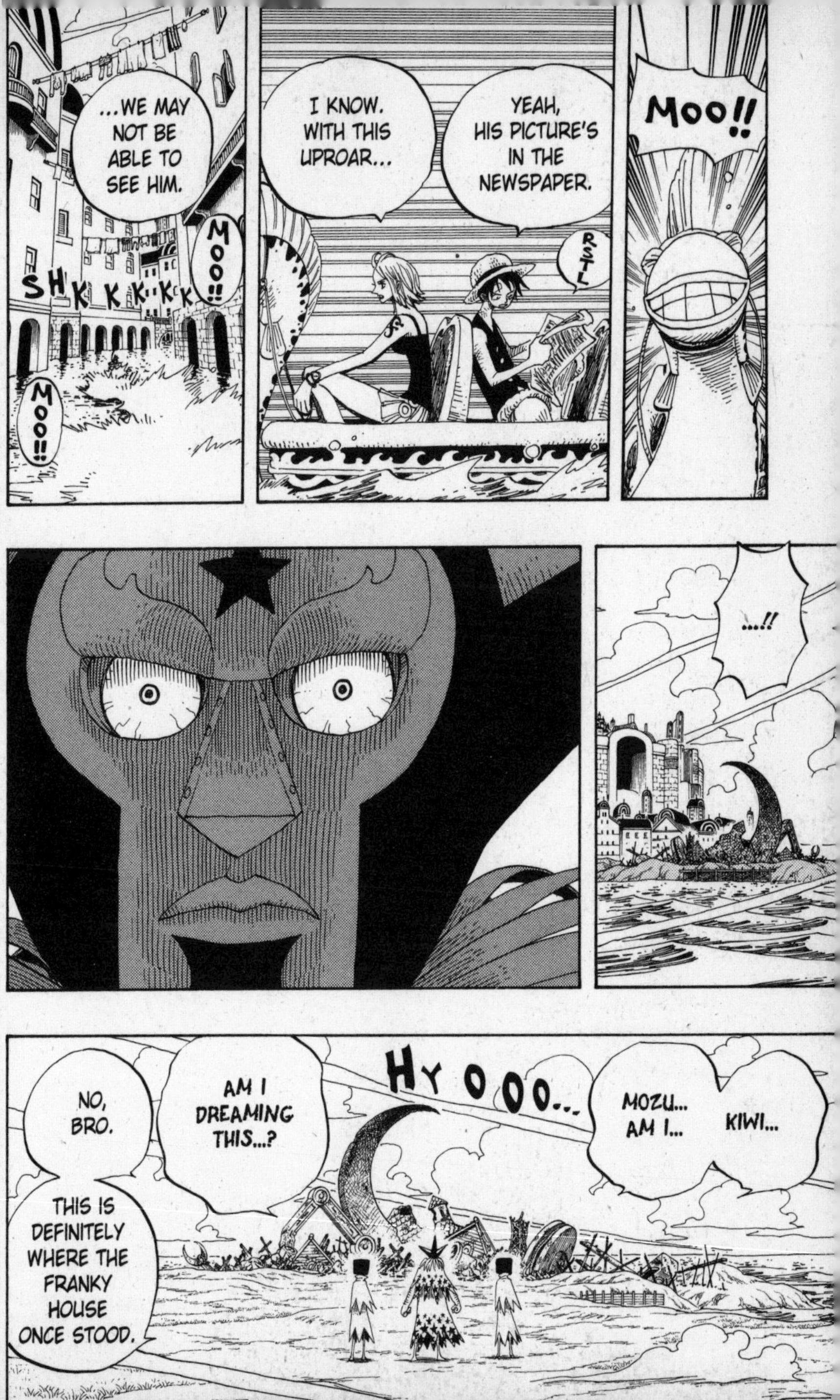
MOO!!
YEAH, HIS PICTURE'S IN THE NEWSPAPER.
RSTL
I KNOW. WITH THIS UPROAR...
...WE MAY NOT BE ABLE TO SEE HIM.
MOO!!
SHKKKKKK
MOO!!
...!!
MOZU... AM I...
KIWI...
HYOOO...
AM I DREAMING THIS...?
NO, BRO.
THIS IS DEFINITELY WHERE THE FRANKY HOUSE ONCE STOOD.

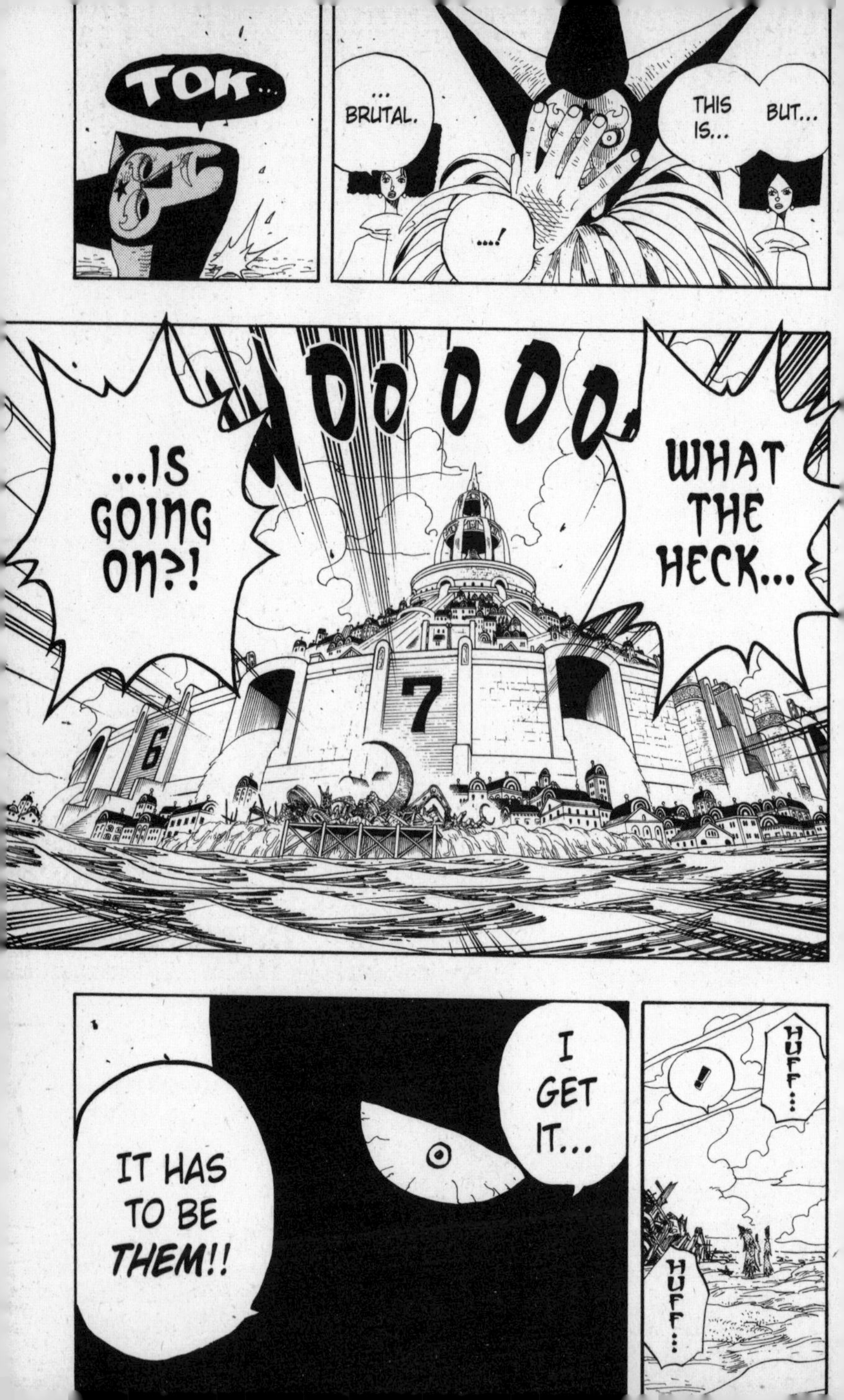
THIS IS... BUT...
...BRUTAL.
...!
TOK...
WHAT THE HECK...
...IS GOING ON?!
!
HUFF...
HUFF...
I GET IT...
IT HAS TO BE THEM!!

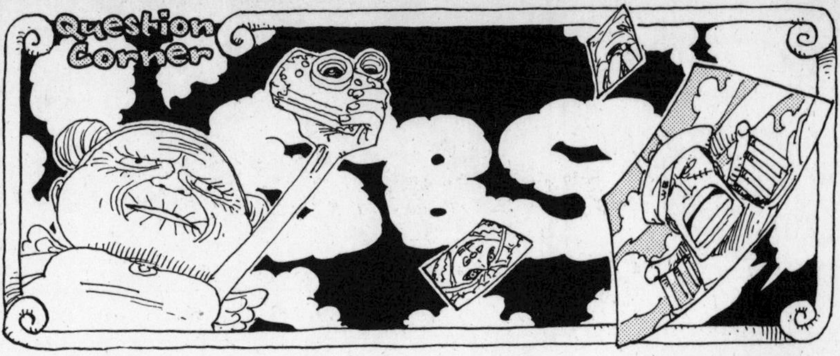
Question Corner

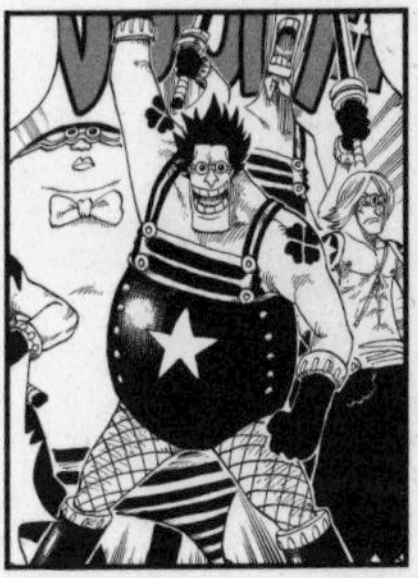

Q: Hello, Oda Sensei. In volume 34, there's a member of the Franky Family who wears fishnet stockings even though he's a guy. Is that just about fashion? Or is it your personal taste? It bothers me so much I can't even sleep in class. Please tell me.

--Sa→ko

A: Let me make this crystal clear, that is not my personal taste at all...

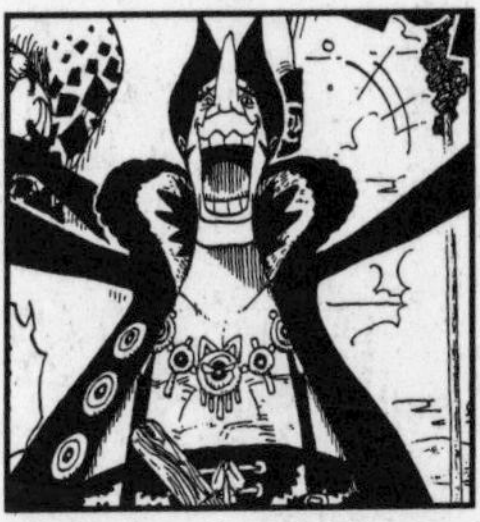

Q: Oda Sensei, I'm really bothered by this, so please tell me. Regarding Foxy the Silver Fox's Slow-Slow Fruit: Please tell me, is it a Logia, Paramythia, or Zoan type? This is weighing on my mind so heavily, I can't even go to the bathroom. Please tell me.

A: It's a Paramythia (super-power) type.
The Logia (element) powers transform the body itself into something different. Zoan (animal) powers transform their holder into animals. Everything else are Paramythia (super-power) types.
However, there are Paramythia types that can transform the body too.

Q: There are so many who have Devil Fruit powers. Have you ever regretted not having Luffy eat something other than the Gum-Gum Fruit?

--Happi

A: Never. I really agonized over that before starting the series, but I never think about it anymore. I love rubber men.
Oh, but I have thought about 13 times that the "Sexy-Sexy Fruit" would've been good too.

Chapter 335:
WARNING

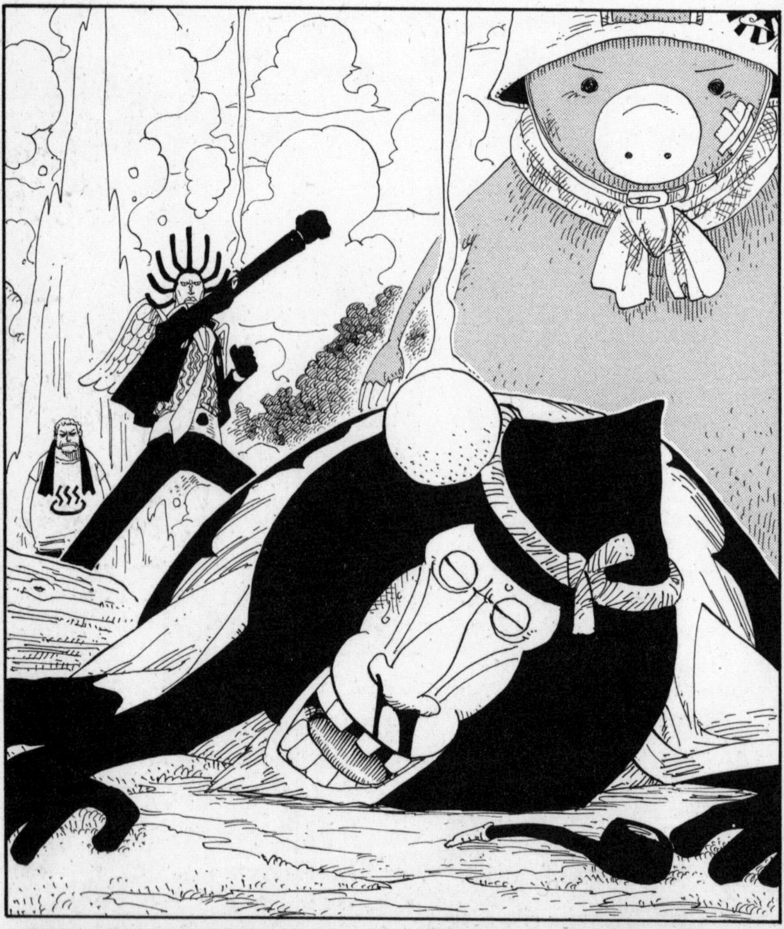

GEDATSU'S UNEXPECTED LIFE ON THE BLUE SEA, VOL. 19:
"THE SKY BOSS WHO MADE THE FOREST BOSS HIS HENCHMAN"

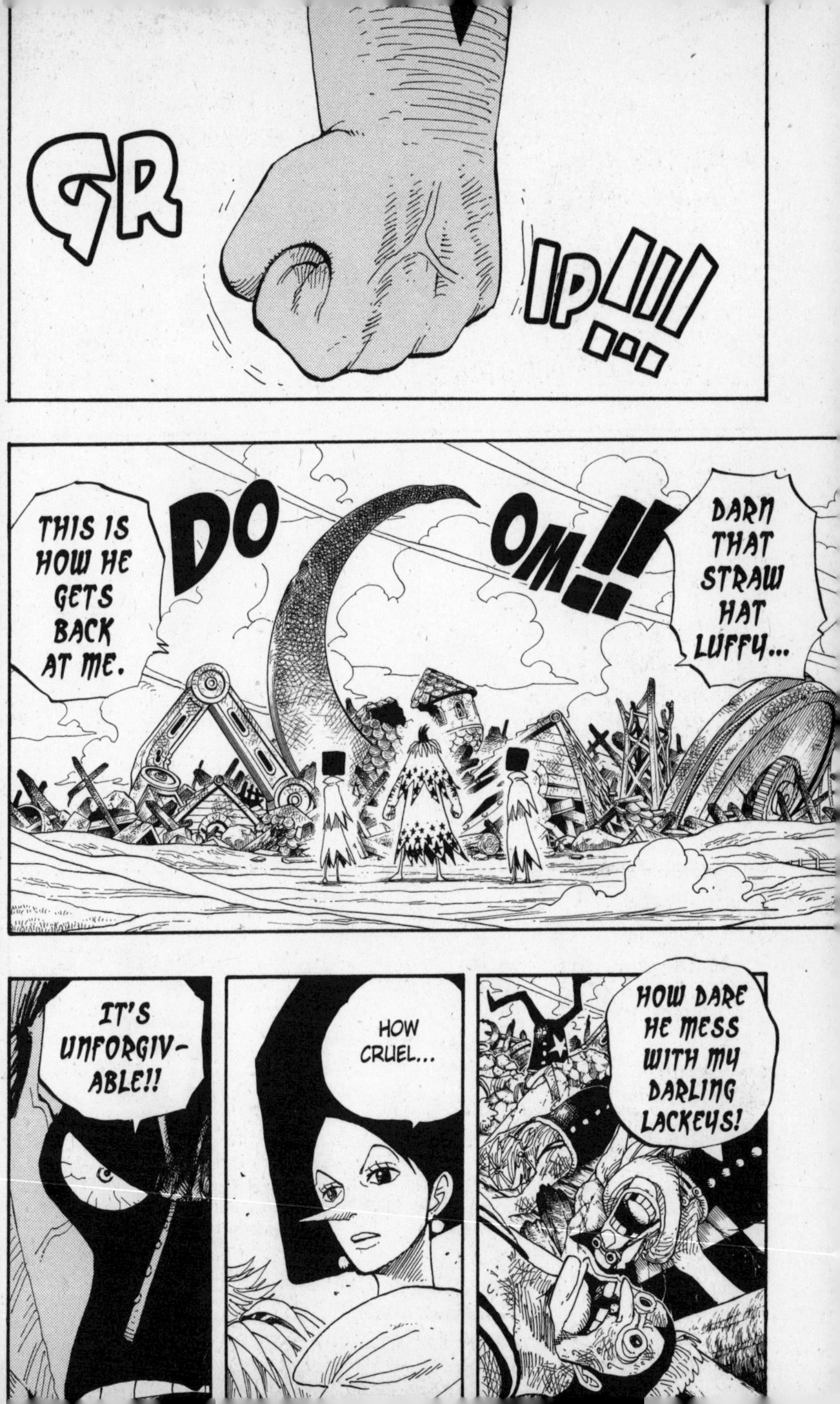
GRIP!!!
DARN THAT STRAW HAT LUFFY...
DOOM!!
THIS IS HOW HE GETS BACK AT ME.
HOW DARE HE MESS WITH MY DARLING LACKEYS!
HOW CRUEL...
IT'S UNFORGIV-ABLE!!

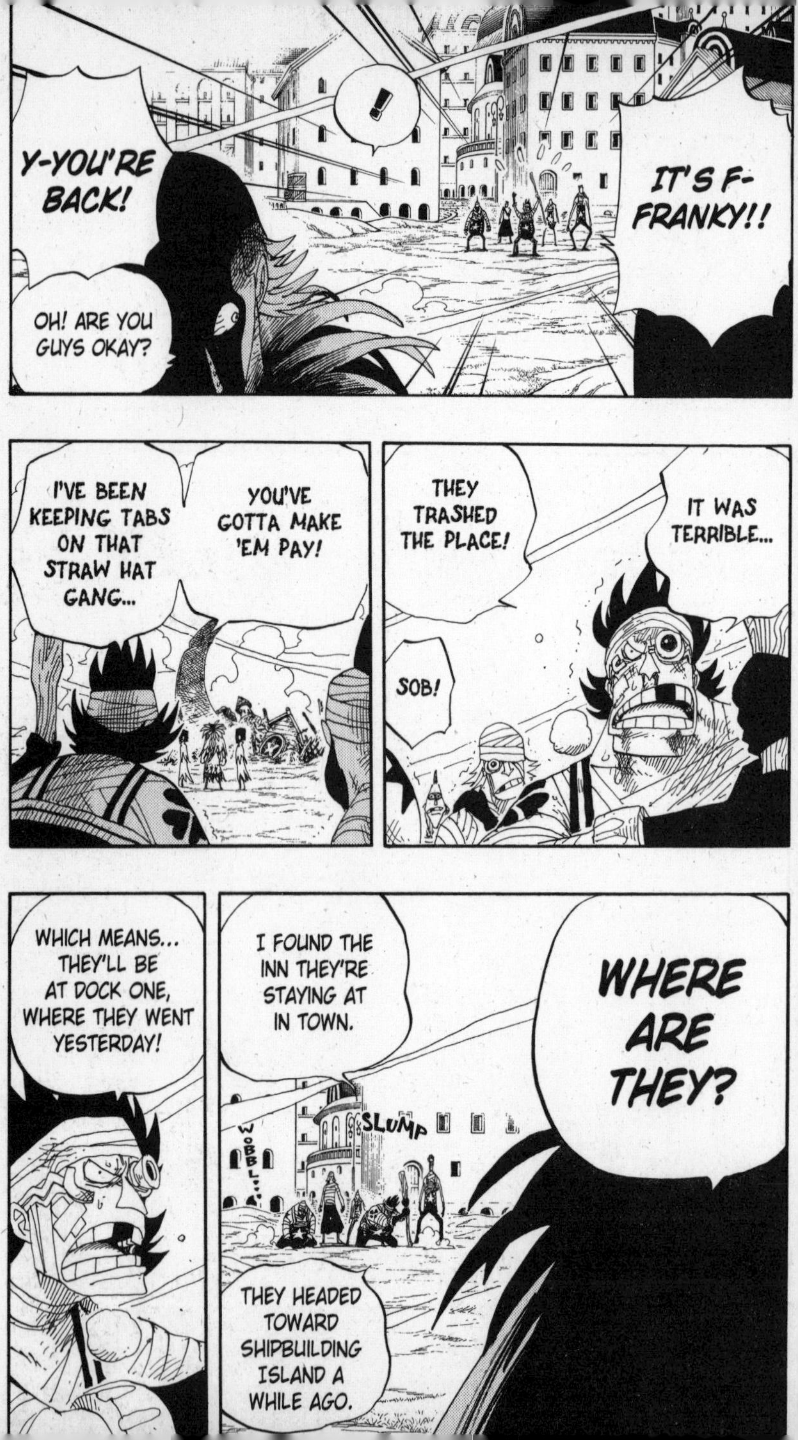
IT'S F-FRANKY!!
!
Y-YOU'RE BACK!
OH! ARE YOU GUYS OKAY?
IT WAS TERRIBLE...
THEY TRASHED THE PLACE!
SOB!
YOU'VE GOTTA MAKE 'EM PAY!
I'VE BEEN KEEPING TABS ON THAT STRAW HAT GANG...
WHERE ARE THEY?
I FOUND THE INN THEY'RE STAYING AT IN TOWN.
SLUMP
WOBBL...
THEY HEADED TOWARD SHIPBUILDING ISLAND A WHILE AGO.
WHICH MEANS... THEY'LL BE AT DOCK ONE, WHERE THEY WENT YESTERDAY!

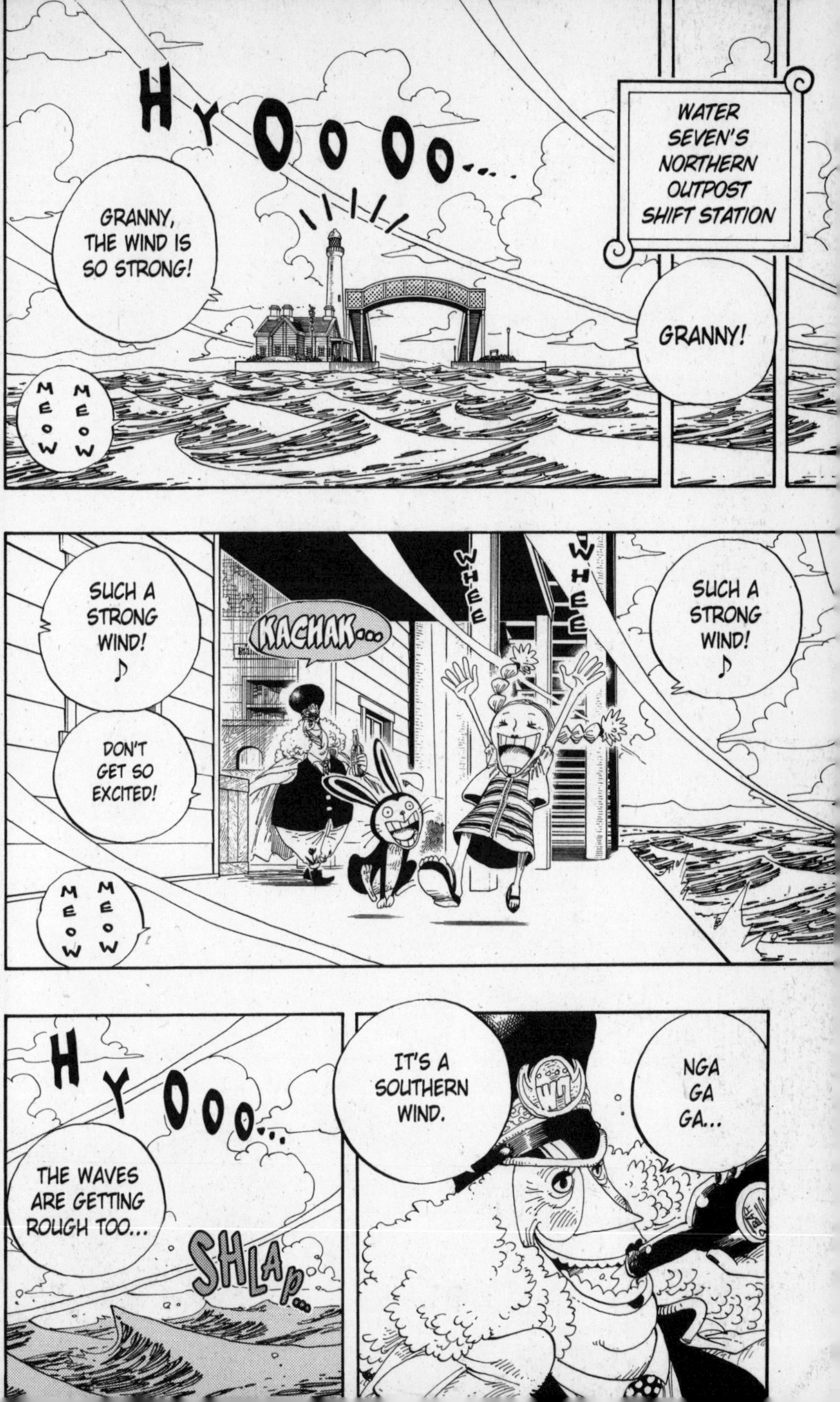
WATER SEVEN'S NORTHERN OUTPOST SHIFT STATION
GRANNY!
HYOOOO...
GRANNY, THE WIND IS SO STRONG!
MEOW MEOW
WHEE WHEE
SUCH A STRONG WIND! ♪
KACHAK...
SUCH A STRONG WIND! ♪
DON'T GET SO EXCITED!
MEOW MEOW
NGA GA GA...
IT'S A SOUTHERN WIND.
HYOOO...
THE WAVES ARE GETTING ROUGH TOO...
SHLAP...

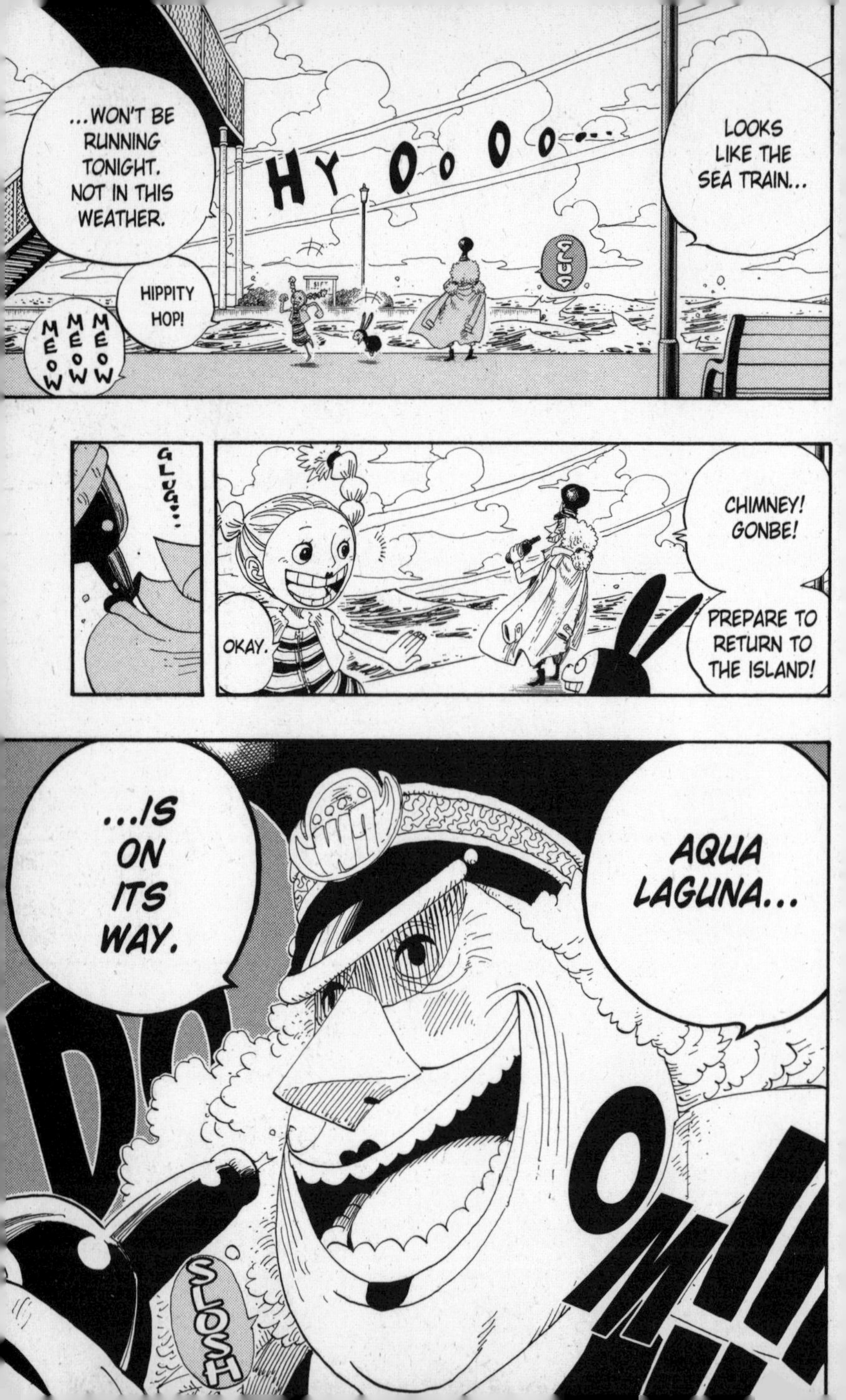
LOOKS LIKE THE SEA TRAIN...
HYOOOO...
GLUG
...WON'T BE RUNNING TONIGHT. NOT IN THIS WEATHER.
HIPPITY HOP!
MEOW MEOW MEOW
CHIMNEY! GONBE!
PREPARE TO RETURN TO THE ISLAND!
OKAY.
GLUG...
AQUA LAGUNA...
...IS ON ITS WAY.
SLOSH

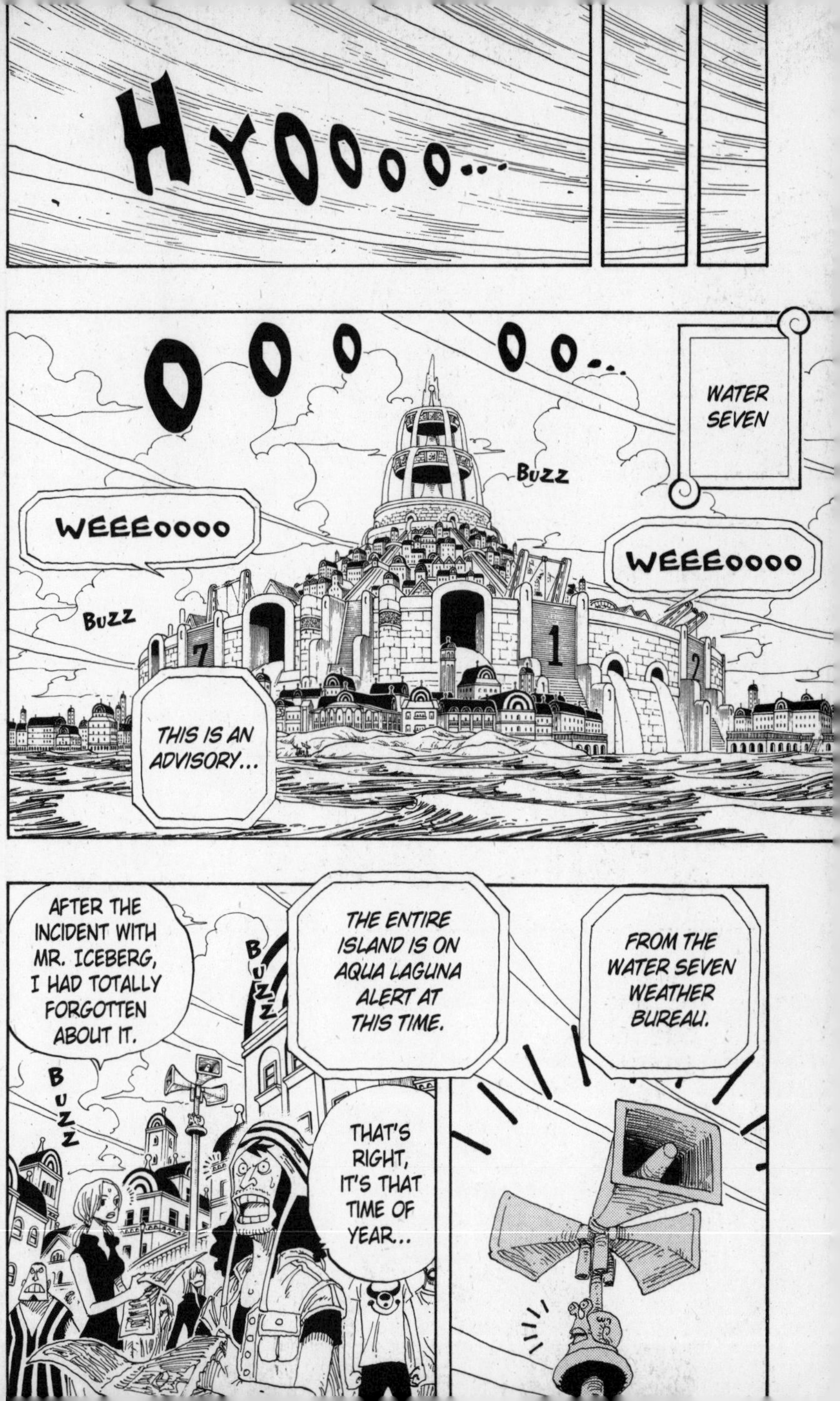
HYOOOO...
OOOOO...
WATER SEVEN
WEEEoooo
BUZZ
WEEEoooo
BUZZ
THIS IS AN ADVISORY...
FROM THE WATER SEVEN WEATHER BUREAU.
THE ENTIRE ISLAND IS ON AQUA LAGUNA ALERT AT THIS TIME.
BUZZ
AFTER THE INCIDENT WITH MR. ICEBERG, I HAD TOTALLY FORGOTTEN ABOUT IT.
BUZZ
THAT'S RIGHT, IT'S THAT TIME OF YEAR...

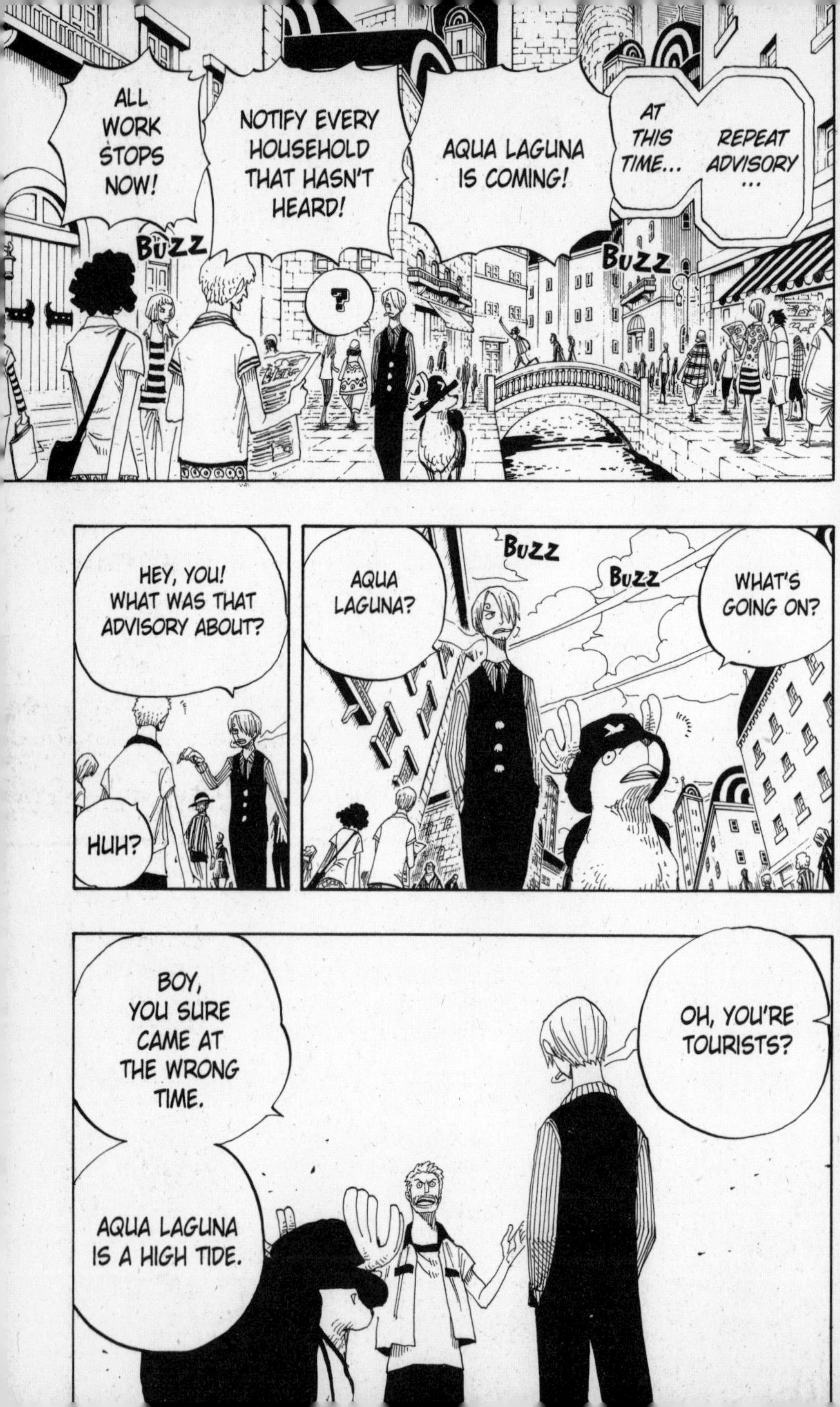
REPEAT ADVISORY...
AT THIS TIME...
AQUA LAGUNA IS COMING!
NOTIFY EVERY HOUSEHOLD THAT HASN'T HEARD!
ALL WORK STOPS NOW!
BUZZ
BUZZ
?
WHAT'S GOING ON?
BUZZ
BUZZ
AQUA LAGUNA?
HEY, YOU! WHAT WAS THAT ADVISORY ABOUT?
HUH?
OH, YOU'RE TOURISTS?
BOY, YOU SURE CAME AT THE WRONG TIME.
AQUA LAGUNA IS A HIGH TIDE.

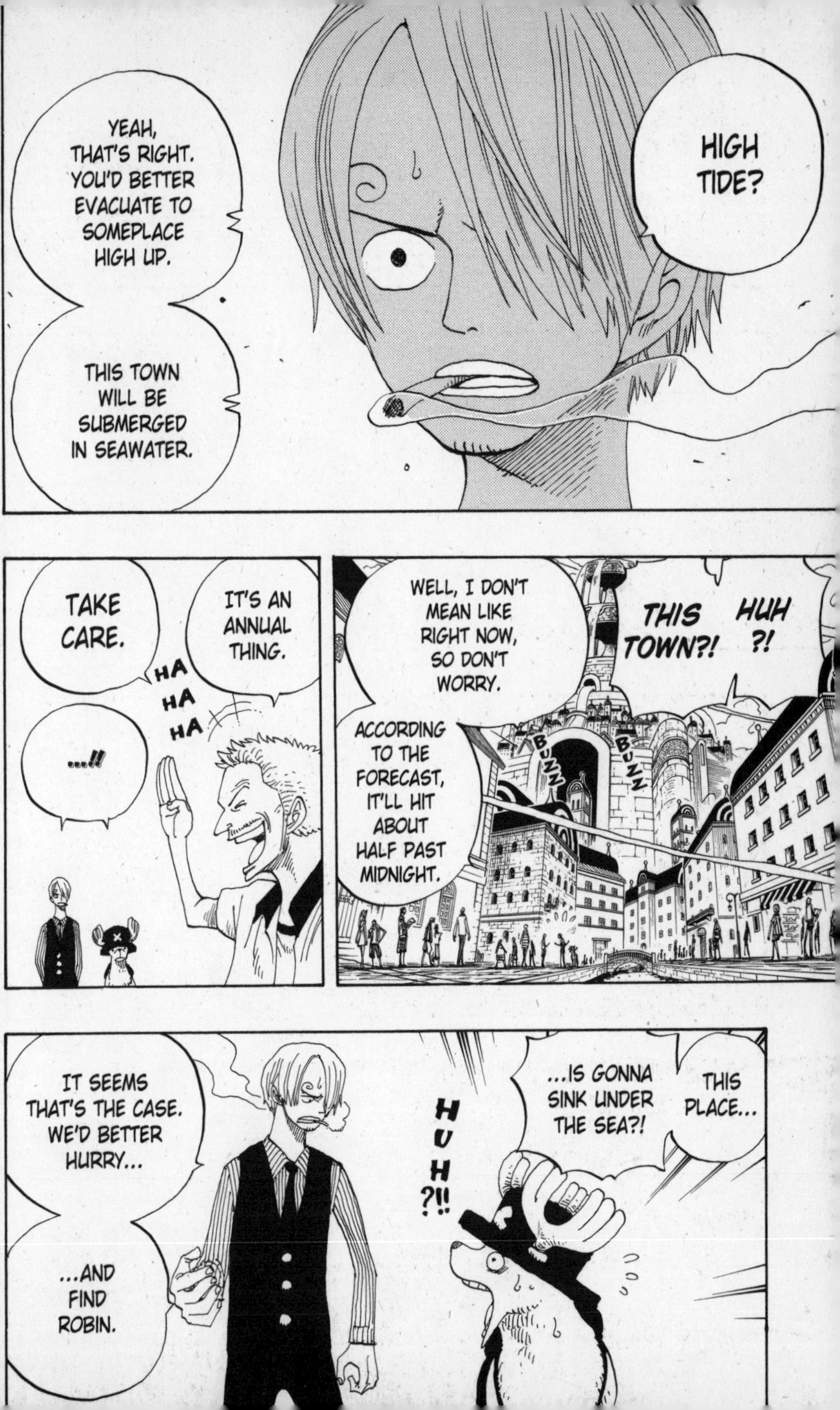
HIGH TIDE?
YEAH, THAT'S RIGHT. YOU'D BETTER EVACUATE TO SOMEPLACE HIGH UP.
THIS TOWN WILL BE SUBMERGED IN SEAWATER.
HUH ?!
THIS TOWN?!
WELL, I DON'T MEAN LIKE RIGHT NOW, SO DON'T WORRY.
ACCORDING TO THE FORECAST, IT'LL HIT ABOUT HALF PAST MIDNIGHT.
BUZZ
BUZZ
IT'S AN ANNUAL THING.
HA HA HA
TAKE CARE.
...!!
THIS PLACE...
...IS GONNA SINK UNDER THE SEA?!
HUH ?!!
IT SEEMS THAT'S THE CASE. WE'D BETTER HURRY...
...AND FIND ROBIN.

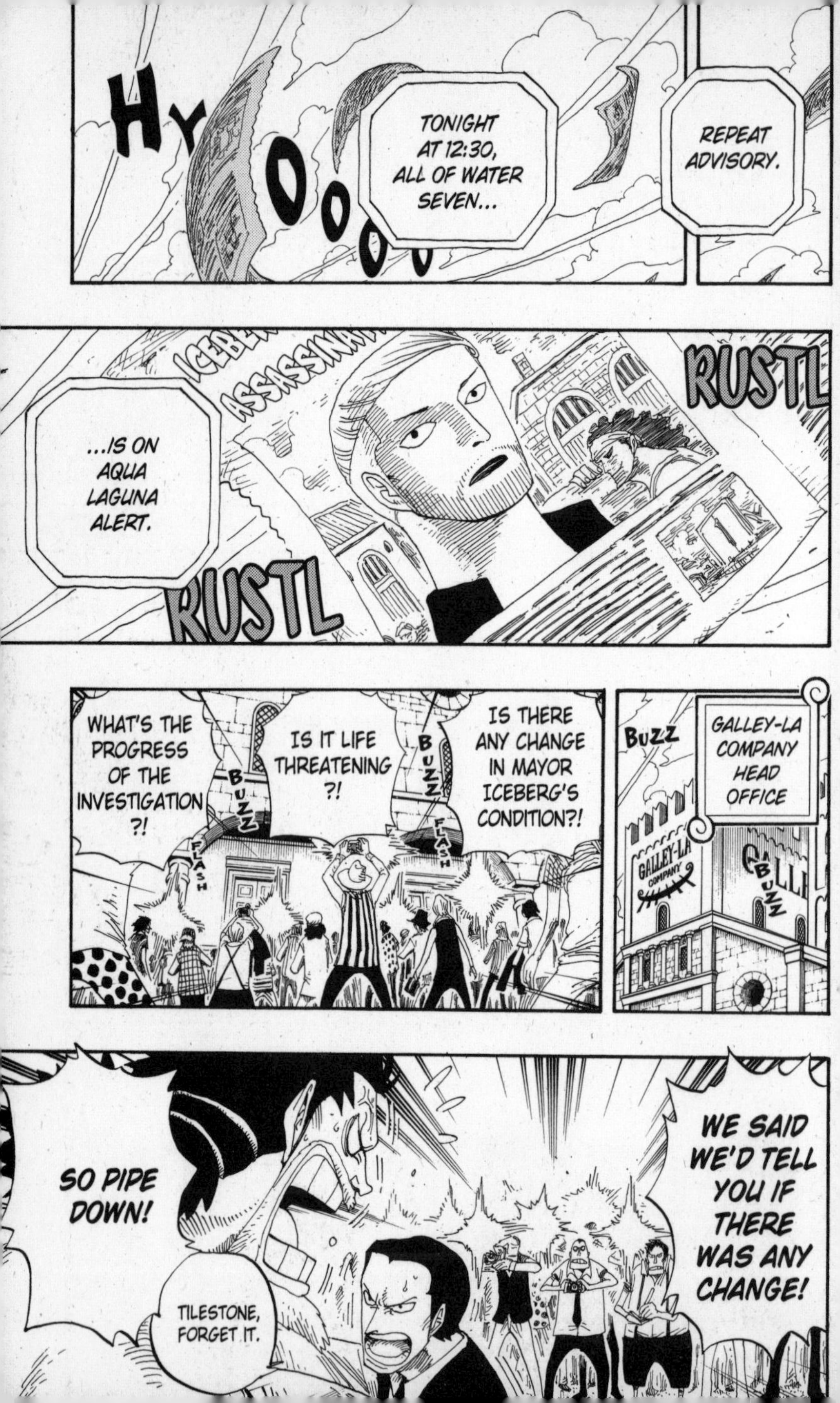
REPEAT ADVISORY.
TONIGHT AT 12:30, ALL OF WATER SEVEN...
HYOOOO
RUSTL
...IS ON AQUA LAGUNA ALERT.
RUSTL
GALLEY-LA COMPANY HEAD OFFICE
BUZZ
GALLEY-LA COMPANY
BUZZ
IS THERE ANY CHANGE IN MAYOR ICEBERG'S CONDITION?!
BUZZ
FLASH
IS IT LIFE THREATENING?!
BUZZ
WHAT'S THE PROGRESS OF THE INVESTIGATION?!
FLASH
WE SAID WE'D TELL YOU IF THERE WAS ANY CHANGE!
SO PIPE DOWN!
TILESTONE, FORGET IT.

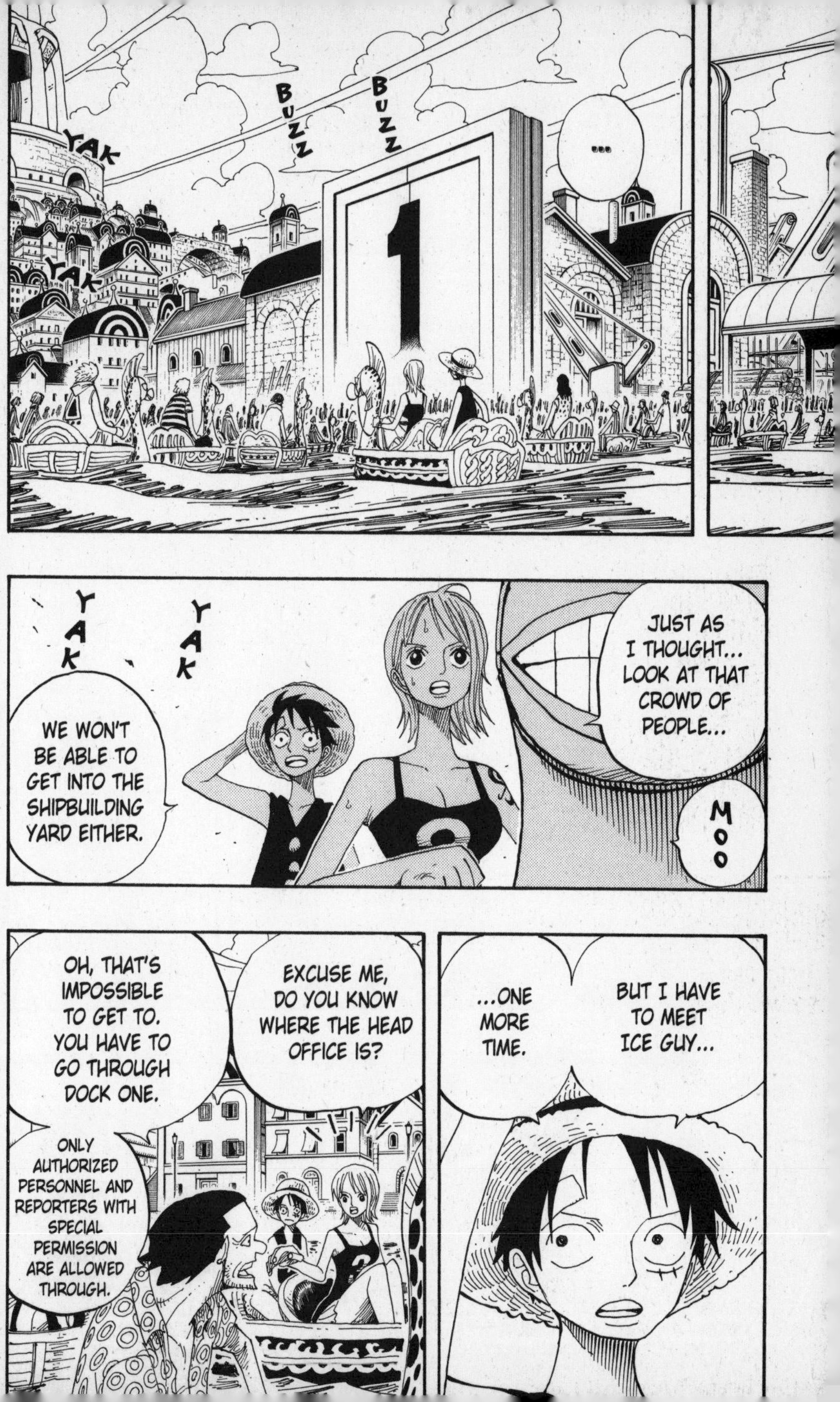
...
BUZZ
BUZZ
YAK
YAK
JUST AS I THOUGHT... LOOK AT THAT CROWD OF PEOPLE...
MOO
YAK
YAK
WE WON'T BE ABLE TO GET INTO THE SHIPBUILDING YARD EITHER.
BUT I HAVE TO MEET ICE GUY...
...ONE MORE TIME.
EXCUSE ME, DO YOU KNOW WHERE THE HEAD OFFICE IS?
OH, THAT'S IMPOSSIBLE TO GET TO. YOU HAVE TO GO THROUGH DOCK ONE.
ONLY AUTHORIZED PERSONNEL AND REPORTERS WITH SPECIAL PERMISSION ARE ALLOWED THROUGH.

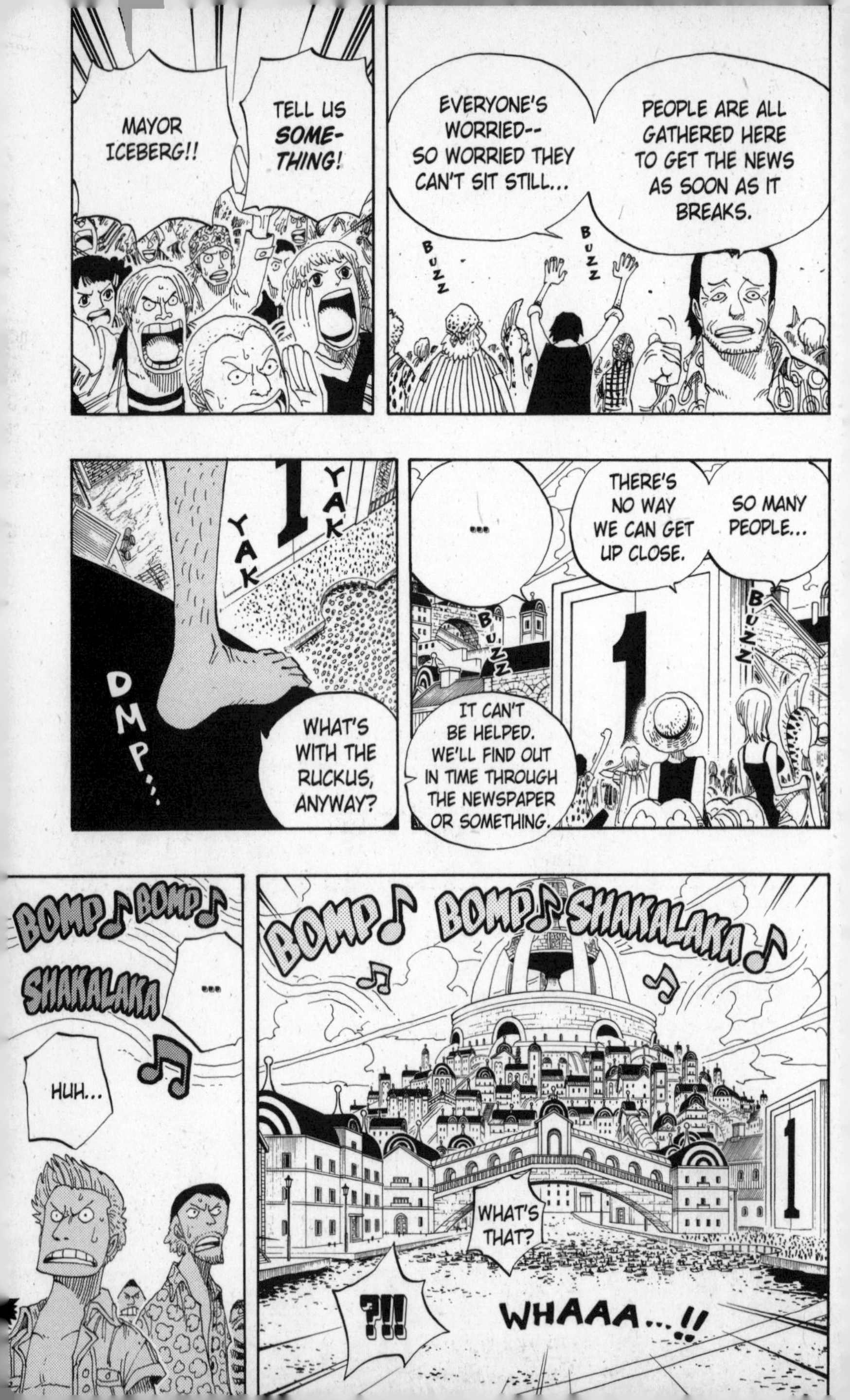
PEOPLE ARE ALL GATHERED HERE TO GET THE NEWS AS SOON AS IT BREAKS.
EVERYONE'S WORRIED-- SO WORRIED THEY CAN'T SIT STILL...
BUZZ
BUZZ
TELL US SOME-THING!
MAYOR ICEBERG!!
SO MANY PEOPLE...
THERE'S NO WAY WE CAN GET UP CLOSE.
...
BUZZ
BUZZ
IT CAN'T BE HELPED. WE'LL FIND OUT IN TIME THROUGH THE NEWSPAPER OR SOMETHING.
YAK
YAK
DMP...
WHAT'S WITH THE RUCKUS, ANYWAY?
BOMP♪ BOMP♪ SHAKALAKA♪
WHAT'S THAT?
?!!
WHAAA...!!
BOMP♪ BOMP♪
SHAKALAKA
...
HUH...

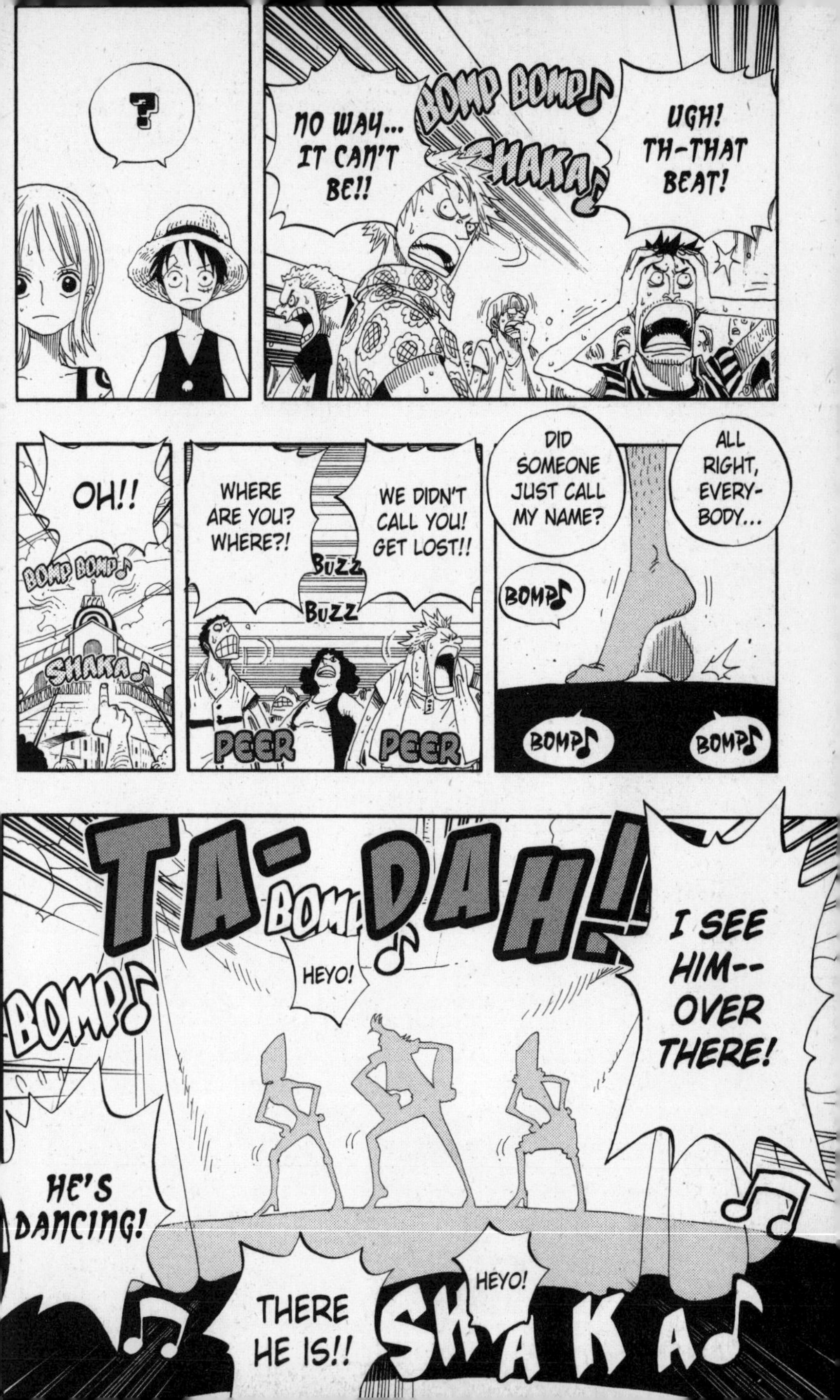

UGH! TH-THAT BEAT!
BOMP BOMP
SHAKA
NO WAY... IT CAN'T BE!!
?
ALL RIGHT, EVERY-BODY...
DID SOMEONE JUST CALL MY NAME?
BOMP
BOMP
BOMP
WE DIDN'T CALL YOU! GET LOST!!
WHERE ARE YOU? WHERE?!
BUZZ
BUZZ
PEER
PEER
OH!!
BOMP BOMP
SHAKA
TA-DAH!!
BOMP
I SEE HIM-- OVER THERE!
HEYO!
BOMP
HE'S DANCING!
HEYO!
SHAKA
THERE HE IS!!

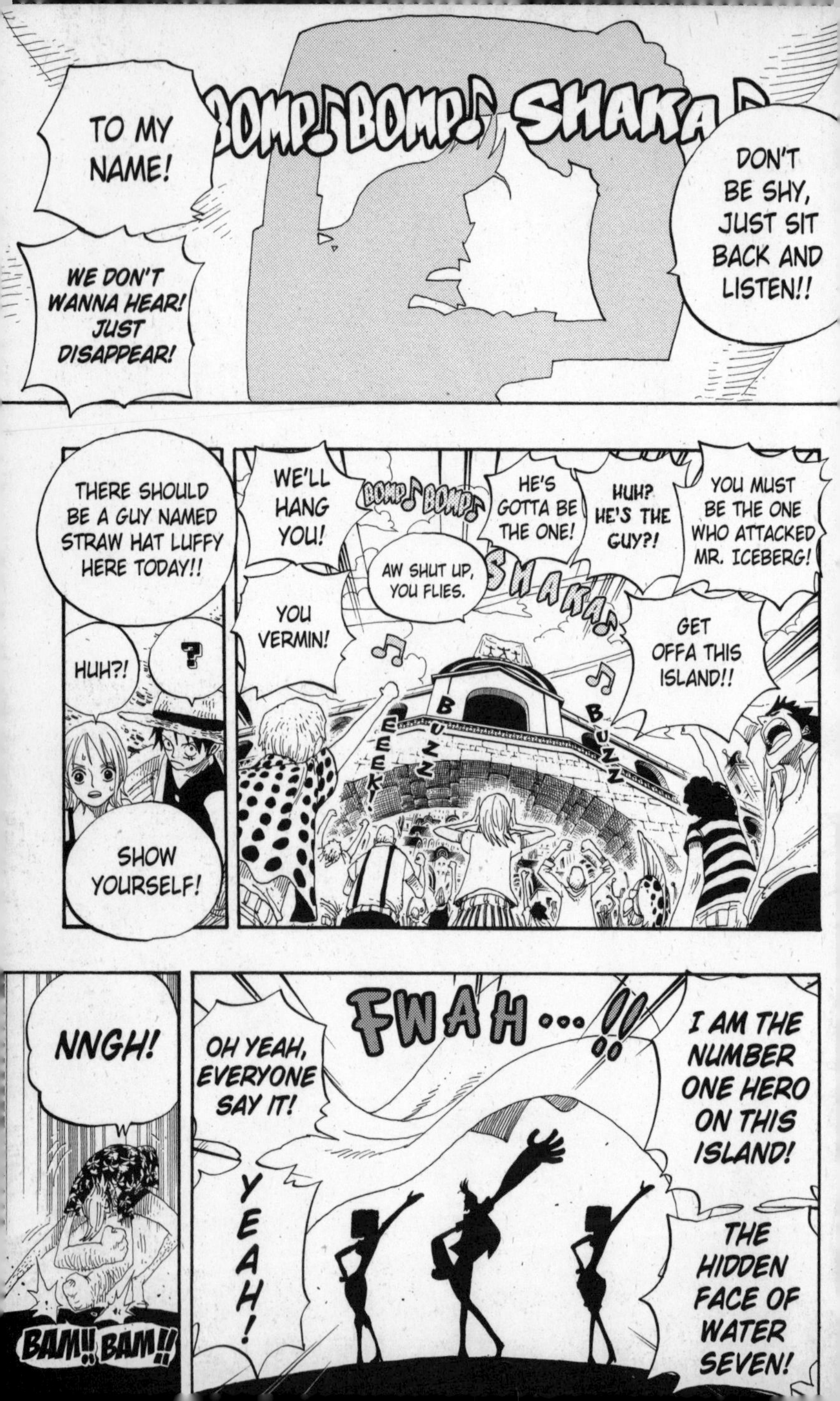

DON'T BE SHY, JUST SIT BACK AND LISTEN!!
BOMP♪ BOMP♪ SHAKA♪
TO MY NAME!
WE DON'T WANNA HEAR! JUST DISAPPEAR!
YOU MUST BE THE ONE WHO ATTACKED MR. ICEBERG!
HUH? HE'S THE GUY?!
HE'S GOTTA BE THE ONE!
BOMP♪ BOMP♪
WE'LL HANG YOU!
AW SHUT UP, YOU FLIES.
SHAKA♪
GET OFFA THIS ISLAND!!
YOU VERMIN!
BUZZ
BUZZ
EEEK!
THERE SHOULD BE A GUY NAMED STRAW HAT LUFFY HERE TODAY!!
?
HUH?!
SHOW YOURSELF!
I AM THE NUMBER ONE HERO ON THIS ISLAND!
FWAH...!!
OH YEAH, EVERYONE SAY IT!
THE HIDDEN FACE OF WATER SEVEN!
YEAH!
NNGH!
BAM!! BAM!!

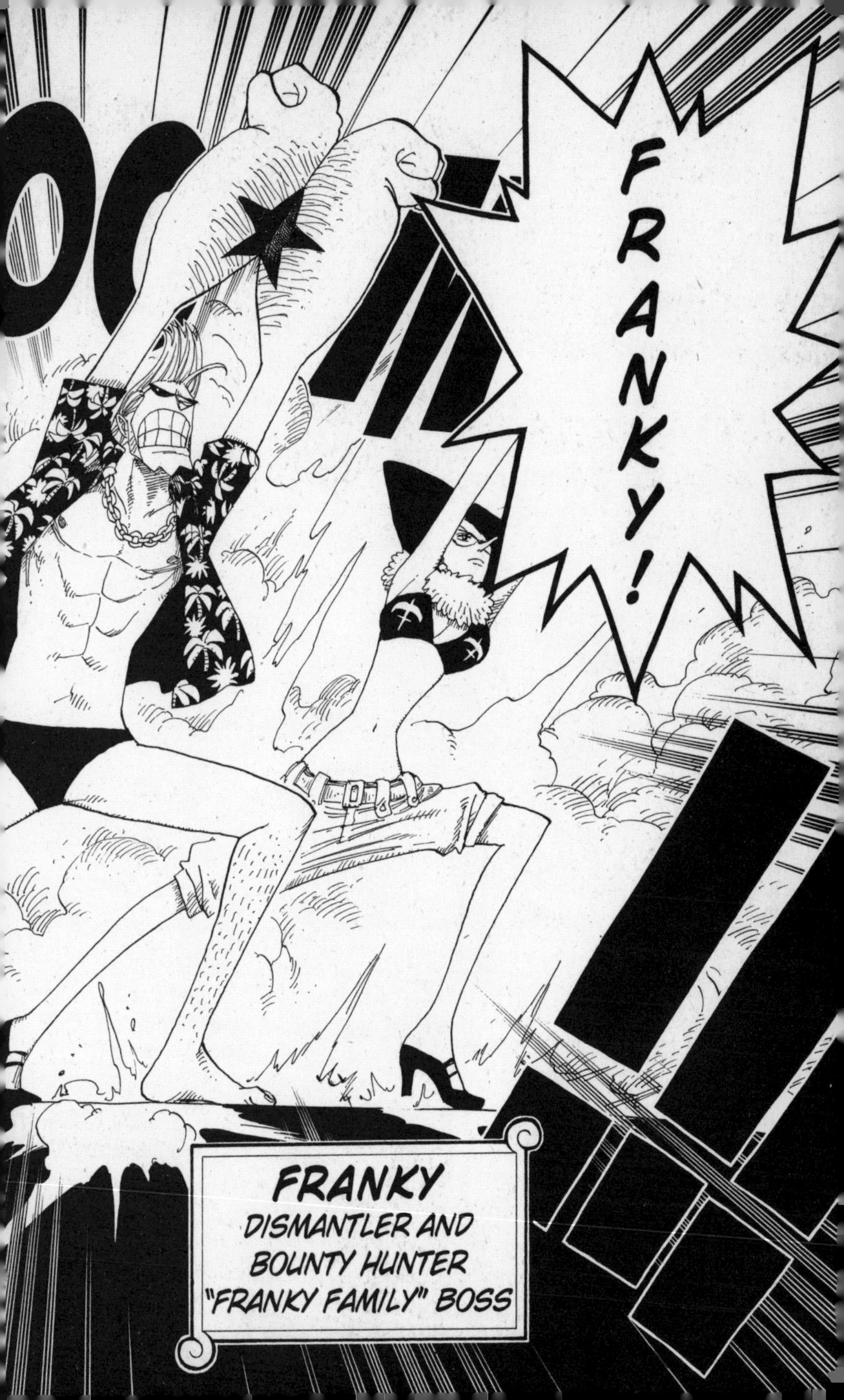
FRANKY!
FRANKY
DISMANTLER AND
BOUNTY HUNTER
"FRANKY FAMILY" BOSS

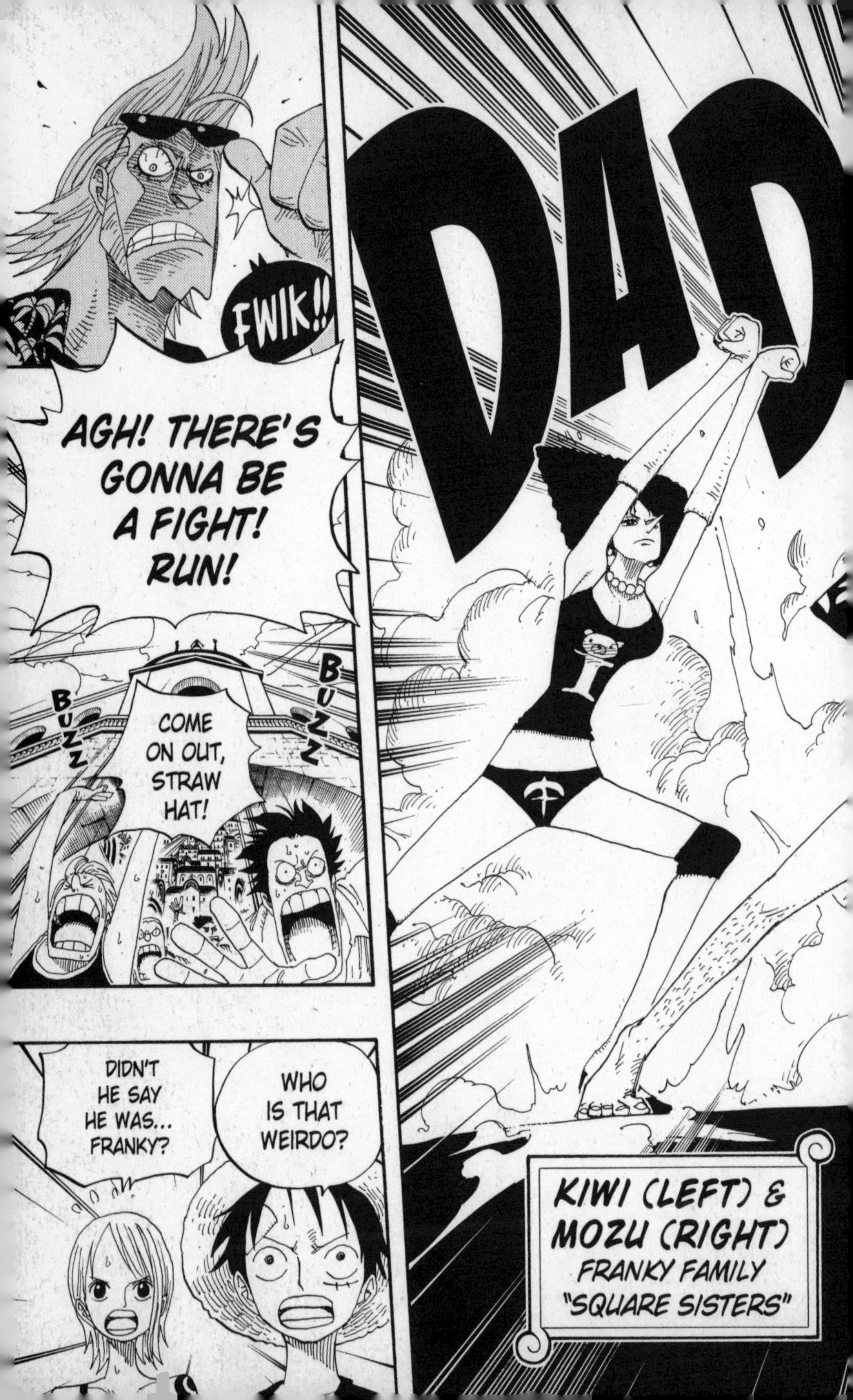
DAD
KIWI (LEFT) & MOZU (RIGHT)
FRANKY FAMILY
"SQUARE SISTERS"
FWIK!!
AGH! THERE'S GONNA BE A FIGHT! RUN!
BUZZ
COME ON OUT, STRAW HAT!
BUZZ
WHO IS THAT WEIRDO?
DIDN'T HE SAY HE WAS... FRANKY?

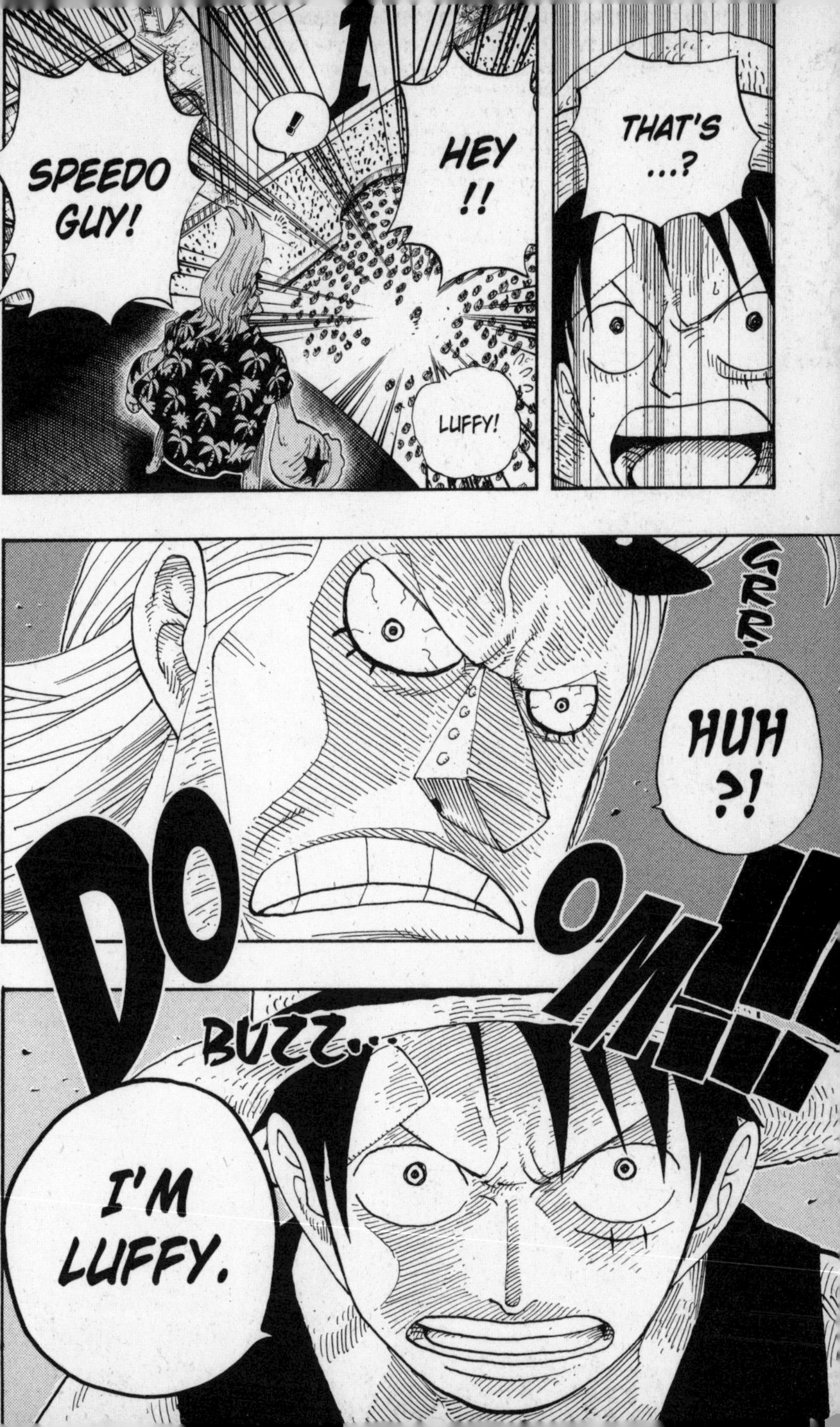
THAT'S ...?
HEY !!
!
SPEEDO GUY!
LUFFY!
SRR...
HUH ?!
DOOM!!!
BUZZ...
I'M LUFFY.

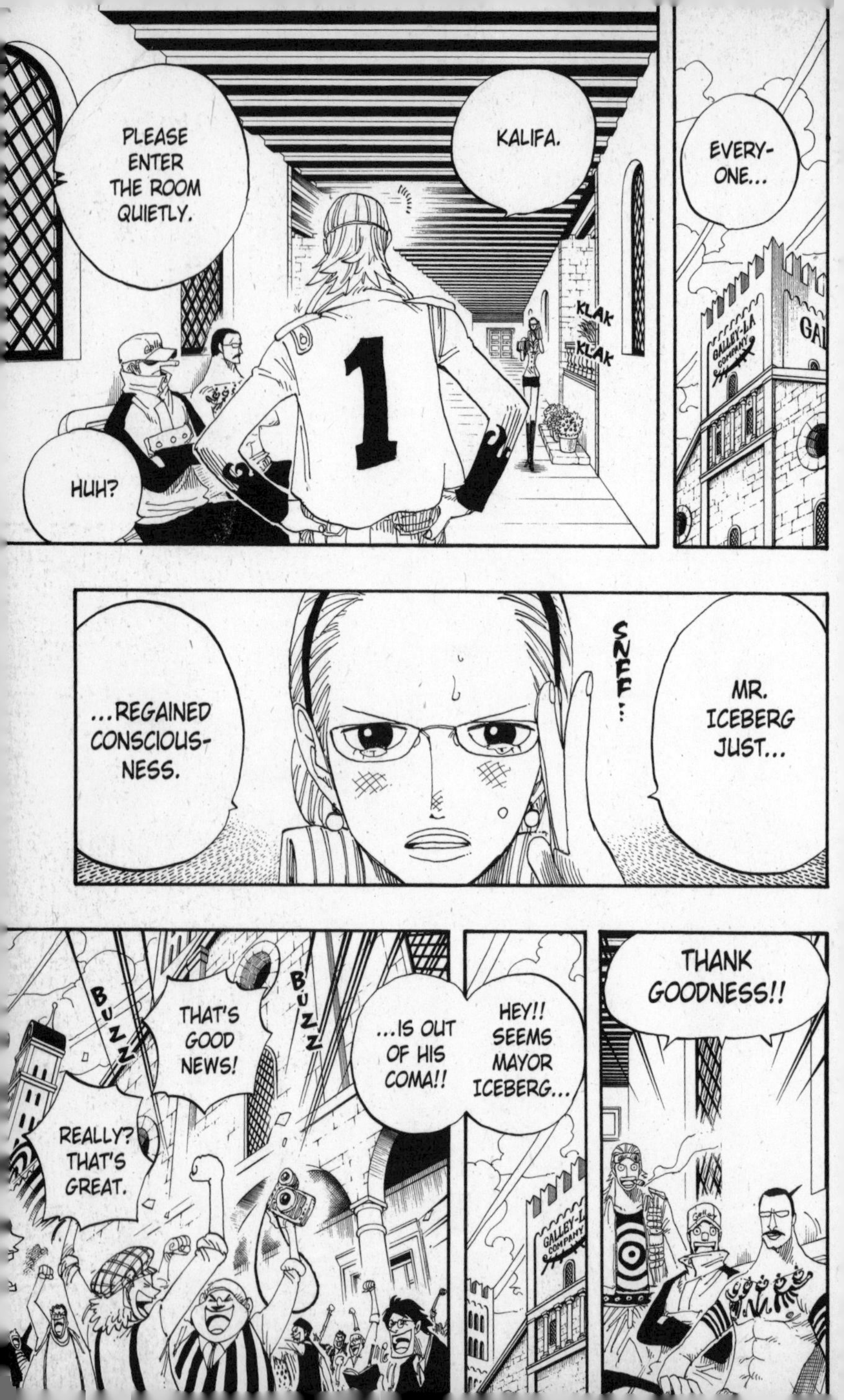
EVERY-ONE...
KALIFA.
KLAK
KLAK
PLEASE ENTER THE ROOM QUIETLY.
HUH?
MR. ICEBERG JUST...
SNFF..
...REGAINED CONSCIOUS-NESS.
THANK GOODNESS!!
HEY!! SEEMS MAYOR ICEBERG...
...IS OUT OF HIS COMA!!
BUZZ
THAT'S GOOD NEWS!
BUZZ
REALLY? THAT'S GREAT.

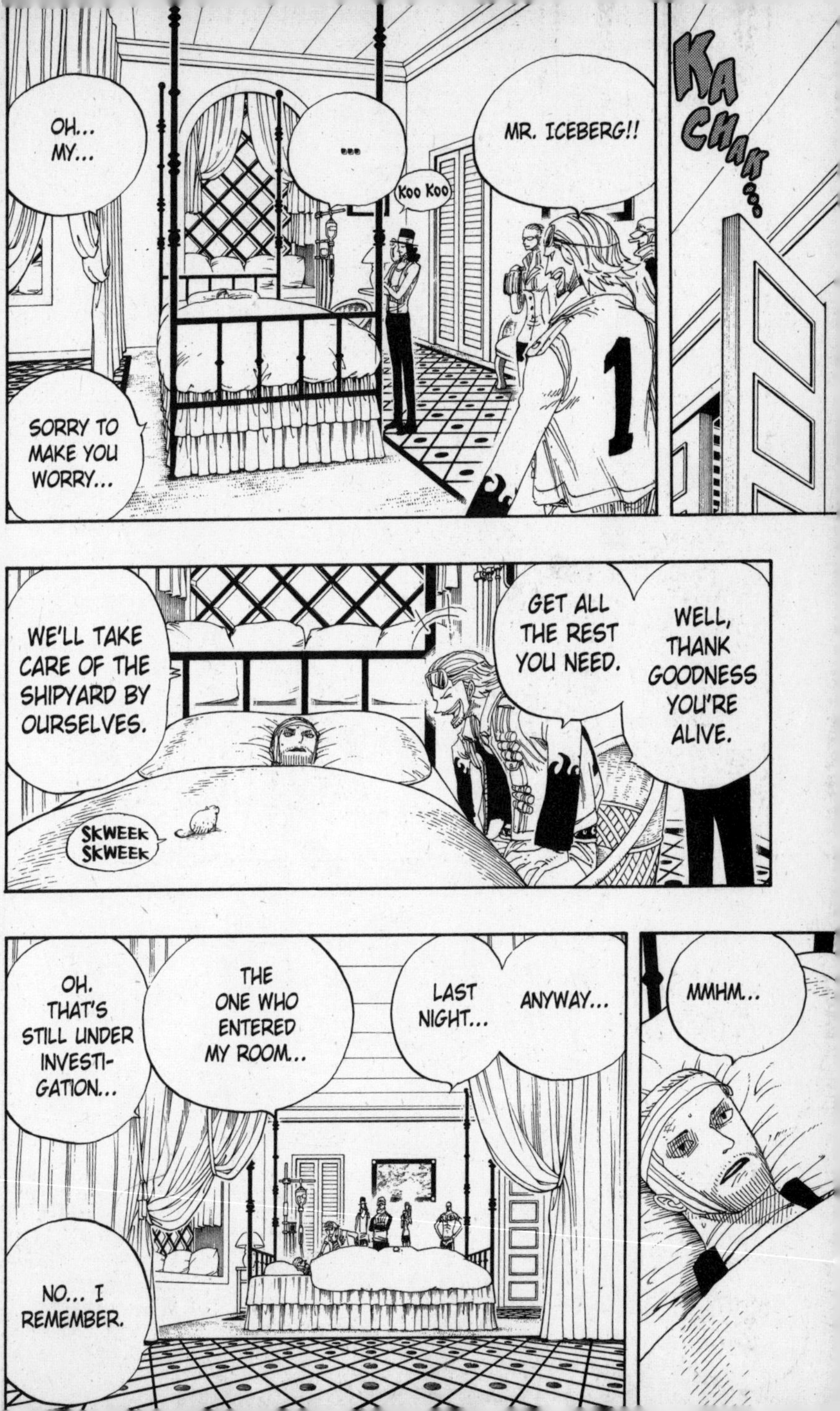
KA CHAK...
MR. ICEBERG!!
Koo Koo
...
OH... MY...
SORRY TO MAKE YOU WORRY...
WELL, THANK GOODNESS YOU'RE ALIVE.
GET ALL THE REST YOU NEED.
WE'LL TAKE CARE OF THE SHIPYARD BY OURSELVES.
SKWEEK SKWEEK
MMHM...
ANYWAY...
LAST NIGHT...
THE ONE WHO ENTERED MY ROOM...
OH. THAT'S STILL UNDER INVESTIGATION...
NO... I REMEMBER.

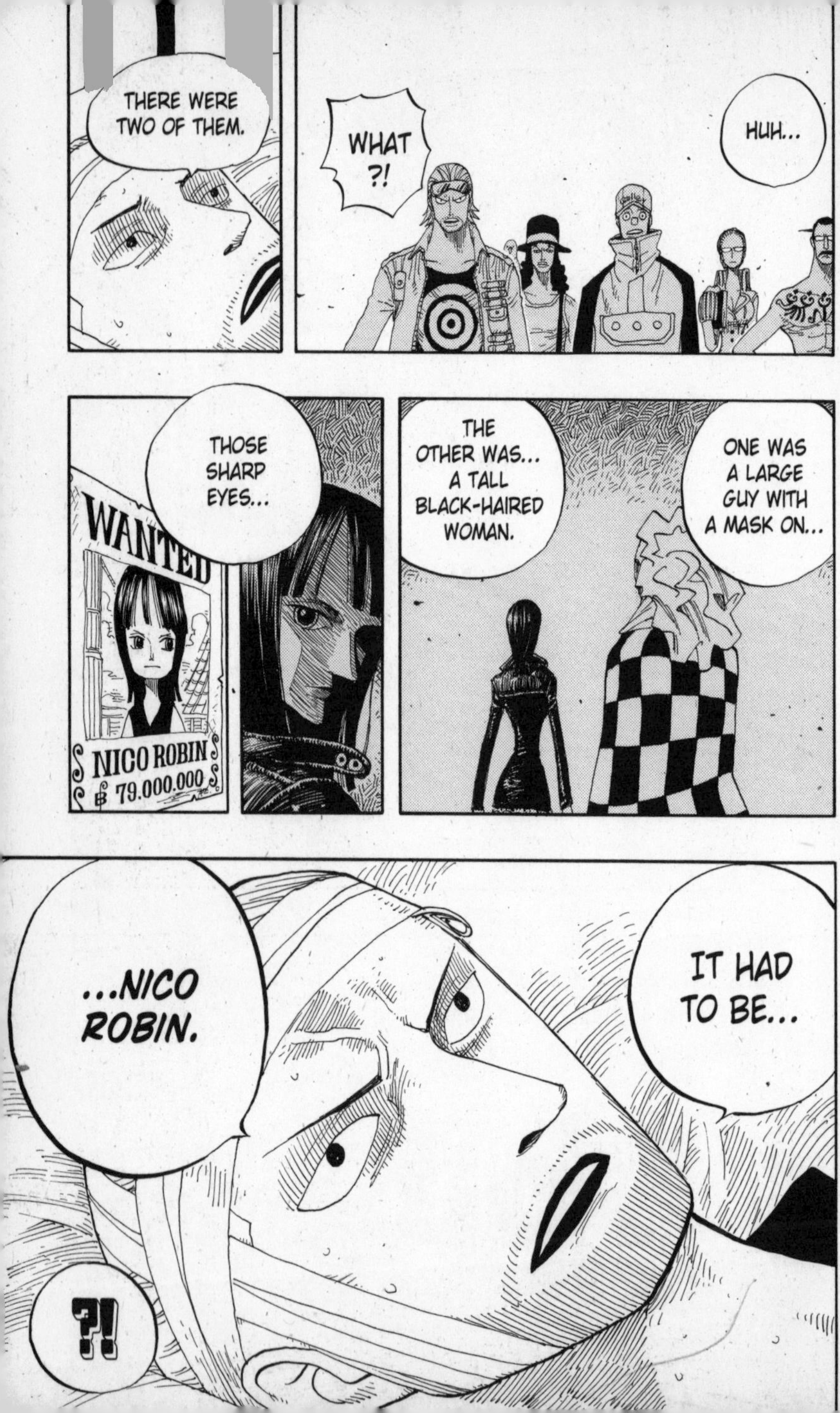
HUH...
WHAT ?!
THERE WERE TWO OF THEM.
ONE WAS A LARGE GUY WITH A MASK ON...
THE OTHER WAS... A TALL BLACK-HAIRED WOMAN.
THOSE SHARP EYES...
WANTED
NICO ROBIN
฿ 79.000.000
IT HAD TO BE...
...NICO ROBIN.
?!

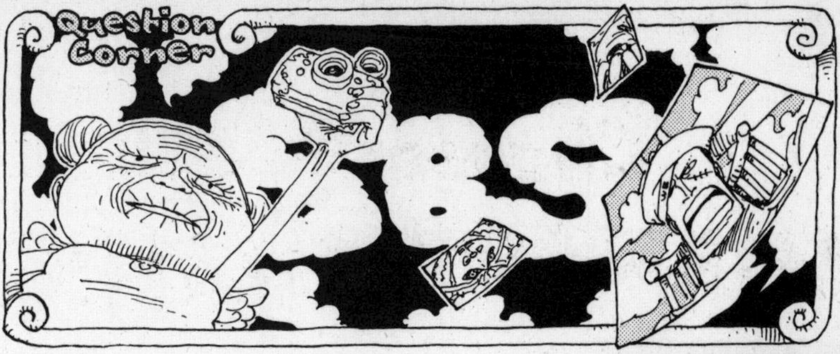
Question Corner

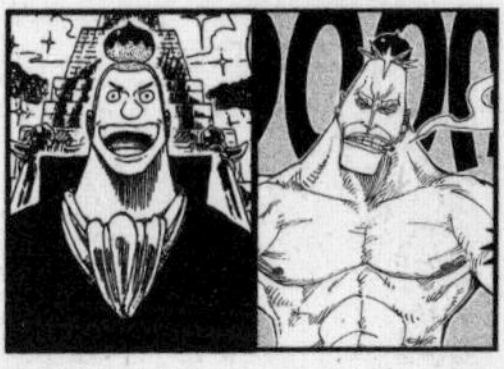

Q: Good evening, Oda Sensei! I was wondering the other day just what's on top of Mont Blanc Noland's and Mont Blanc Cricket's heads? Please answer from the following:

A: A real chestnut
B: Hair
C: Brain
D: Just something I doodled ♥
E: Who the heck knows? (DOOM!!)
F: That's just the way they are.

All right, please answer. And best of luck to you from now on.

--Martian

A: Umm... Well... Let's see... Umm... It's A.

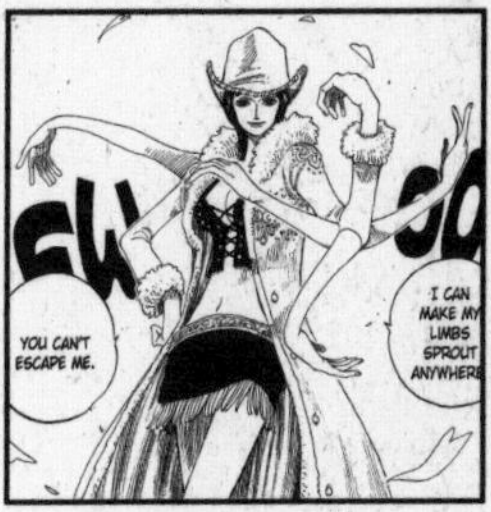
I CAN MAKE MY LIMBS SPROUT ANYWHERE
YOU CAN'T ESCAPE ME.

Q: Hello, Odacchi Sensei! I love, love, love Robin! However, there's one thing that concerns me. Robin has beautiful hands, and when she's using the Flower-Flower Fruit, beautiful hands will blossom, right? So if you're hairy, will using the power of the Flower-Flower Fruit produce really hairy hands? That would be so gross, don't you think?

--Kinoko

A:

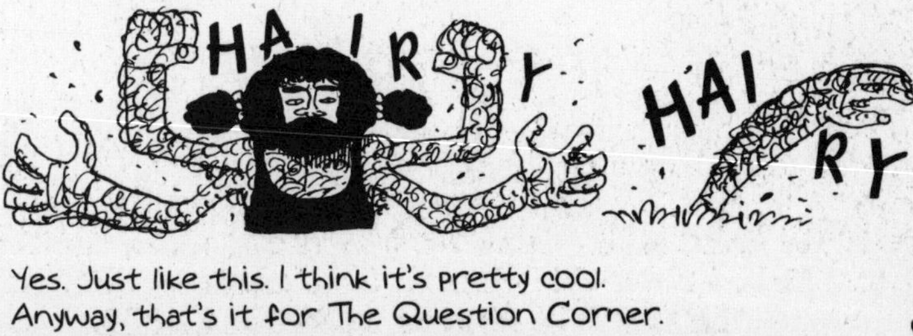
HAIRY
HAIRY

Yes. Just like this. I think it's pretty cool.
Anyway, that's it for The Question Corner.
See you next volume.

Chapter 336:
LUFFY VS. FRANKY

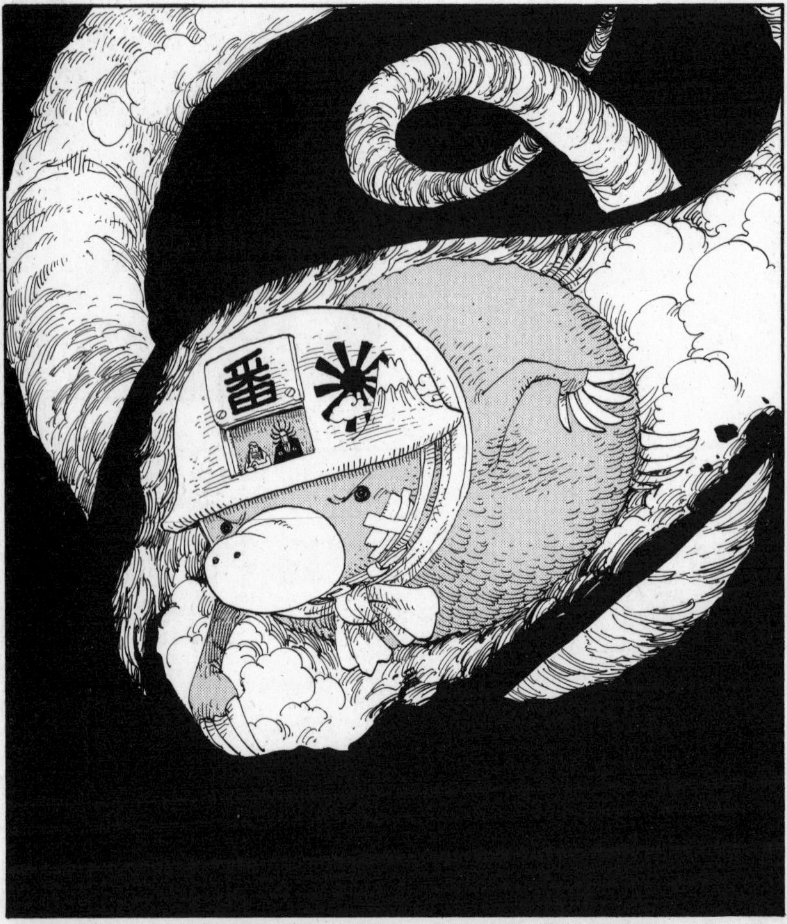
番

GEDATSU'S UNEXPECTED LIFE ON THE BLUE SEA, VOL. 20:
"LEAVE THE FOREST BOSS IN CHARGE
OF THE ISLAND AND KEEP DIGGING, EARTH BOSS"

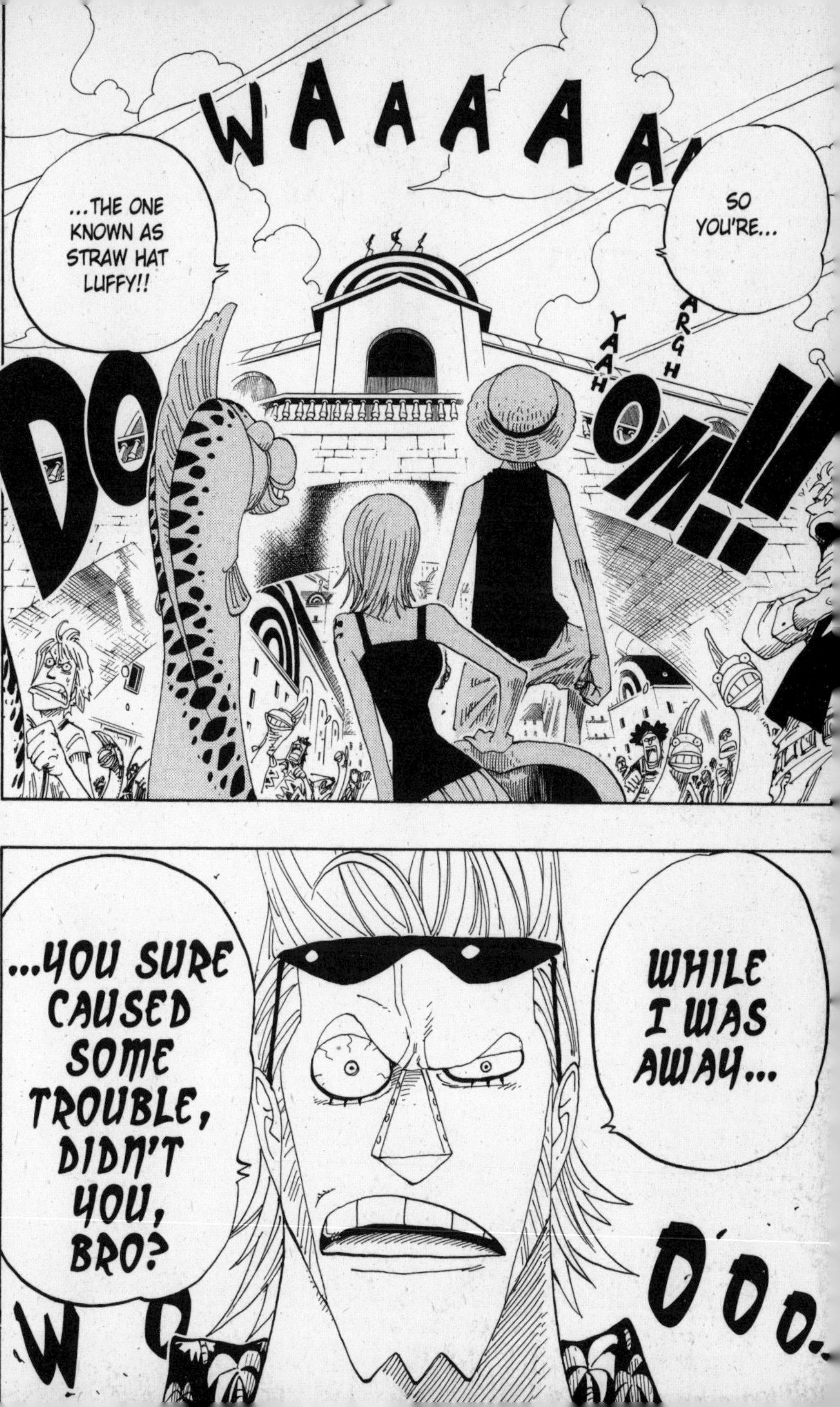
WAAAAA
SO YOU'RE...
...THE ONE KNOWN AS STRAW HAT LUFFY!!
ARGH
YAAH
DOON!!
WHILE I WAS AWAY...
...YOU SURE CAUSED SOME TROUBLE, DIDN'T YOU, BRO?
OOO..

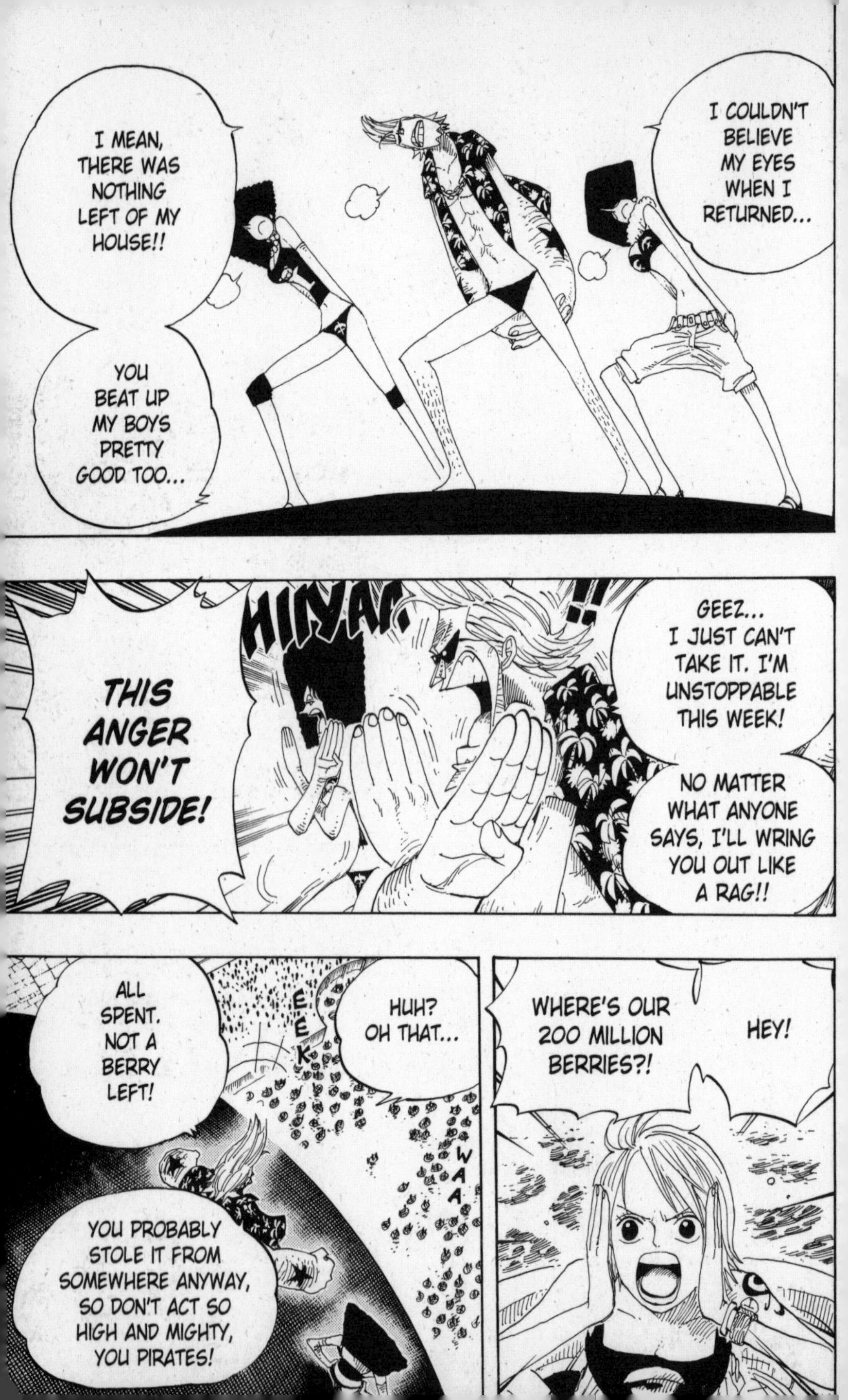

I COULDN'T BELIEVE MY EYES WHEN I RETURNED...
I MEAN, THERE WAS NOTHING LEFT OF MY HOUSE!!
YOU BEAT UP MY BOYS PRETTY GOOD TOO...
GEEZ... I JUST CAN'T TAKE IT. I'M UNSTOPPABLE THIS WEEK!
NO MATTER WHAT ANYONE SAYS, I'LL WRING YOU OUT LIKE A RAG!!
HIIYAH!!
THIS ANGER WON'T SUBSIDE!
HEY!
WHERE'S OUR 200 MILLION BERRIES?!
HUH? OH THAT...
EEEK
ALL SPENT. NOT A BERRY LEFT!
WAAA
YOU PROBABLY STOLE IT FROM SOMEWHERE ANYWAY, SO DON'T ACT SO HIGH AND MIGHTY, YOU PIRATES!

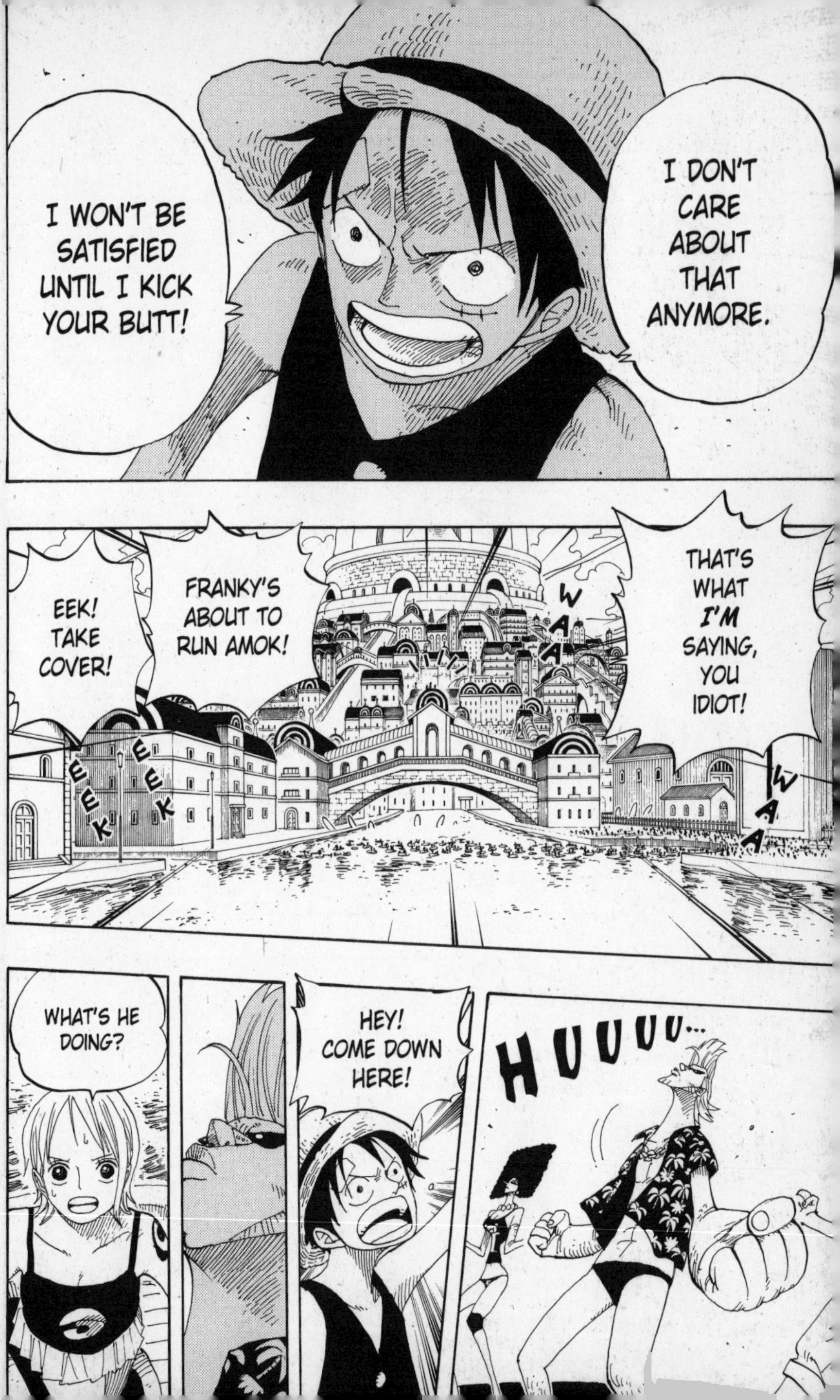
I DON'T CARE ABOUT THAT ANYMORE.
I WON'T BE SATISFIED UNTIL I KICK YOUR BUTT!
THAT'S WHAT *I'M* SAYING, YOU IDIOT!
WAA
WAA
FRANKY'S ABOUT TO RUN AMOK!
EEK! TAKE COVER!
EEEK
EEEK
HUUUU...
HEY! COME DOWN HERE!
WHAT'S HE DOING?

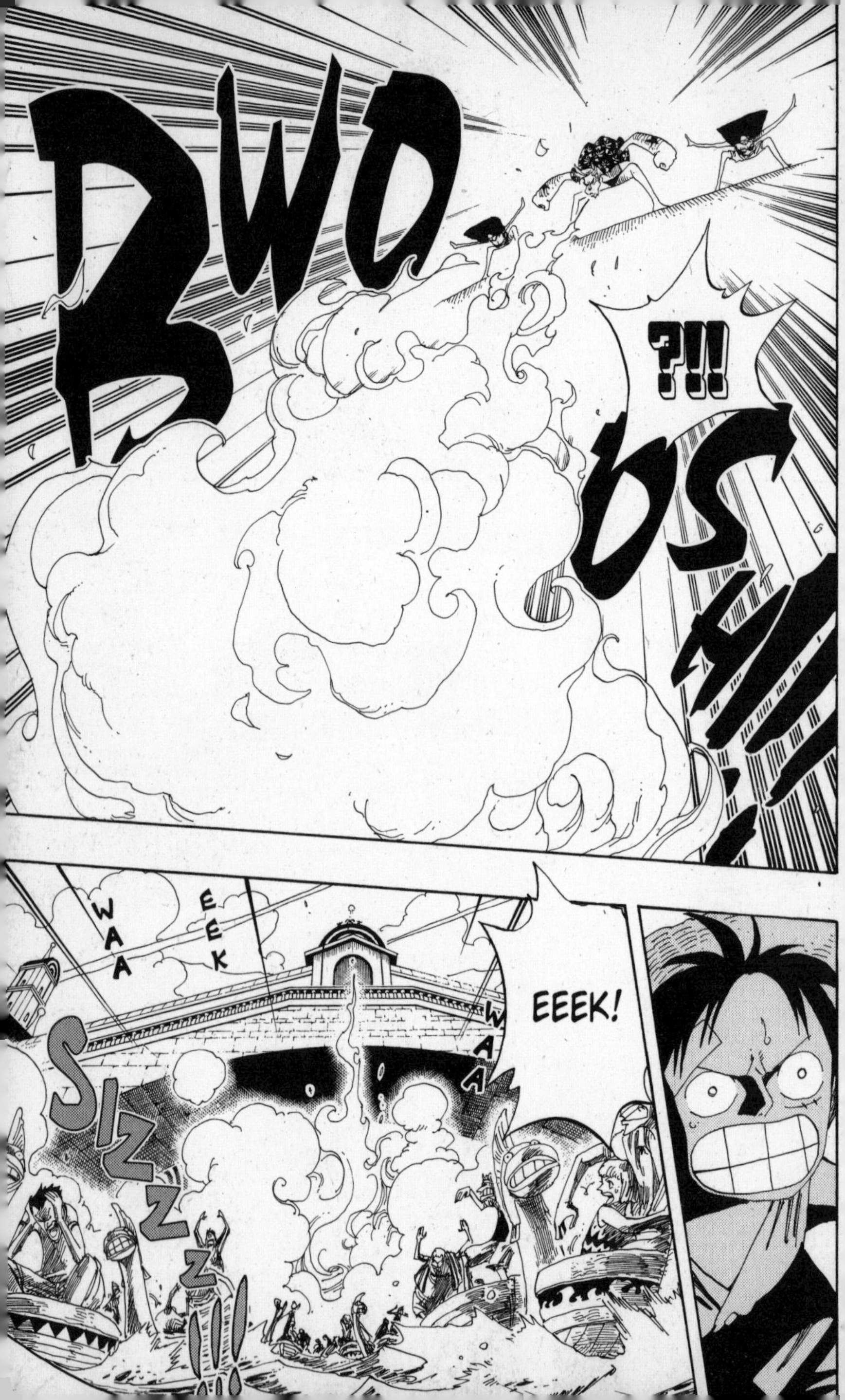
?!!
BSH!!
BWO
EEEK!
WAA
EEK
WAA
SIZZZ!!!

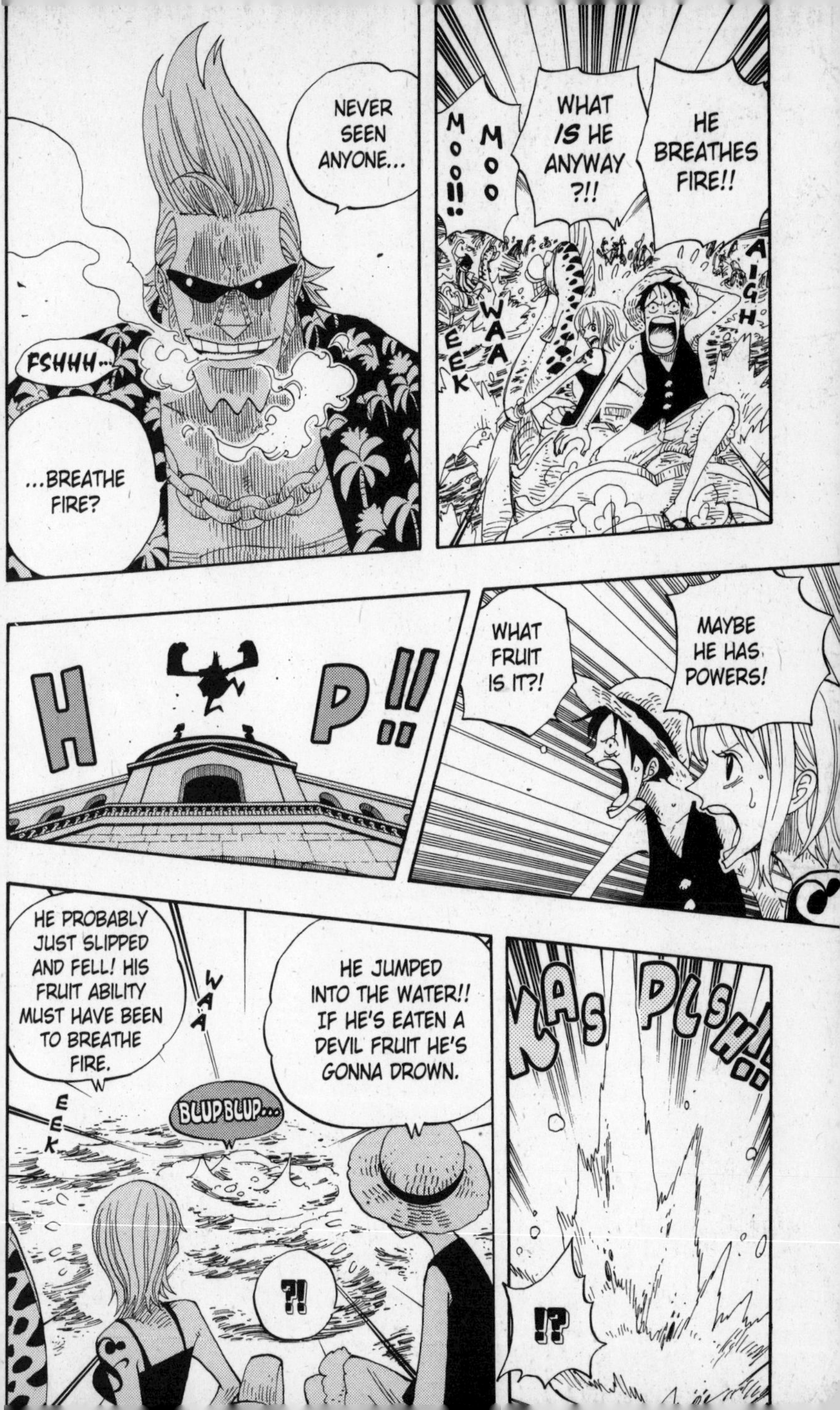
HE BREATHES FIRE!!
WHAT *IS* HE ANYWAY ?!!
MOO
MOOO!!
AIGH
WAA
EEK
NEVER SEEN ANYONE...
FSHHH...
...BREATHE FIRE?
MAYBE HE HAS POWERS!
WHAT FRUIT IS IT?!
H
P!!
KASPLSH!!
!?
HE JUMPED INTO THE WATER!! IF HE'S EATEN A DEVIL FRUIT HE'S GONNA DROWN.
HE PROBABLY JUST SLIPPED AND FELL! HIS FRUIT ABILITY MUST HAVE BEEN TO BREATHE FIRE.
WAA
EEK
BLUPBLUP...
?!

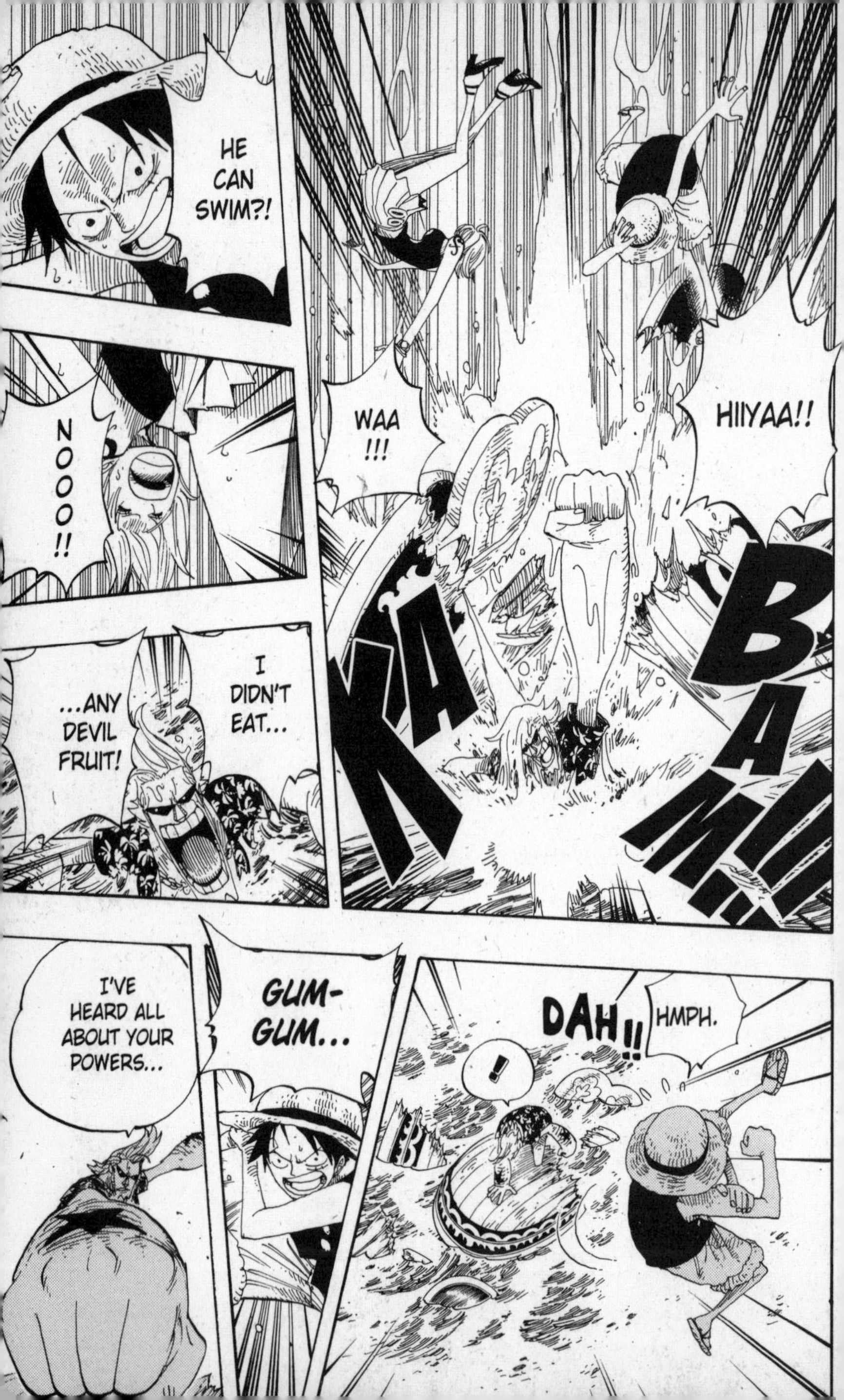
HIIYAA!!
WAA!!!
BAM!!
KA
HE CAN SWIM?!
NOOOO!!
I DIDN'T EAT...
...ANY DEVIL FRUIT!
HMPH.
DAH!!
!
GUM-GUM...
I'VE HEARD ALL ABOUT YOUR POWERS...

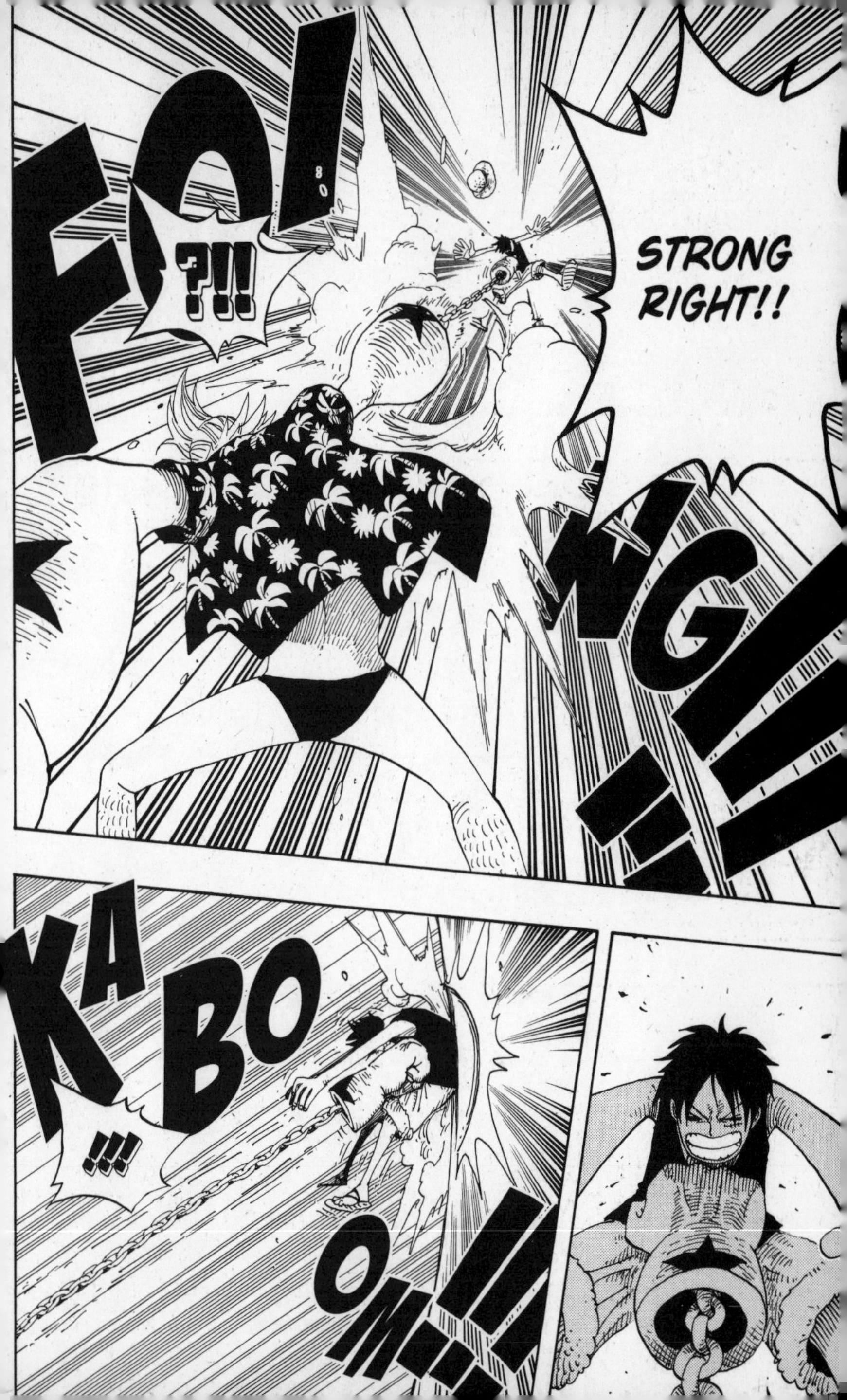
STRONG RIGHT!!
?!!
FO
WG!!
KA
BO
!!!
OM!!

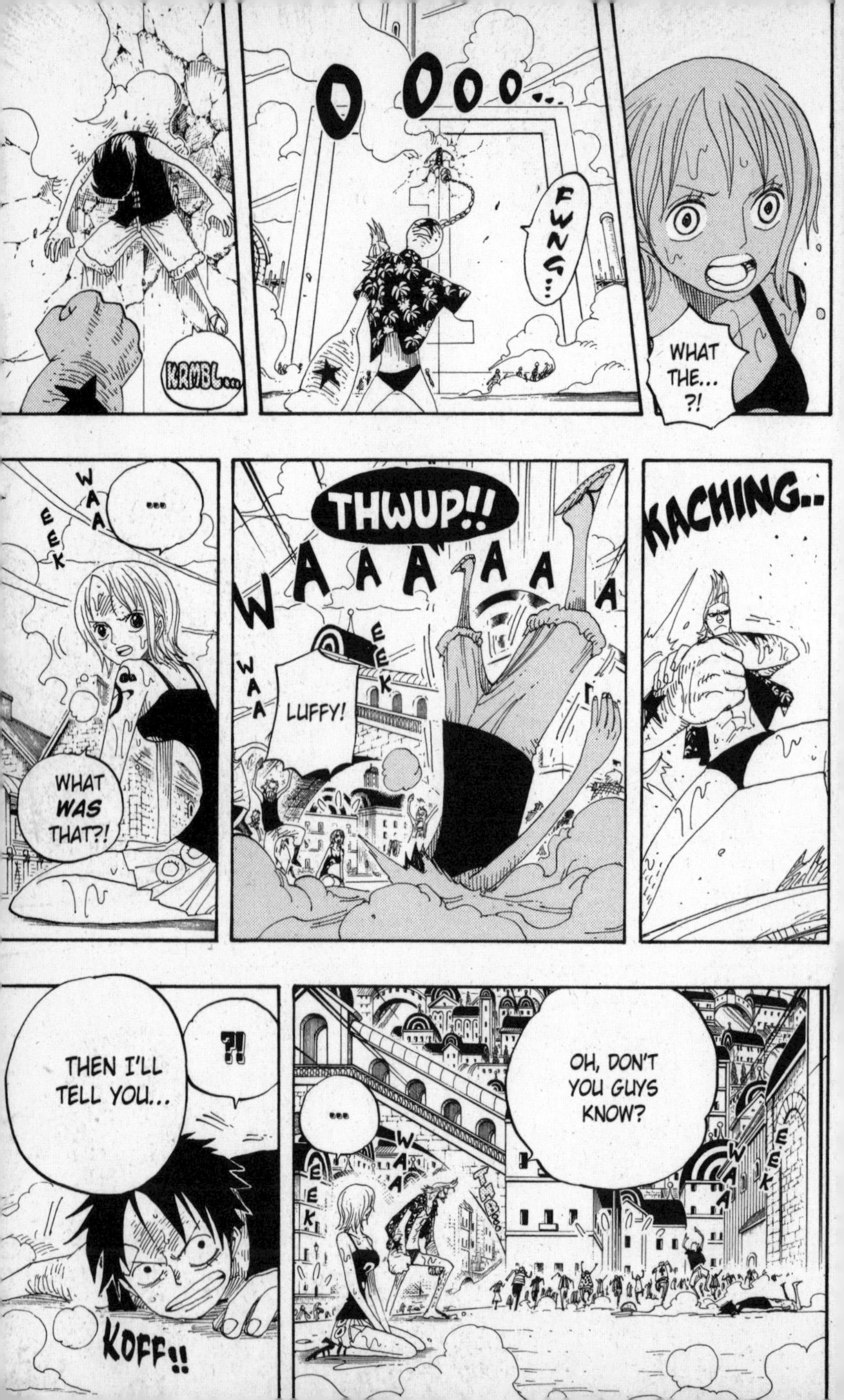
WHAT THE...?!
O OOO...
FWNG...
KRMBL...
KACHING...
THWUP!!
WAAAAAAA
EEK
WAA
LUFFY!
WAA
EEK
...
WHAT WAS THAT?!
OH, DON'T YOU GUYS KNOW?
EEK
WAA
...
WAA
EEK
?!
THEN I'LL TELL YOU...
KOFF!!

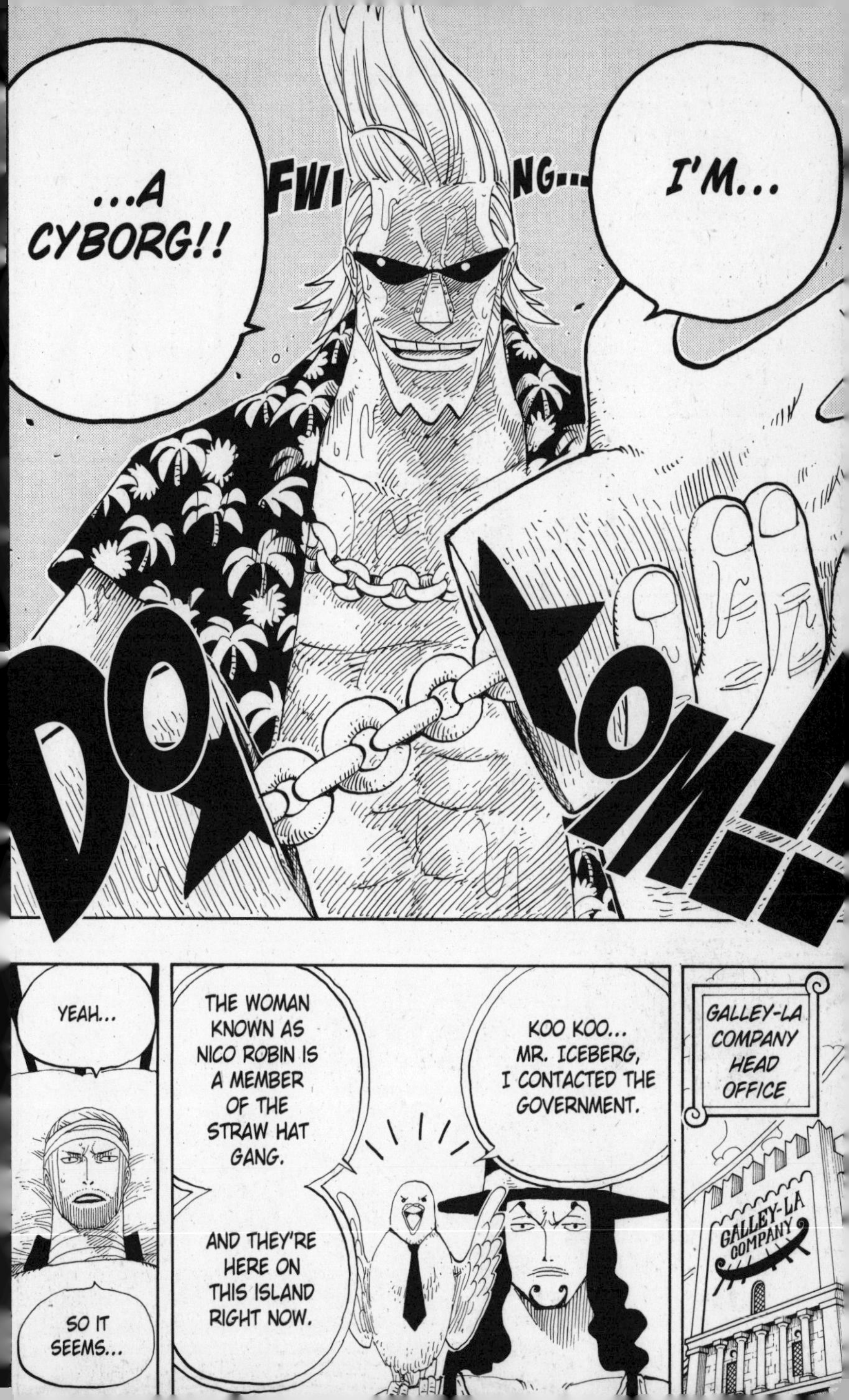
I'M...
FWI NG...
...A CYBORG!!
DON!!
GALLEY-LA COMPANY HEAD OFFICE
GALLEY-LA COMPANY
KOO KOO... MR. ICEBERG, I CONTACTED THE GOVERNMENT.
THE WOMAN KNOWN AS NICO ROBIN IS A MEMBER OF THE STRAW HAT GANG.
AND THEY'RE HERE ON THIS ISLAND RIGHT NOW.
YEAH...
SO IT SEEMS...

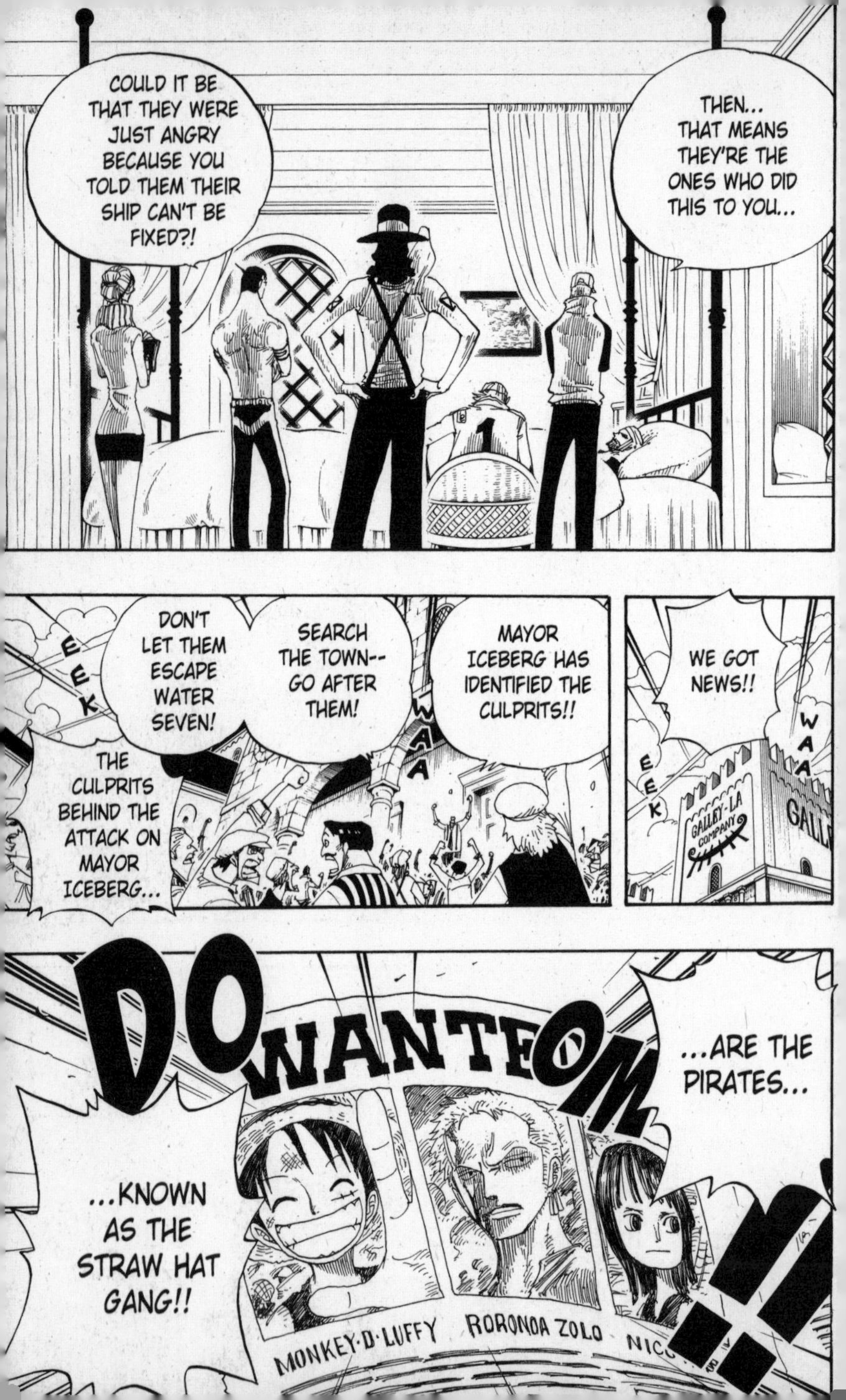
THEN... THAT MEANS THEY'RE THE ONES WHO DID THIS TO YOU...
COULD IT BE THAT THEY WERE JUST ANGRY BECAUSE YOU TOLD THEM THEIR SHIP CAN'T BE FIXED?!
WE GOT NEWS!!
WAA
GALLEY-LA COMPANY
EEK
MAYOR ICEBERG HAS IDENTIFIED THE CULPRITS!!
WAA
SEARCH THE TOWN-- GO AFTER THEM!
DON'T LET THEM ESCAPE WATER SEVEN!
EEK
THE CULPRITS BEHIND THE ATTACK ON MAYOR ICEBERG...
...ARE THE PIRATES...
DOOM
WANTE
...KNOWN AS THE STRAW HAT GANG!!
MONKEY·D·LUFFY
RORONOA ZOLO

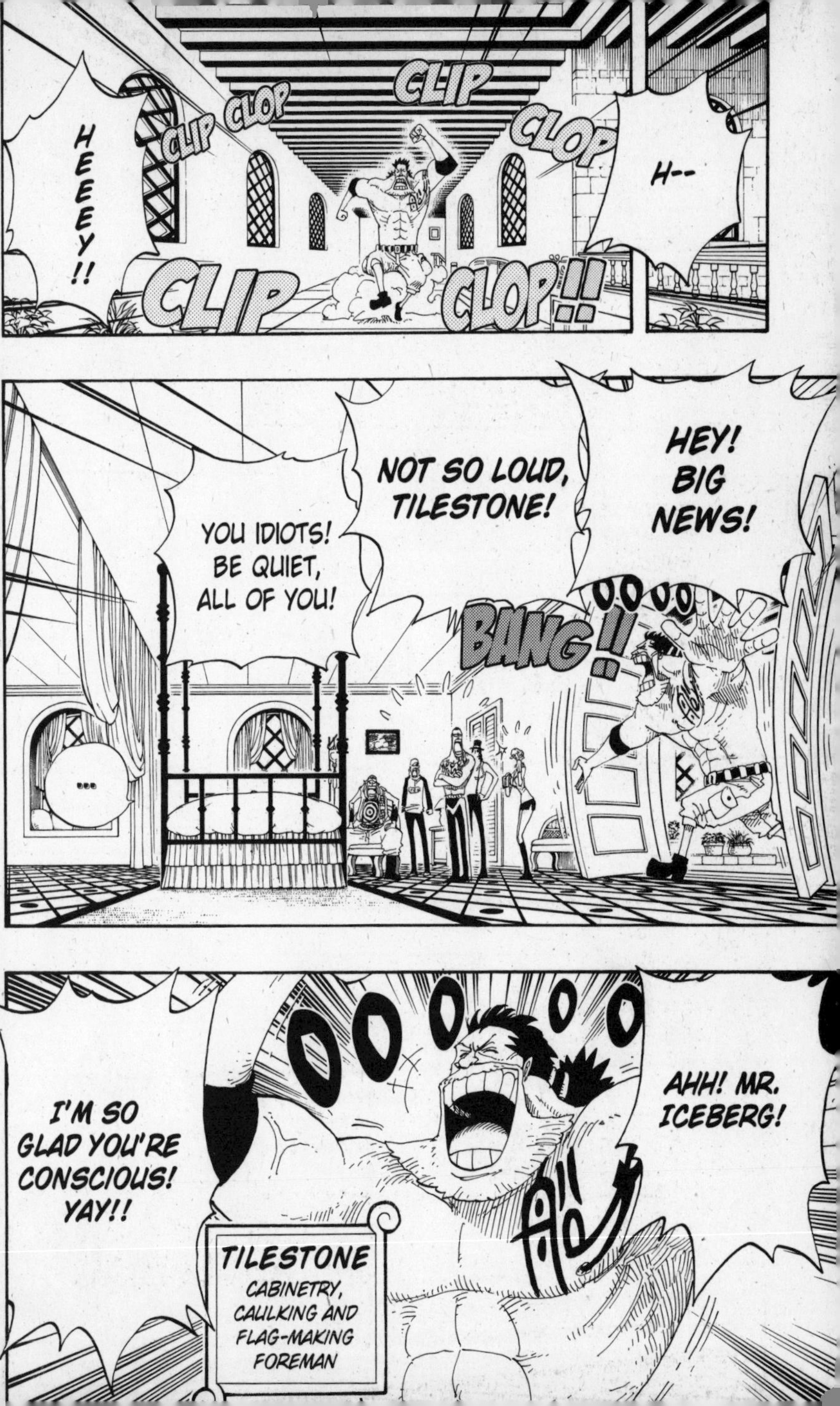
H--
CLIP
CLOP
CLIP CLOP
HEEEEY!!
CLIP CLOP!!
HEY! BIG NEWS!
BANG!!
NOT SO LOUD, TILESTONE!
YOU IDIOTS! BE QUIET, ALL OF YOU!
...
AHH! MR. ICEBERG!
I'M SO GLAD YOU'RE CONSCIOUS! YAY!!
TILESTONE
CABINETRY, CAULKING AND FLAG-MAKING FOREMAN

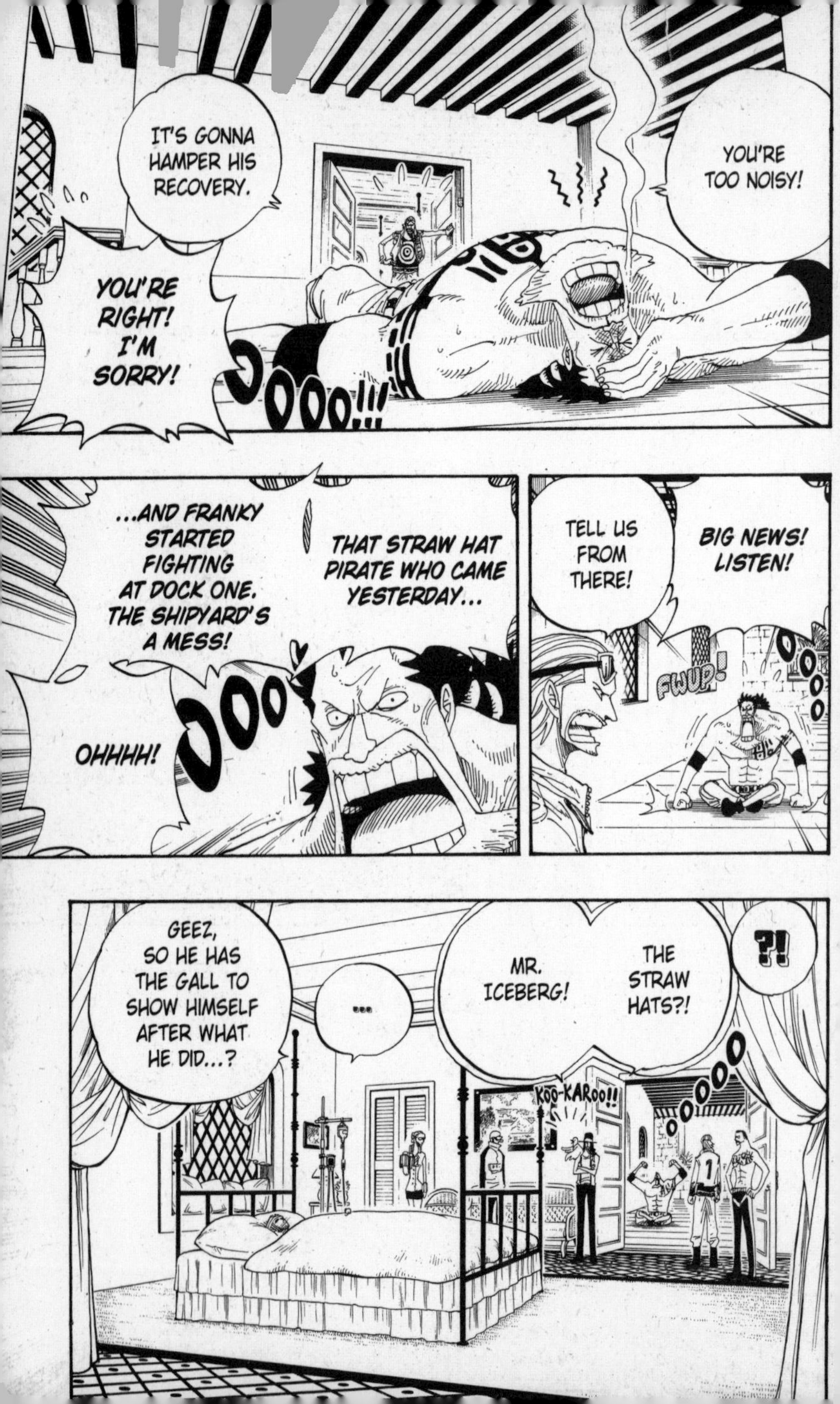
YOU'RE TOO NOISY!
IT'S GONNA HAMPER HIS RECOVERY.
OOOO!!!
YOU'RE RIGHT! I'M SORRY!
BIG NEWS! LISTEN!
TELL US FROM THERE!
OOOO
FWUP!
THAT STRAW HAT PIRATE WHO CAME YESTERDAY...
...AND FRANKY STARTED FIGHTING AT DOCK ONE. THE SHIPYARD'S A MESS!
OOOOHHHH!
?!
THE STRAW HATS?!
MR. ICEBERG!
...
GEEZ, SO HE HAS THE GALL TO SHOW HIMSELF AFTER WHAT HE DID...?
OOOOO
KOO-KAROO!!

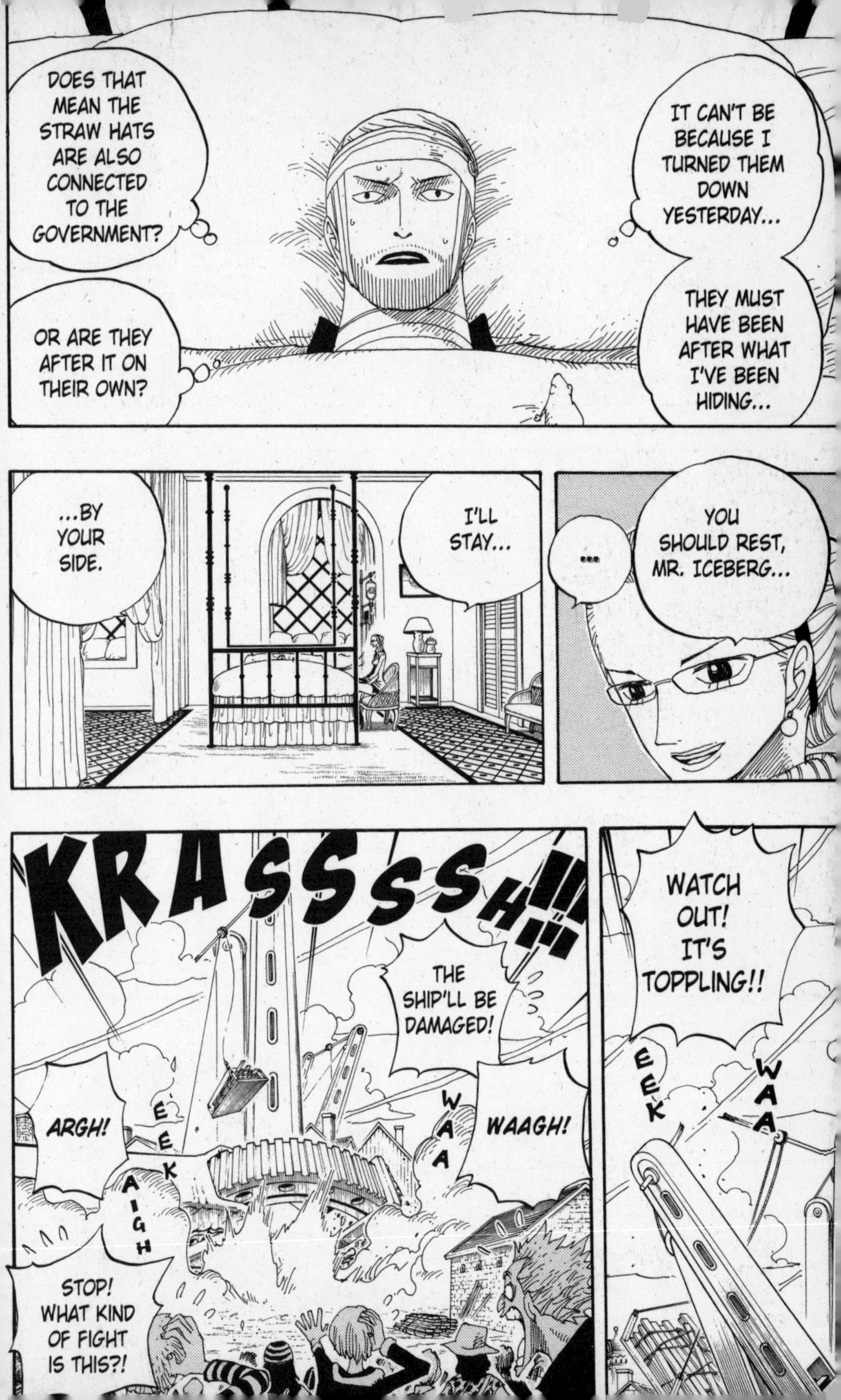
IT CAN'T BE BECAUSE I TURNED THEM DOWN YESTERDAY...
THEY MUST HAVE BEEN AFTER WHAT I'VE BEEN HIDING...
DOES THAT MEAN THE STRAW HATS ARE ALSO CONNECTED TO THE GOVERNMENT?
OR ARE THEY AFTER IT ON THEIR OWN?
YOU SHOULD REST, MR. ICEBERG...
...
I'LL STAY...
...BY YOUR SIDE.
WATCH OUT! IT'S TOPPLING!!
WAA
EEK
KRASSSSH!!
THE SHIP'LL BE DAMAGED!
WAAGH!
WAA
EEK
ARGH!
AIGH
STOP! WHAT KIND OF FIGHT IS THIS?!

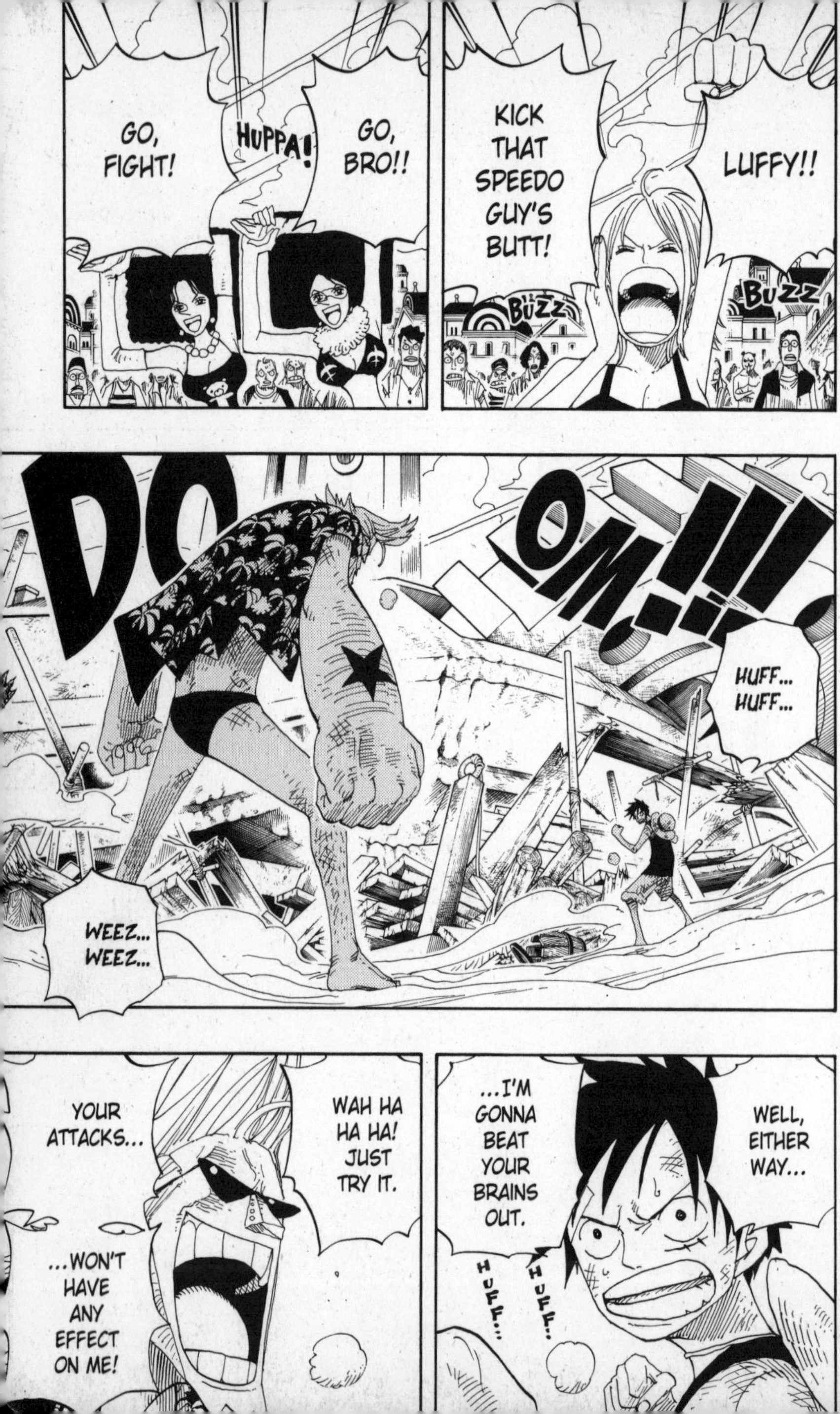
LUFFY!!
KICK THAT SPEEDO GUY'S BUTT!
BUZZ
BÜZZ
GO, BRO!!
HUPPA!
GO, FIGHT!
DOOM!!!
HUFF... HUFF...
WEEZ... WEEZ...
WELL, EITHER WAY...
...I'M GONNA BEAT YOUR BRAINS OUT.
HUFF...
HUFF...
WAH HA HA HA! JUST TRY IT.
YOUR ATTACKS...
...WON'T HAVE ANY EFFECT ON ME!

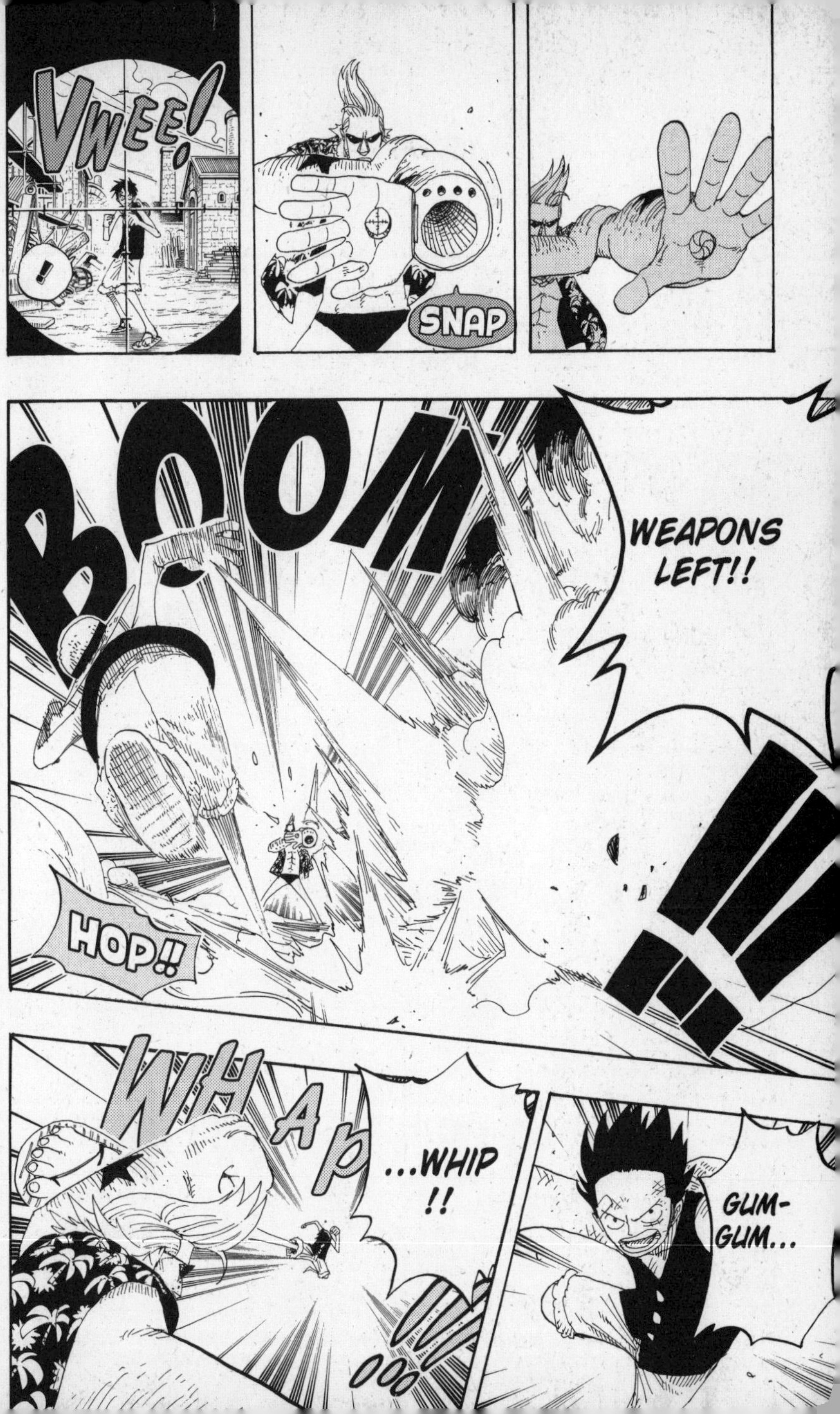
SNAP
VWEE!
!
WEAPONS LEFT!!
BOOM
HOP!!
GUM-GUM...
WHAP
...WHIP !!

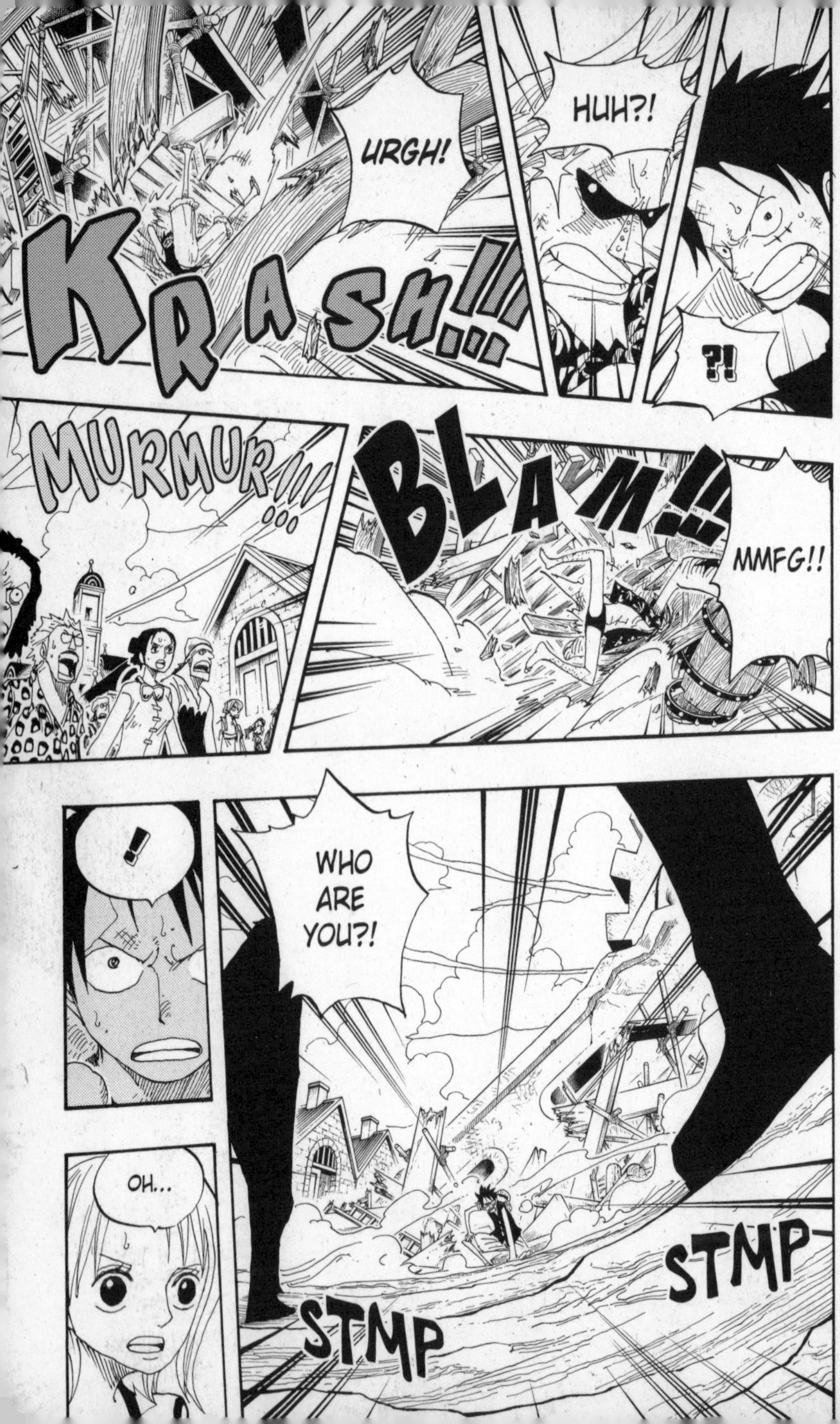
?!
HUH?!
URGH!
KRASH!!!
MMFG!!
BLAM!!
MURMUR
WHO ARE YOU?!
STMP
STMP
!
OH...

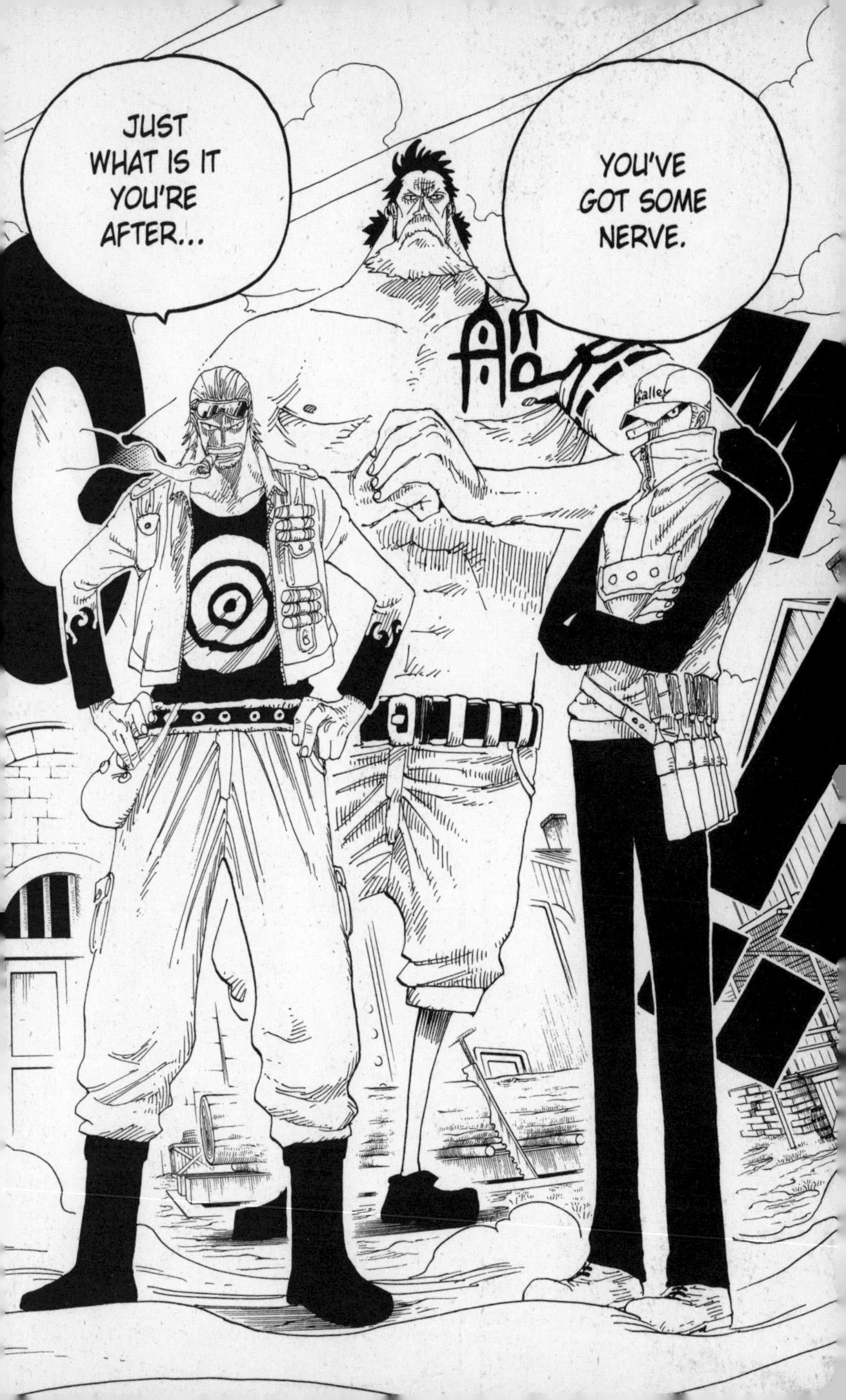
YOU'VE GOT SOME NERVE.
JUST WHAT IS IT YOU'RE AFTER...

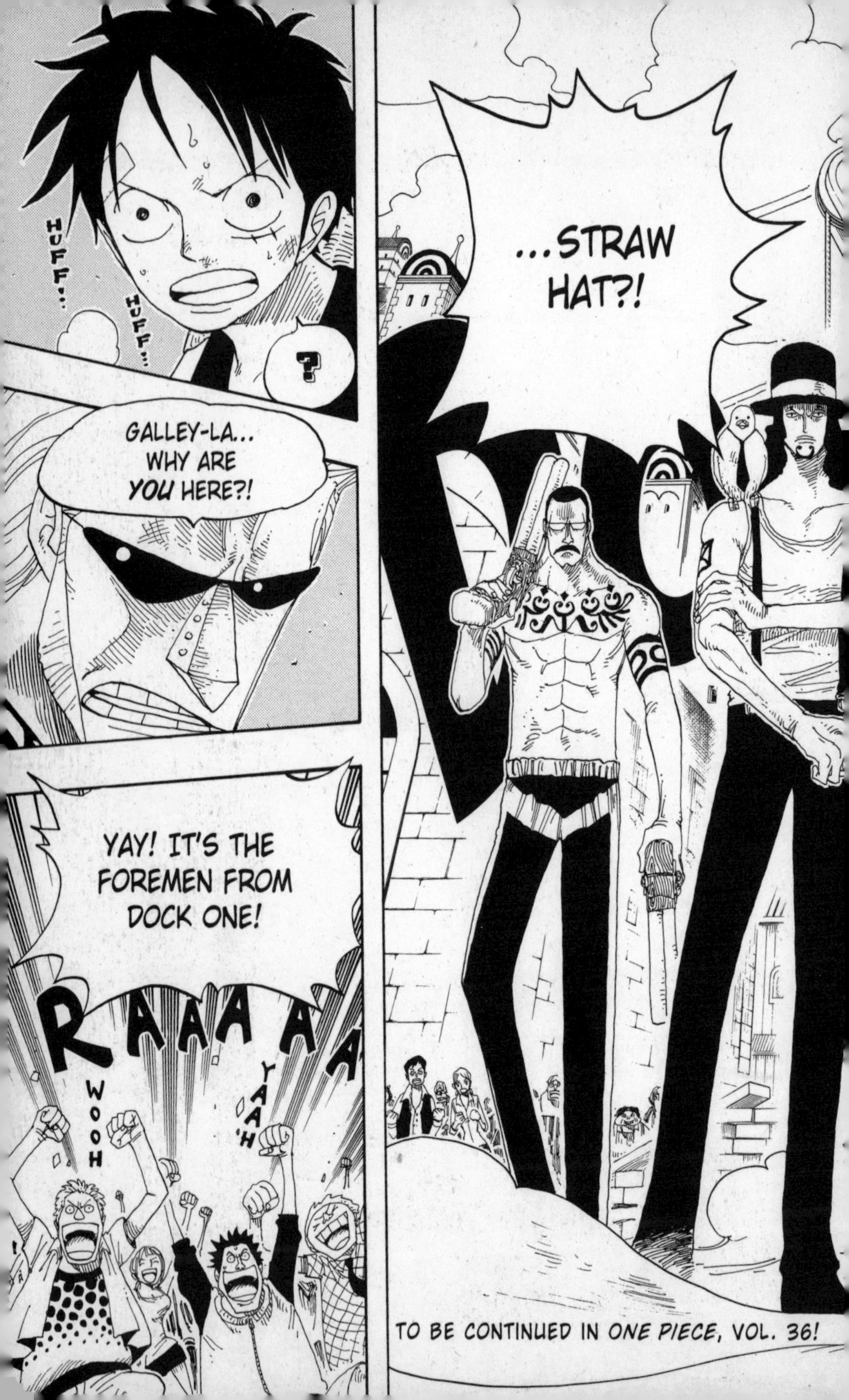
...STRAW HAT?!
TO BE CONTINUED IN ONE PIECE, VOL. 36!
HUFF...
HUFF...
?
GALLEY-LA... WHY ARE YOU HERE?!
YAY! IT'S THE FOREMEN FROM DOCK ONE!
RAAAAA
WOOH
YAAAH

COMING NEXT VOLUME:

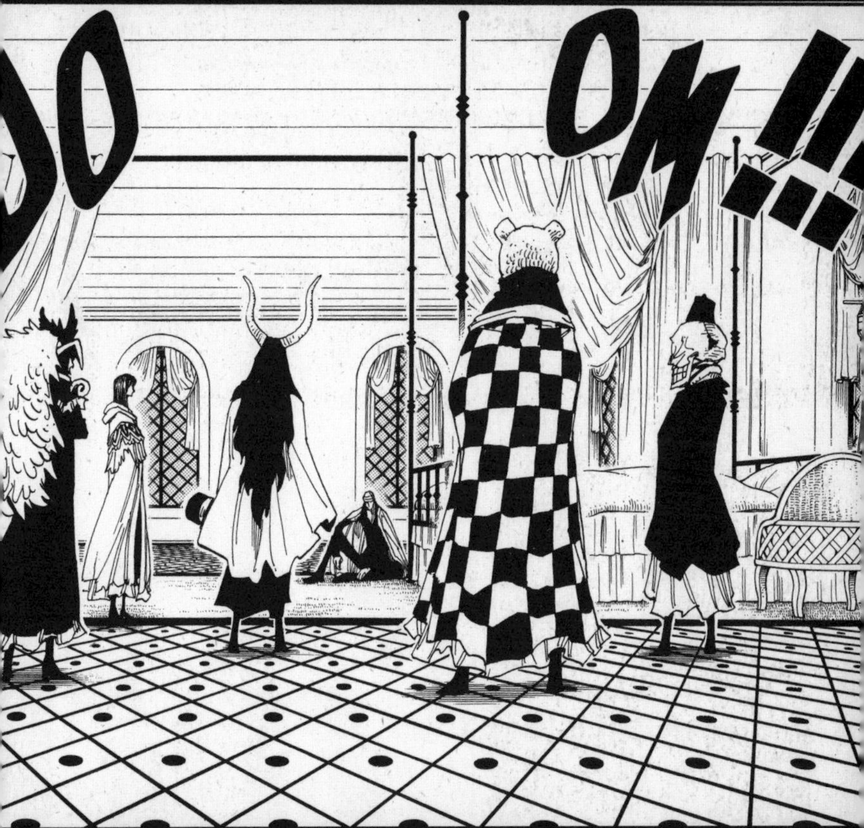
DOOM!!!

As Luffy continues his battle with Franky, the Galley-La Company workers join the fight and accuse the Straw Hat pirates of attempting to assassinate Mayor Iceberg. Luffy tries his best to prove that Robin wasn't involved in the plot, but when the truth is revealed, the city of Water Seven will be turned upside down!

ON SALE NOW!

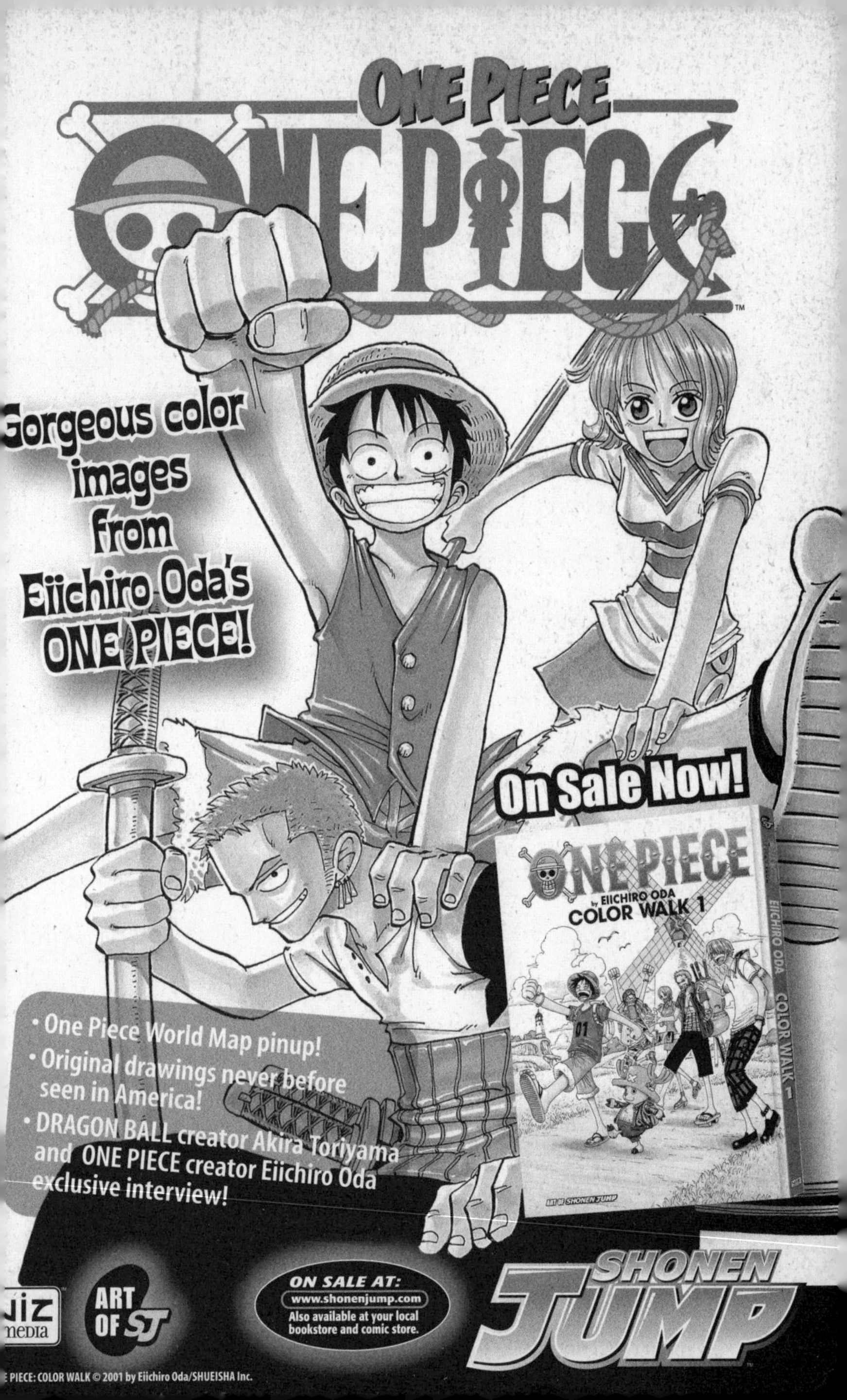
ONE PIECE
ONE PIECE
Gorgeous color images from Eiichiro Oda's ONE PIECE!
On Sale Now!
ONE PIECE by EIICHIRO ODA COLOR WALK 1
EIICHIRO ODA COLOR WALK 1
ART OF SHONEN JUMP
• One Piece World Map pinup!
• Original drawings never before seen in America!
• DRAGON BALL creator Akira Toriyama and ONE PIECE creator Eiichiro Oda exclusive interview!
ART OF SJ
ON SALE AT:
www.shonenjump.com
Also available at your local bookstore and comic store.
SHONEN JUMP
PIECE: COLOR WALK © 2001 by Eiichiro Oda/SHUEISHA Inc.

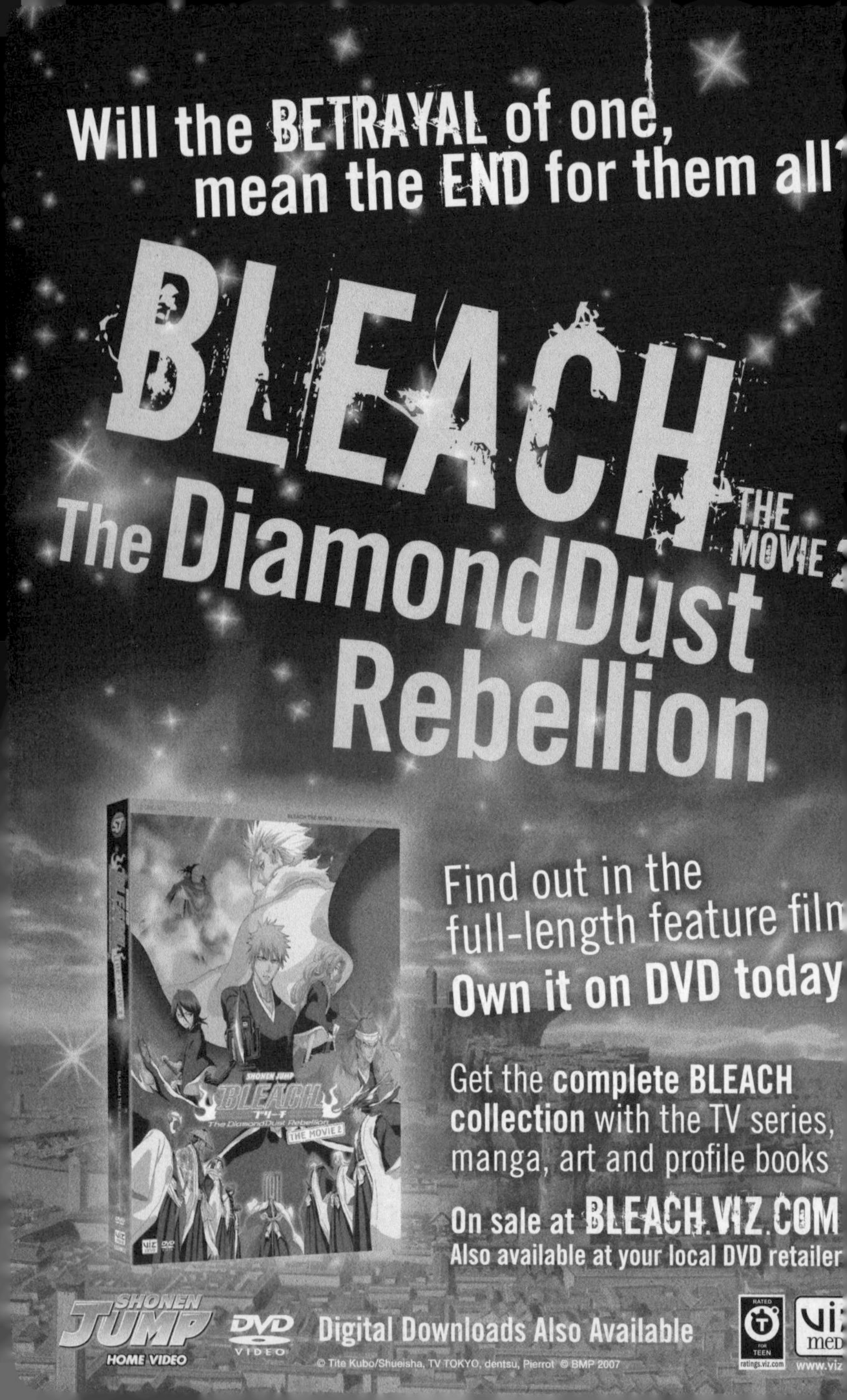
Will the BETRAYAL of one,
mean the END for them all?
BLEACH
THE MOVIE 2
The DiamondDust Rebellion
Find out in the full-length feature film
Own it on DVD today
Get the complete BLEACH collection with the TV series, manga, art and profile books
On sale at BLEACH.VIZ.COM
Also available at your local DVD retailer
SHONEN JUMP HOME VIDEO
DVD VIDEO
Digital Downloads Also Available
RATED T FOR TEEN
ratings.viz.com
© Tite Kubo/Shueisha, TV TOKYO, dentsu, Pierrot © BMP 2007